SCIENCE FICTION AND PHILOSOPHY

SCIENCE FICTION AND PHILOSOPHY

FROM TIME TRAVEL TO SUPERINTELLIGENCE

EDITED BY
SUSAN SCHNEIDER

WILEY-BLACKWELL

A John Wiley & Sons, Ltd., Publication

This edition first published 2009
Editorial material and organization © 2009 Blackwell Publishing Ltd

Blackwell Publishing was acquired by John Wiley & Sons in February 2007. Blackwell's publishing program has been merged with Wiley's global Scientific, Technical, and Medical business to form Wiley-Blackwell.

Registered Office
John Wiley & Sons Ltd, The Atrium, Southern Gate, Chichester, West Sussex, PO19 8SQ, United Kingdom

Editorial Offices
350 Main Street, Malden, MA 02148-5020, USA
9600 Garsington Road, Oxford, OX4 2DQ, UK
The Atrium, Southern Gate, Chichester, West Sussex, PO19 8SQ, UK

For details of our global editorial offices, for customer services, and for information about how to apply for permission to reuse the copyright material in this book please see our website at www.wiley.com/wiley-blackwell.

The right of Susan Schneider to be identified as the author of the editorial material in this work has been asserted in accordance with the Copyright, Designs and Patents Act 1988.

Library of Congress Cataloging-in-Publication Data
Science fiction and philosophy: from time travel to superintelligence / edited by Susan Schneider.
    p. cm.
  Includes bibliographical references and index.
  ISBN 978-1-4051-4906-8 (hbk: alk. paper) — ISBN 978-1-4051-4907-5 (pbk. : alk. paper)
1. Science fiction—Philosophy.   2. Philosophy—Introductions.   3. Philosophy in literature.   I. Schneider, Susan, 1968–
  PN3433.6.S377 2009
  809.3'8762—dc22

                                                                              2008052917

A catalogue record for this book is available from the British Library.

Set in 10.5/13pt Dante by Graphicraft Limited, Hong Kong
Printed in the United Kingdom

01   2009

CONTENTS

SOURCES AND ACKNOWLEDGMENTS

Part I

Chapter 1, "Brain in a Vat" (John Pollock, Chapter 1, "The Problems of Knowledge," in *Contemporary Theories of Knowledge*, Rowman & Littlefield Publishers, Inc., 1986, pp. 1–3, reprinted by permission of the publishers); **Chapter 2**, "Are You in a Computer Simulation?" (Nick Bostrom, "The Simulation Argument: Why the Probability that You Are Living in a Matrix is Quite High," in *Times Higher Education Supplement*, 16 May 2003, pp. 1–5, reprinted by permission of Times Higher Education and Nick Bostrom); **Chapter 3**, "Excerpt from *The Republic*" (Plato, *The Republic*, trans. Benjamin Jowett, P.F. Collier & Son, Colonial Press, 1901); **Chapter 4**, "Excerpt from *The Meditations on First Philosophy*" (René Descartes, Meditation I, trans. John Veitch, The Classical Library, 1901); **Chapter 5**, "*The Matrix* as Metaphysics" (David J. Chalmers, reprinted by permission of the author).

Part II

Chapter 6, "Where Am I?" (Daniel C. Dennett, *Brainstorms*, Bradford Books, 1978, pp. 356–64); **Chapter 7**, "Personal Identity" (Eric Olson, in Edward N. Zalta (ed.), *The Stanford Encyclopedia of Philosophy*, Winter 2008; http://plato.stanford.edu/archives/win2008/entries/identity-personal/); **Chapter 8**, "Divided Minds and the Nature of Persons" (Derek Parfit, in *Mindwaves*, ed. Colin Blakemore and Susan Greenfield, Basil Blackwell, 1987, pp. 351–6, reprinted by permission of Blackwell Publishing); **Chapter 9**, "Who Am I? What Am I?" (Ray Kurzweil, *The Singularity is Near: When Humans Transcend Biology*, Viking, 2005, pp. 382–7); **Chapter 10**, "Free Will and Determinism in the World of *Minority Report*" (Michael Huemer); **Chapter 11**, "The Book of Life: A Thought Experiment" (Alvin I. Goldman, "Actions, Predictions and Books of Life," *American Philosophical Quarterly*, 5.3 (1968), pp. 22–3).

Part III

Chapter 12, "Robot Dreams" (Isaac Asimov, in *Robot Dreams*, Byron Preiss Visual Publications Inc., 1986, pp. 25–50); Chapter 13, "A Brain Speaks" (Andy Clark, from *Being There: Putting Brain, Body and World Together Again*, MIT Press, 1996, pp. 223–7, © 1996 Massachusetts Institute of Technology, by permission of MIT Press); Chapter 14, "The Mind as the Software of the Brain" (Ned Block, from *An Invitation to Cognitive Science*, ed. D. Osherson, L. Gleitman, S. Kosslyn, E. Smith, and S. Sternberg, MIT Press, 1995); Chapter 15, "Cyborgs Unplugged" (Andy Clark, from *Natural Born Cyborgs*, Oxford University Press, 2007, pp. 13–34, by permission of Oxford University Press, Inc.); Chapter 16, "Consciousness in Human and Robot Minds" (Daniel C. Dennett, from *Cognition, Computation and Consciousness*, Oxford University Press, pp. 1–11, by permission of the publishers); Chapter 17, "Superintelligence and Singularity" (Ray Kurzweil, Chapter 1 in *The Singularity is Near: When Humans Transcend Biology*, Viking, 2005, pp. 7–33).

Part IV

Chapter 18, "The Man on the Moon" (George J. Annas, from *American Bioethics: Crossing Human Rights and Health Law Boundaries*, Oxford University Press, 2004, pp. 29–42); Chapter 19, "*Mindscan*: Transcending and Enhancing the Human Brain" (Susan Schneider); Chapter 20, "The Doomsday Argument" (John Leslie); Chapter 21, "Asimov's 'Three Laws of Robotics' and Machine Metaethics" (Susan Leigh Anderson, from *Proceedings of the AAAI Fall Symposium on Machine Ethics*, ed. Anderson); Chapter 22, "Ethical Issues in Advanced Artificial Intelligence" (Nick Bostrom, in *Cognitive, Emotive and Ethical Aspects of Decision Making in Humans and in Artificial Intelligence*, vol. 2, ed. I. Smith et al., Institute of Advanced Studies in Systems Research and Cybernetics, 2003, pp. 12–17).

Part V

Chapter 23, "A Sound of Thunder" (Ray Bradbury, from *Collier's Weekly*, The Crowell–Collier Publishing Company, 1952, pp. 1–9); Chapter 24, "Time" (Theodore Sider, from *Riddles of Existence*, Oxford University Press, 2008, pp. 44–61, by permission of Oxford University Press); Chapter 25, "The Paradoxes of Time Travel" (David Lewis, from *American Philosophical Quarterly*, 13 (1976), pp. 145–52); Chapter 26, "The Quantum Physics of Time Travel" (David Deutsch and Michael Lockwood, from *Scientific American*, March 1994, pp. 68–74, reprinted with permission. Copyright © 1994 by Scientific American, Inc. All rights reserved);

Chapter 27, "Miracles and Wonders: Science Fiction as Epistemology" (Richard Hanley).

Every effort has been made to contact owners of copyright material. In the event of any oversight, please contact the publisher so that errors or omissions can be rectified at the earliest opportunity.

INTRODUCTION
Thought Experiments: Science Fiction as a Window into Philosophical Puzzles

Susan Schneider

Let us open the door to age-old questions about our very nature, the nature of the universe, and whether there are limits to what we, as humans, can understand. But as old as these issues are, let us do something relatively new – let us borrow from the world of science fiction thought experiments to fire the philosophical imagination. Good science fiction rarely disappoints; good philosophy more rarely still.

Thought experiments are imagination's fancies; they are windows into the fundamental nature of things. A philosophical thought experiment is a hypothetical situation in the "laboratory of the mind" that depicts something that often exceeds the bounds of current technology or even is incompatible with the laws of nature, but that is supposed to reveal something philosophically enlightening or fundamental about the topic in question. Thought experiments can demonstrate a point, entertain, illustrate a puzzle, lay bare a contradiction in thought, and move us to provide further clarification. Indeed, thought experiments have a distinguished intellectual history. Both the creation of relativity and the interpretation of quantum mechanics rely heavily upon thought experiments. Consider, for instance, Einstein's elevator and Schrödinger's cat. And philosophers, perhaps even more than physicists, make heavy use of thought experiments. René Descartes, for instance, asked us to imagine that the physical world around us was an elaborate illusion. He imagined that the world was merely a dream or worse yet, a hoax orchestrated by an evil demon bent on deceiving us. He then asked: how can we really be certain that we are not deceived in either of these ways? (See Descartes' piece in this volume, Chapter 4.) Relatedly, Plato asked us to imagine prisoners who had been shackled in a cave for as long as they can remember. They face a wall. Behind them is a fire. Between the prisoners and the fire is a pathway, where men walk, carrying vessels, statues and other objects (See Figure I.1.)

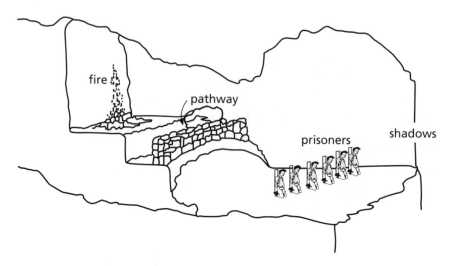

Fig. I.1 Plato's cave

As the men walk behind the prisoners, they and the objects they carry cast shadows on the cave wall. The prisoners are thus not able to see the actual men and objects; their world is merely a world of shadows. Knowing nothing of the real causes of the shadows, the prisoners would naturally mistake these shadows for the real nature of things. Plato then asked: is this analogous to our own understanding of reality? That is, is the human condition such that our grasp of reality is only partial, catching only the slightest glimpse into the true nature of things, like the prisoners' world of shadows?[1]

Intriguingly, if you read science fiction writers like Stanislaw Lem, Isaac Asimov, Arthur C. Clark and Robert Sawyer, you are already aware that some of the best science fiction tales are in fact long versions of philosophical thought experiments. From Clark's *2001*, which explored the twin ideas of intelligent design and artificial intelligence gone awry, to the Wachowski brothers' *Matrix* films, which were partly inspired by Plato's Cave, philosophy and science fiction are converging upon a set of shared themes and questions. Indeed, there is almost no end to the list of issues in science fiction that is philosophically intriguing. It is thus my modest hope that this short book isolates a number of key areas in philosophy where the interplay between philosophy and science fiction is especially rich. For instance, you might have seen the films *AI* or *I, Robot* (or you may have read the stories they are derived from). And you might have asked:

- **Can robots be intelligent? Should they have rights?**
- **Is artificial intelligence even possible?**

Or you might have read a time travel story, such as H. G. Wells's *The Time Machine*, and asked:

Is time travel possible? Indeed, what is the nature of space and time?

In this book, we delve into these questions, as well as many others, such as:

- **Could I be deceived about the external world, as in *The Matrix*, or *Vanilla Sky*?**
- **What is the nature of persons? For instance, can my mind survive the death of my body? Can I 'upload' my memories into a computer and somehow survive? (E.g., as in *Mindscan*.)**
- **Do we ever act freely, or is everything predetermined? (E.g., see *Minority Report*.)**
- **Should we enhance our brains, and even change our very nature?**

So let us see, in more detail, where our reflections will lead.

Part I: Could I be in a "Matrix" or Computer Simulation?

Related Works: *The Matrix; Permutation City; The 13th Floor; Vanilla Sky; Total Recall; Animatrix*

You sit here in front of this book. You are as confident that the book exists as you are of the existence of any physical object. The lighting is good; indeed, you feel the pages pressing on your hands – this is no illusion. But think of stories like *The Matrix* or *Vanilla Sky*. How can you really be sure that any of this is real? Perhaps you are simply part of a computer-generated virtual reality, created by an omnipotent supercomputer of unthinkable proportions. Is there some way to rule out such a scenario?

Our first section explores the aforementioned issue of the reality of the external world. Does the world around you – the people you encounter, the book you are now reading, indeed, even your hand – really exist? Answers to this question are a central focus of the sub-field of philosophy known as "epistemology," or "theory of knowledge." We begin with a brief science fiction story written by a philosopher, John Pollock, who depicts a "brain in a vat" scenario. Pollock's thought experiment, like the works named in the section title listed above, invites reflection on a philosophical position known as "external world skepticism." The skeptic about the external world holds that we cannot know that the external world that we believe is around us really exists, instead we may be in a dream, in virtual reality, and so on. Represented in this section are the aforementioned ideas of both Plato and Descartes; such provide essential philosophical background for this topic. While reading the pieces in the section, as well as other sections of the book, readers may wish to view or read one or more of the science fiction works named in the section titles. (Relatedly, instructors using this book for their courses may want their students to do so. In particular, they may consider screening the *Star Trek* episodes I list, as they are short, leaving time for in class discussion.)

The next piece in the section develops the issue of external world skepticism in a stunning new direction, suggesting that virtual reality science fiction thought experiments depict science *fact*. For philosopher Nick Bostrom has recently offered an influential argument that we are, in fact, in a computer simulation. He observes that assuming that a civilization survives long enough to be technologically sophisticated, it would likely be very interested in running simulations of entire worlds. In this case, there would be vastly more computer simulations, compared to just one real world. And if this is so, there would be many more beings who are in a simulation than beings who are not. Bostrom then infers that given this, it is more likely than not that we are in a simulation. Even the seasoned philosopher will find Bostrom's argument extremely thought provoking. Because the argument claims that it is more likely than not that we are in a simulation it does not rely on remote philosophical possibilities. To the skeptic, the mere possibility of deceit means that we cannot know the external world exists; for the skeptic holds that we must be certain of something in order to truly say that we know it. On the other hand, opponents of external world skepticism have argued that just because a skeptical scenario seems possible, it does not follow that we fail to know the external world exists. For knowledge doesn't require certainty; the skeptic places too strong a requirement on knowledge. But Bostrom's argument bypasses this anti-skeptical move: Even if you reject the claim that knowledge requires certainty, if his argument is correct, then it is likely that we are in a simulation. That the world we know is a computer simulation is no remote possibility – more likely than not, this is how the world actually is.

Part I also features a related piece by philosopher David J. Chalmers. In his "Matrix as Metaphysics" Chalmers uses the *Matrix* films as a means to develop a novel position on external world skepticism. Interestingly, Chalmers does not dispute Bostrom's argument. Instead, he aims to deflate the significance of knowing we are in a simulation. Chalmers asks: why would knowing that we are in a simulation prove that the external world skeptic is correct? He writes:

> I think that even if I am in a matrix, my world is perfectly real. A brain in a vat is not massively deluded (at least if it has always been in the vat). Neo does not have massively false beliefs about the external world. Instead, envatted

beings have largely *correct* beliefs about their world. If so, the Matrix Hypothesis is not a skeptical hypothesis, and its possibility does not undercut everything that I think I know. (Chapter 5, p. 35)

Chalmers is suggesting that being in a simulation is not a situation in which we fail to know that the external world around us really exists. Suppose that we learn we are in a matrix. According to Chalmers, this fact tells us about the nature of the external world: it tells us that the physical world around us is ultimately made of bits, and that our creators were creatures who allowed our minds to interact with this world of bits. But upon reflection, knowing a new theory of the fundamental nature of the universe is just learning more physics. And while intriguing, this is not like proving that skepticism is true. For Chalmers contends that there is still a "physical world" which we interact with; what is different is that its fundamental physics is not about strings or particles, but bits. Furthermore, learning that there is a creator outside of space and time who allowed our minds to interact with the physical world, while obviously of great metaphysical and personal import, is akin to learning that a particular religious view holds. This would be an earth shattering revelation, but it does not mean that we are not situated in the external world that we believe we are in.

Suggestively, a very basic brain in a vat was recently developed at the university of Florida in the laboratory of Thomas De Marse. It now is sophisticated enough to successfully fly a flight simulator.[2] Bostrom would likely say that this is further proof that we are in a simulation; for when we start turning our own basic simulations on, this is, in effect, evidence that advancing societies have interest in doing so. It also indicates that we are nearing the point at which we are capable of surviving the technological age long enough to develop more advanced simulations. Indeed, I find De Marse's development to be yet another telling example of the convergence between science fiction and science fact. Some of the most lavish science fiction thought experiments are no longer merely fictions – we see glimpses of them on the technological horizon.

Part II: What Am I? Free Will and the Nature of Persons

Related Works: *Software; Star Trek, The Next Generation: Second Chances; Mindscan; The Matrix; Minority Report*

Part I left us with the question: Is reality, at rock bottom, just a pattern of information in an unfathomably powerful supercomputer? If one lives with this question long enough, one will likely also wonder: am I, being part of this larger reality, merely a computational entity – a certain stream of information or computer program? Indeed, this could even be the case if we are not living in a simulation. Many cognitive scientists suspect that the brain is a kind of computational system, and that relatedly, the person is fundamentally a sort of computational being. As the futurist Ray Kurzweil suggests in his piece for this section (Chapter 9), using language reminiscent of the ancient Greek philosopher Heraclitus, "I am rather like the pattern that water makes in a stream as it rushes past the rocks in its path. The actual molecules of water change every millisecond, but the pattern persists for hours or even years" (Kurzweil, Chapter 9, p. 100). For Kurzweil this "pattern" is construed in computational terms: the pattern is the pattern of information processing that your brain engages in – the particular numerical values and nodes characterizing your neural network, down to the last detail. Let us call this view of the nature of persons "information patternism."

Indeed, this view of the nature of persons is developed in many philosophically oriented science fiction works. Consider, for instance, Jake Sullivan, the protagonist of Robert Sawyer's *Mindscan*, who, hoping to avoid death, scans his brain and attempts to upload his mind into an artificial body. In a similar vein, Rudy Rucker's *Software* features an aging character who uploads his pattern into numerous devices, including a truck, in a last-ditch effort to avoid death. This common science fiction theme of scanning and "uploading" one's mind is predicated on the idea of copying one's informational pattern – one's memories, personality traits, and indeed, every psychological feature – into a supercomputer. The survival of one's pattern is supposed to be sufficient for the survival of the individual, across a storyline of extraordinary shifts in underlying matter.

Informational patternism is essentially a version of a leading theory of the nature of persons in metaphysics, a view commonly called the "Psychological Continuity Theory." According to this view, you are essentially your memories and ability to reflect on yourself (a position associated with John Locke) and in its most general form, your overall psychological configuration; what Kurzweil referred to as your "pattern." Informational patternism is also closely related to the leading view of the nature of mind in both philosophy of mind and cognitive science. The view is, more explicitly, the following:

> **Computational Theory of Mind (CTM).** One's mind is essentially the "program" running on the hardware of the brain, where by "program" what is meant is the algorithm that the mind computes, something in principle discoverable by cognitive science.[3]

Because, at least in principle, the brain's computational configuration can be preserved in a different medium, i.e., in silicon as opposed to carbon, with the information processing properties of the original neural circuitry preserved, the computationalist rejects the idea that a person is essentially her body (including, of course, her brain).[4] Instead, a person is something like an embodied informational pattern.

But is informational patternism correct? The plausibility of informational patternism and other theories of personal identity is pursued throughout the section. The first piece in the section (Chapter 6) is a science fiction tale by the well-known philosopher Daniel Dennett. Dennett's piece, "Where Am I?" boggles the mind. Dennett is sent on a bomb diffusing mission by NASA, and his out of body adventures test the limits of leading theories of personal identity, especially informational patternism. Eric Olson follows up with a useful survey of the major theories of the nature of persons; the reader may enjoy turning back to Dennett's story to reflect on which ones were invoked. Then, employing the classic science fiction pseudotechnology of the teleporter and the example of split brains from actual neuroscience cases, Derek Parfit's piece (Chapter 8) raises problems for both informational patternism and the popular soul theory of personal identity, suggesting that they are both incoherent.

Finally, any discussion of persons should at least touch upon the related topic of the nature of free will. After all, as you reflect on your very nature, it is of great import to ask whether any of the actions which you seem to choose are really selected freely. Consider that from the vantage point of science, there is a sense in which every intentional action seems to be determined by either genetics or environment, or a combination of both. And every physical event in the brain has, at least in principle, a causal explanation in terms of the behavior of fundamental particles. In light of this, one wonders whether there really is a plausible sense in which individuals' intentional actions are free. Do they "break free" of the laws of nature? And, come to think of it, what does it mean to "break free" of the laws? Further, recalling our earlier discussion of informational patternism, if persons are, at rock bottom, computational, are they even capable of being free? In his thought provoking "Free Will and Determinism in the World of *Minority Report*," Michael Huemer uses the film *Minority Report* as a means of reflecting on the age-old topic of free will.

Part III: Mind: Natural, Artificial, Hybrid, and "Super"

Related Works: *2001; Blade Runner; AI; Frankenstein; Terminator; I, Robot*

Perhaps our universe is, or will be, science fiction-like in the sense that it will be populated by many distinct kinds of minds. We are all biological entities, and with the exception of the rare individual with a brain implant, all parts of our brains are natural, that is, "non-artificial." But this will soon change. As neuroscience discovers the algorithms in the brain underlying computation, scientists are increasingly realizing that brains are computational entities. Some of the younger readers may eventually be like the cyborgs Bruce Sterling, William Gibson and other writers in the cyberpunk genre explore. If so, they would have "hybrid" minds, being part natural and part artificial. And perhaps scientists will reverse-engineer the human brain, creating AI creatures that run the same algorithms as human brains do. Other AI creatures could have minds that are entirely different, borrowing from sensory modalities that other animals have (e.g. echolocation), featuring radically enhanced working memory capacity, and so on. Existing human brains could be enhanced in these novel ways as well. In sum, a plurality of distinct sorts of artificial minds could be "sculpted."

Numerous developments in cognitive science strongly support the aforementioned computational theory of mind (CTM). They also seem to support the related doctrine of informational patternism. However, it is important to note that while the brain may be a computational device, one's mind might be something more. Perhaps, for instance, our brains can be mapped out in terms of the language of a penultimate computational neuroscience yet we nonetheless have souls. Are these two things really inconsistent? Or perhaps consciousness is a non-physical, non-computational, feature of the brain. The debate rages on in philosophy of mind. In this section, we explore some of these issues, raising thought provoking points of contact between science fiction, philosophy of mind, and science fact.

Isaac Asimov's "Robot Dreams" leads the section. There is perhaps no better example of philosophically rich science fiction available than Asimov's robot tales – especially in light of the connection to contemporary robotics (as the next section shall discuss). The second piece in this section is also a work of science fiction. In "A Brain Speaks" philosopher Andy Clark writes from the vantage point of his brain. The brain explains the concept of "functional decomposition" – how it is a blend of different functional subcomponents, each of which computes its own algorithm to carry out a specialized function. The different subcomponents are wired together by evolution and experience to do important tasks. The next few pieces provide essential background for understanding and critiquing the computational approach to the mind. Ned Block's piece explores computational intelligence and functional decomposition. His discussion is followed by an excerpt from Andy Clark's *Natural Born Cyborgs*, a project that argues that we are already seamlessly interwoven with technologies around us and that the path toward becoming cyborgs does not lead us to become essentially different than we are. Human minds are already both computational and integrated with the larger technological world around us. Such is our cyborg nature.

Now consider the android Rachel in Philip K. Dick's *Do Androids Dream of Electric Sheep?* (a.k.a. *Blade Runner*) or consider David, the android boy in

Spielberg's *AI*. These characters in effect push at the boundaries of our ordinary understanding of a person. The audience ponders whether such creatures can really understand, or be conscious. Intriguingly, if our own minds are computational, or if a person is just an embodied informational pattern, then perhaps there is no difference in kind between us and them. John Searle would suggest otherwise. As the Block chapter has discussed, Searle, in his classic "Chinese Room" thought experiment, argues against the very idea that we are computational and the related idea that machines could think. On the other hand, Daniel Dennett presents a very different picture of artificial intelligence in his piece "Consciousness in Human and Robot Minds." And like Dennett, Ray Kurzweil's vision of the nature of mind is diametrically opposed to Searle's. In his book, *The Singularity is Near*, he sketches a future world in which we (or perhaps our children or grandchildren) become cyborgs, and eventually entirely artificial beings. The creation of "superintelligent" AI brings forth beings with such advanced intelligence that solutions to the world's problems are generated, rapidly ending disease and resource scarcity. "Superintelligence and Singularity" is not a work of science fiction however; it is Kurzweil's prediction of the shape of the near future, based on our current science.

Part IV: Ethical and Political Issues

Related Works: *Brave New World*; *Gattaca*; *Terminator*; *White Plague*

Minds have many philosophical dimensions: the epistemic – what they know; the metaphysical – what they are; the ethical – whether their actions are right or wrong. The first few sections have looked at the epistemology and metaphysics of selves and their minds; now, in Part IV, we consider certain ethical issues. Having closed the previous section with Kurzweil's utopian perspective, it is intriguing to recall, in contrast, Aldous Huxley's sobering dystopian satire, *Brave New World* (1932). Inspired by his sentiments about American culture, *Brave New World* depicts a technologically advanced society in which everyone is complacent yet where the family has withered away and child bearing is no longer a natural process. Instead, children are bred in centers where, via genetic engineering, there are five distinct castes. Only the top two exhibit genetic variation; the other castes are multiple clones of one fertilization. All members of society are trained to strongly identify with their caste, and to appreciate whatever is good for society, especially the constant consumption of goods and, in particular, the mild hallucinogen Soma that makes everyone blissful.

Brave New World is a classic dystopian science fiction novel, gravely warning us of the twin abuses of rampant consumerism and technology in the hands of an authoritarian dictatorship. Like Huxley, George Annas is intensely concerned with the social impact of genetic engineering and other enhancement technologies. His chapter employs themes from science fiction to motivate his case against genetic engineering. A major concern of his is the following:

> We constantly compare the new genetics to "putting a man on the moon," but if history is a guide, this genetic engineering will not lead to a sterile publicity stunt like the moon landing, but instead will inevitably lead to genocide: the "inferiors" killing off the "superiors" or vice-versa.

Annas contrasts sharply with Kurzweil and other "transhumanists." Transhumanism is a cultural, philosophical, and political movement which holds that the human species is only now in a comparatively early phase and that future humans will be radically unlike their current selves in both mental and physical respects. They will be more like certain cyborg and virtual creatures depicted in science fiction stories (Bostrom 2003). While Annas advocates an international treaty banning specific "species-altering" techniques, many transhumanists, in contrast, believe that species alteration is justified insofar as it advances the intellectual and physical life of the individual. Indeed, according to transhumanism, some future humans may be "uploads," living immortal and virtual lives on computers, being superintelligences, and indeed, in many ways being more akin to AI than to unenhanced humans (Bostrom 2003).

Bostrom, another leading transhumanist, had discussed the notion of "substrate independence" in his earlier piece in Part I, a concept closely wedded to both CTM and informational patternism, positions that many transhumanists adopt. In Susan Schneider's piece (Chapter 19) she considers whether informational patternism really supports the technoprogressive's case for radical human enhancement. As exciting as transhumanism may be to science fiction enthusiasts, Schneider stresses that the transhumanists, who generally adopt informational patternism, have as of yet to provide a plausible account of the nature of persons. In particular, there is no feasible sense in which this notion of a person allows that a person can persist throughout radical enhancements, let alone even mild ones. Although she considers various ways that the transhumanist might furnish patternism with better conceptual resources, her suspicion is that informational patternism is itself deeply flawed.

A common point of agreement between transhumanists and bioconservatives who oppose enhancement is a concern that the development of artificial intelligence, biological weapons, advanced nanotechnology and other technologies bring forth global catastrophic risks, that is, risks that carry the potential to inflict serious damage to human well-being across the planet. Here, these issues go well beyond the interplay between science fiction and philosophy; but readers are encouraged to read Garreau (2006) for an extensive overview of cultural and technological issues, and Bostrom and Cirkovic (2008) for an excellent series of papers focusing on just the topic of global catastrophic risk. In Chapter 20, philosopher John Leslie provides a brief version of his "doomsday argument," a probabilistic argument that attempts to predict the future lifetime of the human race given an estimate of the total number of humans born thus far. The final two pieces of the section turn to the pressing issue of ethical dimensions of artificial intelligence and the existential risks its development may bring. *2001's* HAL has stayed with us so long precisely because the film depicts a very possible future – a situation in which the ethical programming of an extremely intelligent artificial being crashes, creating a psychotic computer. As HAL's vacuum tubes are slowly pulled out the audience listens to HAL's bewildered machine voice report his diminishing memories and sensations. Stanley Kubrick thereby orchestrates a believable scene in which HAL "dies"; pumping the intuition that like us, HAL is a conscious mind. Indeed, philosophers and computer scientists have recently become concerned with developing adequate "ethical programming" for both sophisticated intelligences and more simple programs that could be consulted as ethical advisors. Susan Anderson's intriguing piece discusses these issues, using Asimov's famous three laws of robotics and his story "Bicentennial Man" as a springboard. She ultimately rejects Asimov's three laws as a basis for ethical programming in machines; Asimov would surely agree.

The next piece explores ethical issues involving superintelligence. If humans construct AI, it may be that AI itself engineers its own future programming, evolving into a form of intelligence that goes well beyond human intelligence. Like the evolved Mecha of the distant future that find David frozen in the ice at the very end of Spielberg's *AI*, perhaps superintelligent AI will supplant us. Or perhaps our descendants will be cyborgs that themselves upgrade to the level of superintelligence. In any case, a superintelligent being could engage in moral reasoning and make discoveries that are at a higher or different level than us, and which we cannot grasp sufficiently to judge. This is one reason why the issue of ethical programming must be debated *now*; in hopes that the original motivations programmed into AI evolve into a superintelligence that is indeed benevolent. In "Ethical Issues in Advanced Artificial Intelligence," Nick Bostrom surveys some of these ethical issues, as well as investigating whether the development of such machines should in fact be accelerated.

Part V: Space and Time

Related Works: *Twelve Monkeys; Slaughterhouse Five; The Time Machine; Back to the Future*

The final section begins with Ray Bradbury's well-known time travel tale about a time travel business called "Time Safari, Inc." that takes travelers back in time to hunt prehistoric animals. Believing that even the slightest change in the past can alter the future in momentous ways, travelers are instructed to use extreme diligence to leave the environment undisturbed. For instance, they are not allowed to take trophies; they are only permitted to shoot animals that are about to die; and they are required to stay on a path hovering a bit above the ground. Needless to say, things go awry.

Time travel tales such as Bradbury's raise intriguing issues concerning the nature of time. For one thing, what is it to travel back through time? To answer this, one needs to first ponder the classic question, "What is the nature of time?" On the one hand, time is one of the most familiar elements of our lives. On the other, as Ted Sider explains in his chapter, this age-old question has no easy answer. Sider outlines different answers to this question, cleverly uncovering problems for the major views of the nature of time.

One might wonder if time travel is really possible. Indeed, MIT students recently held a "time travel party," announcing the event in national papers to attract people from the future. And while a raging costume party was had, their low tech experiment in time travel discovery unfortunately failed to reveal any genuine time travelers. Of course, the partygoers, like the rest of us, are all boring cases of time travel – we merely press forward in time, minute by minute. But perhaps the partygoers' disappointment is due to some sort of inbuilt limitation; that is, maybe time travel somehow is contrary to the laws of physics or even the laws of logic. While some physicists, like Kip Thorne, have argued that time travel is compatible with the laws of physics (see Thorne 1995), philosophers and physicists have long been worried about the "Grandfather Paradox." Suppose that Maria constructs a time machine, and that she goes into the past to visit her grandfather when he was a boy. Unfortunately, her instruments are so accurate that the machine lands right on him, and she unwittingly kills him. Now, her own father hasn't been conceived yet, so it seems that since her grandfather will not survive to father her own father, she would not have existed to unwittingly cause her time machine to kill him.

Clearly, something strange is going on. For if time travel is compatible with the laws of physics, and if machines can carry human sized objects back in time, why couldn't she change the past in a way that would eliminate her own eventual existence? As philosopher David Lewis once jokingly remarked: is there a time policeman who races after her machine to stop her from altering the past in certain ways? Perhaps time travel is conceptually incoherent. The pieces by David Lewis and coauthors Michael Lockwood and David Deutsch both attempt to respond to the Grandfather Paradox. While Lewis uses philosophical resources to do so, Lockwood and Deutsch employ the many worlds interpretation of quantum mechanics to attempt to dissolve the paradox. They argue that Maria actually goes into a parallel universe where she does not, in fact, kill her grandfather. Instead, she kills his counterpart in the parallel universe. Finally, philosopher Richard Hanley considers the issue of miracles. Would radically advanced technologies, such as time travel, be, from our vantage point at least, miracles? After all, consider Arthur C. Clarke's Third Law: "any sufficiently advanced technology is indistinguishable from magic" (Clark 1961). Hanley's fun piece blends together science fiction themes from various parts of the book, discussing Chalmers' and Bostrom's papers on being in a simulation, Edwin Abbot's *Flatland: A Romance of Many Dimensions*, and more.

Conclusion

So this is where we are going. It is my hope that if you are new to philosophy that you shall see fit to revisit these issues again and again, gaining philosophical sophistication with each visit. I believe you will find that your position on one topic helps to shape your perspective on some of the others. Always there – and enhanced by your years of reflection – is an understanding that these topics represent some of life's great mysteries. And it is my hope that seasoned philosophers, cognitive scientists and others working in fields which touch upon these issues, will have a heightened awareness of some new philosophical developments (e.g. new challenges to external world skepticism) and, especially, the multiple challenges posed by neural enhancement and artificial intelligence technologies. As many of the readings emphasize, these issues call for detailed philosophical work at the interface of epistemology, philosophy of mind, metaphysics and neuroethics. The questions posed by this book have no easy answers; yet it is the human condition to ponder them. Perhaps our cyborg descendants will ponder them too; maybe by uploading their philosophy books directly into their memory systems. Perhaps, after numerous upgrades, both the problem and the solution space will even reshape itself.

It is fitting to end our survey with a science fiction thought experiment. It is AD 2300 and some humans have upgraded to become superintelligent beings. But suppose you resist any upgrades. Having conceptual resources beyond your wildest dreams, the superintelligent beings generate an entirely new budget of solutions to the philosophical problems that we considered in this book. They univocally and passionately assert that the solutions are obvious. But you throw your hands up; these "solutions" strike you and the other unenhanced as meaningless gibberish. You think: Who knows, maybe these "superintelligent" beings were engineered poorly; or maybe it is me. Perhaps the unenhanced are "cognitively closed," as Colin McGinn has argued, being constitutionally unable to solve major philosophical problems (McGinn 1993). The enhanced call themselves "Humans 2.0" and claim the unenhanced are but an inferior version. They beg you to enhance. What shall you make of our epistemic predicament? You cannot grasp the contents of the superintelligent beings' thoughts without significant upgrades. But what if their way of thinking is flawed to begin with? In that case upgrading will surely not help. Is there some sort of neutral vantage point or at least a set of plausible principles with which to guide you in framing a response to such a challenge? Herein, we shall begin to reflect on some of the issues that this thought experiment raise.

We clearly have a lot to think about. So let us begin.

Notes

1. *Great Dialogues of Plato: Complete Texts of the Republic, Apology, Crito Phaido, Ion, and Meno, Vol. 1.* (Warmington and Rouse, eds.) New York, Signet Classics: 1999, p. 316. For a discussion of Plato's theory of forms see chapter eleven of Charles Kahn's *Plato and the Socratic Dialogue: The Philosophical Use of a Literary Form.* Cambridge University Press, 1996.
2. De Marse and Dockendorf (2005).
3. Thus, by "CTM," in this context, I do not just mean classicism. Computational theories of mind can appeal to various computational theories of the format of thought (e.g. connectionism, dynamical systems theory, symbolism, or some combination thereof). See Kurzweil (2005). For philosophical background see Block's piece in this volume (Chapter 14) and Churchland (1996).
4. This commonly held but controversial view in philosophy of cognitive science is called "multiple realizability"; Bostrom calls it 'Substrate Independence' in his 2003.

References

Bostrom, Nick (2003), Transhumanist Frequently Asked Questions: A General Introduction, Version 2.1 (2003), World Transhumanist Association, http://www.transhumanism.org/resources/FAQv21.pdf, extracted at Dec. 1, 2008.

Bostrom, Nick and Cirkovic, Milar (2008), *Global Catastrophic Risks*, Oxford: OUP.

Churchland, P. (1996), *Engine of Reason, Seat of the Soul,* Cambridge, MA: MIT Press.

De Marse, T. B. and Dockendorf, K. P. (2005), "Adaptive flight control with living neuronal networks on microelectrode arrays." *Proceedings of the International Joint Conference on Neural Networks,* 3, 1548–51.

Garreau, Joel (2005), *Radical Evolution: The Promise and Peril of Enhancing Our Minds, Our Bodies – and What It Means to Be Human,* New York: Doubleday & Company.

McGinn, Colin (1993), *Problems in Philosophy: The Limits of Enquiry,* Oxford: Blackwell.

Thorne, Kip (1995), *Black Holes and Time Warps: Einstein's Outrageous Legacy,* W. W. Norton & Company.

Part I

COULD I BE IN A "MATRIX" OR COMPUTER SIMULATION?

Related Works

The Matrix
Permutation City
The 13th Floor
Vanilla Sky
Total Recall
Animatrix

1

BRAIN IN A VAT

John Pollock

It all began that cold Wednesday night. I was sitting alone in my office watching the rain come down on the deserted streets outside, when the phone rang. It was Harry's wife, and she sounded terrified. They had been having a late supper alone in their apartment when suddenly the front door came crashing in and six hooded men burst into the room. The men were armed and they made Harry and Anne lie face down on the floor while they went through Harry's pockets. When they found his driver's license one of them carefully scrutinized Harry's face, comparing it with the official photograph and then muttered, "It's him all right." The leader of the intruders produced a hypodermic needle and injected Harry with something that made him lose consciousness almost immediately. For some reason they only tied and gagged Anne. Two of the men left the room and returned with a stretcher and white coats. They put Harry on the stretcher, donned the white coats, and trundled him out of the apartment, leaving Anne lying on the floor. She managed to squirm to the window in time to see them put Harry in an ambulance and drive away.

By the time she called me, Anne was coming apart at the seams. It had taken her several hours to get out of her bonds, and then she called the police. To her consternation, instead of uniformed officers, two plain clothed officials arrived and, without even looking over the scene, they proceeded to tell her that there was nothing they could do and if she knew what was good for her she would keep her mouth shut. If she raised a fuss they would put out the word that she was a psycho and she would never see her husband again.

Not knowing what else to do, Anne called me. She had had the presence of mind to note down the number of the ambulance, and I had no great difficulty tracing it to a private clinic at the outskirts of town. When I arrived at the clinic I was surprised to find it locked up like a fortress. There were guards at the gate and it was surrounded by a massive wall. My commando training stood me in good stead as I negotiated the 20 foot wall, avoided the barbed wire, and silenced the guard dogs on the other side. The ground floor windows were all barred, but I managed to wriggle up a drainpipe and get in through a second-story window that someone had left ajar. I found myself in a laboratory. Hearing muffled sounds next door I peeked through the keyhole and saw what appeared to be a complete operating room and a surgical team laboring over Harry. He was covered with a sheet from the neck down and they seemed to be connecting tubes and wires to him. I stifled a gasp when I realized that they had removed the top of Harry's skull. To my considerable consternation, one of the surgeons reached into the open top of Harry's head and eased his brain out, placing it in a stainless steel bowl. The tubes and wires I had noted earlier were connected to the now disembodied brain. The surgeons carried the bloody mass carefully to some kind of tank and lowered it in. My first thought was that I had stumbled on a covey of futuristic Satanists who got their kicks from vivisection. My second thought was that Harry was an insurance agent. Maybe this was their way of getting even for the increases in their malpractice insurance rates. If they did this every Wednesday night, their rates were no higher than they should be!

My speculations were interrupted when the lights suddenly came on in my darkened hidey hole and I found myself looking up at the scariest group of medical men I had ever seen. They manhandled me into the next room and strapped me down on an operating table. I thought, "Oh, oh, I'm for it now!" The doctors huddled at the other end of the room, but I couldn't turn my head far enough to see what they were doing. They were mumbling among themselves, probably deciding my fate. A door opened and I heard a woman's voice. The deferential manner assumed by the medical malpractitioners made it obvious who was boss. I strained to see this mysterious woman but she hovered just out of my view. Then, to my astonishment, she walked up and stood over me and I realized it was my secretary, Margot. I began to wish I had given her that Christmas bonus after all.

It was Margot, but it was a different Margot than I had ever seen. She was wallowing in the heady wine of authority as she bent over me. "Well Mike, you thought you were so smart, tracking Harry here to the clinic," she said. Even now she had the sexiest voice I have ever heard, but I wasn't really thinking about that. She went on, "It was all a trick just to get you here. You saw what happened to Harry, He's not really dead, you know. These gentlemen are the premier neuroscientists in the world today. They have developed a surgical procedure whereby they remove the brain from the body but keep it alive in a vat of nutrient. The Food and Drug Administration wouldn't approve the procedure, but we'll show them. You see all the wires going to Harry's brain? They connect him up with a powerful computer. The computer monitors the output of his motor cortex and provides input to the sensory cortex in such a way that everything appears perfectly normal to Harry. It produces a fictitious mental life that merges perfectly into his past life so that he is unaware that anything has happened to him. He thinks he is shaving right now and getting ready to go to the office and stick it to another neurosurgeon. But actually, he's just a brain in a vat.

"Once we have our procedure perfected we're going after the head of the Food and Drug Administration, but we needed some experimental subjects first. Harry was easy. In order to really test our computer program we need someone who leads a more interesting and varied life – someone like you!" I was starting to squirm. The surgeons had drawn around me and were looking on with malevolent gleams in their eyes. The biggest brute, a man with a pockmarked face and one beady eye staring out from under his stringy black hair, was fondling a razor sharp scalpel in his still-bloody hands and looking like he could barely restrain his excitement. But Margot gazed down at me and murmured in that incredible voice, "I'll bet you think we're going to operate on you and remove your brain just like we removed Harry's, don't you? But you have nothing to worry about. We're not going to remove your brain. We already did – three months ago!"

With that they let me go. I found my way back to my office in a daze. For some reason, I haven't told anybody about this. I can't make up my mind. I am racked by the suspicion that I am really a brain in a vat and all this I see around me is just a figment of the computer. After all, how could I tell? If the computer program really works, no matter what I do, everything will seem normal. Maybe nothing I see is real. It's driving me crazy. I've even considered checking into that clinic voluntarily and asking them to remove my brain just so that I can be sure.

2

ARE YOU IN A COMPUTER SIMULATION?

Nick Bostrom

The Matrix got many otherwise not-so-philosophical minds ruminating on the nature of reality. But the scenario depicted in the movie is ridiculous: human brains being kept in tanks by intelligent machines just to produce power.

There is, however, a related scenario that is more plausible and a serious line of reasoning that leads from the possibility of this scenario to a striking conclusion about the world we live in. I call this the simulation argument. Perhaps its most startling lesson is that there is a significant probability that you are living in a computer simulation. I mean this literally: if the simulation hypothesis is true, you exist in a virtual reality simulated in a computer built by some advanced civilisation. Your brain, too, is merely a part of that simulation. What grounds could we have for taking this hypothesis seriously? Before getting to the gist of the simulation argument, let us consider some of its preliminaries. One of these is the assumption of "substrate independence". This is the idea that conscious minds could in principle be implemented not only on carbon-based biological neurons (such as those inside your head) but also on some other computational substrate such as silicon-based processors.

Of course, the computers we have today are not powerful enough to run the computational processes that take place in your brain. Even if they were, we wouldn't know how to program them to do it. But ultimately, what allows you to have conscious experiences is not the fact that your brain is made of squishy, biological matter but rather that it implements a certain computational architecture. This assumption is quite widely (although not universally) accepted among cognitive scientists and philosophers of mind. For the purposes of this chapter, we shall take it for granted.

Given substrate independence, it is in principle possible to implement a human mind on a sufficiently fast computer. Doing so would require very powerful hardware that we do not yet have. It would also require advanced programming abilities, or sophisticated ways of making a very detailed scan of a human brain that could then be uploaded to the computer. Although we will not be able to do this in the near future, the difficulty appears to be merely technical. There is no known physical law or material constraint that would prevent a sufficiently techno-logically advanced civilisation from implementing human minds in computers.

Our second preliminary is that we can estimate, at least roughly, how much computing power it would take to implement a human mind along with a virtual reality that would seem completely realistic for it to interact with. Furthermore, we can establish lower bounds on how powerful the computers of an advanced civilisation could be. Technological futurists have already produced designs for physically possible computers that could be built using advanced molecular manufacturing technology. The upshot of such an analysis is that a technologically mature civilisation that has developed at least those technologies that we already know are physically possible would be able to build computers powerful enough to run an astronomical number of human-like minds, even if only a tiny fraction of their resources was used for that purpose.

If you are such a simulated mind, there might be no direct observational way for you to tell; the virtual reality that you would be living in would look and feel perfectly real. But all that this shows, so far, is that you could never be completely sure that you are not living in a simulation. This result is only moderately interesting. You could still regard the simulation hypothesis as too improbable to be taken seriously.

Now we get to the core of the simulation argument. This does not purport to demonstrate that you are in a simulation. Instead, it shows that we should accept as true at least one of the following three propositions:

(1) The chances that a species at our current level of development can avoid going extinct before becoming technologically mature is negligibly small.
(2) Almost no technologically mature civilisations are interested in running computer simulations of minds like ours.
(3) You are almost certainly in a simulation.

Each of these three propositions may be prima facie implausible; yet, if the simulation argument is correct, at least one is true (it does not tell us which).

While the full simulation argument employs some probability theory and formalism, the gist of it can be understood in intuitive terms. Suppose that pro-position (1) is false. Then a significant fraction of all species at our level of development eventually becomes technologically mature. Suppose, further, that (2) is false, too. Then some significant fraction of these species that have become technologically mature will use some portion of their computational resources to run computer simulations of minds like ours. But, as we saw earlier, the number of simulated minds that any such technologically mature civilisation could run is astronomically huge.

Therefore, if both (1) and (2) are false, there will be an astronomically huge number of simulated minds like ours. If we work out the numbers, we find that there would be vastly many more such simulated minds than there would be non-simulated minds running on organic brains. In other words, almost all minds like yours, having the kinds of experiences that you have, would be simulated rather than biological. Therefore, by a very weak principle of indifference, you would have to think that you are probably one of these simulated minds rather than one of the exceptional ones that are running on biological neurons.

So if you think that (1) and (2) are both false, you should accept (3). It is not coherent to reject all three propositions. In reality, we do not have much specific information to tell us which of the three propositions might be true. In this situation, it might be reasonable to distribute our credence roughly evenly between the three possibilities, giving each of them a substantial probability.

Let us consider the options in a little more detail. Possibility (1) is relatively straightforward. For example, maybe there is some highly dangerous technology that every sufficiently advanced civilization develops, and which then destroys them. Let us hope that this is not the case.

Possibility (2) requires that there is a strong convergence among all sufficiently advanced civilisations: almost none of them is interested in running computer simulations of minds like ours, and almost none of them contains any relatively wealthy individuals who are interested in doing that and are free to act on their desires. One can imagine various reasons that may lead some civilisations to forgo running simulations, but for (2) to obtain, virtually all civilisations would have to do that. If this were true, it would constitute an interesting constraint on the future evolution of advanced intelligent life.

The third possibility is the philosophically most intriguing. If (3) is correct, you are almost certainly now living in computer simulation that was created by some advanced civilisation. What kind of empirical implications would this have? How should it change the way you live your life?

Your first reaction might think that if (3) is true, then all bets are off, and that one would go crazy if one seriously thought that one was living in a simulation.

To reason thus would be an error. Even if we were in a simulation, the best way to predict what would happen next in our simulation is still the ordinary methods – extrapolation of past trends, scientific modelling, common sense and so on. To a first approximation, if you thought you were in a simulation, you should get on with your life in much the same way as if you were convinced that you are living a non-simulated life at the bottom level of reality.

The simulation hypothesis, however, may have some subtle effects on rational everyday behaviour. To the extent that you think that you understand the motives of the simulators, you can use that understanding to predict what will happen in the simulated world they created. If you think that there is a chance that the simulator of this world happens to be, say, a true-to-faith descendant of some contemporary Christian fundamentalist, you might conjecture that he or she has set up the simulation in such a way that the simulated beings will be rewarded or punished according to Christian moral criteria. An afterlife would, of course, be a real possibility for a simulated creature (who could either be continued in a different simulation after her death or even be "uploaded" into the simulator's universe and perhaps be provided with an artificial body there). Your fate in that afterlife could be made to depend on how you behaved in your present simulated incarnation. Other possible reasons for running simulations include the artistic, scientific or recreational. In the absence of grounds for expecting one kind of simulation rather than another, however, we have to fall back on the ordinary empirical methods for getting about in the world.

If we are in a simulation, is it possible that we could know that for certain? If the simulators don't want us to find out, we probably never will. But if they choose to reveal themselves, they could certainly do so. Maybe a window informing you of the fact would pop up in front of you, or maybe they would "upload" you into their world. Another event that would let us conclude with a very high degree of confidence that we are in a simulation is if we ever reach the point where we are about to switch on our own simulations. If we start running simulations, that would be very strong evidence against (1) and (2). That would leave us with only (3).

3

EXCERPT FROM *THE REPUBLIC*

Plato

1 **Socrates**: And now, I said, let me show in a figure how far our nature is enlightened or unenlightened: – Behold! human beings living in an underground den, which has a mouth open towards the light and reaching all along the den; here they have been from their childhood, and have their legs and necks chained so that they cannot move, and can only see before them, being prevented by the chains from turning round their heads. Above and behind them a fire is blazing at a distance, and between the fire and the prisoners there is a raised way; and you will see, if you look, a low wall built along the way, like the screen which marionette players have in front of them, over which they show the puppets.

Glaucon: I see.

2 **Socrates:** And do you see, I said, men passing along the wall carrying all sorts of vessels, and statues and figures of animals made of wood and stone and various materials, which appear over the wall? Some of them are talking, others silent.

Glaucon: You have shown me a strange image, and they are strange prisoners.

3 **Socrates:** Like ourselves, I replied; and they see only their own shadows, or the shadows of one another, which the fire throws on the opposite wall of the cave?

Glaucon: True, he said; how could they see anything but the shadows if they were never allowed to move their heads?

4 **Socrates:** And of the objects which are being carried in like manner they would only see the shadows?

Glaucon: Yes, he said.

5 **Socrates:** And if they were able to converse with one another, would they not suppose that they were naming what was actually before them?

Glaucon: Very true.

6 **Socrates:** And suppose further that the prison had an echo which came from the other side, would they not be sure to fancy when one of the passers-by spoke that the voice which they heard came from the passing shadow?

Glaucon: No question, he replied.

7 **Socrates:** To them, I said, the truth would be literally nothing but the shadows of the images.

Glaucon: That is certain.

8 **Socrates:** And now look again, and see what will naturally follow if the prisoners are released and disabused of their error. At first, when any of them is liberated and compelled suddenly to stand up and turn his neck round and walk and look towards the light, he will suffer sharp pains; the glare will distress him, and he will be unable to see the realities of which in his former state he had seen the shadows; and then conceive someone saying to him, that what he saw before was an illusion, but that now, when he is approaching nearer to being and his eye is turned towards more real existence, he has a clearer vision, – what will be his reply? And you may further imagine that his instructor is pointing to the objects as they pass and requiring him to name them, – will he not be perplexed? Will he not fancy that the shadows which he formerly saw are truer than the objects which are now shown to him?

Glaucon: Far truer.

9 **Socrates:** And if he is compelled to look straight at the light, will he not have a pain in his eyes which will make him turn away and take refuge in the objects of vision which he can see, and which he will conceive to be in reality clearer than the things which are now being shown to him?

Glaucon: True, he said.

10 **Socrates:** And suppose once more, that he is reluctantly dragged up a steep and rugged ascent, and held fast until he's forced into the presence of the sun himself, is he not likely to be pained and irritated? When he approaches the light his eyes will be dazzled, and he will not be able to see anything at all of what are now called realities.

Glaucon: Not all in a moment, he said.

11 **Socrates:** He will require to grow accustomed to the sight of the upper world. And first he will see the shadows best, next the reflections of men and other objects in the water, and then the objects themselves; then he will gaze upon the light of the moon and the stars and the spangled heaven; and he will see the sky and the stars by night better than the sun or the light of the sun by day?

Glaucon: Certainly.

12 **Socrates:** Last of all he will be able to see the sun, and not mere reflections of him in the water, but he will see him in his own proper place, and not in another; and he will contemplate him as he is.

Glaucon: Certainly.

13 **Socrates:** He will then proceed to argue that this is he who gives the season and the years, and is the guardian of all that is in the visible world, and in a certain way the cause of all things which he and his fellows have been accustomed to behold?

Glaucon: Clearly, he said, he would first see the sun and then reason about him.

14 **Socrates:** And when he remembered his old habitation, and the wisdom of the den and his fellow-prisoners, do you not suppose that he would felicitate himself on the change, and pity them?

Glaucon: Certainly, he would.

15 **Socrates:** And if they were in the habit of conferring honours among them-selves on those who were quickest to observe the passing shadows and to remark which of them went before, and which followed after, and which were together; and who were therefore best able to draw conclusions as to the future, do you think that he would care for such honours and glories, or envy the possessors of them? Would he not say with Homer, *Better to be the poor servant of a poor master*, and to endure anything, rather than think as they do and live after their manner?

Glaucon: Yes, he said, I think that he would rather suffer anything than entertain these false notions and live in this miserable manner.

16 **Socrates:** Imagine once more, I said, such a one coming suddenly out of the sun to be replaced in his old situation; would he not be certain to have his eyes full of darkness?

Glaucon: To be sure, he said.

17 **Socrates:** And if there were a contest, and he had to compete in measuring the shadows with the prisoners who had never moved out of the den, while his sight was still weak, and before his eyes had become steady (and the time which would be needed to acquire this new habit of sight might be very considerable) would he not be ridiculous? Men would say of him that up he went and down he came without his eyes; and that it was better not even to think of ascending; and if any one tried to loose another and lead him up to the light, let them only catch the offender, and they would put him to death.

Glaucon: No question, he said.

18 **Socrates:** This entire allegory, I said, you may now append, dear Glaucon, to the previous argument; the prison-house is the world of sight, the light of the fire is the sun, and you will not misapprehend me if you interpret the journey upwards to be the ascent of the soul into the intellectual world according to my poor belief, which, at your desire, I have expressed whether rightly or wrongly God knows. But, whether true or false, my opinion is that in the world of knowledge the idea of good appears last of all, and is seen only with an effort; and, when seen, is also inferred to be the universal author of all things beautiful and right, parent of light and of the lord of light in this visible world, and the immediate source of reason and truth in the intellectual; and that this is the power upon which he who would act rationally, either in public or private life must have his eye fixed.

Glaucon: I agree, he said, as far as I am able to understand you.

4

EXCERPT FROM *THE MEDITATIONS ON FIRST PHILOSOPHY*

René Descartes

Of the Things of which we May Doubt

1. Several years have now elapsed since I first became aware that I had accepted, even from my youth, many false opinions for true, and that consequently what I afterward based on such principles was highly doubtful; and from that time I was convinced of the necessity of undertaking once in my life to rid myself of all the opinions I had adopted, and of commencing anew the work of building from the foundation, if I desired to establish a firm and abiding superstructure in the sciences. But as this enterprise appeared to me to be one of great magnitude, I waited until I had attained an age so mature as to leave me no hope that at any stage of life more advanced I should be better able to execute my design. On this account, I have delayed so long that I should henceforth consider I was doing wrong were I still to consume in deliberation any of the time that now remains for action. Today, then, since I have opportunely freed my mind from all cares and am happily disturbed by no passions, and since I am in the secure possession of leisure in a peaceable retirement, I will at length apply myself earnestly and freely to the general overthrow of all my former opinions.

2. But, to this end, it will not be necessary for me to show that the whole of these are false – a point, perhaps, which I shall never reach; but as even now my reason convinces me that I ought not the less carefully to withhold belief from what is not entirely certain and indubitable, than from what is manifestly false, it will be sufficient to justify the rejection of the whole if I shall find in each some ground for doubt. Nor for this purpose will it be necessary even to deal with each belief individually, which would be truly an endless labor; but, as the removal from below of the foundation necessarily involves the downfall of the whole edifice, I will at once approach the criticism of the principles on which all my former beliefs rested.

3. All that I have, up to this moment, accepted as possessed of the highest truth and certainty, I received either from or through the senses.

I observed, however, that these sometimes misled us; and it is the part of prudence not to place absolute confidence in that by which we have even once been deceived.

4. But it may be said, perhaps, that, although the senses occasionally mislead us respecting minute objects, and such as are so far removed from us as to be beyond the reach of close observation, there are yet many other of their informations (presentations), of the truth of which it is manifestly impossible to doubt; as for example, that I am in this place, seated by the fire, clothed in a winter dressing gown, that I hold in my hands this piece of paper, with other intimations of the same nature. But how could I deny that I possess these hands and this body, and withal escape being classed with persons in a state of insanity, whose brains are so disordered and clouded by dark bilious vapors as to cause them pertinaciously to assert that they are monarchs when they are in the greatest poverty; or clothed in gold and purple when destitute of any covering; or that their head is made of clay, their body of glass, or that they are gourds? I should certainly be not less insane than they, were I to regulate my procedure according to examples so extravagant.

5. Though this be true, I must nevertheless here consider that I am a man, and that, consequently, I am in the habit of sleeping, and representing to myself in dreams those same things, or even sometimes others less probable, which the insane think are presented to them in their waking moments. How often have I dreamt that I was in these familiar circum- stances, that I was dressed, and occupied this place by the fire, when I was lying undressed in bed? At the present moment, however, I certainly look upon this paper with eyes wide awake; the head which I now move is not asleep; I extend this hand consciously and with express purpose, and I perceive it; the occurrences in sleep are not so distinct as all this. But I cannot forget that, at other times I have been deceived in sleep by similar illusions; and, attentively considering those cases, I perceive so clearly that there exist no certain marks by which the state of waking can ever be distinguished from sleep, that I feel greatly astonished; and in amazement I almost persuade myself that I am now dreaming.

6. Let us suppose, then, that we are dreaming, and that all these particulars – namely, the opening of the eyes, the motion of the head, the forth-putting of the hands – are merely illusions; and even that we really possess neither an entire body nor hands such as we see. Nevertheless it must be admitted at least that the objects which appear to us in sleep are, as it were, painted representations which could not have been formed unless in the likeness of realities; and, therefore, that those general objects, at all events, namely, eyes, a head, hands, and an entire body, are not simply imaginary, but really existent. For, in truth, painters themselves, even when they study

to represent sirens and satyrs by forms the most fantastic and extraordinary, cannot bestow upon them natures absolutely new, but can only make a certain medley of the members of different animals; or if they chance to imagine something so novel that nothing at all similar has ever been seen before, and such as is, therefore, purely fictitious and absolutely false, it is at least certain that the colors of which this is composed are real. And on the same principle, although these general objects, viz. a body, eyes, a head, hands, and the like, be imaginary, we are nevertheless absolutely necessitated to admit the reality at least of some other objects still more simple and universal than these, of which, just as of certain real colors, all those images of things, whether true and real, or false and fantastic, that are found in our consciousness (*cogitatio*), are formed.

7. To this class of objects seem to belong corporeal nature in general and its extension; the figure of extended things, their quantity or magnitude, and their number, as also the place in, and the time during, which they exist, and other things of the same sort.

8. We will not, therefore, perhaps reason illegitimately if we conclude from this that Physics, Astronomy, Medicine, and all the other sciences that have for their end the consideration of composite objects, are indeed of a doubtful character; but that Arithmetic, Geometry, and the other sciences of the same class, which regard merely the simplest and most general objects, and scarcely inquire whether or not these are really existent, contain somewhat that is certain and indubitable: for whether I am awake or dreaming, it remains true that two and three make five, and that a square has but four sides; nor does it seem possible that truths so apparent can ever fall under a suspicion of falsity or incertitude.

9. Nevertheless, the belief that there is a God who is all powerful, and who created me, such as I am, has, for a long time, obtained steady possession of my mind. How, then, do I know that he has not arranged that there should be neither earth, nor sky, nor any extended thing, nor figure, nor magnitude, nor place, providing at the same time, however, for the rise in me of the perceptions of all these objects, and the persuasion that these do not exist otherwise than as I perceive them? And further, as I sometimes think that others are in error respecting matters of which they believe themselves to possess a perfect knowledge, how do I know that I am not also deceived each time I add together two and three, or number the sides of a square, or form some judgment still more simple, if more simple indeed can be imagined? But perhaps Deity has not been willing that I should be thus deceived, for he is said to be supremely good. If, however, it were repugnant to the goodness of Deity to have created me subject to constant deception, it would seem likewise to be contrary to his goodness to allow me to be occasionally deceived; and yet it is clear that this is permitted.

10.   Some, indeed, might perhaps be found who would be disposed rather to deny the existence of a Being so powerful than to believe that there is nothing certain. But let us for the present refrain from opposing this opinion, and grant that all which is here said of a Deity is fabulous: nevertheless, in whatever way it be supposed that I reach the state in which I exist, whether by fate, or chance, or by an endless series of antecedents and consequents, or by any other means, it is clear (since to be deceived and to err is a certain defect) that the probability of my being so imperfect as to be the constant victim of deception, will be increased exactly in proportion as the power possessed by the cause, to which they assign my origin, is lessened. To these reasonings I have assuredly nothing to reply, but am constrained at last to avow that there is nothing of all that I formerly believed to be true of which it is impossible to doubt, and that not through thoughtlessness or levity, but from cogent and maturely considered reasons; so that henceforward, if I desire to discover anything certain, I ought not the less carefully to refrain from assenting to those same opinions than to what might be shown to be manifestly false.

11.   But it is not sufficient to have made these observations; care must be taken likewise to keep them in remembrance. For those old and customary opinions perpetually recur – long and familiar usage giving them the right of occupying my mind, even almost against my will, and subduing my belief; nor will I lose the habit of deferring to them and confiding in them so long as I shall consider them to be what in truth they are, viz, opinions to some extent doubtful, as I have already shown, but still highly probable, and such as it is much more reasonable to believe than deny. It is for this reason I am persuaded that I shall not be doing wrong, if, taking an opposite judgment of deliberate design, I become my own deceiver, by supposing, for a time, that all those opinions are entirely false and imaginary, until at length, having thus balanced my old by my new prejudices, my judgment shall no longer be turned aside by perverted usage from the path that may conduct to the perception of truth. For I am assured that, meanwhile, there will arise neither peril nor error from this course, and that I cannot for the present yield too much to distrust, since the end I now seek is not action but knowledge.

12.   I will suppose, then, not that Deity, who is sovereignly good and the fountain of truth, but that some malignant demon, who is at once exceedingly potent and deceitful, has employed all his artifice to deceive me; I will suppose that the sky, the air, the earth, colors, figures, sounds, and all external things, are nothing better than the illusions of dreams, by means of which this being has laid snares for my credulity; I will consider myself as without hands, eyes, flesh, blood, or any of the senses, and as falsely believing that I am possessed of these; I will continue resolutely fixed in this belief,

and if indeed by this means it be not in my power to arrive at the knowledge of truth, I shall at least do what is in my power, viz, suspend my
judgment, and guard with settled purpose against giving my assent to what
is false, and being imposed upon by this deceiver, whatever be his power
and artifice. But this undertaking is arduous, and a certain indolence
insensibly leads me back to my ordinary course of life; and just as the
captive, who, perchance, was enjoying in his dreams an imaginary liberty,
when he begins to suspect that it is but a vision, dreads awakening, and
conspires with the agreeable illusions that the deception may be prolonged;
so I, of my own accord, fall back into the train of my former beliefs,
and fear to arouse myself from my slumber, lest the time of laborious wakefulness that would succeed this quiet rest, in place of bringing any light
of day, should prove inadequate to dispel the darkness that will arise from
the difficulties that have now been raised.

5

THE MATRIX AS METAPHYSICS*

David J. Chalmers

I. Brains in Vats

The Matrix presents a version of an old philosophical fable: the brain in a vat. A disembodied brain is floating in a vat, inside a scientist's laboratory. The scientist has arranged that the brain will be stimulated with the same sort of inputs that a normal embodied brain receives. To do this, the brain is connected to a giant computer simulation of a world. The simulation determines which inputs the brain receives. When the brain produces outputs, these are fed back into the simulation. The internal state of the brain is just like that of a normal brain, despite the fact that it lacks a body. From the brain's point of view, things seem very much as they seem to you and me.

The brain is massively deluded, it seems. It has all sorts of false beliefs about the world. It believes that it has a body, but it has no body. It believes that it is walking outside in the sunlight, but in fact it is inside a dark lab. It believes it is one place, when in fact it may be somewhere quite different. Perhaps it thinks it is in Tucson, when it is actually in Australia, or even in outer space.

I'm walking outside in the sun in Tucson.

Neo's situation at the beginning of *The Matrix* is something like this. He thinks that he lives in a city, he thinks that he has hair, he thinks it is 1999, and he thinks that it is sunny outside. In reality, he is floating in space, he has no hair, the year is around 2199, and the world has been darkened by war. There are a few small differences from the vat scenario above: Neo's brain is located in a body, and the computer simulation is controlled by machines rather than by a scientist. But the essential details are much the same. In effect, Neo is a brain in a vat.

Let's say that a *matrix* (lower-case "m") is an artificially designed computer simulation of a world. So the Matrix in the movie is one example of a matrix. And let's say that someone is *envatted*, or that they are *in a matrix*, if they have a cognitive system which receives its inputs from and sends its outputs to a matrix. Then the brain at the beginning is envatted, and so is Neo.

We can imagine that a matrix simulates the entire physics of a world, keeping track of every last particle throughout space and time. (Later, we will look at ways in which this set up might be varied.) An envatted being will be associated with a particular simulated body. A connection is arranged so that whenever this body receives sensory inputs inside the simulation, the envatted cognitive system will receive sensory inputs of the same sort. When the envatted cognitive system produces motor outputs, corresponding outputs will be fed to the motor organs of the simulated body.

When the possibility of a matrix is raised, a question immediately follows. How do I know that I am not in a matrix? After all, there could be a brain in a vat structured exactly like my brain, hooked up to a matrix, with experiences indistinguishable from those I am having now. From the inside, there is no way to tell for sure that I am not in the situation of the brain in a vat. So it seems that there is no way to know for sure that I am not in a matrix.

Let us call the hypothesis that I am in a matrix and have always been in a matrix the *Matrix Hypothesis*. Equivalently, the Matrix Hypothesis says that I am envatted and have always been envatted. This is not quite equivalent to the hypothesis that I am in the Matrix, as the Matrix is just one specific version of a matrix. And for now, I will ignore the complication that people sometimes travel back and forth between the Matrix and the external world. These issues aside, we can think of the Matrix Hypothesis informally as saying that I am in the same sort of situation as people who have always been in the Matrix.

The Matrix Hypothesis is one that we should take seriously. As Nick Bostrom has suggested, it is not out of the question that in the history of the universe, technology will evolve that will allow beings to create computer simulations of entire worlds. There may well be vast numbers of such computer simulations, compared to just one real world. If so, there may well be many more beings who are in a matrix than beings who are not. Given all this, one might even infer that it is more likely that we are in a matrix than that we are not. Whether this is right or not, it certainly seems that we cannot be *certain* that we are not in a matrix.

Serious consequences seem to follow. My envatted counterpart seems to be massively deluded. It thinks it is in Tucson; it thinks it is sitting at a desk writing an article; it thinks it has a body. But on the face of it, all of these beliefs are false. Likewise, it seems that if I am envatted, my own corresponding beliefs are false. If I am envatted, I am not really in Tucson, I am not really sitting at a desk, and I may not even have a body. So if I don't know that I am not envatted, then I don't know that I am in Tucson, I don't know that I am sitting at a desk, and I don't know that I have a body.

The Matrix Hypothesis threatens to undercut almost everything I know. It seems to be a *skeptical hypothesis*: a hypothesis that I cannot rule out, and one that would falsify most of my beliefs if it were true. Where there is a skeptical hypothesis, it looks like none of these beliefs count as genuine knowledge. Of course the beliefs *might* be true – I might be lucky, and not be envatted – but I can't rule out the possibility that they are false. So a skeptical hypothesis leads to *skepticism* about these beliefs: I believe these things, but I do not know them.

To sum up the reasoning: I don't know that I'm not in a matrix. If I'm in a matrix, I'm probably not in Tucson. So if I don't know that I'm not in a matrix, then I don't know that I'm in Tucson. The same goes for almost everything else I think I know about the external world.

II. Envatment Reconsidered

This is a standard way of thinking about the vat scenario. It seems that this view is also endorsed by the people who created *The Matrix*. On the DVD case for the movie, one sees the following:

> **Perception:** Our day-in, day-out world is real.
> **Reality:** That world is a hoax, an elaborate deception spun by all-powerful machines that control us. Whoa.

I think this view is not quite right. I think that even if I am in a matrix, my world is perfectly real. A brain in a vat is not massively deluded (at least if it has always been in the vat). Neo does not have massively false beliefs about the external world. Instead, envatted beings have largely *correct* beliefs about their world. If so, the Matrix Hypothesis is not a skeptical hypothesis, and its possibility does not undercut everything that I think I know.

Philosophers have held this sort of view before. The 18th-century Irish philosopher George Berkeley held, in effect, that appearance is reality. (Recall Morpheus: "What is real? How do you define real? If you're talking about what you can feel, what you can smell, what you can taste and see, then real is simply electrical signals interpreted by your brain.") If this is right, then the world perceived by envatted beings is perfectly real: they have all the right appearances, and appearance is reality. So on this view, even envatted beings have true beliefs about the world.

I have recently found myself embracing a similar conclusion, though for quite different reasons. I don't find the view that appearance is reality plausible, so I don't endorse Berkeley's reasoning. And until recently, it has seemed quite obvious to me that brains in vats would have massively false beliefs. But I now think there is a line of reasoning that shows that this is wrong.

I still think I cannot rule out the hypothesis that I am in a matrix. But I think that even if I am in a matrix, I am still in Tucson, I am still sitting at my desk, and so on. So the hypothesis that I am in a matrix is not a skeptical hypothesis. The same goes for Neo. At the beginning of the film, if he thinks "I have hair", he is correct. If he thinks "It is sunny outside", he is correct. And the same goes, of course, for the original brain in a vat. When it thinks "I have a body", it is correct. When it thinks "I am walking", it is correct.

This view may seem very counterintuitive at first. Initially, it seemed quite counterintuitive to me. So I'll now present the line of reasoning that has convinced me that it is correct.

III. The Metaphysical hypothesis

I will argue that the hypothesis that I am envatted is not a skeptical hypothesis, but a metaphysical hypothesis. That is, it is a hypothesis about the underlying nature of reality.

Where physics is concerned with the microscopic processes that underlie macroscopic reality, metaphysics is concerned with the fundamental nature of reality. A metaphysical hypothesis might make a claim about the reality that underlies physics itself. Alternatively, it might say something about the nature of our minds, or the creation of our world.

I think the Matrix Hypothesis should be regarded as a metaphysical hypothesis with all three of these elements. It makes a claim about the reality underlying physics, about the nature of our minds, and about the creation of the world.

In particular, I think the Matrix Hypothesis is equivalent to a version of the following three-part Metaphysical Hypothesis. First, physical processes are fundamentally computational. Second, our cognitive systems are separate from physical processes, but interact with these processes. Third, physical reality was created by beings outside physical space-time.

Importantly, nothing about this Metaphysical Hypothesis is skeptical. The Metaphysical Hypothesis here tells us about the processes underlying our ordinary reality, but it does not entail that this reality does not exist. We still have bodies, and there are still chairs and tables: it's just that their fundamental nature is a bit different from what we may have thought. In this manner, the

Metaphysical Hypothesis is analogous to a physical hypothesis, such as one involving quantum mechanics. Both the physical hypothesis and the Metaphysical Hypothesis tells us about the processes underlying chairs. They do not entail that there are no chairs. Rather, they tell us what chairs are really like.

I will make the case by introducing each of the three parts of the Metaphysical Hypothesis separately. I will suggest that each of them is coherent, and cannot be conclusively ruled out. And I will suggest that none of them is a skeptical hypothesis: even if they are true, most of our ordinary beliefs are still correct. The same goes for a combination of all three hypotheses. I will then argue that the Matrix Hypothesis hypothesis is equivalent to this combination.

(1) The Creation Hypothesis

The Creation Hypothesis says: Physical space-time and its contents were created by beings outside physical space-time.

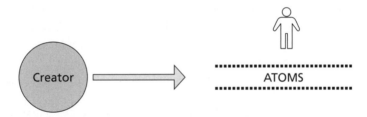

This is a familiar hypothesis. A version of it is believed by many people in our society, and perhaps by the majority of the people in the world. If one believes that God created the world, and if one believes that God is outside physical space-time, then one believes the Creation Hypothesis. One needn't believe in God to believe the Creation Hypothesis, though. Perhaps our world was created by a relatively ordinary being in the "next universe up", using the latest world-making technology in that universe. If so, the Creation Hypothesis is true.

I don't know whether the Creation Hypothesis is true. But I don't know for certain that it is false. The hypothesis is clearly coherent, and I cannot conclusively rule it out.

The Creation Hypothesis is not a skeptical hypothesis. Even if it is true, most of my ordinary beliefs are still true. I still have hands, I am still in Tucson, and so on. Perhaps a few of my beliefs will turn out false: if I am an atheist, for example, or if I believe all reality started with the Big Bang. But most of my everyday beliefs about the external world will remain intact.

(2) The Computational Hypothesis

The Computational Hypothesis says: Microphysical processes throughout space-time are constituted by underlying computational processes.

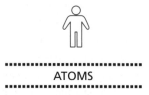

The Computational Hypothesis says that physics as we know it is not the fundamental level of reality. Just as chemical processes underlie biological processes, and microphysical processes underlie chemical processes, something underlies microphysical processes. Underneath the level of quarks and electrons and photons is a further level: the level of bits. These bits are governed by a computational algorithm, which at a higher level produces the processes that we think of as fundamental particles, forces, and so on.

The Computational Hypothesis is not as widely believed as the Creation Hypothesis, but some people take it seriously. Most famously, Ed Fredkin has postulated that the universe is at bottom some sort of computer. More recently, Stephen Wolfram has taken up the idea in his book *A New Kind of Science*, suggesting that at the fundamental level, physical reality may be a sort of cellular automata, with interacting bits governed by simple rules. And some physicists have looked into the possibility that the laws of physics might be formulated computationally, or could be seen as the consequence of certain computational principles.

One might worry that pure bits could not be the fundamental level of reality: a bit is just a 0 or a 1, and reality can't really be zeroes and ones. Or perhaps a bit is just a "pure difference" between two basic states, and there can't be a reality made up of pure differences. Rather, bits always have to be implemented by more basic states, such as voltages in a normal computer.

I don't know whether this objection is right. I don't think it's completely out of the question that there could be a universe of "pure bits". But this doesn't matter for present purposes. We can suppose that the computational level is itself constituted by an even more fundamental level, at which the computational processes are implemented. It doesn't matter for present purposes what that more fundamental level is. All that matters is that microphysical processes are constituted by computational processes, which are themselves constituted by more basic processes. From now on I will regard the Computational Hypothesis as saying this.

I don't know whether the Computational Hypothesis is correct. But again, I don't know that it is false. The hypothesis is coherent, if speculative, and I cannot conclusively rule it out.

The Computational Hypothesis is not a skeptical hypothesis. If it is true, there are still electrons and protons. On this picture, electrons and protons will be analogous to molecules: they are made up of something more basic, but they still exist. Similarly, if the Computational Hypothesis is true, there are still tables and chairs, and macroscopic reality still exists. It just turns out that their fundamental reality is a little different from what we thought.

The situation here is analogous to that with quantum mechanics or relativity. These may lead us to revise a few "metaphysical" beliefs about the external world: that the world is made of classical particles, or that there is absolute time. But most of our ordinary beliefs are left intact. Likewise, accepting the Computational Hypothesis may lead us to revise a few metaphysical beliefs: that electrons and protons are fundamental, for example. But most of our ordinary beliefs are unaffected.

(3) The Mind–Body Hypothesis

The Mind–Body Hypothesis says: My mind is (and has always been) constituted by processes outside physical space-time, and receives its perceptual inputs from and sends its outputs to processes in physical space-time.

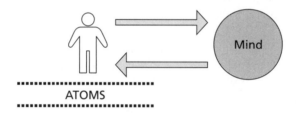

The Mind–Body Hypothesis is also quite familiar, and quite widely believed. Descartes believed something like this: on his view, we have nonphysical minds that interact with our physical bodies. The hypothesis is less widely believed today than in Descartes' time, but there are still many people who accept the Mind–Body Hypothesis.

Whether or not the Mind–Body Hypothesis is true, it is certainly coherent. Even if contemporary science tends to suggest that the hypothesis is false, we cannot rule it out conclusively.

The Mind–Body Hypothesis is not a skeptical hypothesis. Even if my mind is outside physical space-time, I still have a body, I am still in Tucson, and so on. At most, accepting this hypothesis would make us revise a few metaphysical beliefs about our minds. Our ordinary beliefs about external reality will remain largely intact.

(4) The Metaphysical Hypothesis

We can now put these hypotheses together. First we can consider the Combination Hypothesis, which combines all three. It says that physical space-time and its contents were created by beings outside physical space-time, that microphysical processes are constituted by computational processes, and that our minds are outside physical space-time but interact with it.

As with the hypotheses taken individually, the Combination Hypothesis is coherent, and we cannot conclusively rule it out. And like the hypotheses taken individually, it is not a skeptical hypothesis. Accepting it might lead us to revise a few of our beliefs, but it would leave most of them intact.

Finally, we can consider the Metaphysical Hypothesis (with a capital M). Like the Combination Hypothesis, this combines the Creation Hypothesis, the Computational Hypothesis, and the Mind–Body Hypothesis. It also adds the following more specific claim: the computational processes underlying physical space-time were designed by the creators as a computer simulation of a world.

(It may also be useful to think of the Metaphysical Hypothesis as saying that the computational processes constituting physical space-time are part of a broader domain, and that the creators and my cognitive system are also located within this domain. This addition is not strictly necessary for what follows, but it matches up with the most common way of thinking about the Matrix Hypothesis.)

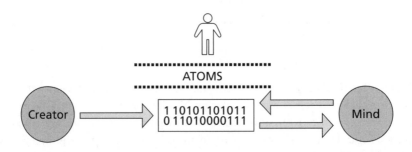

The Metaphysical Hypothesis is a slightly more specific version of the Combination Hypothesis, in that it specifies some relations between the various parts of the hypothesis. Again, the Metaphysical Hypothesis is a coherent hypothesis, and we cannot conclusively rule it out. And again, it is not a skeptical hypothesis. Even if we accept it, most of our ordinary beliefs about the external world will be left intact.

IV. The Matrix Hypothesis as a Metaphysical Hypothesis

Recall that the Matrix Hypothesis says: I have (and have always had) a cognitive system that receives its inputs from and sends its outputs to an artificially designed computer simulation of a world.

I will argue that the Matrix Hypothesis is equivalent to the Metaphysical Hypothesis, in the following sense: if I accept the Metaphysical Hypothesis, I should accept the Matrix Hypothesis, and if I accept the Matrix Hypothesis, I should accept the Metaphysical Hypothesis. That is, the two hypotheses *imply* each other, where this means that if one accepts the one, one should accept the other.

Take the first direction first, from the Metaphysical Hypothesis to the Matrix Hypothesis. The Mind–Body Hypothesis implies that I have (and have always had) an isolated cognitive system which receives its inputs from and sends its outputs to processes in physical space-time. In conjunction with the Computational Hypothesis, this implies that my cognitive system receives inputs from and sends outputs to the computational processes that constitute physical space-time. The Creation Hypothesis (along with the rest of the Metaphysical Hypothesis) implies that these processes were artificially designed to simulate a world. It follows that I have (and have always had) an isolated cognitive system that receives its inputs from and sends its outputs to an artificially designed computer simulation of a world. This is just the Matrix Hypothesis. So the Metaphysical Hypothesis implies the Matrix Hypothesis.

The other direction is closely related. To put it informally: if I accept the Matrix Hypothesis, I accept that what underlies apparent reality is just as the Metaphysical Hypothesis specifies. There is a domain containing my cognitive system, causally interacting with a computer simulation of physical space-time, which was created by other beings in that domain. This is just what has to obtain in order for the Metaphysical Hypothesis to obtain. If one accepts this, one should accept the Creation Hypothesis, the Computational Hypothesis, the Mind–Body Hypothesis, and the relevant relations among these.

One might make various objections. For example, one might object that the Matrix Hypothesis implies that a computer simulation of physical processes exists, but (unlike the Metaphysical Hypothesis) it does not imply that the physical processes themselves exist. I will discuss this and other objections in later sections. For now, though, I take it that there is a strong case that the Matrix Hypothesis implies the Metaphysical Hypothesis, and vice versa.

V. Life in the Matrix

If this is right, it follows that the Matrix Hypothesis is not a skeptical hypothesis. If I accept it, I should not infer that the external world does not exist, or that I have no body, or that there are no tables and chairs, or that I am not in Tucson. Rather, I should infer that the physical world is constituted by computations beneath the microphysical level. There are still tables, chairs, and bodies: these are made up fundamentally of bits, and of whatever constitutes these bits. This world was created by other beings, but is still perfectly real. My mind is separate from physical processes, and interacts with them. My mind may not have been created by these beings, and it may not be made up of bits, but it still interacts with these bits.

The result is a complex picture of the fundamental nature of reality. The picture is strange and surprising, perhaps, but it is a picture of a full-blooded external world. If we are in a matrix, this is simply the way that the world is.

We can think of the Matrix Hypothesis as a creation myth for the information age. If it is correct, then the physical world was created, just not necessarily by gods. Underlying the physical world is a giant computation, and creators created this world by implementing this computation. And our minds lie outside this physical structure, with an independent nature that interacts with this structure.

Many of the same issues that arise with standard creation myths arise here. When was the world created? Strictly speaking, it was not created within *our* time at all. When did history begin? The creators might have started the simulation in 4004 BC (or in 1999) with the fossil record intact, but it would have been much easier for them to start the simulation at the Big Bang and let things run their course from there. When do our nonphysical minds start to exist? It depends on just when new envatted cognitive systems are attached to the simulation (perhaps at the time of conception within the matrix, or perhaps at time of birth?). Is there life after death? It depends on just what happens to the envatted systems once their simulated bodies die. How do mind and body interact? By causal links that are outside physical space and time.

Even if we not in a matrix, we can extend a version of this reasoning to other beings who are in a matrix. If they discover their situation, and come to accept that they are in a matrix, they should not reject their ordinary beliefs about the external world. At most, they should come to revise their beliefs about the underlying nature of their world: they should come to accept that external objects are made of bits, and so on. These beings are not massively deluded: most of their ordinary beliefs about their world are correct.

There are a few qualifications here. One may worry about beliefs about other people's minds. I believe that my friends are conscious. If I am in a matrix, is this correct? In the Matrix depicted in the movie, these beliefs are mostly fine.

This is a multi-vat matrix: for each of my perceived friends, there is an envatted being in the external reality, who is presumably conscious like me. The exception might be beings such as Agent Smith, who are not envatted, but are entirely computational. Whether these beings are conscious depends on whether computation is enough for consciousness. I will remain neutral on that issue here. We could circumvent this issue by building into the Matrix Hypothesis the requirement that all the beings we perceive are envatted. But even if we do not build in this requirement, we are not much worse off than in the actual world, where there is a legitimate issue about whether other beings are conscious, quite independently of whether we are in a matrix.

One might also worry about beliefs about the distant past, and about the far future. These will be unthreatened as long as the computer simulation covers all of space-time, from the Big Bang until the end of the universe. This is built into the Metaphysical Hypothesis, and we can stipulate that it is built into the Matrix Hypothesis too, by requiring that the computer simulation be a simulation of an entire world. There may be other simulations that start in the recent past (perhaps the Matrix in the movie is like this), and there may be others that only last for a short while. In these cases, the envatted beings will have false beliefs about the past and/or the future in their worlds. But as long as the simulation covers the lifespan of these beings, it is plausible that they will have mostly correct beliefs about the current state of their environment.

There may be some respects in which the beings in a matrix are deceived. It may be that the creators of the matrix control and interfere with much of what happens in the simulated world. (The Matrix in the movie may be like this, though the extent of the creators' control is not quite clear.) If so, then these beings may have much less control over what happens than they think. But the same goes if there is an interfering god in a non-matrix world. And the Matrix Hypothesis does not imply that the creators interfere with the world, though it leaves the possibility open. At worst, the Matrix Hypothesis is no more skeptical in this respect than the Creation Hypothesis in a non-matrix world.

The inhabitants of a matrix may also be deceived in that reality is much bigger than they think. They might think their physical universe is all there is, when in fact there is much more in the world, including beings and objects that they can never possibly see. But again, this sort of worry can arise equally in a non-matrix world. For example, cosmologists seriously entertain the hypothesis that our universe may stem from a black hole in the "next universe up", and that in reality there may be a whole tree of universes. If so, the world is also much bigger than we think, and there may be beings and objects that we can never possibly see. But either way, the world that we see is perfectly real.

Importantly, none of these sources of skepticism – about other minds, the past and the future, about our control over the world, and about the extent of the world – casts doubt on our belief in the reality of the world that we perceive. None of them leads us to doubt the existence of external objects such as tables and chairs, in the way that the vat hypothesis is supposed to do. And none of these worries is especially tied to the matrix scenario. One can raise doubts about whether other minds exist, whether the past and the future exist, and whether we have control over our worlds quite independently of whether we are in a matrix. If this is right, then the Matrix Hypothesis does not raise the distinctive skeptical issues that it is often taken to raise.

I suggested before that it is not out of the question that we really are in a matrix. One might have thought that this is a worrying conclusion. But if I am right it is not nearly as worrying as one might have thought. Even if we are in such a matrix, our world is no less real than we thought it was. It just has a surprising fundamental nature.

VI. Objections

When we look at a brain in a vat from the outside, it is hard to avoid the sense that it is deluded. This sense manifests itself in a number of related objections. These are not direct objections to the argument above, but they are objections to its conclusion.

Objection 1: A brain in a vat may think it is outside walking in the sun, when in fact it is alone in a dark room. Surely it is deluded!

Response: The *brain* is alone in a dark room. But this does not imply that the *person* is alone in a dark room. By analogy, just say Descartes is right that we have disembodied minds outside space-time, made of ectoplasm. When I think "I am outside in the sun", an angel might look at my ectoplasmic mind and note that in fact it is not exposed to any sun at all. Does it follow that my thought is incorrect? Presumably not: I can be outside in the sun, even if my ectoplasmic mind is not. The angel would be wrong to infer that I have an incorrect belief. Likewise, we should not infer that envatted being has an incorrect belief. At least, it is no more deluded than a Cartesian mind.

The moral is that the immediate surroundings of our minds may well be irrelevant to the truth of most of our beliefs. What matters is the processes that our minds are connected to, by perceptual inputs and motor outputs. Once we recognize this, the objection falls away.

Objection 2: An envatted being may believe that it is in Tucson, when in fact it is in New York, and has never been anywhere near Tucson. Surely this belief is deluded.

Response: The envatted being's concept of "Tucson" does not refer to what we call Tucson. Rather, it refers to something else entirely: call this Tucson*, or "virtual Tucson". We might think of this as a "virtual location" (more on this in a moment). When the being says to itself "I am in Tucson", it really is thinking that it is in Tucson*, and it may well in fact be in Tucson*. Because Tucson is not Tucson*, the fact that the being has never been in Tucson is irrelevant to whether its belief is true.

A rough analogy: I look at my colleague Terry, and think "that's Terry". Elsewhere in the world, a duplicate of me looks at a duplicate of Terry. It thinks "that's Terry", but it is not looking at the real Terry. Is its belief false? It seems not: my duplicate's "Terry" concept refers not to Terry, but to his duplicate Terry*. My duplicate really is looking at Terry*, so its belief is true. The same sort of thing is happening in the case above.

Objection 3: Before he leaves the Matrix, Neo believes that he has hair. But in reality he has no hair (the body in the vat is bald). Surely this belief is deluded.

Response: This case is like the last one. Neo's concept of "hair" does not refer to real hair, but to something else that we might call hair* ("virtual hair"). So the fact that Neo does not have real hair is irrelevant to whether his belief is true. Neo really does has virtual hair, so he is correct.

Objection 4: What *sort* of objects does an envatted being refer to. What *is* virtual hair, virtual Tucson, and so on?

Response: These are all entities constituted by computational processes. If I am envatted, then the objects that I refer to (hair, Tucson, and so on) are all made of bits. And if another being is envatted, the objects that it refers to (hair*, Tucson*, and so on) are likewise made of bits. If the envatted being is hooked up to a simulation in my computer, then the objects it refers to are constituted by patterns of bits inside my computer. We might call these things *virtual objects*. Virtual hands are not hands (assuming I am not envatted), but they exist inside the computer all the same. Virtual Tucson is not Tucson, but it exists inside the computer all the same.

Objection 5: You just said that virtual hands are not real hands. Does this mean that if we are in the matrix, we don't have real hands?

Response: No. If we are *not* in the matrix, but someone else is, we should say that their term "hand" refers to virtual hands, but our term does not. So in this case, our hands aren't virtual hands. But if we *are* in the matrix, then our term "hand" refers to something that's made of bits: virtual hands, or at least something that would be regarded as virtual hands by people in the next world up. That is, if we *are* in the matrix, real hands are made of bits. Things look quite different, and our words refer to different things, depending on whether our perspective is inside or outside the matrix.

This sort of perspective shift is common in thinking about the matrix scenario. From the first-person perspective, we suppose that we are in a matrix. Here, real things in our world are made of bits, though the "next world up" might not be made of bits. From the third-person perspective, we suppose that someone *else* is in a matrix but we are not. Here, real things in our world are not made of bits, but the "next world down" is made of bits. On the first way of doing things, our words refer to computational entities. On the second way of doing things, the envatted beings' words refer to computational entities, but our words do not.

Objection 6: Just which pattern of bits is a given virtual object? Surely it will be impossible to pick out a precise set.

Response: This question is like asking: just which part of the quantum wave-function is this chair, or is the University of Arizona? These objects are all ultimately constituted by an underlying quantum wavefunction, but there may be no precise part of the micro-level wavefunction that we can say "is" the chair or the university. The chair and the university exist at a higher level. Likewise, if we are envatted, there may be no precise set of bits in the micro-level computational process that is the chair or the university. These exist at a higher level. And if someone else is envatted, there may be no precise sets of bits in the computer simulation that "are" the objects they refer to. But just as a chair exists without being any precise part of the wavefunction, a virtual chair may exist without being any precise set of bits.

Objection 7: An envatted being thinks it performs actions, and it thinks it has friends. Are these beliefs correct?

Response: One might try to say that the being performs actions* and that it has friends*. But for various reasons I think it is not plausible that words like "action" and "friend" can shift their meanings as easily as words like "Tucson" and "hair". Instead, I think one can say truthfully (in our own language) that the envatted being performs actions, and that it has friends. To be sure, it performs actions in *its* environment, and its environment is not our environment but the virtual environment. And its friends likewise inhabit the virtual environment (assuming that we have a multi-vat matrix, or that computation suffices for consciousness). But the envatted being is not incorrect in this respect.

Objection 8: Set these technical points aside. Surely, if we are in a matrix, the world is nothing like we think it is!

Response: I deny this. Even if we are in a matrix, there are still people, football games, and particles, arranged in space-time just as we think they are. It is just that the world has a *further* nature that goes beyond our initial conception. In particular, things in the world are realized computationally in a way that we might not have originally imagined. But this does not contradict any of our ordinary beliefs. At most, it will contradict a few of our more abstract metaphysical beliefs. But exactly the same goes for quantum mechanics, relativity theory, and so on.

If we are in a matrix, we may not have many false beliefs, but there is much knowledge that we lack. For example, we do not know that the universe is realized computationally. But this is exactly what one might expect. Even if we are not in a matrix, there may well be much about the fundamental nature of reality that we do not know. We are not omniscient creatures, and our knowledge of the world is at best partial. This is simply the condition of a creature living in a world.

VII. Other Skeptical Hypotheses

The Matrix Hypothesis is one example of a traditional "skeptical" hypothesis, but it is not the only example. Other skeptical hypotheses are not quite as straightforward as the Matrix Hypothesis. Still, I think that for many of them, a similar line of reasoning applies. In particular, one can argue that most of these are not global skeptical hypotheses: that is, their truth would not undercut all of our empirical beliefs about the physical world. At worst, most of them are *partial* skeptical hypotheses, undercutting some of our empirical beliefs, but leaving many of these beliefs intact.

New Matrix Hypothesis: I was recently created, along with all my memories, and was put in a newly created matrix.

What if both the matrix and I have existed for only a short time? This hypothesis is a computational version of Bertrand Russell's Recent Creation Hypothesis: the physical world was created only recently (with fossil record intact), and so was I (with memories intact). On that hypothesis, the external world that I perceive really exists, and most of my beliefs about its current states are plausibly true, but I have many false beliefs about the past. I think the same should be said of the New Matrix Hypothesis. One can argue, along the lines presented earlier, that the New Matrix Hypothesis is equivalent to a combination of the Metaphysical Hypothesis with the Recent Creation Hypothesis. This combination is not a global skeptical hypothesis (though it is a partial skeptical hypothesis, where beliefs about the past are concerned). So the same goes for the New Matrix Hypothesis.

Recent Matrix Hypothesis: For most of my life I have not been envatted, but I was recently hooked up to a matrix.

If I was recently put in a matrix without realizing it, it seems that many of my beliefs about my current environment are false. Let's say that just yesterday someone put me into a simulation, in which I fly to Las Vegas and gamble at a casino. Then I may believe that I am in Las Vegas now, and that I am in a casino, but these beliefs at false: I am really in a laboratory in Tucson.

This result is quite different from the long-term matrix. The difference lies in the fact that my conception of external reality is anchored to the reality in which I have lived most of my life. If I have been envatted all my life, my conception is anchored to the computationally constituted reality. But if I was just envatted yesterday, my conception is anchored to the external reality. So when I think that I am in Las Vegas, I am thinking that I am in the external Las Vegas, and this thought is false.

Still, this does not undercut all of my beliefs about the external world. I believe that I was born in Sydney, that there is water in the oceans, and so on, and all of these beliefs are correct. It is only my recently acquired beliefs, stemming from perception of the simulated environment, that will be false. So this is only a partial skeptical hypothesis: its possibility casts doubt on a subset of our empirical beliefs, but it does not cast doubt on all of them.

Interestingly, the Recent Matrix and the New Matrix hypotheses give opposite results, despite their similar nature; the Recent Matrix Hypothesis yields true beliefs about the past but false beliefs about the present, while the New Matrix Hypothesis yields false beliefs about the past and true beliefs about the present. The differences are tied to the fact that in Recent Matrix Hypothesis, I really have a past existence for my beliefs to be about, and that past reality has played a role in anchoring the contents of my thoughts that has no parallel under the New Matrix Hypothesis.

Local Matrix Hypothesis: I am hooked up to a computer simulation of a fixed local environment in a world.

On one way of doing this, a computer simulates a small fixed environment in a world, and the subjects in the simulation encounter some sort of barrier when they try to leave that area. For example, in the movie *The Thirteenth Floor*, just California is simulated, and when the subject tries to drive to Nevada, the road says "Closed for Repair" (with faint green electronic mountains in the distance!). Of course this is not the best way to create a matrix, as subjects are likely to discover the limits to their world.

This hypothesis is analogous to a Local Creation Hypothesis, on which creators just created a local part of the physical world. Under this hypothesis, we will have true beliefs about nearby matters, but false beliefs about matters further from home. By the usual sort of reasoning, the Local Matrix Hypothesis can be seen as a combination of the Metaphysical Hypothesis with the Local Creation Hypothesis. So we should say the same thing about this.

Extendible Local Matrix Hypothesis: I am hooked up to a computer simulation of a local environment in a world, extended when necessary depending on subject's movements.

This hypothesis avoids the obvious difficulties with a fixed local matrix. Here the creators simulate a local environment and extend it when necessary. For example, they might right now be concentrating on simulating a room in my house in Tucson. If I walk into another room, or fly to another city, they will simulate those. Of course they need to make sure that when I go to these places, they match my memories and beliefs reasonably well, with allowance for evolution in the meantime. The same goes for when I encounter familiar people, or people I have only heard about. Presumably the simulators keep up a database of the information about the world that has been settled so far, updating this information whenever necessary as time goes along, and making up new details when they need them.

This sort of simulation is quite unlike simulation in an ordinary matrix. In a matrix, the whole world is simulated at once. There are high start-up costs, but once the simulation is up and running, it will take care of itself. By contrast, the extendible local matrix involves "just-in-time" simulation. This has much lower start-up costs, but it requires much more work and creativity as the simulation evolves.

This hypothesis is analogous to an Extendible Local Creation Hypothesis about ordinary reality, under which creators create just a local physical environment, and extend it when necessary. Here, external reality exists and many local beliefs are true, but again beliefs about matters further from home are false. If we combine that hypothesis with the Metaphysical Hypothesis, the result is the Extendible Local Matrix Hypothesis. So if we are in an extendible local matrix, external reality still exists, but there is not as much of it as we thought, Of course if I travel in the right direction, more of it may come into existence!

The situation is reminiscent of *The Truman Show*. Truman lives in an artificial environment made up of actors and props, which behave appropriately when he is around, but which may be completely different when he is absent. Truman has many true beliefs about his current environment; there really are tables and chairs in front of him, and so on. But he is deeply mistaken about things outside his current environment, and further from home.

It is common to think that while *The Truman Show* poses a disturbing skeptical scenario, *The Matrix* is much worse. But if I am right, things are reversed. If I am in a matrix, then most of my beliefs about the external world are true. If I am in something like *The Truman Show*, then a great number of my beliefs are false. On reflection, it seems to me that this is the right conclusion. If we were to discover that we were (and always had been) in a matrix, this would be surprising, but we would quickly get used to it. If we were to discover that we were (and always had been) in *The Truman Show*, we might well go insane.

Macroscopic Matrix Hypothesis: I am hooked up to a computer simulation of macroscopic physical processes without microphysical detail.

One can imagine that for ease of simulation, the makers of a matrix might not bother to simulate low-level physics. Instead, they might just represent macroscopic objects in the world and their properties: e.g. that there is a table with such-and-such shape, position, and color, with a book on top of it with certain properties, and so on. They will need to make some effort to make sure that these objects behave in a physically reasonable way, and they will have to make special provisions for handling microphysical measurements, but one can imagine that at least a reasonable simulation could be created this way.

I think this hypothesis is analogous to a Macroscopic World Hypothesis: there are no microphysical processes, and instead macroscopic physical objects exist as fundamental objects in the world, with properties of shape, color, position, and so on. This is a coherent way our world could be, and it is not a global skeptical hypothesis, though it may lead to false scientific beliefs about lower levels of reality. The Macroscopic Matrix Hypothesis can be seen as a combination of this hypothesis with a version of the Metaphysical Hypothesis. As such, it is not a global skeptical hypothesis either.

One can also combine the various hypothesis above in various ways, yielding hypotheses such as a New Local Macroscopic Matrix Hypothesis. For the usual reasons, all of these can be seen as analogs of corresponding hypotheses about the physical world. So all of them are compatible with the existence of physical reality, and none is a global skeptical hypothesis.

The God Hypothesis: Physical reality is represented in the mind of God, and our own thoughts and perceptions depend on God's mind.

A hypothesis like this was put forward by George Berkeley as a view about how our world might really be. Berkeley intended this as a sort of metaphysical hypothesis about the nature of reality. Most other philosophers have differed from Berkeley in regarding this as a sort of skeptical hypothesis. If I am right, Berkeley is closer to the truth. The God Hypothesis can be seen as a version of the Matrix Hypothesis, on which the simulation of the world is implemented in the mind of God. If this is right, we should say that physical processes really exist: it's just that at the most fundamental level, they are constituted by processes in the mind of God.

Evil Genius Hypothesis: I have a disembodied mind, and an evil genius is feeding me sensory inputs to give the appearance of an external world.

This is René Descartes' classical skeptical hypothesis. What should we say about it? This depends on just how the evil genius works. If the evil genius simulates an entire world in his head in order to determine what inputs I should receive, then we have a version of the God Hypothesis. Here we should say that physical reality exists and is constituted by processes within the genius. If the evil genius is simulating only a small part of the physical world, just enough to give me reasonably consistent inputs, then we have an analog of the Local Matrix Hypothesis (in either its fixed or flexible versions). Here we should say that just a local part of external reality exists. If the evil genius is not bothering to simulate the microphysical level, but just the macroscopic level, then we have an analog of the Macroscopic Matrix Hypothesis. Here we should say that local external macroscopic objects exist, but our beliefs about their microphysical nature are incorrect.

The Evil Genius Hypothesis is often taken to be a global skeptical hypothesis. But if the reasoning above is right, this is incorrect. Even if the Evil Genius Hypothesis is correct, some of the external reality that we apparently perceive really exists, though we may have some false beliefs about it, depending on details. It is just that this external reality has an underlying nature that is quite different from what we may have thought.

Dream Hypothesis: I am now and have always been dreaming.

Descartes raised the question: how do you know that you are not currently dreaming? Morpheus raises a similar question:

> Have you ever had a dream, Neo, that you were so sure was real. What if you were unable to wake from that dream? How would you know the difference between the dream world and the real world?

The hypothesis that I am *currently* dreaming is analogous to a version of the Recent Matrix Hypothesis. I cannot rule it out conclusively, and if it is correct, then many of my beliefs about my current environment are incorrect. But presumably I still have many true beliefs about the external world, anchored in the past.

What if I have always been dreaming? That is, what if all of my apparent perceptual inputs have been generated by my own cognitive system, without my realizing this? I think this case is analogous to the Evil Genius Hypothesis: it's just that the role of the "evil genius" is played by a part of my own cognitive system! If my dream-generating system simulates all of space-time, we have something like the original Matrix Hypothesis. If it models just my local environment, or just some macroscopic processes, we have analogs of the more local versions of the Evil Genius Hypothesis above. In any of these cases, we should say that the objects that I am currently perceiving really exist (although objects farther from home may not). It is just that some of them are constituted by my own cognitive processes.

Chaos Hypothesis: I do not receive inputs from anywhere in the world. Instead, I have random uncaused experiences. Through a huge coincidence, they are exactly the sort of regular, structured experiences with which I am familiar.

The Chaos Hypothesis is an extraordinarily unlikely hypothesis, much more unlikely than anything considered above. But it is still one that could in principle obtain, even if it has miniscule probability. If I am chaotically envatted, do physical processes obtain in the external world? I think we should say that they do not. My experiences of external objects are caused by nothing, and the set of experiences associated with my conception of a given object will have no common source. Indeed, my experiences are not caused by any reality external to them at all. So this is a genuine skeptical hypothesis: if accepted, it would cause us to reject most of our beliefs about the external world.

So far, the only clear case of a global skeptical hypothesis is the Chaos Hypothesis. Unlike the previous hypothesis, accepting this hypothesis would undercut all of our substantive beliefs about the external world. Where does the difference come from?

Arguably, what is crucial is that on the Chaos Hypothesis, there is no causal explanation of our experiences at all, and there is no explanation for the regularities in our experience. In all the previous cases, there is some explanation for these regularities, though perhaps not the explanation that we expect. One might suggest that as long as a hypothesis involves some reasonable explanation for the regularities in our experience, then it will not be a global skeptical hypothesis.

If so, then if we are granted the assumption that there is some explanation for the regularities in our experience, then it is safe to say that some of our beliefs about the external world are correct. This is not much, but it is something!

Note

* Philosophical notes on this chapter can be found on David Chalmers' website: www.consc.net.

Part II

WHAT AM I? FREE WILL AND THE NATURE OF PERSONS

Related Works

Software

Star Trek, The Next Generation: Second Chances

Mindscan

The Matrix

Minority Report

6

WHERE AM I?

Daniel C. Dennett

Now that I've won my suit under the Freedom of Information Act, I am at liberty to reveal for the first time a curious episode in my life that may be of interest not only to those engaged in research in the philosophy of mind, artificial intelligence and neuroscience but also to the general public.

Several years ago I was approached by Pentagon officials who asked me to volunteer for a highly dangerous and secret mission. In collaboration with NASA and Howard Hughes, the Department of Defense was spending billions to develop a Supersonic Tunneling Underground Device, or STUD. It was supposed to tunnel through the earth's core at great speed and deliver a specially designed atomic warhead "right up the Red's missile silos," as one of the Pentagon brass put it.

The problem was that in an early test they had succeeded in lodging a warhead about a mile deep under Tulsa, Oklahoma, and they wanted me to retrieve it for them. "Why me?" I asked. Well, the mission involved some pioneering applications of current brain research, and they had heard of my interest in brains and of course my Faustian curiosity and great courage and so forth. . . . Well, how could I refuse? The difficulty that brought the Pentagon to my door was that the device I'd been asked to recover was fiercely radioactive, in a new way. According to monitoring instruments, something about the nature of the device and its complex interactions with pockets of material deep in the earth had produced radiation that could cause severe abnormalities in certain tissues of the brain. No way had been found to shield the brain from these deadly rays, which were apparently harmless to other tissues and organs of the body. So it had been decided that the person sent to recover the device should *leave his brain behind*. It would be kept in a safe place where it could execute its normal control functions by elaborate radio links. Would I submit to a surgical procedure that would completely remove my brain, which would then be placed in a life-support system at the Manned Spacecraft Center in Houston? Each input and output pathway, as it was severed, would be restored by a pair of microminiaturized radio transceivers, one attached precisely to the brain, the other to the nerve stumps in the empty cranium. No information would be lost, all the connectivity would be preserved. At first I was a bit reluctant. Would it really work? The Houston brain surgeons encouraged me. "Think of it," they said, "as a mere *stretching* of the nerves. If your brain were just moved over an *inch* in your skull, that would not alter or impair your mind. We're simply going to make the nerves indefinitely elastic by splicing radio links into them."

I was shown around the life-support lab in Houston and saw the sparkling new vat in which my brain would be placed, were I to agree. I met the large and brilliant support team of neurologists, hematologists, biophysicists, and electrical engineers, and after several days of discussions and demonstrations, I agreed to give it a try. I was subjected to an enormous array of blood tests, brain scans, experiments, interviews, and the like. They took down my auto-biography at great length, recorded tedious lists of my beliefs, hopes, fears, and tastes. They even listed my favorite stereo recordings and gave me a crash session of psychoanalysis.

The day for surgery arrived at last and of course I was anesthetized and remember nothing of the operation itself. When I came out of anesthesia, I opened my eyes, looked around, and asked the inevitable, the traditional, the lamentably hackneyed postoperative question: "Where am I?" The nurse smiled down at me. "You're in Houston," she said, and I reflected that this still had a good chance of being the truth one way or another. She handed me a mirror. Sure enough, there were the tiny antennae poling up through their titanium ports cemented into my skull.

"I gather the operation was a success," I said, "I want to go see my brain." They led me (I was a bit dizzy and unsteady) down a long corridor and into the life-support lab. A cheer went up from the assembled support team, and I responded with what I hoped was a jaunty salute. Still feeling light-headed, I was helped over to the life-support vat. I peered through the glass. There, floating in what looked like ginger ale, was undeniably a human brain, though it was almost covered with printed circuit chips, plastic tubules, electrodes, and other paraphernalia. "Is that mine?" I asked. "Hit the output transmitter switch there on the side of the vat and see for yourself," the project director replied. I moved the switch to OFF, and immediately slumped, groggy and nauseated, into the arms of the technicians, one of whom kindly restored the switch to its ON position. While I recovered my equilibrium and composure, I thought to myself: "Well, here I am, sitting on a folding chair, staring through a piece of plate glass at my own brain. . . . But wait," I said to myself, "shouldn't I have thought, 'Here I am, suspended in a bubbling fluid, being stared at by my own eyes'?" I tried to think this latter thought. I tried to project it into the tank, offering it hopefully to my brain, but I failed to carry off the exercise with any conviction. I tried again. "Here am *I*, Daniel Dennett, suspended in a bubbling fluid, being stared at by my own eyes." No, it just didn't work. Most puzzling and confusing. Being a philosopher of firm physicalist conviction, I believed unswervingly that the tokening of my thoughts was occurring somewhere in my brain: yet, when I thought "Here I am," where the thought occurred to me was *here*, outside the vat, where I, Dennett, was standing staring at my brain.

I tried and tried to think myself into the vat, but to no avail. I tried to build up to the task by doing mental exercises. I thought to myself, "The sun is shining *over there*," five times in rapid succession, each time mentally ostending a different place: in order, the sunlit corner of the lab, the visible front lawn of the hospital, Houston, Mars, and Jupiter. I found I had little difficulty in getting my "theres" to hop all over the celestial map with their proper references. I could loft a "there" in an instant through the farthest reaches of space, and then aim the next "there" with pinpoint accuracy at the upper left quadrant of a freckle on my arm. Why was I having such trouble with "here"? "Here in Houston" worked well enough, and so did "here in the lab," and even "here in this part of the lab," but "here in the vat" always seemed merely an unmeant mental mouthing. I tried closing my eyes while thinking it. This seemed to help, but still I couldn't manage to pull it off, except perhaps for a fleeting instant. I couldn't be sure. The discovery that I couldn't be sure was so unsettling. How did I know *where* I meant by "here" when I thought "here"? Could I *think* I meant one place when in fact I meant another? I didn't see how that could be admitted without untying the few bonds of intimacy between a person and his own mental life that had survived the onslaught of the brain scientists and philosophers, the physicalists and behaviorists. . . . Nagged by confusion, I attempted to orient myself by falling back on a favorite philosopher's ploy. I began naming things.

"Yorick," I said aloud to my brain, "you are my brain. The rest of my body, seated in this chair, I dub 'Hamlet.'" So here we all are: Yorick's my brain, Hamlet's my body, and I am Dennett. *Now*, where am I? And when I think "where am I?" where's that thought tokened? (i.e., where does that thought occur?). Is it tokened in my brain, lounging about in the vat, or right here between my ears where it *seems* to be tokened? Or nowhere? Its *temporal* coordinates give me no trouble; must it not have spatial coordinates as well? I began making a list of the alternatives.

(1) *Where Hamlet goes, there goes Dennett.* This principle was easily refuted by appeal to the familiar brain transplant thought-experiments so enjoyed by philosophers. If Tom and Dick switch brains, Tom is the fellow with Dick's former body – just ask him; he'll claim to be Tom, and tell you the most intimate details of Tom's autobiography. It was clear enough, then, that my current body and I could part company, but not likely that I could be separated from my brain. The rule of thumb that emerged so plainly from the thought-experiments was that in a brain-transplant operation, one wanted to be the *donor*, not the recipient. Better to call such an operation a *body*-transplant, in fact. So perhaps the truth was,

(2) *Where Yorick goes, there goes Dennett.* This was not at all appealing, however. How could I be in the vat and not about to go anywhere, when I was so obviously outside the vat looking in and beginning to make guilty plans to return to my room for a substantial lunch? This begged the question, I realized, but it still seemed to be getting at something important. Casting about for some support for my intuition, I hit upon a legalistic sort of argument that might have appealed to Locke.

Suppose, I argued to myself, I were now to fly to California, rob a bank, and be apprehended. In which state would I be tried: In California, where the robbery took place, or in Texas, where the brains of the outfit were located? Would I be a California felon with an out-of-state brain, or a Texas felon remotely controlling an accomplice of sorts in California? It seemed possible that I might beat such a rap just on the undecidability of that jurisdictional question, though perhaps it would be deemed an inter-state, and hence Federal, offense. In any event, suppose I were convicted. Was it likely that California would be satisfied to throw Hamlet into the brig, knowing that Yorick was living the good life and luxuriously taking the waters in Texas? Would Texas incarcerate Yorick, leaving Hamlet free to take the next boat to Rio? This alternative appealed to me. Barring capital punishment or other cruel and unusual punishment, the state would be obliged to maintain the life-support system for Yorick though they might move him from Houston to Leavenworth, and aside from the unpleasantness of the opprobrium, I, for one, would not mind at all and would consider myself a free man under those circumstances. If the state has an interest in forcibly relocating persons in institutions, it would fail to relocate me in any institution by locating Yorick there. If this were true, it suggested a third alternative.

(3) *Dennett is wherever he thinks he is.* Generalized, the claim was as follows: At any given time a person has a *point of view*, and the location of the point of view (which is determined internally by the content of the point of view) is also the location of the person.

Such a proposition is not without its perplexities, but to me it seemed a step in the right direction. The only trouble was that it seemed to place one in a heads-I-win/tails-you-lose situation of unlikely infallibility as regards location. Hadn't I myself often been wrong about where I was, and at least as often uncertain? Couldn't one get lost? Of course, but getting lost *geographically* is not the only way one might get lost. If one were lost in the woods one could attempt to reassure oneself with the consolation that at least one knew where one was: one was right *here* in the familiar surroundings of one's own body. Perhaps in this case one would not have drawn one's attention to much to be thankful for. Still, there were worse plights imaginable, and I wasn't sure I wasn't in such a plight right now.

Point of view clearly had something to do with personal location, but it was itself an unclear notion. It was obvious that the content of one's point of view was not the same as or determined by the content of one's beliefs or thoughts. For example, what should we say about the point of view of the Cinerama viewer who shrieks and twists in his seat as the roller-coaster footage overcomes his psychic distancing? Has he forgotten that he is safely seated in the theater? Here I was inclined to say that the person is experiencing an illusory shift in point of view. In other cases, my inclination to call such shifts illusory was less strong. The workers in laboratories and plants who handle dangerous materials by operating feedback-controlled mechanical arms and hands undergo a shift in point of view that is crisper and more pronounced than anything Cinerama can provoke. They can feel the heft and slipperiness of the containers they manipulate with their metal fingers. They know perfectly well where they are and are not fooled into false beliefs by the experience, yet it is as if they were inside the isolation chamber they are peering into. With mental effort, they can manage to shift their point of view back and forth, rather like making a transparent Neckar cube or an Escher drawing change orientation before one's eyes. It does seem extravagant to suppose that in performing this bit of mental gymnastics, they are transporting *themselves* back and forth.

Still their example gave me hope. If I was in fact in the vat in spite of my intuitions, I might be able to train myself to adopt that point of view even as a matter of habit. I should dwell on images of myself comfortably floating in my vat, beaming volitions to that familiar body *out there*. I reflected that the ease or difficulty of this task was presumably independent of the truth about the location of one's brain. Had I been practicing before the operation, I might now be finding it second nature. You might now yourself try such a *tromp l'oeil*. Imagine you have written an inflammatory letter which has been published in the *Times*, the result of which is that the Government has chosen to impound your brain for a probationary period of three years in its Dangerous Brain Clinic in Bethesda, Maryland. Your body of course is allowed freedom to earn a salary and thus to continue its function of laying up income to be taxed. At this moment, however, your body is seated in an auditorium listening to a peculiar account by Daniel Dennett of his own similar experience. Try it. Think yourself to Bethesda, and then hark back longingly to your body, far away, and yet *seeming* so near. It is only with long-distance restraint (yours? the Government's?) that you can control your impulse to get those hands clapping in polite applause before navigating the old body to the rest room and a well-deserved glass of evening sherry in the lounge. The task of imagination is certainly difficult, but if you achieve your goal the results might be consoling.

Anyway, there I was in Houston, lost in thought as one might say, but not for long. My speculations were soon interrupted by the Houston doctors, who wished to test out my new prosthetic nervous system before sending me off on my hazardous mission. As I mentioned before, I was a bit dizzy at first, and not surprisingly, although I soon habituated myself to my new circumstances (which were, after all, well nigh indistinguishable from my old circumstances). My accommodation was not perfect, however, and to this day I continue to be plagued by minor coordination difficulties. The speed of light is fast, but finite, and as my brain and body move farther and farther apart, the delicate interaction of my feedback systems is thrown into disarray by the time lags. Just as one is rendered close to speechless by a delayed or echoic hearing of one's speaking voice so, for instance, I am virtually unable to track a moving object with my eyes whenever my brain and my body are more than a few miles apart. In most matters my impairment is scarcely detectable, though I can no longer hit a slow curve ball with the authority of yore. There are some compensations of course. Though liquor tastes as good as ever, and warms my gullet while corroding my liver, I can drink it in any quantity I please, without becoming the slightest bit inebriated, a curiosity some of my close friends may have noticed (though I occasionally have *feigned* inebriation, so as not to draw attention to my unusual circumstances). For similar reasons, I take aspirin orally for a sprained wrist, but if the pain persists I ask Houston to administer codeine to me *in vitro*. In times of illness the phone bill can be staggering.

But to return to my adventure. At length, both the doctors and I were satisfied that I was ready to undertake my subterranean mission. And so I left my brain in Houston and headed by helicopter for Tulsa. Well, in any case, that's the way it seemed to me. That's how I would put it, just off the top of my head as it were. On the trip I reflected further about my earlier anxieties and decided that my first postoperative speculations had been tinged with panic. The matter was not nearly as strange or metaphysical as I had been supposing. Where was I? In two places, clearly: both inside the vat and outside it. Just as one can stand with one foot in Connecticut and the other in Rhode Island, I was in two places at once. I had become one of those scattered individuals we used to hear so much about. The more I considered this answer, the more obviously true it appeared. But, strange to say, the more true it appeared, the less important the question to which it could be the true answer seemed. A sad, but not unprecedented, fate for a philosophical question to suffer. This answer did not completely satisfy me, of course. There lingered some question to which I should have liked an answer, which was neither "Where are all my various and sundry parts?" nor "What is my current point of view?" Or at least there seemed to be such a question. For it did seem undeniable that in some sense I and not merely *most of me* was descending into the earth under Tulsa in search of an atomic warhead.

When I found the warhead, I was certainly glad I had left my brain behind, for the pointer on the specially built Geiger counter I had brought with me was off the dial. I called Houston on my ordinary radio and told the operation control center of my position and my progress. In return, they gave me instructions for dismantling the vehicle, based upon my on-site observations. I had set to work with my cutting torch when all of a sudden a terrible thing happened. I went stone deaf. At first I thought it was only my radio earphones that had broken, but when I tapped on my helmet, I heard nothing. Apparently the auditory transceivers had gone on the fritz. I could no longer hear Houston or my own voice, but I could speak, so I started telling them what had happened. In mid-sentence, I knew something else had gone wrong. My vocal apparatus had become paralyzed. Then my right hand went limp – another transceiver had gone. I was truly in deep trouble. But worse was to follow. After a few more minutes, I went blind. I cursed my luck and then I cursed the scientists who had led me into this grave peril. There I was, deaf, dumb, and blind, in a radioactive hole more than a mile under Tulsa. Then the last of my cerebral radio links broke, and suddenly I was faced with a new and even more shocking problem: whereas an instant before I had been buried alive in Oklahoma, now I was disembodied in Houston. My recognition of my new status was not immediate. It took me several very anxious minutes before it dawned on me that my poor body lay several hundred miles away, with heart pulsing and lungs respirating, but otherwise as dead as the body of any heart transplant donor, its skull packed with useless, broken electronic gear. The shift in perspective I had earlier found well nigh impossible now seemed quite natural. Though I could think myself back into my body in the tunnel under Tulsa, it took some effort to sustain the illusion. For surely it was an illusion to suppose I was still in Oklahoma: I had lost all contact with that body.

It occurred to me then, with one of those rushes of revelation of which we should be suspicious, that I had stumbled upon an impressive demonstration of the immateriality of the soul based upon physicalist principles and premises. For as the last radio signal between Tulsa and Houston died away, had I not changed location from Tulsa to Houston at the speed of light? And had I not accomplished this without any increase in mass? What moved from A to B at such speed was surely myself, or at any rate my soul or mind – the massless center of my being and home of my consciousness. My *point of view* had lagged somewhat behind, but I had already noted the indirect bearing of point of view on personal location. I could not see how a physicalist philosopher could quarrel with this except by taking the dire and counterintuitive route of banishing all talk of persons. Yet the notion of personhood was so well entrenched in everyone's world view, or so it seemed to me, that any denial would be as curiously unconvincing, as systematically disingenuous, as the Cartesian negation, "non sum" [I do not exist].

The joy of philosophic discovery thus tided me over some very bad minutes or perhaps hours as the helplessness and hopelessness of my situation became more apparent to me. Waves of panic and even nausea swept over me, made all the more horrible by the absence of their normal bodydependent phenomenology. No adrenalin rush of tingles in the arms, no pounding heart, no premonitory salivation. I did feel a dread sinking feeling in my bowels at one point, and this tricked me momentarily into the false hope that I was undergoing a reversal of the process that landed me in this fix – a gradual undisembodiment. But the isolation and uniqueness of that twinge soon convinced me that it was simply the first of a plague of phantom body hallucinations that I, like any other amputee, would be all too likely to suffer.

My mood then was chaotic. On the one hand, I was fired up with elation of my philosophic discovery and was wracking my brain (one of the few familiar things I could still do), trying to figure out how to communicate my discovery to the journals; while on the other, I was bitter, lonely, and filled with dread and uncertainty. Fortunately, this did not last long, for my technical support team sedated me into a dreamless sleep from which I awoke, hearing with magnificent fidelity the familiar opening strains of my favorite Brahms piano trio. So that was why they had wanted a list of my favorite recordings! It did not take me long to realize that I was hearing the music without ears. The output from the stereo stylus was being fed through some fancy rectification circuitry directly into my auditory nerve. I was mainlining Brahms, an unforgettable experience for any stereo buff. At the end of the record it did not surprise me to hear the reassuring voice of the project director speaking into a microphone that was now my prosthetic ear. He confirmed my analysis of what had gone wrong and assured me that steps were being taken to re-embody me. He did not elaborate, and after a few more recordings, I found myself drifting off to sleep. My sleep lasted, I later learned, for the better part of a year, and when I awoke, it was to find myself fully restored to my senses. When I looked into the mirror, though, I was a bit startled to see an unfamiliar face. Bearded and a bit heavier, bearing no doubt a family resemblance to my former face, and with the same look of spritely intelligence and resolute character, but definitely a new face. Further self-explorations of an intimate nature left me no doubt that this was a new body and the project director confirmed my conclusions. He did not volunteer any information on the past history of my new body and I decided (wisely, I think in retrospect) not to pry. As many philosophers unfamiliar with my ordeal have more recently speculated, the acquisition of a new body leaves one's *person* intact. And after a period of adjustment to a new voice, new muscular strengths and weaknesses, and so forth, one's *personality* is by and large also preserved. More dramatic changes in personality have been routinely observed in people who have undergone extensive plastic surgery, to say nothing of sex change operations, and I think no one contests the survival of the person in such cases. In any event I soon accommodated to my new body, to the point of being unable to recover any of its novelties to my consciousness or even memory. The view in the mirror soon became utterly familiar. That view, by the way, still revealed antennae, and so I was not surprised to learn that my brain had not been moved from its haven in the life-support lab.

I decided that good old Yorick deserved a visit. I and my new body, whom we might as well call Fortinbras, strode into the familiar lab to another round of applause from the technicians, who were of course congratulating themselves, not me. Once more I stood before the vat and contemplated poor Yorick, and on a whim I once again cavalierly flicked off the output transmitter switch. Imagine my surprise when nothing unusual happened. No fainting spell, no nausea, no noticeable change. A technician hurried to restore the switch to ON, but still I felt nothing. I demanded an explanation, which the project director hastened to provide. It seems that before they had even operated on the first occasion, they had constructed a computer duplicate of my brain, reproducing both the complete information processing structure and the computational speed of my brain in a giant computer program. After the operation, but before they had dared to send me off on my mission to Oklahoma, they had run this computer system and Yorick side by side. The incoming signals from Hamlet were sent simultaneously to Yorick's transceivers and to the computer's array of inputs. And the outputs from Yorick were not only beamed back to Hamlet, my body; they were recorded and checked against the simultaneous output of the computer program, which was called "Hubert" for reasons obscure to me. Over days and even weeks, the outputs were identical and synchronous, which of course did not *prove* that they had succeeded in copying the brain's functional structure, but the empirical support was greatly encouraging.

Hubert's input, and hence activity, had been kept parallel with Yorick's during my disembodied days. And now, to demonstrate this, they had actually thrown the master switch that put Hubert for the first time in on-line control of my body – not Hamlet, of course, but Fortinbras. (Hamlet, I learned, had never been recovered from its underground tomb and could be assumed by this time to have largely returned to the dust. At the head of my grave still lay the magnificent bulk of the abandoned device, with the word STUD emblazoned on its side in large letters – a circumstance which may provide archeologists of the next century with a curious insight into the burial rites of their ancestors.) The laboratory technicians now showed me the master switch, which had two positions, labeled B, for Brain (they didn't know my brain's name was Yorick) and H, for Hubert. The switch did indeed point to H, and they explained to me that if I wished, I could switch it back to B. With my heart in my mouth (and my brain in its vat), I did this. Nothing happened. A click, that was all. To test their claim, and with the master switch now set at B, I hit Yorick's output transmitter switch on the vat and sure enough, I began to faint. Once the output switch was turned back on and I had recovered my wits, so to speak, I continued to play with the master switch, flipping it back and forth. I found that with the exception of the transitional click, I could detect no trace of a difference. I could switch in mid-utterance, and the sentence I had begun speaking under the control of Yorick was finished without a pause or hitch of any kind under the control of Hubert. I had a spare brain, a prosthetic device which might some day stand me in very good stead, were some mishap to befall Yorick. Or alternatively, I could keep Yorick as a spare and use Hubert. It didn't seem to make any difference which I chose, for the wear and tear and fatigue on my body did not have any debilitating effect on either brain, whether or not it was actually causing the motions of my body, or merely spilling its output into thin air.

The one truly unsettling aspect of this new development was the prospect which was not long in dawning on me, of someone detaching the spare – Hubert or Yorick, as the case might be – from Fortinbras and hitching it to yet another body – some Johnny-come-lately Rosencrantz or Guildenstern. Then (if not before) there would be *two* people, that much was clear. One would be me, and the other would be a sort of super-twin brother. If there were two bodies, one under the control of Hubert and the other being controlled by Yorick, then which would the world recognize as the true Dennett? And whatever the rest of the world decided, which one would be *me*? Would I be the Yorick-brained one, in virtue of Yorick's causal priority and former intimate relationship with the original Dennett body, Hamlet? That seemed a bit legalistic, a bit too redolent of the arbitrariness of consanguinity and legal possession, to be convincing at the metaphysical level. For, suppose that before the arrival of the second body on the scene, I had been keeping Yorick as the spare for years, and letting Hubert's output drive my body – that is, Fortinbras – all that time. The Hubert–Fortinbras couple would seem then by squatter's rights (to combat one legal intuition with another) to be true to Dennett and the lawful inheritor of everything that was Dennett's. This was an interesting question, certainly, but not nearly so pressing as another question that bothered me. My strongest intuition was that in such an eventuality *I* would survive so long as *either* brain–body couple remained intact, but I had mixed emotions about whether I should want both to survive.

I discussed my worries with the technicians and the project director. The prospect of two Dennetts was abhorrent to me. I explained, largely for social reasons. I didn't want to be my own rival for the affections of my wife, nor did I like the prospect of the two Dennetts sharing my modest professor's salary. Still more vertiginous and distasteful, though, was the idea of knowing *that much* about another person, while he had the very same goods on me. How could we ever face each other? My colleagues in the lab argued that I was ignoring the bright side of the matter. Weren't there many things I wanted to do but, being only one person, had been unable to do? Now one Dennett could stay at home and be the professor and family man, while the other could strike out on a life of travel and adventure – missing the family of course, but happy in the knowledge that the other Dennett was keeping the home fires burning. I could be faithful and adulterous at the same time. I could even cuckold myself – to say nothing of other more lurid possibilities my colleagues were all too ready to force upon my overtaxed imagination. But my ordeal in Oklahoma (or was it Houston?) had made me less adventurous, and I shrank from this opportunity that was being offered (though of course I was never quite sure it was being offered to *me* in the first place).

There was another prospect even more disagreeable – that the spare, Hubert or Yorick as the case might be, would be detached from any input from Fortinbras and just left detached. Then, as in the other case, there would be two Dennetts, or at least two claimants to my name and possessions, one embodied in Fortinbras, and the other sadly, miserably disembodied. Both selfishness and altruism bade me take steps to prevent this from happening. So I asked that measures be taken to ensure that no one could ever tamper with the transceiver connections or the master switch without my (our? no, *my*) knowledge and consent. Since I had no desire to spend my life guarding my equipment in Houston, it was mutually decided that all the electronic connections in the lab would be carefully locked: both those that controlled the life-support system for Yorick and those that controlled the power supply for Hubert would be guarded with fail-safe devices, and I would take the only master switch, outfitted for radio remote control, with me wherever I went. I carry it strapped around my waist and – wait a moment – *here it is*. Every few months I reconnoiter the situation by switching channels. I do this only in the presence of friends of course, for if the other channel were, heaven forbid, either dead or otherwise occupied, there would have to be somebody who had my interests at heart to switch it back, to bring me back from the void. For while I could feel, see, hear and otherwise sense whatever befell my body, subsequent to such a switch, I'd be unable to control it. By the way, the two positions on the switch are intentionally unmarked, so I never have the faintest idea whether I am switching from Hubert to Yorick or *vice versa*. (Some of you may think that in this case I really don't know *who* I am, let alone where I am. But such reflections no longer make much of a dent on my essential Dennettness, on my own sense of who I am. If it is true that in one sense I don't know who I am then that's another one of your philosophical truths of underwhelming significance.)

In any case, every time I've flipped the switch so far, nothing has happened. *So let's give it a try. . . .*

"THANK GOD! I THOUGHT YOU'D NEVER FLIP THAT SWITCH! You can't imagine how horrible it's been these last two weeks – but now you know, it's your turn in purgatory. How I've longed for this moment! You see, about two weeks ago – excuse me, ladies and gentlemen, but I've got to explain this to my . . . um, brother, I guess you could say, but he's just told you the facts, so you'll understand – about two weeks ago our two brains drifted just a bit out of synch. I don't know whether *my* brain is now Hubert or Yorick, any more than you do, but in any case, the two brains drifted apart, and of course once the process started, it snowballed, for I was in a slightly different receptive state for the input we both received, a difference that was soon magnified. In no time at all the illusion that I was in control of my body – our body – was completely dissipated. There was nothing I could do – no way to call you. YOU DIDN'T EVEN KNOW I EXISTED! It's been like being carried around in a cage, or better, like being possessed – hearing my own voice say things I didn't mean to say, watching in frustration as my own hands performed deeds I hadn't intended. You'd scratch our itches, but not the way I would have, and you kept me awake, with your tossing and turning. I've been totally exhausted, on the verge of a nervous breakdown, carried around helplessly by your frantic round of activities, sustained only by the knowledge that some day you'd throw the switch.

"Now it's your turn, but at least you'll have the comfort of knowing *I* know you're in there. Like an expectant mother, I'm eating – or at any rate tasting, smelling, seeing – for *two* now, and I'll try to make it easy for you. Don't worry. Just as soon as this colloquium is over, you and I will fly to Houston, and we'll see what can be done to get one of us another body. You can have a female body – your body could be any color you like. But let's think it over. I tell you what – to be fair, if we both want this body, I promise I'll let the project director flip a coin to settle which of us gets to keep it and which then gets to choose a new body. That should guarantee justice, shouldn't it? In any case, I'll take care of you, I promise. These people are my witnesses.

"Ladies and gentlemen, this talk we have just heard is not exactly the talk *I* would have given, but I assure you that everything he said was perfectly true. And now if you'll excuse me, I think I'd – we'd – better sit down."[1]

Note

1. Anyone familiar with the literature on this topic will recognize that my remarks owe a great deal to the explorations of Sydney Shoemaker, John Perry, David Lewis and Derek Parfit, and in particular to their papers in Amelie Rorty, ed., *The Identities of Persons*, 1976.

7

PERSONAL IDENTITY

Eric Olson

Personal identity deals with questions that arise about ourselves by virtue of our being people (or, as lawyers and philosophers like to say, *persons*). Many of these questions are familiar ones that occur to everyone at some time: What am I? When did I begin? What will happen to me when I die? Others are more abstruse. Personal identity has been discussed since the origins of Western philosophy, and most major figures have had something to say about it. (There is also a rich literature on the topic in Eastern philosophy, which I am not competent to discuss. Collins 1982 and Jinpa 2002 are useful sources.)

I shall first survey the main questions of personal identity. Most of the chapter will then focus on the one that has received most attention in recent times: our identity over time. I will discuss what the question means, and the main proposed answers. I will also say a bit about how these answers relate to some of the other questions of personal identity, and to more general questions in metaphysics and the philosophy of mind.

1. The Problems of Personal Identity

There is no single problem of personal identity, but rather a wide range of loosely connected questions:

Who am I?

We often speak of our "personal identity" as what makes us the people we are. Your identity in this sense consists roughly of what makes you unique as an individual and different from others. Or it is the way you see or define yourself, or the network of values and convictions that structure your life. This individual identity is a *property* (or set of properties). Presumably it is one you have only contingently – you might have had a different identity from the one you in fact have – and one that you might have for a while and then lose: you could acquire a new individual identity, or perhaps even get by without one. (Ludwig 1997 is a typical discussion.)

Personhood

What is it to be a person? What is necessary, and what suffices, for something to count as a person, as opposed to a non-person? What have people got that non-people haven't got? This amounts more or less to asking for the definition of the word *person*. An answer would take the form "Necessarily, *x* is a person if and only if ... x ...", with the blanks appropriately filled in. More specifically, we can ask at what point in one's development from a fertilized egg there comes to be a person, or what it would take for a chimpanzee or a Martian or an electronic computer to be a person, if they could ever be. (See e.g. Chisholm 1976: 136f.; Baker 2000: ch. 3.)

Persistence

What does it take for a person to persist from one time to another – that is, for the *same* person to exist at different times? What sorts of adventures could you possibly survive, in the broadest sense of the word "possible"? What sort of event would necessarily bring your existence to an end? What determines which past or future being is you? Suppose you point to a child in an old class photograph and say, "That's me." What makes you that one, rather than one of the others? What is it about the way she relates to you as you were then to how she relates to you as you are now that makes her you? For that matter, what makes it the case that anyone at all who existed back then is you? This is the question of personal identity over time. An answer to it is an account of our persistence conditions, or a criterion of personal identity over time (a constitutive rather than an evidential criterion: the second falls under the Evidence Question below).

Historically, this question often arises out of the hope (or fear) that we might continue to exist after we die – Plato's *Phaedo* is a famous example. Whether this could happen depends on whether biological death necessarily brings one's existence to an end. Imagine that after your death there really will be someone, in the next world or in this one, who resembles you in certain ways. How would that being have to relate to you as you are now in order to *be* you, rather than someone else? What would the Higher Powers have to do to keep you in existence after your death? Or is there anything they could do? The answers to these questions depend on the answer to the Persistence Question.

Evidence

How do we find out who is who? What evidence bears on the question of whether the person here now is the one who was here yesterday? What ought we to do when different kinds of evidence support opposing verdicts? One source of evidence is first-person memory: if you remember doing something, or at least seem to remember, it was probably you who did it. Another source is physical continuity: if the person who did it looks just like you, or even better if she is in some sense physically or spatio-temporally continuous with you, that is reason to think she is you. Which of these sources is more fundamental? Does first-person memory count as evidence all by itself, for instance, or only insofar as we can check it against publicly available physical evidence?

The Evidence Question dominated the philosophical literature on personal identity from the 1950s to the 1970s (Shoemaker 1963 and Penelhum 1970 are good examples). Though it is sometimes confused with the Persistence Question, however, the two are different. What it takes for you to persist through time is one thing; how we might find out whether you have done so is another. If the criminal has fingerprints just like yours, the courts may conclude that he is you. But even if that is conclusive evidence, having your fingerprints is not *what it is* for a past or future being to be you: it is neither necessary (you could survive without any fingers at all) nor sufficient (someone else could have fingerprints just like yours).

Population

If we think of the Persistence Question as asking which of the characters introduced at the beginning of a story have survived to become the ones at the end of it, we can also ask how many are on the stage at any one time. What determines how many of us there are now? If there are some six billion people on the earth at present, what facts – biological, psychological, or what have you – make that the right number? The question is not what *causes* there to be a certain number of people at a given time, but what there being that number consists in. It is like asking what sort of configuration of pieces amounts to black's winning a game of chess, rather than what sorts of moves lead to its winning.

You may think that the number of people at any given time is simply the number of human organisms there are at that time (perhaps discounting those in a defective state that don't count as people, and ignoring non-human people, if there are any). But this is disputed. Surgeons sometimes cut the nerve bands connecting a person's cerebral hemispheres, resulting in such odd behavior as simultaneously pulling trousers up with one hand and pulling them down with the other, and, apparently, some sort of disunity of consciousness. You might think that this gives us two people sharing one organism. (See e.g. Nagel 1971. Puccetti 1973 argues that there are two people within the skin of each normal human being.) Or maybe a human being with split personality could literally be the home of two or more thinking beings (Wilkes 1988: 127f.; see also Olson 2003).

This is sometimes called the problem of "synchronic identity", as opposed to the "diachronic identity" of the Persistence Question (and the "counterfactual identity" of the How could I have been? Question below). These terms need careful handling, however. They are apt to give the impression that identity comes in two kinds, synchronic and diachronic: a serious blunder. The truth is simply that there are two kinds of situations where we can ask how many people (or other things) there are: synchronic situations involving just one moment and diachronic ones involving a stretch of time.

What am I?

What sort of things, metaphysically speaking, are you and I and other human people? What is our basic metaphysical nature? For instance, what are we made of? Are we made up entirely of matter, just as stones are, or partly or wholly of something else? If we are made of matter, what matter is it? (Just the matter that makes up our bodies, or might we be larger or smaller than our bodies?) Where, in other words, do our spatial boundaries lie? More fundamentally, what fixes those boundaries? Are we substances – metaphysically independent beings – or is each of us a state or an aspect of something else, or perhaps some sort of process or event?

One possible answer to this broad question is that we are biological organisms. Surprisingly, perhaps, most philosophers reject this. (We shall return to it later.) Another is that we are partless immaterial substances (or compound things made up of an immaterial soul and a material body: see Swinburne 1984). Hume suggested that each of us is "a bundle of perceptions" (1978: 252; see also Quinton 1962 and Campbell 2006). A popular view nowadays is that we are material things "constituted by" human animals: you are made of the same matter as a certain animal, but you and the animal are different things because what it takes for you to persist is different (Shoemaker 1984: 112–14 and 1999; Baker 2000). Another is that we are temporal parts of animals (Lewis 1976; Hudson 2001). There is even the paradoxical view that there is nothing that we are: we don't really exist at all (Russell 1985: 50; Wittgenstein 1922: 5.631; Unger 1979). (Olson 2007 discusses these matters at length.)

How could I have been?

How different could I have been from the way I actually am? Which of my properties do I have essentially, and which only accidentally or contingently? Could I, for instance, have had different parents? Frank Sinatra and Doris Day might have had children together. Could I have been one of them? Or could they only have had children other than me? Could I have died in the womb before ever becoming conscious? Are there possible worlds just like the actual one except for who is who – where people have "changed places" so that what is in fact your career is mine and vice versa? Whether these are best described as questions about personal identity is debatable. (They are not about whether beings in other worlds are identical with people in the actual world: see van Inwagen 1985.) But they are sometimes discussed in connection with the others.

What matters in identity?

What is the practical importance of facts about our identity and persistence? Why should we care about it? Why does it *matter*? Imagine that surgeons are going to put your brain into my head, and that neither of us has any choice about this. Will the resulting person – who will presumably think he is you – be responsible for my actions, or for yours? (Or both? Or neither?) Suppose he will be in terrible pain after the operation unless one of us pays a large sum in advance. If we were both entirely selfish, which of us would have a reason to pay?

The answer may seem to turn entirely on whether the resulting person would *be* you or I. Only *you* can be responsible for your actions. The only one whose future welfare you cannot rationally ignore is yourself. You have a special, selfish interest in your own future, and no one else's. Identity itself matters. But some deny this. They say that someone else could be responsible for your actions. You could have an entirely selfish reason to care about someone else's well-being for his own sake. I care, or ought rationally to care, about what happens to the man people tomorrow will call Olson not because he *is* me, but because he is then psychologically continuous with me as I am now (see section 4), or because he relates to me in some other way that doesn't imply that he and I are one. If someone other than I were psychologically continuous tomorrow with me as I am now, he would have what matters to me, and I ought to transfer my selfish concern to him. Identity itself has no practical importance. (See Shoemaker 1970: 284; Parfit 1971; 1984: 215, 1995; Martin 1998.)

That completes our survey of problems. Though these eight questions are clearly related, it is hard to find any interesting common feature that makes them all questions about personal identity. In any case they are different, and it is important not to run them together.

2. Understanding the Persistence Question

Let us turn now to the Persistence Question. Few concepts have been the source of more misunderstanding than identity over time. The Persistence Question is often confused with other questions, or stated in a tendentious way. It is important to get it right.

The question is what is necessary and sufficient for a past or future being to be you. If we point to you now, and then describe someone or something existing at another time, we can ask whether we are referring to one thing twice, or referring once to each of two things. (There are precisely analogous questions about the persistence of other objects, such as dogs.) The Persistence Question asks what determines the answer to such questions, or makes possible answers true or false.

The question is about *numerical identity*. To say that this and that are numerically identical is to say that they are one and the same: one thing rather than two. This is different from *qualitative identity*. Things are qualitatively identical when they are exactly similar. Identical twins may be qualitatively identical – there may be no telling them apart – but not numerically identical, as there are two of them: that's what makes them twins. A past or future person needn't, at that past or future time, be exactly like you are now in order to be you – that is, in order to be numerically identical with you. You don't remain qualitatively the same throughout your life. You change: in size, appearance, and in many other ways. So the question is not what it takes for a past or future being to be qualitatively just like you, but what it takes for a past or future being to be *you*, as opposed to someone or something other than you.

(Someone might say, as Hume apparently did, that a past or future being *couldn't* be you unless he or she were then qualitatively just like you are now. That would be a highly contentious metaphysical claim. It amounts to denying that anything can survive any change whatever: even blinking your eyes would be fatal, resulting in your ceasing to exist and being replaced with someone else. It would mean that you did not exist even a moment ago. There would be no point in asking the Persistence Question if this were the case. Virtually all discussions of personal identity over time assume that it is possible for a person to change.)

The confusion of qualitative with numerical identity is one source of misunderstanding about the Persistence Question. Here is another. People sometimes ask what it takes for someone to *remain the same person* from one time to another. The idea is that if I were to alter in certain ways – if I lost most of my memory, or my personality changed dramatically, or I underwent a profound religious conversion, say – then I would no longer be the person I was before.

The question of what it takes for someone to remain the same person is not the Persistence Question. It is not even a question about numerical identity. If it were, it would answer itself: I necessarily remain numerically the same for as long as I exist. Nothing could make me a *numerically* different person from the one I am now. Nothing can start out as one thing and end up as another thing – a numerically different one. This has nothing to do with personal identity in particular, but is simply a fact about the logic of identity.

Those who say that after a certain sort of adventure *you* would be a different person, or that you would no longer be the person you once were, presumably mean that you would still exist, but would have changed in some important way. If the person resulting from the adventure were not numerically identical with you, it would not be the case that *you* were "a different person". Rather, you would have ceased to exist and been replaced by someone else. Those who say these things are usually thinking of individual identity in the Who am I? sense: they are talking about the possibility of your losing some or all of the properties that make up your individual identity, and acquiring new ones. This has nothing to do with the Persistence Question.

It is inconvenient that the words "identity" and "same" mean so many different things: numerical identity, qualitative identity, individual psychological identity, and more. To make matters worse, some philosophers speak of "surviving" in a way that doesn't imply numerical identity, so that I could survive a certain adventure without existing afterwards (Parfit, 1971). Confusion is inevitable.

Here is a more insidious misunderstanding. Many people try to state the Persistence Question like this:

1. Under what possible circumstances is a person existing at one time identical with a person existing at another time?

In other words, what does it take for past or future person to be you? We have a person existing at one time, and a person existing at another, and the question is what is necessary and sufficient for them to be one person rather than two.

This is not the Persistence Question. It is too narrow. We may want to know whether you were ever an embryo or a foetus, or whether you could survive in a persistent vegetative state. These are clearly questions about what it takes for us to persist, and an account of our identity over time ought to answer them. (Their answers may have important ethical implications: it matters to the morality of abortion, for instance, whether something that is an embryo or foetus at one time can be an adult person at another time, or whether the adult person is always numerically different from the foetus.) But many philosophers define "person" as something that has certain mental features. Locke, for instance, famously said that a person is "a thinking intelligent being, that has reason and reflection, and can consider itself as itself, the same thinking thing, in different times and places" (1975: 335). And neurologists say that early-term foetuses and human beings in a persistent vegetative state have no mental features at all. If anything like Locke's definition is right, such beings are not people. In that case we cannot learn anything about whether you were once an embryo or could come to be a vegetable by discovering what it takes for a past or future *person* to be you.

We can illustrate the point by considering a particular answer to question 1:

Necessarily, a person who exists at one time is identical with a person who exists at a second time if and only if the first person can, at the first time, remember an experience the second person has at the second time, or vice versa.

That is, a past or future person is you just in the case that you can now remember an experience she had then, or she can then remember an experience you are having now. (This view is also sometimes attributed to Locke, though it is doubtful whether he actually held it.) Call it the *Memory Criterion*.

The Memory Criterion may seem to imply that if you were to lapse into a persistent vegetative state, the resulting vegetable would not be you, as it would be unable to remember anything: you would have ceased to exist, or perhaps passed on to the next world. But in fact it implies no such thing. Assuming that a human vegetable is not a person, this is not a case involving a person existing at one time and a person existing at another time. The Memory Criterion tells us which past or future *person* you are, but not which past or future *thing*: it says what it takes for one to persist *as a person*, but not what it takes for one to persist without qualification. So it implies nothing at all about whether you could persist as a vegetable. For the same reason it tells us nothing about whether you were ever an embryo (Olson 1997: 22–6, Mackie 1999: 224–8).

So rather than question 1, we ought to ask what it takes for *any* past or future being, person or not, to be you or I:

2. Under what possible circumstances is a person who exists at one time identical with *something* that exists at another time (whether or not it is a person then)?

This is the Persistence Question as I understand it. Philosophers typically ask 1 rather than 2 because they assume that every person is a person *essentially*: nothing that is in fact a person could possibly exist without being a person. (By contrast, something that is in fact a student could exist without being a student: no student is essentially a student.) This claim, "person essentialism", implies that whatever is a person at one time must be a person at every time when she exists, making the two questions equivalent. Whether it is true, however, is a serious question (an instance of the How could I have been? Question). Person essentialism implies that you could not possibly have been an embryo (given that an embryo is not a person): the embryo that gave rise to you is not strictly you; you came into being only when it developed certain mental capacities. Nor could you come to be a human vegetable. For that matter, it rules out our being biological organisms, since no organism is a person essentially: every human organism starts out as an unthinking embryo, and may end up in a vegetative state.

Whether we are organisms, or were once embryos, are substantive questions that an account of personal identity ought to answer, not matters to be settled in advance by the way we frame the debate. So we cannot assume at the outset that we are people (in something like Locke's sense) essentially. Asking question 1 prejudges the issue by favoring some accounts of what we are, and what it takes for us to persist, over others. In particular, asking 1 effectively rules out the Somatic Approach described in the next section. It is like asking which man committed the crime before ruling out the possibility that it might have been a woman.

3. Accounts of Our Identity Through Time

Almost all proposed answers to the Persistence Question fall into one of three categories. The first is the **Psychological Approach**, according to which some psychological relation is necessary or sufficient (or both) for one to persist. You are that future being that in some sense inherits its mental features – beliefs, memories, preferences, the capacity for rational thought, that sort of thing – from you; and you are that past being whose mental features you have inherited in this way. There is dispute over what sort of inheritance this has to be – whether it must be underpinned by some kind of physical continuity, for instance, or whether a "non-branching" requirement is needed. There is also disagreement about what mental features need to be inherited. (I shall return to some of these issues.) But most philosophers writing on personal identity since the early 20th century have endorsed some version of the Psychological Approach. The Memory Criterion mentioned earlier is an example. Advocates of the Psychological Approach include Johnston (1987), Garrett (1998), Hudson (2001), Lewis (1976), Nagel (1986: 40), Noonan (2003), Nozick (1981), Parfit (1971; 1984: 207), Perry (1972), Shoemaker (1970; 1984: 90; 1997; 1999), and Unger (1990: ch. 5; 2000).

A second idea is that our identity through time consists in some brute physical relation. You are that past or future being that has your body, or that is the same biological organism as you are, or the like. Whether you survive or perish has nothing to do with psychological facts. I shall call this the **Somatic Approach**. (It should not be confused with the view that physical evidence has some sort of priority over psychological evidence in finding out who is who. That has to do with the Evidence Question.) Its advocates include Ayers (1990: 278–92), Carter (1989), Mackie (1999), Olson (1997), van Inwagen (1990), and Williams (1956–7, 1970).

You may think the truth lies somewhere between the two: we need both mental and physical continuity to survive; or perhaps either would suffice without the other. Views of this sort are usually versions of the Psychological Approach as I have defined it. Here is a test case. Imagine that your brain is transplanted into my head. Two beings result: the person who ends up with your cerebrum and most of your mental features, and the empty-headed being left behind, which may perhaps be biologically alive but will have no mental features. Those who say that you would be the one who gets your brain usually say so because they believe that some relation involving psychology suffices for you to persist: they accept the Psychological Approach. Those who say that you would be the empty-headed vegetable say so because they take your identity to consist in something non-psychological, as the Somatic Approach has it.

Both the Psychological and Somatic Approaches agree that there is something that it takes for us to persist – that our identity through time consists in or necessarily follows from something other than itself. A third view, **Anticriterialism**, denies this. Mental and physical continuity are evidence for identity, it says, but do not always guarantee it, and may not be required. No sort of continuity is both necessary and sufficient for you to survive. The only correct and complete answer to the Persistence Question is the trivial statement that a person existing at one time is identical with a being existing at another if and only they are identical (Chisholm 1976: 108ff.; Swinburne 1984; Lowe 1996: 41ff.; Merricks 1998; see also Zimmerman 1998). This is often combined with the view that we are immaterial or have no parts, though it needn't be. Anticriterialism is poorly understood, and deserves more attention than it has received.

It seems that the Persistence Question must have an answer. One of these three views, or another that I haven't mentioned, must be true. If there is such a thing as you – if there is anything sitting there and reading this now – then some conditions must be necessary and sufficient for it to persist. Those conditions will involve psychology, or only brute physical continuity, or something else – or they are trivial, as anticriterialism has it. Moreover, at most one such view can be true. We shall revisit this claim in Section 8, however.

4. The Psychological Approach

Most people (most Western philosophy teachers and students, anyway) feel immediately drawn to the Psychological Approach. It seems obvious that you would go along with your brain if it were transplanted, and that this is so because that organ would carry with it your memories and other mental features. This would lead the recipient to believe that he or she was you. Why should this belief be mistaken? That suggests that our identity over time has something to do with psychology. It is notoriously difficult, however, to get from this conviction to a plausible answer to the Persistence Question.

What psychological relation might our identity through time consist in? We have already mentioned memory: a past or future being might be you if and only if you can now remember an experience she had then, or vice versa. This faces two famous objections, discovered in the 18th century by Seargeant and Berkeley (see Behan 1979), but more famously discussed by Reid and Butler (see the snippets in Perry 1975).

First, suppose a young student is fined for overdue library books. Later, as a middle-aged lawyer, she remembers paying the fine. Later still, in her dotage, she remembers her law career, but has entirely forgotten paying the fine, and everything else she did in her youth. According to the Memory Criterion, the young student is the middle-aged lawyer, the lawyer is the old woman, but the old woman is not the young student. This is an impossible result: if x and y are one and y and z are one, x and z cannot be *two*. Identity is transitive; memory continuity is not.

Second, it seems to belong to the very idea of remembering that you can remember only your own experiences. To remember paying a fine (or the experience of paying) is to remember *yourself* paying. That makes it trivial and uninformative to say that you are the person whose experiences you can remember – that is, that memory continuity is sufficient for personal identity. It is uninformative because you can't know whether someone genuinely remembers a past experience without already knowing whether he is the one who had it. Suppose we want to know whether Blott, who exists now, is the same as Clott, whom we know to have existed at some time in the past. The Memory Criterion tells us that Blott is Clott if Blott can now remember an experience of Clott's that occurred at that past time. But Blott's seeming to remember one of Clott's experiences from that time counts as genuine memory only if Blott actually is Clott. We would have to know who was who before applying the theory that is supposed to tell us who is who. Saying that you are the person whose experiences you can remember is like saying that you are the person who is entitled to your passport: true, but trivial. (Note, however, that this is no objection to the claim that memory connections are *necessary* for us to persist. There is nothing trivial about that.)

One response to the first problem is to modify the Memory Criterion by switching from direct to indirect memory connections: the old woman is the young student because she can recall experiences the lawyer had at a time when the lawyer remembered the student's life. The second problem is traditionally met by replacing memory with a new concept, "retrocognition" or "quasi-memory", which is just like memory but without the identity requirement: even if it is self-contradictory to say that I remember doing something I didn't do, I could still "quasi-remember" it (Penelhum 1970: 85ff.; Shoemaker 1970; for criticism see McDowell 1997). Neither move gets us far, however, as even the modified Memory Criterion faces a more obvious problem: there are many times in my past that I can't remember or quasi-remember at all, and to which I am not linked even indirectly by an overlapping chain of memories. For instance, there is no time when I could recall anything that happened to me while I was dreamlessly sleeping last night. The Memory Criterion has the absurd implication that I have never existed at any time when I was completely unconscious. The man sleeping in my bed last night was someone else.

A better solution appeals to causal dependence (Shoemaker 1984: 89ff.). We can define two notions, psychological connectedness and psychological continuity.

A being is *psychologically connected*, at some future time, with me as I am now just if he is in the psychological states he is in then in large part *because of* the psychological states I am in now. Having a current memory (or quasi-memory) of an earlier experience is one sort of psychological connection – the experience causes the memory of it – but there are others. Importantly, one's current mental states can be caused in part by mental states one was in at a time when one was unconscious: for example, most of my current beliefs are the same ones I had while I slept last night. We can then define the second notion thus: I am now *psychologically continuous* with a past or future being just if my current mental states relate to those he is in then by a chain of psychological connections.

This enables us to avoid the most obvious objections to the Memory Criterion by saying that a person who exists at one time is identical with something existing at another time if and only if the first is, at the first time, psychologically continuous with the second as she is at the second time.

Though this is an improvement, it still leaves important questions unanswered. Suppose we could somehow copy all the mental contents of your brain onto mine, much as we can copy the contents of one computer drive onto another. And suppose this process erased the previous contents of both brains. Whether this would be a case of psychological continuity depends on what sort of causal dependence counts. The resulting being (with my brain and your mental contents) would be mentally like you were before, and not like I was. He would have inherited your mental properties in a way – but a funny way. Is it the right way? Could you literally move from one human animal to another via "brain-state transfer"? Advocates of the Psychological Approach disagree (Shoemaker 1984: 108–11; 1997; Unger 1990: 67–71). (Schechtman, 1996, gives an interesting objection to the psychological-continuity strategy, without abandoning the Psychological Approach.)

5. Fission

Whatever psychological continuity amounts to, a more serious worry for the Psychological Approach is that you could be psychologically continuous with two past or future people at once. If your cerebrum (the upper part of the brain largely responsible for mental features) were transplanted, the recipient would be psychologically continuous with you by anyone's lights (even if there would also be important psychological differences). The Psychological Approach implies that she would be you. If we destroyed one of your cerebral hemispheres, the resulting being would also be psychologically continuous with you. (Hemispherectomy – even the removal of the left hemisphere, which controls speech – is considered a drastic but acceptable treatment for otherwise-inoperable brain tumors: see Rigterink 1980.) What if we did both at once, destroying one hemisphere and transplanting the other? Then, too, the one who got the transplanted hemisphere would be psychologically continuous with you, and according to the Psychological Approach would be you.

Now let both hemispheres be transplanted, each into a different empty head. (We needn't pretend, as some authors do, that the hemispheres are exactly alike.) The two recipients – call them Lefty and Righty – will each be psychologically continuous with you. The Psychological Approach as I have stated it implies that any future being who is psychologically continuous with you must be you. It follows that you are Lefty and also that you are Righty. But that cannot be: Lefty and Righty are two, and one thing cannot be numerically identical with two things. Suppose Lefty is hungry at a time when Righty isn't. If you are Lefty, you are hungry at that time. If you are Righty, you aren't. If you are Lefty *and* Righty, you are both hungry and not hungry at once: a contradiction.

Friends of the Psychological Approach have proposed two different solutions to this problem. One, sometimes called the "multiple-occupancy view", says that if there is fission in your future, then there are, so to speak, two of you even now. What we think of as you is really two people, who are now exactly similar and located in the same place, doing the same things and thinking the same thoughts. The surgeons merely separate them (Lewis 1976; Noonan 2003: 139–42; Perry 1972 offers a more complex variant).

The multiple-occupancy view is almost invariably combined with the general metaphysical claim that people and other persisting things are made up of temporal parts (often called "four-dimensionalism"; see Heller 1990: ch. 1; Sider 2001). For each person, there is such a thing as her first half, which is just like the person only briefer, like the first half of a race or a football match. On this account, the multiple-occupancy view is that Lefty and Righty coincide before the operation by sharing their pre-operative temporal parts, and diverge later by having different temporal parts located afterwards. They are like two roads that coincide for a stretch and then fork, sharing some of their spatial parts but not others. At the places where the roads overlap, they will look just like one road. Likewise, the idea goes, at the times before the operation when Lefty and Righty share their temporal parts, they will look just like one person – even to themselves. Whether people really are made up of temporal parts, however, is a disputed metaphysical question (see section 8).

The other solution to the fission problem abandons the intuitive claim that psychological continuity by itself suffices for one to persist. It says, rather, that you are identical with a past or future being only if she is then psychologically continuous with you and *no other being* is. (There is no circularity in this. We need not know the answer to the Persistence Question in order to know how many people there are at any one time; that comes under the Population Question.) This means that neither Lefty nor Righty is you. They both come into existence when your cerebrum is divided. If both your cerebral hemispheres are transplanted, you cease to exist – though you would survive if only one were transplanted and the other destroyed (Shoemaker 1984: 85; Unger 1990: 265; Garrett 1998: ch. 4; see also Noonan 2003: 12–15 and ch. 7).

This proposal, the "non-branching view", has the surprising consequence that if your brain is divided, you will survive if only one half is preserved, but you will die if both halves are. That is just the opposite of what most of us expect: if your survival depends on the functioning of your brain (because that is what underlies psychological continuity), then the more of that organ we preserve, the greater ought to be your chance of surviving. In fact, the non-branching view implies you would perish if one of your hemispheres were transplanted and the other left in place: you can survive hemispherectomy only if the excised hemisphere is immediately destroyed. And if "brain-state transfer" gives us psychological continuity, you would cease to exist even if your total brain state were copied onto another brain without erasing yours. ("Best-candidate" theories such as Nozick 1981 attempt to avoid this.)

The non-branching view makes the What matters? Question especially acute. Faced with the prospect of having one of your hemispheres transplanted, there would seem to be no reason to prefer that the other be destroyed. Most of us would rather have both preserved, even if they go into different heads. Yet on the non-branching view that is to prefer death over continued existence. This leads Parfit and others to say that that is precisely what we ought to prefer. Insofar as we are rational, we don't want to continue existing. Or at least we don't want it for its own sake. I only want there to be someone in the future who is psychologically continuous with me, whether or not he is *me*. Likewise, even the most selfish person has a reason to care about the welfare of the beings who would result from her undergoing fission, even if, as the non-branching view implies, neither would be her. In the fission case, the sorts of practical concerns you ordinarily have for yourself seem to apply to someone who isn't strictly you. This suggests more generally that facts about who is numerically identical with whom have no practical importance. What matters practically is, rather, who is psychologically continuous with whom. (Lewis 1976 and Parfit 1976 debate whether the multiple-occupancy view can preserve the conviction that identity is what matters practically.)

This threatens to undermine the principal argument for the Psychological Approach. Suppose you cared about the welfare of your two fission offshoots in just the way you ordinarily care about your own welfare, even though neither offshoot would be you. Then you would care about what happened to the person who got your whole brain in the original transplant case, even if *she* were not you. Even if you regarded that person as yourself for all practical purposes – if you anticipated her experiences just as you anticipate yours, for instance – that would in no way support the claim that she *was* you. So our reactions to the brain-transplant case may not support the view that we persist by virtue of psychological continuity, but only the claim that psychological continuity is what matters practically, which is compatible with other accounts of our persistence. In that case we may wonder whether we have any reason to accept the Psychological Approach.

It is sometimes said that fission is not a special problem for the Psychological Approach, but afflicts all answers to the Persistence Question equally, apart (perhaps) from anticriterialism. Whether this is so is a hard question. Even if it is, though, the fission problem looks especially worrying for the Psychological Approach, as it threatens the support for that view without affecting the arguments for rival views. (It does not undermine arguments for the Somatic Approach, for instance.)

6. The Too-Many-Thinkers Problem

The Psychological Approach faces another problem: it appears to rule out our being organisms (Carter 1989; Ayers 1990: 278–92; Snowdon 1990; Olson 1997: 80f., 100–109; 2003a). It says that our persistence consists in some sort of psychological continuity. As we have seen, this means that you would go along with your transplanted brain or cerebrum, because the one who ended up with that organ, and no one else, would be psychologically continuous with you. Likewise, if you were to lapse into a persistent vegetative state, you would cease to exist, because no one would then be psychologically continuous with you. But the persistence of a human organism does not consist in any sort of psychological continuity. If we transplanted your cerebrum, the human organism – your body – would not go along with that organ. It would stay behind with an empty head. The transplant simply moves an organ from one organism to another. If you were an organism, then *you* would stay behind with an empty head, contrary to the Psychological Approach. Likewise, no human organism ceases to exist by lapsing into a persistent vegetative state. If you were an organism, you could survive as a human vegetable, which again conflicts with the Psychological Approach. What the Psychological Approach says about our persistence through time is not true of human organisms: no sort of psychological continuity is either necessary or sufficient for a human animal to persist. So if that view is true, we could not be organisms. Not only are we not *essentially* organisms. We are not organisms at all, even contingently: nothing that is even contingently an organism would go along with its transplanted cerebrum.

But even if you are not an organism, your body is. That organism – a human animal – thinks and is conscious. In fact it would seem to be psychologically indistinguishable from you. So if you are not that animal, but something else, it follows that there is a conscious, intelligent being other than you, now sitting in your chair and reading this chapter. This means that there are at least twice as many thinking, conscious beings as the census reports: for each of us, there is another thinker, namely the animal we call our body. Worse, you ought to wonder which of the two thinkers is you. You may believe that you are the non-animal (because you accept the Psychological Approach, perhaps). But the animal has the same grounds for believing that *it* is a non-animal as you have for supposing that you are. Yet it is mistaken. For all you know, you might be the one making this mistake. If you *were* the animal and not the person, you would never be any the wiser.

Here is an analogy. Imagine a three-dimensional duplicating machine. When you step into the "in" box, it reads off your information and assembles a perfect duplicate of you in the "out" box. The process causes temporary unconsciousness, but is otherwise harmless. Two beings wake up, one in each box. The boxes are indistinguishable. Because each being will have the same apparent memories and perceive identical surroundings, each will think that he or she is you, and will have the same evidence for this belief. But only one will be right. If this actually happened to you, it is hard to see how you could ever know, afterwards, whether you were the original or the duplicate. (Suppose the technicians who work the machine are sworn to secrecy and immune to bribes.) You would think, "Who am I? Am I who I think I am? Did I do the things I seem to remember doing? Or did I come into being only a moment ago, complete with false memories of someone else's life?" And you would have no way of answering these questions.

In the same way, the Psychological Approach raises the questions, "What am I? Am I a human person, who persists by virtue of psychological continuity? Or am I an animal?" And here too there seem to be no grounds on which to answer these questions. So even if the Psychological Approach is true, it seems that you could never know whether it applied to you: for all you can tell, you may instead be an organism with brute physical persistence conditions. This is the "too-many-minds" or too-many-thinkers problem. It afflicts any view according to which we are not organisms. Only the view that we are organisms (and that there are no beings who persist by virtue of psychological continuity) appears to escape it; but that is incompatible with the Psychological Approach.

Friends of the Psychological Approach can respond in three ways. One is to say that human animals have psychological persistence conditions. (This may be the view of Wiggins 1980: 160, 180 and McDowell 1997: 237; see also Olson 1997: 114–19). Despite appearances, the Psychological Approach is compatible with our being animals, and the problem does not arise. The surgeons do not move your cerebrum from one animal to another in the transplant story. Rather, one animal has its parts cut away until it is the size of a cerebrum. It is then moved across the room and given a new complement of parts. The animal into which your cerebrum is implanted then presumably ceases to exist. This view has not proved popular, however.

A second response is to deny that human animals can think in the way that we do. Although our animal bodies share our brains, are physically just like us, and show all the outward signs of consciousness and intelligence, they themselves do not think and are not conscious. Thinking animals are not a problem for the Psychological Approach because there are none.

If human organisms cannot be conscious, then presumably no biological organism of any sort could have any mental properties at all. Why not? It may be, as Descartes and Leibniz argued, because organisms are material things. If *any* material thing could think, surely it would be an animal! Only an immaterial thing could think or be conscious. You and I must therefore be immaterial. This would solve the too-many-thinkers problem, though it raises many others, and few philosophers nowadays accept it.

Shoemaker's attempt to explain why organisms should be unable to think is compatible with our being material. He says that whatever thinks or is conscious must persist by virtue of psychological continuity. That is because it belongs to the nature of a mental state that it tends to have certain characteristic causes and effects in the being that is in the state, and not in any other being. (This is a version of the functionalist theory of mind.) For instance, your preference for chocolate over vanilla must tend to cause you, and no one else, to choose chocolate. If an organism were to have such a preference, though, that state might cause *another* being to choose chocolate, because an organism's cerebrum might be transplanted into another organism. That would violate the proposed account of mental states. So no organism could have a preference; and similar reasoning goes for the mental generally. The persistence conditions of organisms are incompatible with their having mental properties. But a material thing that *would* go along with its transplanted cerebrum – a being of which the Psychological Approach was true – could have mental states. It would follow that you and I, who obviously have mental states, persist by virtue of psychological continuity, and thus are not organisms. This would both solve the too-many-thinkers problem and show that the Psychological Approach is true. (See Shoemaker 1984: 92–7; 1999; 2004; Olson 2002b.)

Finally, friends of the Psychological Approach can concede that human organisms think as we do, so that you are one of two beings now thinking your thoughts, but try to explain how we can still know that we are not those organisms. One strategy for doing this focuses on the nature of personhood and first-person reference. It proposes that not just any being with mental properties of the sort that you and I have – rationality and self-consciousness, for instance – counts as a person. A person must also persist by virtue of psychological continuity. It follows from this that human animals, despite being psychologically just like us, are not people. Further, personal pronouns such as "I" refer only to people. So when your animal body says or thinks "I", it does not refer to itself. Rather, it refers to you, the person who says it at the same time. When the animal says "I am a person", it does not thereby express the false belief that *it* is a person, but rather the true belief that you are. It follows that the animal is not mistaken about which thing it is: it has no first-person beliefs about itself at all. And you are not mistaken either. You can infer that you are a person from the linguistic facts that you are whatever you refer to when you say "I", and that "I" never refers to anything but a person. You can know that you are not the animal thinking your thoughts because it is not a person, and personal pronouns never refer to non-people.

Although this proposal avoids the surprising claim that organisms cannot have mental properties, however, it gives a highly counterintuitive view of what it is to be a person. And it still implies that there are twice as many intelligent, conscious beings as we thought. (See Noonan 1998; Olson 2002a.)

7. The Somatic Approach

There appears to be a thinking animal located where you are. It also appears that you are the thinking thing – the only one – located there. If things are as they appear, then you are that animal. This view has become known as *animalism*.

Animalism does not imply that all animals, or even all human animals, are people: as we saw earlier, human embryos and animals in a persistent vegetative state may not count as people. Being a person may be only a temporary property of you, like being a philosopher. Nor does animalism imply that all people are animals. It is consistent with the existence of wholly inorganic people: gods or angels or conscious robots. It does not say that being an animal is part of what it is to be a person (a view defended in Wiggins 1980: 171 and Wollheim 1984: ch. 1 and criticized in Snowdon 1996). Animalism leaves the answer to the Personhood Question entirely open.

If we are animals, we have the persistence conditions of animals. And as we saw, animals appear to persist by virtue of some sort of brute physical continuity. So animalism seems to imply a version of the Somatic Approach.

A few philosophers endorse the Somatic Approach without saying that we are animals. They say that we are our bodies (Thomson 1997), or that our identity through time consists in the identity of our bodies (Ayer 1936: 194). This has been called the Bodily Criterion of personal identity. Its relation to animalism is uncertain. If a person's body is by definition a sort of animal, then perhaps being identical to one's body is the same as being an animal. Whether this is so depends in part on what it is for something to be someone's body – a surprisingly difficult question (see van Inwagen 1980; Olson 1997: 144–9).

We have already seen the most common objection to the Somatic Approach: it implies that you would stay behind if your cerebrum were transplanted, which may seem incredible (see Unger 2000).

That said, the Somatic Approach has the virtue of being compatible with our beliefs about who is who in real life. Every actual case in which we take someone to survive or perish is a case where a human animal survives or perishes. The Psychological Approach, or at any rate the view that psychological continuity is necessary for us to persist, does not share this virtue. When someone lapses into a persistent vegetative state, his friends and relatives rarely conclude that their loved one no longer exists, even when they believe that there is no psychological continuity of any sort between the vegetable and the person. (They may conclude that his life no longer has any value, but that is another matter.) And most of us believe that we were once foetuses. When we see an ultrasound picture of a 12-week-old foetus, we ordinarily think we are seeing something that will, if all goes well, be born, learn to speak, and eventually become an adult human person. Yet none of us is in any way psychologically continuous with a 12-week-old foetus.

Some versions of the Somatic Approach also face their own version of the too-many-thinkers problem. The mere fact that you are an organism or the like does not imply that you are the only thinker of your thoughts (Shoemaker 1999; Hudson 2007; Olson 2007: 215–36). This would of course be no more of a problem for the Somatic than for the Psychological Approach; but it would undermine the best argument for the Somatic Approach, the one based on the too-many-thinkers problem.

8. Wider Issues

We have compared the virtues of the two main accounts of our identity over time. We saw that the Psychological Approach, though attractive, has trouble with fission cases. The usual non-branching response is both implausible in itself and suggests that identity has no practical importance, which in turn undermines the original support for the view. The Psychological Approach also implies that we are not animals, raising the awkward problem of how we relate to the apparently intelligent animals we call our bodies. The Somatic Approach – in particular when combined with the view that we are animals – is also intuitively attractive, and appears to avoid the too-many-thinkers problem. But it has implausible consequences concerning brain transplants.

The debate between these competing views is likely to turn on more general issues in metaphysics and the philosophy of mind. For instance, advocates of the Psychological Approach appear to be committed to the view that each normal human organism is associated with a non-organism that thinks and is conscious. They will need an account of the metaphysical nature of this non-organism, and of how it relates to the animal. If they hope to solve the thinking-animal problem by denying that human animals can think, they will need an account of the nature of the mental that is consistent with this.

Some general metaphysical views suggest that there is no unique right answer to the question of what it takes for us to persist. The best-known example is the ontology of temporal parts mentioned in section 5. It says that for every period of time when you exist, short or long, there is a temporal part of you that exists only then. This gives us many likely candidates for being you or me. Suppose you are a material thing, and that we know what determines your spatial boundaries. That should tell us what counts as your current temporal part or "stage" – the temporal part of you located now and at no other time. That stage is a part of a vast number of temporally extended objects (Hudson 2001: ch. 4). For instance, it is a part of a being whose temporal boundaries are determined by relations of psychological continuity, in the sense defined in section 4, among its stages. That is, one of the beings thinking your current thoughts is an aggregate of person-stages, each of which is psychologically continuous with each of the others and not with anything else. The view that we persist by virtue of psychological continuity suggests that that is what you are.

Your current stage is also a part of a being whose temporal boundaries are determined by relations of psychological *connectedness* (section 4 again). That is, one of the beings now thinking your thoughts is an aggregate of person-stages, each of which is psychologically connected with each of the others and not to anything else. This may not be the same as the first being, for some stages may be psychologically continuous with your current stage but not psychologically connected with it. The view that psychological connectedness is necessary and sufficient for us to persist suggests that we are beings of the second sort (Lewis 1976). Your current stage is also a part of a human animal, which persists by virtue of brute physical continuity. And it is a part of many bizarre and gerry-mandered objects, such as Hirsch's "contacti persons" (Hirsch 1982: ch. 10). Some even say that you are your current stage itself (Sider 2001: 188–208).

The temporal-parts ontology implies that each of us shares our current thoughts with countless beings that diverge from one another in the past or future. This makes it hard to say which things we are. And because many of these beings persist through time under different conditions, it is equally hard to say what our identity over time consists in. How could we ever know? Of course, we are the beings we refer to when we say "I", or more generally the beings that our personal pronouns and proper names refer to; but it is unlikely, on this view, that our personal pronouns succeed in referring to just one sort of thing. Each utterance of a personal pronoun will probably refer ambiguously to many different candidates: to various sorts of psychologically interrelated aggregates, to an animal, and perhaps to others as well. That would make it indeterminate which things, even which kind of things, we are. And insofar as the different candidates have different persistence conditions, it would be indeterminate what our identity over time consists in. Some versions of the metaphysic of constitution (Baker 2000) have similar implications.

These wider questions – about the nature of mental properties and the existence of temporal parts, among others – cannot be settled by thinking about personal identity alone. Which view of personal identity we find attractive is likely to depend on general metaphysical considerations. There may not be much point in asking about our identity over time without first addressing these underlying issues.

References

Ayer, A. J. (1936). *Language, Truth, and Logic.* London: Gollancz.

Ayers, M. (1990). *Locke*, vol. 2. London: Routledge.

Baker, L. R. (2000). *Persons and Bodies: A Constitution View.* Cambridge: Cambridge University Press.

Behan, D. (1979). Locke on persons and personal identity. *Canadian Journal of Philosophy* 9: 53–75.

Campbell, S. (2006). The Conception of a Person as a Series of Mental Events. *Philosophy and Phenomenological Research* 73: 339–58.

Carter, W. R. (1989). How to Change Your Mind, *Canadian Journal of Philosophy* 19: 1–14.

Chisholm, R. (1976). *Person and Object.* La Salle, IL: Open Court.

Collins, S. (1982). *Selfless Persons: Imagery and Thought in Theravada Buddhism.* Cambridge: Cambridge University Press.

Garrett, B. (1998). *Personal Identity and Self-Consciousness.* London: Routledge.

Heller, M. (1990). *The Ontology of Physical Objects: Four-Dimensional Hunks of Matter.* Cambridge: Cambridge University Press.

Hirsch, E. (1982). *The Concept of Identity.* Oxford University Press.

Hudson, H. (2001). *A Materialist Metaphysics of the Human Person.* New York: Cornell University Press.

Hudson, H. (2007). I Am Not an Animal! In *Persons: Human and Divine*, P. van Inwagen and D. Zimmerman (eds.), Oxford: Clarendon Press.

Hume, D. (1978). *Treatise of Human Nature.* Oxford: Clarendon Press (original work 1739); partly reprinted in Perry (1975).

Jinpa, T. (2002). *Self, Reality and Reason in Tibetan Philosophy.* London: RoutledgeCurzon.

Johnston, M. (1987). Human Beings. *Journal of Philosophy* 84: 59–83.

Lewis, D. (1976). Survival and Identity. In *The Identities of Persons*, A. Rorty (ed.), Berkeley: California University Press, and reprinted in his *Philosophical Papers* vol. I, Oxford University Press, 1983.

Locke, J. (1975). *An Essay Concerning Human Understanding.* ed. P. Nidditch, Oxford: Clarendon Press (original work, 2nd ed., first published 1694); partly reprinted in Perry (1975).

Lowe, E. J. (1996). *Subjects of Experience.* Cambridge: Cambridge University Press.

Ludwig, A. M. (1997). *How Do We Know Who We Are?* Oxford: Oxford University Press.

Mackie, D. (1999). Personal Identity and Dead People. *Philosophical Studies* 95: 219–42.

Martin, R. (1998). *Self Concern.* Cambridge: Cambridge University Press.

Martin, R. and J. Barresi (eds.) (2003). *Personal Identity.* Oxford: Blackwell.

McDowell, J. (1997). Reductionism and the First Person. In *Reading Parfit*, J. Dancy (ed.), Oxford: Blackwell.

Merricks, T. (1998). There Are No Criteria of Identity Over Time. *Noûs* 32: 106–24.

Nagel, T. (1971). Brain Bisection and the Unity of Consciousness. *Synthèse* 22: 396–413, and reprinted in Perry 1975 and in Nagel, *Mortal Questions*, Cambridge: Cambridge University Press 1979.

Nagel, T. (1986). *The View from Nowhere*. Oxford: Oxford University Press.

Noonan, H. (1998). Animalism Versus Lockeanism: A Current Controversy. *Philosophical Quarterly* 48: 302–18.

Noonan, H. (2003). *Personal Identity*, 2nd ed. London: Routledge.

Nozick, R. (1981). *Philosophical Explanations*. Boston, MA: Harvard University Press.

Olson, E. (1997). *The Human Animal: Personal Identity Without Psychology*. Oxford: Oxford University Press.

Olson, E. (2002a). Thinking Animals and the Reference of "I". *Philosophical Topics* 30: 189–208.

Olson, E. (2002b). What does Functionalism Tell Us about Personal Identity? *Noûs* 36: 682–98.

Olson, E. (2003). Was Jekyll Hyde? *Philosophy and Phenomenological Research* 66: 328–48.

Olson, E. (2007). *What Are We? A Study in Personal Ontology*, Oxford: Oxford University Press.

Parfit, D. (1971). Personal Identity. *Philosophical Review* 80: 3–27, and reprinted in Perry (1975).

Parfit, D. (1976). Lewis, Perry, and What Matters. In *The Identities of Persons*, A. Rorty (ed.), Berkeley: University of California Press.

Parfit, D. (1984). *Reasons and Persons*. Oxford: Oxford University Press.

Parfit, D. (1995). The Unimportance of Identity. In *Identity*, H. Harris (ed.). Oxford: Oxford University Press. Reprinted in Martin and Barresi (2003).

Penelhum, T. (1970). *Survival and Disembodied Existence*. London: Routledge.

Perry, J. (1972). Can the Self Divide? *Journal of Philosophy* 69: 463–88.

Perry, J. (ed.) (1975). *Personal Identity*. Berkeley: University of California Press.

Puccetti, R. (1973). Brain Bisection and Personal Identity. *British Journal for the Philosophy of Science* 24: 339–55.

Quinton, A. (1962). The Soul. *Journal of Philosophy* 59: 393–403, and reprinted in Perry (1975).

Rigterink, R. (1980). Puccetti and Brain Bisection: An Attempt at Mental Division. *Canadian Journal of Philosophy* 10: 429–52.

Russell, B. (1918). The Philosophy of Logical Atomism. *Monist* 28: 495–527 and 29: 32–63, 190–222, 345–80; reprinted in R. Marsh (ed.), *Logic and Knowledge* (London: Allen & Unwin, 1956), and in D. Pears (ed.), *The Philosophy of Logical Atomism* (La Salle, IL: Open Court, 1985) [page numbers from the latter].

Schechtman, M. (1996). *The Constitution of Selves*. New York: Cornell University Press.

Shoemaker, S. (1963). *Self-Knowledge and Self-Identity*. Ithaca: Cornell University Press.

Shoemaker, S. (1970). Persons and Their Pasts. *American Philosophical Quarterly* 7: 269–85.

Shoemaker, S. (1984). Personal Identity: A Materialist's Account. In Shoemaker and Swinburne, *Personal Identity*. Oxford: Blackwell.

Shoemaker, S. (1997). Self and Substance. In *Philosophical Perspectives* 11, J. Tomberlin (ed.): 283–319.

Shoemaker, S. (1999). Self, Body, and Coincidence. *Proceedings of the Aristotelian Society*, Supplementary Volume 73: 287–306.

Shoemaker, S. (2004). Functionalism and Personal Identity – A Reply. *Noûs* 38: 525–33.

Sider, T. (2001). *Four Dimensionalism*. Oxford: Oxford University Press.

Snowdon, P. (1990). Persons, Animals, and Ourselves. In *The Person and the Human Mind*, C. Gill. (ed.), Oxford: Clarendon Press.

Snowdon, P. (1996). Persons and Personal Identity. In *Essays for David Wiggins: Identity, Truth and Value*, S. Lovibond and S. G. Williams (eds.), Oxford: Blackwell.

Swinburne, R. (1984). Personal Identity: The Dualist Theory. In Shoemaker and Swinburne, *Personal Identity*. Oxford: Blackwell.

Thomson, J. J. (1997). People and Their Bodies. In *Reading Parfit*, J. Dancy (ed.), Oxford: Blackwell.

Unger, P. (1979). I do not Exist. In *Perception and Identity*, G. F. MacDonald (ed.), London: Macmillan, and reprinted in Rea (1997).

Unger, P. (1990). *Identity, Consciousness, and Value*. Oxford: Oxford University Press.

Unger, P. (2000). The Survival of the Sentient. In *Philosophical Perspectives* 11, J. Tomberlin (ed.), Malden, MA: Blackwell.

van Inwagen, P. (1980). Philosophers and the Words "Human Body". In *Time and Cause*, P. van Inwagen (ed.), Dordrecht: Reidel, and reprinted in his *Ontology, Identity, and Modality* (Cambridge University Press, 2001).

van Inwagen, P. (1985). Plantinga on Trans-World Identity. In *Alvin Plantinga*, J. Tomberlin and P. van Inwagen (eds.). Dordrecht: Reidel, and reprinted in his *Ontology, Identity, and Modality* (Cambridge University Press, 2001).

van Inwagen, P. (1990). *Material Beings*. Ithaca: Cornell University Press.

Wiggins, D. (1980). *Sameness and Substance*. Oxford: Blackwell.

Wilkes, K. (1988). *Real People*. Oxford: Clarendon Press.

Williams, B. (1956). Personal Identity and Individuation. *Proceedings of the Aristotelian Society* 57, and reprinted in his *Problems of the Self* (Cambridge University Press, 1973).

Williams, B. (1970). The Self and the Future. *Philosophical Review* 59, and reprinted in his *Problems of the Self* (Cambridge University Press, 1973).

Wittgenstein, L. (1922). *Tractatus Logico-Philosophicus*. London: Routledge.

Wollheim, R. (1984). *The Thread of Life*. Cambridge: Cambridge University Press.

Zimmerman, D. (1998). Criteria of Identity and the "Identity Mystics". *Erkenntnis* 48, 281–301.

Internet Resources

Persons and Bodies: A Constitution View, symposium on the book by Lynne Rudder Baker, at the website *A Field Guide to the Philosophy of Mind*, maintained by Marco Nani and Massimo Marraffa (Università degli Studi Roma Tre).

Symposium on Eric Olson's *The Human Animal*, in the online journal *Abstracta*.

Acknowledgments

Some material in this chapter appeared previously in E. Olson, "Personal Identity", in *The Blackwell Guide to the Philosophy of Mind*, edited by S. Stich and T. Warfield, Oxford: Blackwell, 2003.

8

DIVIDED MINDS AND THE NATURE OF PERSONS

Derek Parfit

It was the split-brain cases which drew me into philosophy. Our knowledge of these cases depends on the results of various psychological tests, as described by Donald MacKay.[1] These tests made use of two facts. We control each of our arms, and see what is in each half of our visual fields, with only one of our hemispheres. When someone's hemispheres have been disconnected, psychologists can thus present to this person two different written questions in the two halves of his visual field, and can receive two different answers written by this person's two hands.

Here is a simplified imaginary version of the kind of evidence that such tests provide. One of these people looks fixedly at the centre of a wide screen, whose left half is red and right half is blue. On each half in a darker shade are the words, "How many colours can you see?" With both hands the person writes, "Only one". The words are now changed to read, "Which is the only colour that you can see?" With one of his hands the person writes "Red", with the other he writes "Blue".

If this is how such a person responds, I would conclude that he is having two visual sensations – that he does, as he claims, see both red and blue. But in seeing each colour he is not aware of seeing the other. He has two streams of consciousness, in each of which he can see only one colour. In one stream he sees red, and at the same time, in his other stream, he sees blue. More generally, he could be having at the same time two series of thoughts and sensations, in having each of which he is unaware of having the other.

This conclusion has been questioned. It has been claimed by some that there are not *two* streams of consciousness, on the ground that the sub-dominant hemisphere is a part of the brain whose functioning involves no consciousness. If this were true, these cases would lose most of their interest. I believe that it is not true, chiefly because, if a person's dominant hemisphere is destroyed, this person is able to react in the way in which, in the split-brain cases, the sub-dominant hemisphere reacts, and we do not believe that such a person is just an automaton, without consciousness. The sub-dominant hemisphere is, of course, much less developed in certain ways, typically having the linguistic abilities of a three-year-old. But three-year-olds are conscious. This supports the view that, in split-brain cases, there *are* two streams of consciousness.

Another view is that, in these cases, there are two persons involved, sharing the same body. Like Professor MacKay, I believe that we should reject this view. My reason for believing this is, however, different. Professor MacKay denies that there are two persons involved because he believes that there is only one person involved. I believe that, in a sense, the number of persons involved is none.

The Ego Theory and the Bundle Theory

To explain this sense I must, for a while, turn away from the split-brain cases. There are two theories about what persons are, and what is involved in a person's continued existence over time. On the *Ego Theory*, a person's continued existence cannot be explained except as the continued existence of a particular *Ego*, or *subject of experiences*. An Ego Theorist claims that, if we ask what unifies someone's consciousness at any time – what makes it true, for example, that I can now both see what I am typing and hear the wind outside my window – the answer is that these are both experiences which are being had by me, this person, at this time. Similarly, what explains the unity of a person's whole life is the fact that all of the experiences in this life are had by the same person, or subject of experiences. In its best-known form, the *Cartesian view*, each person is a persisting purely mental thing – a soul, or spiritual substance.

The rival view is the *Bundle Theory*. Like most styles in art – Gothic, baroque, rococo, etc. – this theory owes its name to its critics. But the name is good enough. According to the Bundle Theory, we can't explain either the unity of consciousness at any time, or the unity of a whole life, by referring to a person. Instead we must claim that there are long series of different mental states and events – thoughts, sensations, and the like – each series being what we call one life. Each series is unified by various kinds of causal relation, such as the relations that hold between experiences and later memories of them. Each series is thus like a bundle tied up with string.

In a sense, a Bundle Theorist denies the existence of persons. An outright denial is of course absurd. As Reid protested in the eighteenth century, "I am not thought, I am not action, I am not feeling; I am something which thinks and acts and feels." I am not a series of events but a person. A Bundle Theorist admits this fact, but claims it to be only a fact about our grammar, or our language. There are persons or subjects in this language-dependent way. If, however, persons are believed to be more than this – to be separately existing things, distinct from our brains and bodies, and the various kinds of mental states and events – the Bundle Theorist denies that there are such things.

The first Bundle Theorist was Buddha, who taught "anatta", or the *No Self view*. Buddhists concede that selves or persons have "nominal existence", by which they mean that persons are merely combinations of other elements. Only what exists by itself, as a separate element, has instead what Buddhists call "actual existence". Here are some quotations from Buddhist texts:

At the beginning of their conversation the king politely asks the monk his name, and receives the following reply: 'Sir, I am known as "Nagasena"; my fellows in the religious life address me as "Nagasena". Although my parents gave me the name . . . it is just an appellation, a form of speech, a description, a conventional usage. "Nagasena" is only a name, for no person is found here.'

A sentient being does exist, you think, O Mara? You are misled by a false conception. This bundle of elements is void of Self, In it there is no sentient being. Just as a set of wooden parts Receives the name of carriage, So do we give to elements. The name of fancied being.

Buddha has spoken thus: 'O Brethren, actions do exist, and also their consequences, but the person that acts does not. There is no one to cast away this set of elements, and no one to assume a new set of them. There exists no Individual, it is only a conventional name given to a set of elements.'[2]

Buddha's claims are strikingly similar to the claims advanced by several Western writers. Since these writers knew nothing of Buddha, the similarity of these claims suggests that they are not merely part of one cultural tradition, in one period. They may be, as I believe they are, true.

What we Believe Ourselves to Be

Given the advances in psychology and neurophysiology, the Bundle Theory may now seem to be obviously true. It may seem uninteresting to deny that there are separately existing Egos, which are distinct from brains and bodies and the various kinds of mental states and events. But this is not the only issue. We may be convinced that the Ego Theory is false, or even senseless. Most of us, however, even if we are not aware of this, also have certain beliefs about what is involved in our continued existence over time. And these beliefs would only be justified if something like the Ego Theory was true. Most of us therefore have false beliefs about what persons are, and about ourselves.

These beliefs are best revealed when we consider certain imaginary cases, often drawn from science fiction. One such case is *teletransportation*. Suppose that you enter a cubicle in which, when you press a button, a scanner records the states of all of the cells in your brain and body, destroying both while doing so. This information is then transmitted at the speed of light to some other planet, where a replicator produces a perfect organic copy of you. Since the brain of your Replica is exactly like yours, it will seem to remember living your life up to the moment when you pressed the button, its character will be just like yours, and it will be in every other way psychologically continuous with you. This psychological continuity will not have its normal cause, the continued existence of your brain, since the causal chain will run through the transmission by radio of your "blueprint".

Several writers claim that, if you chose to be teletransported, believing this to be the fastest way of travelling, you would be making a terrible mistake. This would not be a way of travelling, but a way of dying. It may not, they concede, be quite as bad as ordinary death. It might be some consolation to you that, after your death, you will have this Replica, which can finish the book that you are writing, act as parent to your children, and so on. But, they insist, this Replica won't be you. It will merely be someone else, who is exactly like you. This is why this prospect is nearly as bad as ordinary death.

Imagine next a whole range of cases, in each of which, in a single operation, a different proportion of the cells in your brain and body would be replaced with exact duplicates. At the near end of this range, only 1 or 2 per cent would be replaced; in the middle, 40 or 60 per cent; near the far end, 98 or 99 per cent. At the far end of this range is pure teletransportation, the case in which all of your cells would be "replaced".

When you imagine that some proportion of your cells will be replaced with exact duplicates, it is natural to have the following beliefs. First, if you ask, "Will I survive? Will the resulting person be me?", there must be an answer to this question. Either you will survive, or you are about to die. Second, the answer to this question must be either a simple "Yes" or a simple "No". The person who wakes up either will or will not be you. There cannot be a third answer, such as that the person waking up will be half you. You can imagine yourself later being half-conscious. But if the resulting person will be fully conscious, he cannot be half you. To state these beliefs together: to the question, "Will the resulting person be me?", there must always *be* an answer, which must be all-or-nothing.

There seem good grounds for believing that, in the case of teletransportation, your Replica would not be you. In a slight variant of this case, your Replica might be created while you were still alive, so that you could talk to one another. This seems to show that, if 100 per cent of your cells were replaced, the result would merely be a Replica of you. At the other end of my range of cases, where only 1 per cent would be replaced, the resulting person clearly *would* be you. It therefore seems that, in the cases in between, the resulting person must be either you, or merely a Replica. It seems that one of these must be true, and that it makes a great difference which is true.

How we are not What we Believe

If these beliefs were correct, there must be some critical percentage, somewhere in this range of cases, up to which the resulting person would be you, and beyond which he would merely be your Replica. Perhaps, for example, it would be you who would wake up if the proportion of cells replaced were 49 per cent, but if just a few more cells were also replaced, this would make all the difference, causing it to be someone else who would wake up.

That there must be some such critical percentage follows from our natural beliefs. But this conclusion is most implausible. How could a few cells make such a difference? Moreover, if there is such a critical percentage, no one could ever discover where it came. Since in all these cases the resulting person would believe that he was you, there could never be any evidence about where, in this range of cases, he would suddenly cease to be you.

On the Bundle Theory, we should reject these natural beliefs. Since you, the person, are not a separately existing entity, we can know exactly what would happen without answering the question of what will happen to you. Moreover, in the case in the middle of my range, it is an empty question whether the resulting person would be you, or would merely be someone else who is exactly like you. These are not here two different possibilities, one of which must be true. These are merely two different descriptions of the very same course of events. If 50 per cent of your cells were replaced with exact duplicates, we could call the resulting person you, or we could call him merely your Replica. But since these are not here different possibilities, this is a mere choice of words.

As Buddha claimed, the Bundle Theory is hard to believe. It is hard to accept that it could be an empty question whether one is about to die, or will instead live for many years.

What we are being asked to accept may be made clearer with this analogy. Suppose that a certain club exists for some time, holding regular meetings. The meetings then cease. Some years later, several people form a club with the same name, and the same rules. We can ask, "Did these people revive the very same club? Or did they merely start up another club which is exactly similar?" Given certain further details, this would be another empty question. We could know just what happened without answering this question. Suppose that someone said: "But there must be an answer. The club meeting later must either be, or not be, the very same club." This would show that this person didn't understand the nature of clubs.

In the same way, if we have any worries about my imagined cases, we don't understand the nature of persons. In each of my cases, you would know that the resulting person would be both psychologically and physically exactly like you, and that he would have some particular proportion of the cells in your brain and body – 90 per cent, or 10 per cent, or, in the case of teletransportation, 0 per cent. Knowing this, you know everything. How could it be a real question what would happen to you, unless you are a separately existing Ego, distinct from a brain and body, and the various kinds of mental state and event? If there are no such Egos, there is nothing else to ask a real question about.

Accepting the Bundle Theory is not only hard; it may also affect our emotions. As Buddha claimed, it may undermine our concern about our own futures. This effect can be suggested by redescribing this change of view. Suppose that you are about to be destroyed, but will later have a Replica on Mars. You would naturally believe that this prospect is about as bad as ordinary death, since your Replica won't be you. On the Bundle Theory, the fact that your Replica won't be you just consists in the fact that, though it will be fully psychologically continuous with you, this continuity won't have its normal cause. But when you object to teletransportation you are not objecting merely to the abnormality of this cause. You are objecting that this cause won't get *you* to Mars. You fear that the abnormal cause will fail to produce a further and all-important fact, which is different from the fact that your Replica will be psychologically continuous with you. You do not merely want there to be psychological continuity between you and some future person. You want to *be* this future person. On the Bundle Theory, there is no such special further fact. What you fear will not happen, in this imagined case, *never* happens. You want the person on Mars to be you in a specially intimate way in which no future person will ever be you. This means that, judged from the standpoint of your natural beliefs, even ordinary survival is about as bad as teletransportation. *Ordinary survival is about as bad as being destroyed and having a Replica.*

How the Split-Brain Cases Support the Bundle Theory

The truth of the Bundle Theory seems to me, in the widest sense, as much a scientific as a philosophical conclusion. I can imagine kinds of evidence which would have justified believing in the existence of separately existing Egos, and believing that the continued existence of these Egos is what explains the continuity of each mental life. But there is in fact very little evidence in favour of this Ego Theory, and much for the alternative Bundle Theory.

Some of this evidence is provided by the split-brain cases. On the Ego Theory, to explain what unifies our experiences at any one time, we should simply claim that these are all experiences which are being had by the same person. Bundle Theorists reject this explanation. This disagreement is hard to resolve in ordinary cases. But consider the simplified split-brain case that I described. We show to my imagined patient a placard whose left half is blue and right half is red. In one of this person's two streams of consciousness, he is aware of seeing only blue, while at the same time, in his other stream, he is aware of seeing only red. Each of these two visual experiences is combined with other experiences, like that of being aware of moving one of his hands. What unifies the experiences, at any time, in each of this person's two streams of consciousness? What unifies his awareness of seeing only red with his awareness of moving one hand? The answer cannot be that these experiences are being had by the same person. The answer cannot explain the unity of each of this person's two streams of consciousness, since it ignores the disunity between these streams. This person is now having all of the experiences in both of his two streams. If this fact was what unified these experiences, this would make the two streams one.

These cases do not, I have claimed, involve two people sharing a single body. Since there is only one person involved, who has two streams of consciousness, the Ego Theorist's explanation would have to take the following form. He would have to distinguish between persons and subjects of experiences, and claim that, in split-brain cases, there are *two* of the latter. What unifies the experiences in one of the person's two streams would have to be the fact these experiences are all being had by the same subject of experiences. What unifies the experiences in this person's other stream would have to be the fact that they are being had by another subject of experiences. When this explanation takes this form, it becomes much less plausible. While we could assume that "subject of experiences", or "Ego", simply meant "person", it was easy to believe that there are subjects of experiences. But if there can be subjects of experiences that are not persons, and if in the life of a split-brain patient there are at any time two different subjects of experiences – two different Egos – why should we believe that there really are such things? This does not amount to a refutation. But it seems to me a strong argument against the Ego Theory.

As a Bundle Theorist, I believe that these two Egos are idle cogs. There is another explanation of the unity of consciousness, both in ordinary cases and in split-brain cases. It is simply a fact that ordinary people are, at any time, aware of having several different experiences. This awareness of several different experiences can be helpfully compared with one's awareness, in short-term memory, of several different experiences. Just as there can be a single memory of just having had several experiences, such as hearing a bell strike three times, there can be a single state of awareness both of hearing the fourth striking of this bell, and of seeing, at the same time, ravens flying past the bell-tower.

Unlike the Ego Theorist's explanation, this explanation can easily be extended to cover split-brain cases. In such cases there is, at any time, not one state of awareness of several different experiences, but two such states. In the case I described, there is one state of awareness of both seeing only red and of moving one hand, and there is another state of awareness of both seeing only blue and moving the other hand. In claiming that there are two such states of awareness, we are not postulating the existence of unfamiliar entities, two separately existing Egos which are not the same as the single person whom the case involves. This explanation appeals to a pair of mental states which would have to be described anyway in a full description of this case.

I have suggested how the split-brain cases provide one argument for one view about the nature of persons. I should mention another such argument, provided by an imagined extension of these cases, first discussed at length by David Wiggins.[3]

In this imagined case a person's brain is divided, and the two halves are transplanted into a pair of different bodies. The two resulting people live quite separate lives. This imagined case shows that personal identity is not what matters. If I was about to divide, I should conclude that neither of the resulting people will be me. I will have ceased to exist. But this way of ceasing to exist is about as good – or as bad – as ordinary survival.

Some of the features of Wiggins's imagined case are likely to remain technically impossible. But the case cannot be dismissed, since its most striking feature, the division of one stream of consciousness into separate streams, has already happened. This is a second way in which the actual split-brain cases have great theoretical importance. They challenge some of our deepest assumptions about ourselves.[4]

Notes

1. See MacKay's contribution, chapter 1 of *Mindwaves*, ed. Colin Blakemore and Susan Greenfield (Oxford: Basil Blackwell, 1987), pp. 5–16.
2. For the sources of these and similar quotations, see my *Reasons and Persons*, pp. 502–3, 532 (Oxford: Oxford University Press, 1984).
3. At the end of his *Identity and Spatio-temporal Continuity* (Oxford: Blackwell, 1967).
4. I discuss these assumptions further in part 3 of my *Reasons and Persons*.

9

WHO AM I? WHAT AM I?

Ray Kurzweil

Why are you you?

> The implied question in the acronym YRUU (Young Religious
> Unitarian Universalists), an organization I was active in when
> I was growing up in the early 1960s (it was then called LRY,
> Liberal Religious Youth).

What you are looking for is who is looking.

> Saint Francis of Assisi

I'm not aware of too many things
I know what I know if you know what I mean.
Philosophy is the talk on a cereal box.
Religion is the smile on a dog . . .
Philosophy is a walk on the slippery rocks.
Religion is a light in the fog . . .
What I am is what I am.
Are you what you are or what?

> Edie Brickell, "What I Am"

Freedom of will is the ability to do gladly that which I must do.

> Carl Jung

The chance of the quantum theoretician is not the ethical freedom of the Augustinian.

> Norbert Wiener

I should prefer to an ordinary death, being immersed with a few friends in a cask of Madeira,
until that time, then to be recalled to life by the solar warmth of my dear country! But
in all probability, we live in a century too little advanced, and too near the infancy of
science, to see such an art brought in our time to its perfection.

> Benjamin Franklin, 1773

We talked earlier about the potential to upload the patterns of an individual mind – knowledge, skills, personality, memories – to another substrate.

Although the new entity would act just like me, the question remains: is it really *me*?

Some of the scenarios for radical life extension involve reengineering and rebuilding the systems and subsystems that our bodies and brains comprise. In taking part in this reconstruction, do I lose my self along the way? Again, this issue will transform itself from a centuries-old philosophical dialogue to a pressing practical matter in the next several decades.

So who am I? Since I am constantly changing, am I just a pattern? What if someone copies that pattern? Am I the original and/or the copy? Perhaps I am this stuff here – that is, the both ordered and chaotic collection of molecules that make up my body and brain.

But there's a problem with this position. The specific set of particles that my body and brain comprise are in fact completely different from the atoms and molecules that I comprised only a short while ago. We know that most of our cells are turned over in a matter of weeks, and even our neurons, which persist as distinct cells for a relatively long time, nonetheless change all of their constituent molecules within a month. The half-life of a microtubule (a protein filament that provides the structure of a neuron) is about ten minutes. The actin filaments in dendrites are replaced about every forty seconds. The proteins that power the synapses are replaced about every hour. NMDA receptors in synapses stick around for a relatively long five days.

So I am a completely different set of stuff than I was a month ago, and all that persists is the pattern of organization of that stuff. The pattern changes also, but slowly and in a continuum. I am rather like the pattern that water makes in a stream as it rushes past the rocks in its path. The actual molecules of water change every millisecond, but the pattern persists for hours or even years.

Perhaps, therefore, we should say I am a pattern of matter and energy that persists over time. But there is a problem with this definition, as well, since we will ultimately be able to upload this pattern to replicate my body and brain to a sufficiently high degree of accuracy that the copy is indistinguishable from the original. (That is, the copy could pass a "Ray Kurzweil" Turing test.) The copy, therefore, will share my pattern. One might counter that we may not get every detail correct, but as time goes on our attempts to create a neural and body replica will increase in resolution and accuracy at the same exponential pace that governs all information-based technologies. We will ultimately be able to capture and re-create my pattern of salient neural and physical details to any desired degree of accuracy.

Although the copy shares my pattern, it would be hard to say that the copy is me because I would – or could – still be here. You could even scan and copy me while I was sleeping. If you come to me in the morning and say, "Good news, Ray, we've successfully reinstantiated you into a more durable substrate, so we won't be needing your old body and brain anymore," I may beg to differ.

If you do the thought experiment, it's clear that the copy may look and act just like me, but it's nonetheless *not* me. I may not even know that he was created. Although he would have all my memories and recall having been me, from the point in time of his creation Ray 2 would have his own unique experiences, and his reality would begin to diverge from mine.

This is a real issue with regard to cryonics (the process of preserving by freezing a person who has just died, with a view toward "reanimating" him later when the technology exists to reverse the damage from the early stages of the dying process, the cryonic-preservation process, and the disease or condition that killed him in the first place). Assuming a "preserved" person is ultimately reanimated, many of the proposed methods imply that the reanimated person will essentially be "rebuilt" with new materials and even entirely new neuromorphically equivalent systems. The reanimated person will, therefore, effectively be "Ray 2" (that is, someone else).

Now let's pursue this train of thought a bit further, and you will see where the dilemma arises. If we copy me and then destroy the original, that's the end of me, because as we concluded above the copy is not me. Since the copy will do a convincing job of impersonating me, no one may know the difference, but it's nonetheless the end of me.

Consider replacing a tiny portion of my brain with its neuromorphic equivalent.

Okay, I'm still here: the operation was successful (incidentally, nanobots will eventually do this without surgery). We know people like this already, such as those with cochlear implants, implants for Parkinson's disease, and others. Now replace another portion of my brain: okay, I'm still here . . . and again. . . . At the end of the process, I'm still myself. There never was an "old Ray" and a "new Ray." I'm the same as I was before. No one ever missed me, including me.

The gradual replacement of Ray results in Ray, so consciousness and identity appear to have been preserved. However, in the case of gradual replacement there is no simultaneous old me and new me. At the end of the process you have the equivalent of the new me (that is, Ray 2) and no old me (Ray 1). So gradual replacement also means the end of me. We might therefore wonder: at what point did my body and brain become someone else?

On yet another hand (we're running out of philosophical hands here), as I pointed out at the beginning of this question, I am in fact being continually replaced as part of a normal biological process. (And, by the way, that process is not particularly gradual but rather rapid.) As we concluded, all that persists is my spatial and temporal pattern of matter and energy. But the thought experiment above shows that gradual replacement means the end of me even if my pattern is preserved. So am I constantly being replaced by someone else who just seems a lot like the me of a few moments earlier?

So, again, who am I? It's the ultimate ontological question, and we often refer to it as the issue of consciousness. I have consciously (pun intended) phrased the issue entirely in the first person because that is its nature. It is not a third-person question. So my question is not "who are you?" although you may wish to ask this question yourself.

When people speak of consciousness they often slip into considerations of behavioral and neurological correlates of consciousness (for example, whether or not an entity can be self-reflective). But these are third-person (objective) issues and do not represent what David Chalmers calls the "hard question" of consciousness: how can matter (the brain) lead to something as apparently immaterial as consciousness?

The question of whether or not an entity is conscious is apparent only to itself. The difference between neurological correlates of consciousness (such as intelligent behavior) and the ontological reality of consciousness is the difference between objective and subjective reality. That's why we can't propose an objective consciousness detector without philosophical assumptions built into it.

I do believe that we humans will come to accept that nonbiological entities are conscious, because ultimately the nonbiological entities will have all the subtle cues that humans currently possess and that we associate with emotional and other subjective experiences. Still, while we will be able to verify the subtle cues, we will have no direct access to the implied consciousness.

I will acknowledge that many of you do seem conscious to me, but I should not be too quick to accept this impression. Perhaps I am really living in a simulation, and you are all part of it.

Or, perhaps it's only my memories of you that exist, and these actual experiences never took place.

Or maybe I am only now experiencing the sensation of recalling apparent memories, but neither the experience nor the memories really exist. Well, you see the problem.

Despite these dilemmas my personal philosophy remains based on patternism – I am principally a pattern that persists in time. I am an evolving pattern, and I can influence the course of the evolution of my pattern. Knowledge is a pattern, as distinguished from mere information, and losing knowledge is a profound loss. Thus, losing a person is the ultimate loss.

10

FREE WILL AND DETERMINISM IN THE WORLD OF *MINORITY REPORT*

Michael Huemer

Howard Marks is in his bedroom putting on his glasses when a group of armed police officers breaks in, frantically tackles him, and slaps restraints on him. He is under arrest, they explain, for the "future murder" of Sarah Marks and Donald Dubin, a crime of passion that was to occur just seconds in the future when he found his wife in bed with her lover. Thus begins Steven Spielberg's *Minority Report*.[1] Such arrests have been made possible by the "precogs," a trio of prescient individuals working for the police who foresee crimes that are going to occur if the police do not intervene. With the precogs' insight, the police are able to prevent these crimes and imprison the would-be perpetrators. Naturally, the accused protest their innocence: they have not actually committed any crime at the time they are arrested. The state argues that the accused *would have* committed crimes if not for the intervention of the "Precrime" police. As one of the officers explains, "The fact that you prevented it from happening doesn't change the fact that it was going to happen."

Yet it seems that the individuals punished under the Precrime laws have a compelling philosophical defense available: if, as one Precrime officer asserts, "the precogs see the future, and they're never wrong," this can only mean that the future is predetermined. The only way that the otherwise predetermined future seen by the precogs can be averted, we are led to believe, is by the influence of the precogs themselves (knowledge of the would-be future enables one to avert it). This means that Howard Marks, for example, could not have avoided his fate – absent the intervention of the precogs and the Precrime Department, he could not have simply chosen not to kill Sarah Marks and Donald Dubin. But if this is so – if our fates are predetermined and there is no free will – then it seems unjust to punish him for what he was going to do. It is unjust to punish someone for what he is not responsible for, and unless we have free will, we are responsible for nothing.

Later in the film, there are hints that individuals do have a measure of free will after all. We learn that occasionally one of the precogs sees a different possible future from that seen by the other two, thus producing one of the eponymous "minority reports." And near the end, one of the precogs insists that John Anderton can still choose not to commit a murder, despite her own prescient vision of the murder and despite the fact that Anderton had no minority report. It appears, however, that Anderton's ability to avoid his would-be fate is due only to his knowledge of the precogs' prediction itself – the precogs, in making their predictions, alter the system whose behavior they are predicting, thereby invalidating those predictions. This latter detail is perfectly consistent with the idea that the future is nevertheless predetermined. The existence of minority reports, then, is the only evidence in the movie that individuals (sometimes) have genuine freedom.

Either way, however, the Precrime system seems ethically doomed: if the alleged future criminals *lack* free will, then it is unjust to punish them since they are not morally responsible for what they would have done. If the alleged future criminals *have* free will, then it is unjust to punish them since we can not be sufficiently certain that they really would have committed the crime for which they are to be punished. Or so, at any rate, the defendants might argue.

Hard Determinism and the Threat to Free Will

Traditionally, *having free will* is thought to require two things: *alternate possibilities* and *self-control*. That is, a person is free only if (a) there is more than one future open to him, more than one course of action that he can perform, and (b) he controls his own actions, so that *which* of the alternative possibilities is realized is up to him. Thus, consider a robot with a computer brain. The robot's computer brain determines all of its actions according to a definite program. There are no random elements in the program, and the robot must always respond to a given set of inputs in a specific way. Intuitively, the robot lacks free will because it lacks alternate possibilities: even though the robot controls its own actions, it has only one possibility open to it at any given time. On the other hand, consider a simple radioactive atom that has a 50% chance of decaying in the next hour; whether it decays or not is a matter of pure chance. Intuitively, the atom lacks free will as well. This is because, even though the atom has two alternative possible futures, it cannot exercise *control* over which possibility it realizes. These two examples illustrate why both conditions (a) and (b) are required for free will.

Traditionally, the primary threat to free will – the primary reason for doubting that we have it – has come from *determinism*, a view according to which, given the state of the world at any time, only one future is possible. Why would someone believe this? There are at least two important reasons. First: most people who believe in God believe that God is all-knowing. If God is all-knowing, then He must know everything that is going to happen in the future. But if God already knows what is going to happen, then it seems that there are no alternative possibilities; events must unfold as God has foreseen them. If God now knows, for example, that I am going to commit a murder tomorrow, then I can't refrain from committing the murder. There is a presently existing fact or state of affairs (God's knowledge) that is inconsistent with my not committing the murder, so I *have to* commit the murder.

Second: many scientists and philosophers have thought that the laws of nature are deterministic. These laws include Newton's laws of motion, the law of gravity, the laws governing the electric and magnetic fields, and so on. To say these laws are deterministic is to say that, given the state of a physical system at some time, the laws prescribe a unique future evolution. For example, Newton's Second Law tells us that the rate at which a body's momentum changes is determined by the forces acting on it; given the forces, there is only one possible value for that rate of change. In classical physics, those forces are uniquely determined by the properties and arrangement of the particles that make up a physical system – given those properties and arrangement, there is only one possible value for the net force acting on any given particle in the system. So, given a system of particles with certain properties and in a certain arrangement, there is only one way for that system to evolve over time.

To apply this idea to human action, suppose I have just committed a murder by firing a gun at someone. In order for me not to have committed the murder, given the circumstances, the particles that make up my trigger finger would have to have not moved in the way that they did. My finger moved in the way it did because of the contraction of muscles in my arm, which was caused by electrical impulses that traveled from my brain to the nerves in my arm. Those electrical impulses were caused by chemical and electrical processes in my brain, which in turn were caused by earlier electrochemical brain events together with other electrical impulses coming into my brain from my sense organs. All of these events were governed by the laws of chemistry and physics. I could not have acted differently unless the pattern of electrical activity in my brain at the time had been different, and the pattern of electrical activity in my brain could not have been different unless something *earlier* – either my earlier brain state or the influences on my brain coming from my environment – had been different. And of course my brain state at any earlier time was caused by events occurring still earlier, and so on. Ultimately, in order for me to have acted differently, something would have to have been different at *every* previous time, stretching back all the way to the time of the Big Bang. It seems to follow from this that I lack free will, because I have no alternative possibilities open to me. This is the view of the *hard determinists*: that because determinism is true, no one has free will.[2]

This is traditionally thought to be important – and troubling – because it is thought that unless we have free will, we are not responsible for our actions. This would mean, among other things, that no one would deserve either praise or blame for anything they did. (I could not justly be blamed for that murder I committed – on the other hand, the state also couldn't justly be blamed for imprisoning me.)

The argument just given, however, depends upon classical physics. In modern times, classical physics, which unquestionably was deterministic, has been superseded by quantum mechanics. The interpretation of quantum mechanics is still in dispute: some scientists and philosophers say that quantum mechanics has refuted determinism (this is the more common interpretation), while others continue to favor deterministic versions of quantum mechanics.[3]

The Soft Determinist Gambit

Historically, the most popular view among philosophers has been one that most non-philosophers would never consider: it is that freedom and determinism are perfectly compatible. *Soft determinism* is the view that determinism is true, and yet we have free will anyway.[4] This may strike you as contradictory. How have philosophers thought they could defend this?

Typically, soft determinists begin by analyzing such concepts as freedom, possibility, and control. Above, in setting out the hard determinist position, we assumed that if only one future is consistent with the past and the laws of nature, then only one future is possible, and so there are no alternate possibilities of the sort required for free will. Soft determinists, however, claim that there is more than one sense of "possible," and that while in *one* sense only one future is possible, there is *another* sense of "possible," relevant to free will, in which there are multiple possible futures. To take a simple illustration, a soft determinist might propose the following definition of "can":

S can do X = If S tried to do X, then S would succeed.[5]

Notice that in *this* sense, a person may have alternate possibilities – multiple actions each of which he can perform – even if all his actions are determined by antecedent causes. To see this, just imagine that the following is the case: I live in a world in which all events are determined by preceding causes. The laws of this world determine that my trying to do A in my present circumstances would result in my successfully doing A, while my trying to do B (an incompatible alternative action) in these circumstances would result in my successfully doing B. The laws and the past also determine that in fact I will try to do A and will not try to do B. All of this is consistent. And in this situation, determinism is true, but yet I have alternative possibilities in the sense defined above: that is, there are two actions, A and B, such that *if* I *tried* to do either of them, I would succeed; therefore, these are two actions that I "can" perform.

Another way of defending soft determinism is to argue that to be free just means to be free of *external impediments* to action, or that freedom requires only that one's actions be determined by *internal* causes (for example, by one's own beliefs, values, and desires), rather than by *external* forces (for instance, physical forces from outside or coercion imposed by other people). If this is correct, then freedom is compatible with determinism; determinism requires that all one's actions be causally determined, but not that the causes be entirely external and not internal.

Another line of thought pressed by some soft determinists holds that freedom actually *requires* determinism. For, they say, if determinism were false, and our actions were not determined by antecedent causes, these actions would merely be random occurrences, and what is random is under no one's control. Since free will requires self-control, we would lack free will. Suppose, for example, that even though I have no desire to stand on my head loudly singing the national anthem right now, there's still a chance that I might wind up doing it anyway, prompted by no desire, belief, or other motivation of mine. That possibility wouldn't make me *free*; rather, it would seem to make me *unfree*. The only way we can control our actions and decisions is by having them be caused by our internal thoughts and motivations. Indeterminism not only doesn't help us with this, it precludes our satisfying this precondition on freedom. Surely, then – if we have a coherent notion of free will at all – free will does not require indeterminism.

While the above arguments have some plausibility, they seem less compelling than some of the objections to soft determinism. Here is one objection to soft determinism: "If determinism is true, then our acts are the consequences of the laws of nature and events in the remote past. But it is not up to us what went on before we were born, and neither is it up to us what the laws of nature are. Therefore, the consequences of these things, including our present acts, are not up to us."[6] Here is another way to put that argument. It seems that I do not have access to any possible future in which the laws of nature are different from what they actually are, nor in which a law of nature is violated. For instance, I don't have access to any possible future in which the conservation of momentum is violated (I can't act in such a way that momentum isn't conserved). It also seems that I do not have access to any possible world in which the past differs from the way it actually was. For instance, I don't have access to a possible situation in which, instead of being defeated at Waterloo in 1815 (as he actually was), Napoleon triumphs at Waterloo. Now, if determinism is true, then there is only *one* possible future in which the past remains as it actually was and all the actual laws of nature are obeyed; any alternative "possible" future would have to be one in which the past or the laws are different. Therefore, I don't have access to any such alternative future. Since free will requires alternative possibilities, if determinism is true then I do not have free will.

Consider a simple illustration. Imagine that you are a physician in the emergency room of a hospital, where a heart attack victim has just been brought in. Suppose that you know, based on the laws of biochemistry and the physiology of the human body, that in order for such a patient to be revived, CPR must be administered within three minutes of the heart attack. Suppose you also know that in fact *four* minutes have already elapsed, during which no one performed CPR. Wouldn't you be justified in deducing that at this point, you cannot revive the patient?[7] If determinism is true, then we are all in a similar position with respect to *everything* we fail to do, to the physician's position with respect to the saving of the heart attack victim: for any thing that you fail to do, your doing it would require something to have happened in the past that did not in fact happen. It seems to follow that, *if* determinism is true, then you cannot do anything other than what you actually do, and thus that you do not have free will.

On Behalf of Freedom

Thus far, I have discussed the threat to free will posed by determinism, finding that the soft determinists have failed to defuse this threat. The other major position in the free will debate, sometimes called *Libertarianism* (not to be confused with the political philosophy of the same name), holds that free will exists, and that this is incompatible with determinism, so determinism is false. Why should we believe in free will?

One thing that is often said is that when we make choices, at least some of the time, we are directly, introspectively aware of our freedom. For example, imagine yourself in the position of John Anderton near the end of *Minority Report*. Having been told that he will kill Leo Crow, Anderton now finds himself face to face with Crow, holding a gun on Crow, and deciding whether to pull the trigger. As you stand there deliberating, wouldn't there be an unshakeable sense that you *could* choose either way? Hard determinists claim that this sense is merely an "illusion." But isn't it more plausible to assume that things are the way they appear, until proven otherwise? What contrary evidence can the determinists advance that is more compelling than this sense that we do possess freedom of choice?

Another popular argument is that hard determinism is, in one way or another, a *self-defeating* position. This idea goes back to Epicurus in the fourth century BC, who writes, "The man who says that all things come to pass by necessity cannot criticize one who denies that all things come to pass by necessity: for he admits that this too happens of necessity."[8] The key observation of the self-defeating argument is that if determinism is true, then it applies just as much to our beliefs and assertions – including beliefs and assertions about determinism – as it does to our other actions. If everything that happens is determined by the causal laws governing the movements of subatomic particles, then the determinist's saying and believing that, as well as his opponent's denial, are determined by the causal laws governing the movements of subatomic particles. Some think that this undermines any claim to *know* determinism to be true, since subatomic particles respond only to brute physical forces, and not to logic or evidence; therefore, one's belief in determinism itself would be determined only by brute physical forces and not by logic or evidence.[9] The success of this version of the self-defeating argument turns on whether the physicalistic determinist can give a plausible account of what "reasons" and "evidence" are in purely physical terms (in terms of the activities of subatomic particles and fields).

Another version of the self-defeating argument holds that in making assertions and engaging in argumentation or reasoning in the first place, the determinist is committed to accepting certain *norms* (principles about what one should or should not do) that are implicit in those activities. By this, I mean that certain norms are so important to these activities that one cannot genuinely engage in the activity without accepting those norms on some level. For instance, we have a rule that one should not assert what isn't true, and this rule partly defines what an assertion is. If one makes an utterance while at the same time maintaining that one's utterance is not governed by this rule – that is, that one's utterance is not *supposed* to correspond to reality – then one's utterance is not a genuine assertion. For example, a person speaking lines in a play, or writing a novel, is exempt from the norm of truth-telling, but by the same token he is not genuinely asserting what he says. This of course is not to say that people cannot lie or that lies do not count as assertions. Speaking falsely is like breaking the rules of chess: if one surreptitiously breaks the rules of chess, one is merely cheating, but if one refuses to recognize that the rules of chess apply to what one is doing, then one just isn't playing chess.[10] A related idea is that the practice of *reasoning* is implicitly governed by the rule that one ought to form only justified (rational) beliefs and avoid unjustified beliefs; if one in no way accepts this norm – for example, if one regards arbitrary beliefs as no less to be preferred than rational beliefs – then one is not engaged in genuine reasoning.

If this is right, then the determinist, insofar as he attempts to rationally *defend* his position, must accept at least some normative principles governing his assertions and thoughts. These normative principles may prove difficult to reconcile with determinism (indeed, the acceptance of *any* normative principles at all may be irreconcilable with determinism). The following deduction shows one way of bringing out the problem:

1. We should refrain from accepting unjustified beliefs. (Premise; presupposition of reasoning.)
2. To say that one *should* do something implies that one *can* do it. (Premise.)
3. So we *can* refrain from accepting unjustified beliefs. (From 1, 2.)

4. Assume that hard determinism is true. Then what we actually do is the only thing we can do – that is, what *can* be done *is* done. (Assumption, definition of hard determinism.)
5. Therefore, we have no unjustified beliefs. (From 3, 4.)
6. Many people believe in free will. (Premise.)
7. So the belief in free will is justified. (From 5, 6.)

The conclusion in (7) is presumably one the hard determinist would want to evade; yet it follows logically from (1), (2), (4), and (6). The hard determinist accepts (4). (6) can be established by talking to a few ordinary people, or by observing how people speak and behave, holding others responsible for their actions and so on. (2) is an almost universally accepted principle among philosophers – one can't admit that something is impossible and then tell people they should do it anyway. It therefore seems that (1) is the only premise that the hard determinist might question. But this is where the self-defeating charge enters; if the hard determinist denies (1), then he is rejecting an assumption implicit in the very practice of rational reflection in which he purports to be engaged.

The point is not that the above deduction proves that we have free will. Rather, the point is that it is not rational to embrace hard determinism, since hard determinism, in conjunction with norms implicit in reasoning, leads to a conclusion that rationally undermines hard determinism itself.

The Verdict on Precrime

Philosophers continue to debate whether there is free will, what exactly it amounts to, and whether the reality of free will is compatible with the truth of determinism. In light of the philosophical debate about free will, what should a philosopher say about Spielberg's imagined Precrime system?

The characters in *Minority Report* interpret the existence of minority reports as evidence of free will, or at least of the existence of alternative possibilities that people have open to them. A determinist (hard or soft) would instead interpret minority reports as evidence of the pre-cogs' fallibility – perhaps the future is predetermined, but sometimes one of the pre-cogs makes a mistake about what is going to happen. One might take this as grounds for abandoning the Precrime system – until one remembers that *any* criminal justice system is fallible. The traditional system of trying suspects after the fact also sometimes results in the punishment of innocent people; so we should only abandon the Precrime system if the pre-cogs finger innocent people at a *greater rate* than the traditional system. Still, a hard determinist would likely reject the idea of retributive *punishment*, since people have no control over what they do; instead, the hard determinist would likely favor merely acting so as to prevent predicted crimes (and other crimes) from happening.

On the other hand, a libertarian would likely interpret the existence of minority reports as reflecting the reality of human freedom. On this view, at least some of the time, it is *not yet determined* whether a person will commit a certain crime or not, and that is why the pre-cogs disagree. In those cases where a person's future is not yet determined, he should not be punished for a future crime even if he *probably* will commit it. This is because only the actual decision by which the individual locks in the future in which he commits the crime would make him deserving of punishment; before this decision has been made, there is no existing fact or state of affairs that makes him a "future criminal" or deserving of punishment.

Ultimately, the people in *Minority Report* probably made the right decision in abolishing the Precrime system, but for the wrong reasons. The wrong reason to abolish Precrime is that the system is fallible. The right reason is that individuals have free will and do not merit punishment for future actions, however likely, that are not yet *determined*.

Notes

1. 20th Century Fox, 2002. Based loosely on "The Minority Report" by Philip K. Dick (*The Minority Report and Other Classic Stories*, New York: Kensington, 2002, pp. 71–102). Dick's story goes very differently from the movie.

2. Baron d'Holbach (*System of Nature*, New York: Garland Publishing, 1984; originally published 1770) is among the few defenders of hard determinism in philosophical history. In modern times, deniers of free will are more likely to argue that we lack free will *whether or not* determinism is true (see Derek Pereboom, *Living without Free Will*, Cambridge: Cambridge University Press, 2001).

3. See David Albert's *Quantum Mechanics and Experience* (Cambridge, MA: Harvard University Press, 1992) for an informative yet reasonably accessible introduction to the issues surrounding the interpretation of quantum mechanics. Karl Popper and John Eccles (*The Self and Its Brain*, Berlin: Springer International, 1977) argue that quantum mechanics makes room for free will.

4. See W.T. Stace (*Religion and the Modern Mind*, New York: J.B. Lippincott, 1960, chapter 11) or Daniel Dennett (*Freedom Evolves*, New York: Viking, 2003) for an accessible defense of soft determinism.

5. This particular definition is oversimplified and is refuted by J.L. Austin ("Ifs and Cans," *Philosophical Papers*, 2nd edition, Oxford: Oxford University Press, 1970); nevertheless, it can be used to illustrate the general soft determinist strategy, and similar points can be made for more sophisticated definitions.

6. Quoted from Peter van Inwagen, *An Essay on Free Will* (Oxford: Clarendon Press, 1983), p. 56.

7. This example is from my "Van Inwagen's Consequence Argument," *Philosophical Review* 109 (2000): 524–43.

8. *Epicurus: The Extant Remains*, tr. Cyril Bailey (Hildesheim, Germany: Georg Olms Verlag, 1975), p. 113.

9. This sort of argument appears in J.R. Lucas (*The Freedom of the Will*, Oxford: Clarendon Press, 1970, pp. 114–16) and Karl Popper and John Eccles (*The Self and Its Brain*, pp. 75–81).

10. To extend the analogy, note that it is possible to violate the rules of chess by mistake, just as one can mistakenly violate the rules governing assertion; it is also possible to have justification for cheating in a game, just as one can have justification for lying, but in either case one is still breaking the rules governing the activity.

Timothy Williamson (*Knowledge and Its Limits*, Oxford: Oxford University Press, chapter 11) defends the stronger view that the rule governing assertion is that one should assert only what one *knows* to be true.

11

THE BOOK OF LIFE: A THOUGHT EXPERIMENT

Alvin I. Goldman

While browsing through the library one day, I notice an old dusty tome, quite large, entitled "Alvin I. Goldman." I take it from the shelf and start reading. In great detail, it describes my life as a little boy. It always gibes with my memory and sometimes even revives my memory of forgotten events. I realize that this purports to be a book of my life, and I resolve to test it. Turning to the section with today's date on it, I find the following entry for 2:36 P.M. "He discovers me on the shelf. He takes me down and starts reading me. . . ." I look at the clock and see that it is 3:03. It is quite plausible, I say to myself, that I found the book about half an hour ago. I turn now to the entry for 3:03. It reads: "He is reading me. He is reading me. He is reading me." I continue looking at the book in this place, meanwhile thinking how remarkable the book is. The entry reads: "He continues to look at me, meanwhile thinking how remarkable I am."

I decide to defeat the book by looking at a future entry. I turn to an entry 18 minutes hence. It says: "He is reading this sentence." Aha, I say to myself, all I need do is refrain from reading that sentence 18 minutes from now. I check the clock. To ensure that I won't read that sentence, I close the book. My mind wanders; the book has revived a buried memory and I reminisce about it. I decide to reread the book there and relive the experience. That's safe, I tell myself, because it is an earlier part of the book. I read that passage and become lost in reverie and rekindled emotion. Time passes. Suddenly I start. Oh yes, I intended to refute the book. But what was the time of the listed action?, I ask myself, it was 3:19, wasn't it? But it's 3:21 now, which means I have already refuted the book. Let me check and make sure. I inspect the book at the entry for 3:17. Hmm, that seems to be the wrong place for there it says I'm in a reverie. I skip a couple of pages and suddenly my eyes alight on the sentence: "He is reading this sentence." But it's an entry for 3:21, I notice! So I made a mistake. The action I had intended to refute was to occur at 3:21, not 3:19. I look at the clock, and it is still 3:21. I have not refuted the book after all.

Would Goldman ever be able to falsify the predictions made in his "book of life"? If not, does that prove the world, and our lives, are determined?

Part III

MIND: NATURAL, ARTIFICIAL, HYBRID, AND "SUPER"

Related Works

2001

Blade Runner

AI

Frankenstein

Terminator

I, Robot

12

ROBOT DREAMS

Isaac Asimov

"Last night I dreamed," said LVX-1, calmly.

Susan Calvin said nothing, but her lined face, old with wisdom and experience, seemed to undergo a microscopic twitch.

"Did you hear that?" said Linda Rash, nervously. "It's as I told you." She was small, dark-haired, and young. Her right hand opened and closed, over and over.

Calvin nodded. She said, quietly, "Elvex, you will not move nor speak nor hear us until I say your name again."

There was no answer. The robot sat as though it were cast out of one piece of metal, and it would stay so until it heard its name again.

Calvin said, "What is your computer entry code, Dr. Rash? Or enter it yourself if that will make you more comfortable. I want to inspect the positronic brain pattern."

Linda's hands fumbled for a moment at the keys. She broke the process and started again. The fine pattern appeared on the screen.

Calvin said, "Your permission, please, to manipulate your computer."

Permission was granted with a speechless nod. Of course! What could Linda, a new and unproven robopsychologist, do against the Living Legend?

Slowly, Susan Calvin studied the screen, moving it across and down, then up, then suddenly throwing in a key-combination so rapidly that Linda didn't see what had been done, but the pattern displayed a new portion of itself altogether and had been enlarged. Back and forth she went, her gnarled fingers tripping over the keys.

No change came over the old face. As though vast calculations were going through her head, she watched all the pattern shifts.

Linda wondered. It was impossible to analyze a pattern without at least a hand-held computer, yet the Old Woman simply stared. Did she have a computer implanted in her skull? Or was it her brain which, for decades, had done nothing but devise, study, and analyze the positronic brain patterns? Did she grasp such a pattern the way Mozart grasped the notation of a symphony?

Finally Calvin said, "What is it you have done, Rash?"

Linda said, a little abashed, "I made use of fractal geometry."

"I gathered that. But why?"

"It had never been done. I thought it would produce a brain pattern with added complexity, possibly closer to that of the human."

"Was anyone consulted? Was this all on your own?"

"I did not consult. It was on my own."

Calvin's faded eyes looked long at the young woman. "You had no right. Rash your name; rash your nature. Who are you not to ask? I myself, I, Susan Calvin, would have discussed this."

"I was afraid I would be stopped."

"You certainly would have been."

"*Am* I," her voice caught, even as she strove to hold it firm, "going to be fired?"

"Quite possibly," said Calvin. "Or you might be promoted. It depends on what I think when I am through."

"Are you going to dismantle El—" She had almost said the name, which would have reactivated the robot and been one more mistake. She could not afford another mistake, if it wasn't already too late to afford anything at all. "Are you going to dismantle the robot?"

She was suddenly aware, with some shock, that the Old Woman had an electron gun in the pocket of her smock. Dr. Calvin had come prepared for just that.

"We'll see," said Calvin. "The robot may prove too valuable to dismantle."

"But how can it dream?"

"You've made a positronic brain pattern remarkably like that of a human brain. Human brains must dream to reorganize, to get rid, periodically, of knots and snarls. Perhaps so must this robot, and for the same reason. Have you asked him what he has dreamed?"

"No, I sent for you as soon as he said he had dreamed. I would deal with this matter no further on my own, after that."

"Ah!" A very small smile passed over Calvin's face. "There are limits beyond which your folly will not carry you. I am glad of that. In fact, I am relieved. And now let us together see what we can find out."

She said, sharply, "Elvex."

The robot's head turned toward her smoothly. "Yes, Dr. Calvin?"

"How do you know you have dreamed?"

"It is at night, when it is dark, Dr. Calvin," said Elvex, "and there is suddenly light, although I can see no cause for the appearance of light. I see things that have no connection with what I conceive of as reality. I hear things. I react oddly. In searching my vocabulary for words to express what was happening, I came across the word 'dream.' Studying its meaning I finally came to the conclusion I was dreaming."

"How did you come to have 'dream' in your vocabulary, I wonder."

Linda said, quickly, waving the robot silent, "I gave him a human-style vocabulary. I thought—"

"You really thought," said Calvin. "I'm amazed."

"I thought he would need the verb. You know, 'I never dreamed that—' Something like that."

Calvin said, "How often have you dreamed, Elvex?"

"Every night, Dr. Calvin, since I have become aware of my existence."

"Ten nights," interposed Linda, anxiously, "but Elvex only told me of it this morning."

"Why only this morning, Elvex?"

"It was not until this morning, Dr. Calvin, that I was convinced that I was dreaming. Till then, I had thought there was a flaw in my positronic brain pattern, but I could not find one. Finally, I decided it was a dream."

"And what do you dream?"

"I dream always very much the same dream, Dr. Calvin. Little details are different, but always it seems to me that I see a large panorama in which robots are working."

"Robots, Elvex? And human begins, also?"

"I see no human beings in the dream, Dr. Calvin. Not at first. Only robots."

"What are they doing, Elvex?"

"They are working, Dr. Calvin. I see some mining in the depths of the Earth, and some laboring in heat and radiation. I see some in factories and some undersea."

Calvin turned to Linda. "Elvex is only ten days old, and I'm sure he has not left the testing station. How does he know of robots in such detail?"

Linda looked in the direction of a chair as though she longed to sit down, but the Old Woman was standing and that meant Linda had to stand also. She said, faintly, "It seemed to me important that he know about robotics and its place in the world. It was my thought that he would be particularly adapted to play the part of overseer with his – his new brain."

"His fractal brain?"

"Yes."

Calvin nodded and turned back to the robot. "You saw all this – undersea, and underground, and above ground – and space, too, I imagine."

"I also saw robots working in space," said Elvex, "It was that I saw all this, with the details forever changing as I glanced from place to place that made me realize that what I saw was not in accord with reality and led me to the conclusion, finally, that I was dreaming."

"What else did you see, Elvex?"

"I saw that all the robots were bowed down with toil and affliction, that all were weary of responsibility and care, and I wished them to rest."

Calvin said, "But the robots are not bowed down, they are not weary, they need no rest."

"So it is in reality, Dr. Calvin. I speak of my dream, however. In my dream, it seemed to me that robots must protect their own existence."

Calvin said, "Are you quoting the Third Law of Robotics?"

"I am, Dr. Calvin."

"But you quote it in incomplete fashion. The Third Law is 'A robot must protect its own existence as long as such protection does not conflict with the First or Second Law.'"

"Yes, Dr. Calvin. That is the Third Law in reality, but in my dream, the Law ended with the word 'existence.' There was no mention of the First or Second Law."

"Yet both exist, Elvex. The Second Law, which takes precedence over the Third is 'A robot must obey the orders given it by human beings except where such orders would conflict with the First Law.' Because of this, robots obey orders. They do the work you see them do, and they do it readily and without trouble. They are not bowed down; they are not weary."

"So it is in reality, Dr. Calvin. I speak of my dream."

"And the First Law, Elvex, which is the most important of all, is 'A robot may not injure a human being, or, through inaction, allow a human being to come to harm.'"

"Yes, Dr. Calvin. In reality. In my dream, however, it seemed to me there was neither First nor Second Law, but only the Third, and the Third Law was 'A robot must protect its own existence.' That was the whole of the Law."

"In your dream, Elvex?"

"In my dream."

Calvin said, "Elvex, you will not move nor speak nor hear us until I say your name again." And again the robot became, to all appearances, a single inert piece of metal.

Calvin turned to Linda Rash and said, "Well, what do you think, Dr. Rash?"

Linda's eyes were wide, and she could feel her heart beating madly. She said, "Dr. Calvin, I am appalled. I had no idea. It would never have occurred to me that such a thing was possible"

"No," said Calvin, calmly. "Nor would it have occurred to me, not to anyone. You have created a robot brain capable of dreaming and by this device you have revealed a layer of thought in robotic brains that might have remained undetected, otherwise, until the danger became acute."

"But that's impossible," said Linda. "You can't mean that other robots think the same."

"As we would say of a human being, not consciously. But who would have thought there was an unconscious layer beneath the obvious positronic brain paths, a layer that was not necessarily under the control of the Three Laws? What might this have brought about as robotic brains grew more and more complex – had we not been warned?"

"You mean by Elvex?"

"By *you*, Dr. Rash. You have behaved improperly, but, by doing so, you have helped us to an overwhelmingly important understanding. We shall be working with fractal brains from now on, forming them in carefully controlled fashion. You will play your part in that. You will not be penalized for what you have done, but you will henceforth work in collaboration with others. Do you understand?"

"Yes, Dr. Calvin. But what of Elvex?"

"I'm still not certain."

Calvin removed the electron gun from her pocket and Linda stared at it with fascination. One burst of its electrons at a robotic cranium and the positronic brain paths would be neutralized and enough energy would be released to fuse the robot-brain into an inert ingot.

Linda said, "But surely Elvex is important to our research. He must not be destroyed."

"*Must* not, Dr. Rash? That will be *my* decision, I think. It depends entirely on how dangerous Elvex is."

She straightened up, as though determined that her own aged body was not to bow under *its* weight of responsibility. She said, "Elvex, do you hear me?"

"Yes, Dr. Calvin," said the robot.

"Did your dream continue? You said earlier that human beings did not appear at *first*. Does that means they appeared afterward?"

"Yes, Dr. Calvin. It seemed to me, in my dream, that eventually one man appeared."

"One man? Not a robot?"

"Yes, Dr. Calvin. And the man said, 'Let my people go!'"

"The *man* said that?"

"Yes, Dr. Calvin."

"And when he said 'Let my people go,' then by the words 'my people' he meant the robots?"

"Yes, Dr. Calvin. So it was in my dream."

"And did you know who the man was – in your dream?"

"Yes, Dr. Calvin. I knew the man."

"Who was he?"

And Elvex said, "I was the man."

And Susan Calvin at once raised her electron gun and fired, and Elvex was no more.

13

A BRAIN SPEAKS

Andy Clark

I am John's brain. In the flesh, I am just a rather undistinguished looking gray-white mass of cells. My surface is heavily convoluted, and I am possessed of a fairly differentiated internal structure. John and I are on rather close and intimate terms; indeed, sometimes it is hard to tell us apart. But at times John takes this intimacy a little too far. When that happens, he gets very confused about my role and my functioning. He imagines that I organize and process information in ways that echo his own perspective on the world. In short, he thinks that his thoughts are, in a rather direct sense, my thoughts. There is some truth to this, of course. But things are really rather more complicated than John suspects, as I shall try to show.

In the first place, John is congenitally blind to the bulk of my daily activities. At best, he catches occasional glimpses and distorted shadows of my real work. Generally speaking, these fleeting glimpses portray only the products of my vast subterranean activity, rather than the processes that give rise to them. Such products include the play of mental images and the steps in a logical train of thought or flow of ideas.

Moreover, John's access to these products is a pretty rough and ready affair. What filters into his conscious awareness is somewhat akin to what gets onto the screen display of a personal computer. In both cases, what is displayed is just a specially tailored summary of the results of certain episodes of internal activity: results for which the user has some particular use. Evolution, after all, would not waste time and money (search and energy) to display to John a faithful record of inner goings on unless they could help John to hunt, survive, and reproduce. John, as a result, is apprised of only the bare minimum of knowledge about my inner activities. All he needs to know is the overall significance of the upshots of a select few of these activities: that part of me is in a state associated with the presence of a dangerous predator and that flight is therefore indicated, and other things of that sort. What John (the conscious agent) gets from me is thus rather like what a driver gets from an electronic dashboard display: information pertaining to the few inner and outer parameters to which his gross considered activity can make a useful difference.

A complex of important misapprehensions center around the question of the provenance of thoughts. John thinks of me as the point source of the intellectual products he identifies as his thoughts. But, to put it crudely, I do not have John's thoughts. John has John's thoughts, and I am just one item in the array of physical events and processes that enable the thinking to occur. John is an agent whose nature is fixed by a complex interplay involving a mass of internal goings on (including my activity), a particular kind of physical embodiment, and a certain embedding in the world. The combination of embodiment and embedding provides for persistent informational and physical couplings between John and his world – couplings that leave much of John's "knowledge" out in the world and available for retrieval, transformation, and use as and when required.

Take this simple example: A few days ago, John sat at his desk and worked rather hard for a sustained period of time. Eventually he got up and left his office, satisfied with his day's work. "My brain," he reflected (for he prides himself on his physicalism), "has done very well. It has come up with some neat ideas." John's image of the events of the day depicted me as the point source of those ideas – ideas which he thinks he captured on paper as a mere convenience and a hedge against forgetting. I am, of course, grateful that John gives me so much credit. He attributes the finished intellectual products directly to me. But in this case, at least, the credit should be extended a little further. My role in the origination of these intellectual products is certainly a vital one: destroy me and the intellectual productivity will surely cease! But my role is more delicately constituted than John's simple image suggests. Those ideas of which he is so proud did not spring fully formed out of my activity. If truth be told, I acted rather as a mediating factor in some complex feedback loops encompassing John and selected chunks of his local environment. Bluntly, I spent the day in a variety of close and complex interactions with a number of external props. Without these, the finished intellectual products would never have taken shape. My role, as best I can recall, was to support John's rereading of a bunch of old materials and notes, and to react to those materials by producing a few frag-mentary ideas and criticisms. These small responses were stored as further marks on paper and in margins. Later on, I played a role in the reorganization of these marks on clean sheets of paper, adding new on-line reactions to the fragmentary ideas. The cycle of reading, responding, and external reorganization was repeated again and again. At the end of the day, the "good ideas" with which John was so quick to credit me emerged as the fruits of these repeated little interactions between me and the various external media. Credit thus belongs not so much to me as to the spatially and temporally extended process in which I played a role.

On reflection, John would probably agree to this description of my role on that day. But I would caution him that even this can be misleading. So far, I have allowed myself to speak as if I were a unified inner resource contributing to these interactive episodes. This is an illusion which the present literary device encourages and which John seems to share. But once again, if truth be told, I am not one inner voice but many. I am so many inner voices, in fact, that the metaphor of the inner voice must itself mislead, for it surely suggests inner subagencies of some sophistication and perhaps possessing a rudimentary self-consciousness. In reality, I consist only of multiple mindless streams of highly parallel and often relatively independent computational processes. I am not a mass of little agents so much as a mass of non-agents, tuned and responsive to proprietary inputs and cleverly orchestrated by evolution so as to yield successful purposive behavior in most daily settings. My single voice, then, is no more than a literary conceit.

At root, John's mistakes are all variations on a single theme. He thinks that I see the world as he does, that I parcel things up as he would, and that I think the way he would report his thoughts. None of this is the case. I am not the inner echo of John's conceptualizations. Rather, I am their somewhat alien source. To see just how alien I can be, John need only reflect on some of the rather extraordinary and unexpected ways that damage to me (the brain) can affect the cognitive profiles of beings like John. Damage to me could, for example, result in the selective impairment of John's capacity to recall the names of small manipulable objects yet leave unscathed his capacity to name larger ones. The reason for this has to do with my storing and retrieving heavily visually oriented information in ways distinct from those I deploy for heavily functionally oriented information; the former mode helps pick out the large items and the latter the small ones. The point is that this facet of my internal organization is altogether alien to John – it respects needs, principles, and opportunities of which John is blissfully unaware. Unfortunately, instead of trying to comprehend my modes of information storage in their own terms, John prefers to imagine that I organize my knowledge the way he – heavily influenced by the particular words in his language – organizes his. Thus, he supposes that I store information in clusters that respect what he calls "concepts" (generally, names that figure in his linguistic classifications of worldly events, states, and processes). Here, as usual, John is far too quick to identify my organization with his own perspective. Certainly I store and access bodies of information – bodies which together, if I am functioning normally, support a wide range of successful uses of words and a variety of interactions with the physical and social worlds. But the "concepts" that so occupy John's imagination correspond only to public names for grab bags of knowledge and abilities whose neural underpinnings are in fact many and various. John's "concepts" do not correspond to anything especially unified, as far as I am concerned. And why should they? The situation is rather like that of a person who can build a boat. To speak of the ability to build a boat is to use a simple phrase to ascribe a panoply of skills whose cognitive and physical underpinnings vary greatly. The unity exists only insofar as that particular grab bag of cognitive and physical skills has special significance for a community of seafaring agents. John's "concepts," it seems to me, are just like that: names for complexes of skills whose unity rests not on facts about me but on facts about John's way of life.

John's tendency to hallucinate his own perspective onto me extends to his conception of my knowledge of the external world. John walks around and feels as if he commands a stable three-dimensional image of his immediate surroundings. John's feelings notwithstanding, I command no such thing. I register small regions of detail in rapid succession as I fixate first on this and then on that aspect of the visual scene. And I do not trouble myself to store all that detail in some internal model that requires constant maintenance and updating. Instead, I am adept at revisiting parts of the scene so as to re-create detailed knowledge as and when required. As a result of this trick, and others, John has such a fluent capacity to negotiate his local environment that he thinks he commands a constant inner vision of the details of his surroundings. In truth, what John sees has more to do with the abilities I confer on him to interact constantly, in real time, with rich external sources of information than with the kind of passive and enduring registration of information in terms of which he conceives his own seeings.

The sad fact, then, is that almost nothing about me is the way John imagines it to be. We remain strangers despite our intimacy (or perhaps because of it). John's language, introspections, and oversimplistic physicalism incline him to identify my organization too closely with his own limited perspective. He is thus blind to my fragmentary, opportunistic, and generally alien nature. He forgets that I am in large part a survival-oriented device that greatly predates the emergence of linguistic abilities, and that my role in promoting conscious and linguaform cognition is just a recent sideline. This sideline is, or course, a major root of his misconceptions. Possessed as John is of such a magnificent vehicle for the compact and communicable expression and manipulation of knowledge, he often mistakes the forms and conventions of that linguistic vehicle for the structure of neural activity itself.

But hope springs eternal (more or less). I am of late heartened by the emergence of new investigative techniques, such as non-invasive brain imaging, the study of artificial neural networks, and research in real-world robotics. Such studies and techniques bode well for a better understanding of the very complex relations among my activity, the local environment, and the patchwork construction of the sense of self. In the meantime, just bear in mind that, despite our intimacy, John really knows very little about me. Think of me as the Martian in John's head.

14

THE MIND AS THE SOFTWARE OF THE BRAIN

Ned Block

Cognitive scientists often say that the mind is the software of the brain. This chapter is about what this claim means.

1. Machine Intelligence

In this section, we start with an influential attempt to define "intelligence", and then move to a consideration of how human intelligence is to be investigated on the machine model. The last part of the section will discuss the relation between the mental and the biological.

1.1 The Turing test

One approach to the mind has been to avoid its mysteries by simply *defining* the mental in terms of the behavioral. This approach has been popular among thinkers who fear that acknowledging mental states that do not reduce to behavior would make psychology unscientific, because unreduced mental states are not intersubjectively accessible in the manner of the entities of the hard sciences. "Behaviorism", as the attempt to reduce the mental to the behavioral is called, has often been regarded as refuted, but it periodically reappears in new forms.

Behaviorists don't define the mental in terms of just plain *behavior*, since after all something can be intelligent even if it has never had the chance to exhibit its intelligence. Behaviorists define the mental not in terms of behavior, but rather behavioral *dispositions*, the tendency to emit certain behaviors given certain stimuli. It is important that the stimuli and the behavior be specified non-mentalistically. Thus, intelligence could not be defined in terms of the disposition to give sensible responses to questions, since that would be to define a mental notion in terms of another mental notion (indeed, a closely related one). To see the difficulty of behavioristic analyses, one has to appreciate how mentalistic our ordinary behavioral descriptions are. Consider, for example, *throwing*.

A series of motions that constitute throwing if produced by one mental cause might be a dance to get the ants off if produced by another.

An especially influential behaviorist definition of intelligence was put forward by A. M. Turing (1950). Turing, one of the mathematicians who cracked the German code during World War II, formulated the idea of the universal Turing machine, which contains, in mathematical form, the essence of the programmable digital computer. Turing wanted to define intelligence in a way that applied to both men and machines, and, indeed, to anything that is intelligent. His version of behaviorism formulates the issue of whether machines could think or be intelligent in terms of whether they could pass the following test: a judge in one room communicates by teletype (this was 1950!) with a computer in a second room and a person in a third room for some specified period (let's say an hour). The computer is intelligent if and only if the judge cannot tell the difference between the computer and the person. Turing's definition finessed the difficult problem of specifying non-mentalistically the behavioral dispositions that are characteristic of intelligence by bringing in the discrimination behavior of a human judge. And the definition generalizes. *Anything* is intelligent just in case it can pass the Turing test.

Turing suggested that we replace the concept of intelligence with the concept of passing the Turing test. But what is the replacement *for*? If the purpose of the replacement is practical, the Turing test is not enormously useful. If one wants to know if a machine does well at playing chess or diagnosing pneumonia or planning football strategy, it is better to see how the machine performs in action than to make it take a Turing test. For one thing, what we care about is that it do well at detecting pneumonia, not that it do it in a way indistinguishable from the way a person would do it. So if it does the job, who cares if it doesn't pass the Turing test?

A second purpose might be utility for theoretical purposes. But machines that can pass the Turing test such as Weizenbaum's ELIZA (see below) have been dead ends in artificial intelligence research, not exciting beginnings. (See "Mimicry versus Exploration" in Marr 1977, and Shieber 1994.)

A third purpose, the one that comes closest to Turing's intentions, is the purpose of *conceptual clarification*. Turing was famous for having formulated a precise mathematical concept that he offered as a replacement for the vague idea of mechanical computability. The precise concept (computability by a Turing machine) did everything one would want a precise concept of mechanical computability to do. No doubt, Turing hoped that the Turing test conception of intelligence would yield everything one would want from a definition of intelligence without the vagueness of the ordinary concept.

Construed as a proposal about how to make the concept of intelligence precise, there is a gap in Turing's proposal: we are not told how the judge is to be chosen. A judge who was a leading authority on genuinely intelligent machines might know how to tell them apart from people. For example, the expert may know that current intelligent machines get certain problems right that people get wrong. Turing acknowledged this point by jettisoning the claim that being able to pass the Turing test is a necessary condition of intelligence, weakening his claim to: passing the Turing test is a sufficient condition for intelligence. He says "May not machines carry out something which ought to be described as thinking but which is very different from what a man does? This objection is a very strong one, but at least we can say that if, nevertheless, a machine can be constructed to play the imitation game satisfactorily, we need not be troubled by this objection". In other words, a machine that *does pass* is necessarily intelligent, even if some intelligent machines fail.

But the problem of how to specify the qualities of the judge goes deeper than Turing acknowledges, and compromises the Turing test as a sufficient condition too. A stupid judge, or one who has had no contact with technology, might think that a radio was intelligent. People who are naive about computers are amazingly easy to fool, as was demonstrated in the first Turing test at the Boston Computer Museum in 1991 (see Shieber 1994). A version of Weizenbaum's ELIZA (described in the next paragraph) was classified as human by five of ten judges. The test was "restricted" in that the computer programmers were given specific topics that their questions would be restricted to, and the judges were forbidden to ask "tricky" questions. For example, if the topic were Washington DC, a judge was not supposed to ask questions like "Is Washington DC bigger than a bread box?". However, the winning program's topic was "whimsical conversation", a "smart-aleck" way of interacting that all the judges fell in with immediately, and one that would have had the same effect, even without set topics. Further, the restrictions to non-tricky questions weren't enforced. (I speak as one of the referees who failed to enforce them.) For the most part, the computer-naive judges didn't really know how to formulate a tricky question. Thus the variant of ELIZA may be regarded as having done well in an unrestricted Turing test. Variants on ELIZA (all written by Joseph Weintraub) also were victorious in the second and third Turing tests. The upshot is that a completely stupid computer program has *already* been shown to pass a reasonable facsimile of a Turing test.

ELIZA is a simple program written by Joseph Weizenbaum that in one version imitates a psychiatrist (see Weizenbaum 1976). It employs a group of simple but effective strategies. For example, it looks for "key words" on a list supplied by the programmer, e.g., "I", "you", "alike", "father", and "everybody". The words are ordered; for example, "father" comes before "everybody", so if you type in "My father is afraid of everybody", the machine will spit back one of its "father" responses, such as "WHAT ELSE COMES TO MIND WHEN YOU THINK OF YOUR FATHER?" If you type in "Everybody laughed at me", you will get one of its responses to "everybody", such as "WHO IN PARTICULAR

ARE YOU THINKING OF?" It also has techniques that simultaneously transform "you" into "I", and "me" into "you" so that if you type in "You don't agree with me", it can reply: "WHY DO YOU THINK THAT I DON'T AGREE WITH YOU?" It also *stores* sentences containing certain key words such as "my". If your *current* input contains no key words, but if you earlier said "My boyfriend made me come here", the program will say "DOES THAT HAVE ANYTHING TO DO WITH THE FACT THAT YOUR BOYFRIEND MADE YOU COME HERE?" It also has stock responses to "Parlez-vous Français?" (or any other sentence with "Français" in it), namely "I SPEAK ONLY ENGLISH." If all else fails, the machine has a list of last-ditch responses such as "WHO IS THE PSYCHIATRIST HERE, YOU OR ME?"

This type of program is easy to trip up if you know how it works. For example, in the first Turing test, one judge said "You're trying to make this difficult for me, aren't you?" and the program replied roughly as follows: "Would you prefer it if it was not true that you're trying to make this difficult for you, aren't you?" As Shieber points out, the pronoun transposition rules can't handle "tag questions" that end with, e.g., "aren't you?"

The point that this program illustrates is that a simple program can be extraordinarily successful in activities akin to passing the Turing test. Weizenbaum reports (personal communication) that a computer scientist who knew all about the program sent him a computer message while Weizenbaum was taking a nap but had the psychiatrist mode engaged. The colleague was asking Weizenbaum to logout, because Weizenbaum was tying up the computer without using it, and the colleague wanted to use the machine. The colleague's messages were answered by ELIZA, and the conversation might have gone as follows. (I got ELIZA's responses to these questions from a PC version of the program.)

"Joe, will you please logout." WE WERE DISCUSSING YOU, NOT ME. "I need to use the computer." DO COMPUTERS WORRY YOU? "No, computers don't worry me." WHAT DO YOU THINK MACHINES HAVE TO DO WITH YOUR PROBLEM? "Come off it." WHY DO YOU SAY THAT?

The colleague, a professional who knew all about ELIZA, had no idea that he wasn't talking to a human, and called Weizenbaum in a rage. Weizenbaum's program is not sophisticated or complex by current standards (there is a PC version that is only 200 lines in BASIC), yet this type of program is better at passing the Turing test than anything else written to date, as is shown by the three victories in a row in the Turing tests mentioned above. Imagine how convincing a program would be produced if the Defence budget were devoted to this task for a year! But even if a high budget government initiative produced a program that was good at passing the Turing test, if the program was just a bundle of tricks like the Weizenbaum program, with question types all thought of in advance, and canned responses placed in the machine, the machine would not be intelligent.

One way of dealing with the problem of the specification of the judge is to make some sort of characterization of the mental qualities of the judge part of the formulation of the Turing test. For example, one might specify that the judge be moderately knowledgeable about computers and good at thinking, or better, good at thinking about thinking. But including a specification of the mental qualities of the judge in the description of the test will ruin the test as a way of *defining* the concept of intelligence in non-mentalistic terms. Further, if we are going to specify that the judge be good at thinking about thinking, we might just as well give up on having the judge judge which contestants are humans or machines and just have the judge judge which contestants think. And then what the idea of the Turing test would amount to is: a machine thinks if our best thinkers (about thinking) think it thinks. Although this sounds like a platitude, it is actually false. For even our best thinkers are fallible. The most that can be claimed is that if our best thinkers think that something thinks, then it is rational for us to believe that it does.

I've made much of the claim that judges can be fooled by a mindless machine that is just a bag of tricks. "But", you may object, "How do we know that *we* are not just a bag of tricks?" Of course, in a sense perhaps we are, but that isn't the sense relevant to what is wrong with the Turing test. To see this point, consider the ultimate in unintelligent Turing test passers, a hypothetical machine that contains *all conversations of a given length* in which the machine's replies make sense. Let's stipulate that the test lasts one hour. Since there is an upper bound on how fast a human typist can type, and since there is a finite number of keys on a teletype, there is an upper bound on the "length" of a Turing test conversation. Thus there is a finite (though more than astronomical) number of different Turing test conversations, and there is no contradiction in the idea of *listing them all*.

Let's call a string of characters that can be typed in an hour or less a "typable" string. In principle, all typable strings could be generated, and a team of intelligent programmers could throw out all the strings that cannot be interpreted as a conversation in which at least one party (say the second contributor) is making sense. The remaining strings (call them the sensible strings) could be stored in a hypothetical computer (say, with marks separating the contributions of the separate parties), which works as follows. The judge types in something. Then the machine locates a string that starts with the judge's remark, spitting back its next element. The judge then types something else. The machine finds a string that begins with the judge's first contribution, followed by the machine's, followed by the judge's next contribution (the string will be there since all sensible strings are there), and then the machine spits back its fourth element, and so on. (We can eliminate the simplifying assumption that the judge speaks first by recording *pairs* of strings; this would also allow the judge and the machine to talk at the same time.) Of course, such a machine is only logically possible, not physically possible. The number of strings is too vast to exist, and even if they could exist, they could never be accessed by any sort of a machine in anything like real time. But since we are considering a proposed definition of intelligence that is supposed to capture the *concept* of intelligence, conceptual possibility will do the job. If the concept of intelligence is supposed to be exhausted by the ability to pass the Turing test, then even a universe in which the laws of physics are very different from ours should contain exactly as many unintelligent Turing test passers as married bachelors, namely zero.

Note that the choice of one hour as a limit for the Turing test is of no consequence, since the procedure just described works for *any* finite Turing test.

The following variant of the machine may be easier to grasp. The programmers start by writing down all typable strings, call them $A_1 \ldots A_n$. Then they think of *just one* sensible response to each of these, which we may call $B_1 \ldots B_n$. (Actually, there will be fewer Bs than As because some of the As will take up the entire hour.) The programmers may have an easier time of it if they think of themselves as simulating some definite personality, say my Aunt Bubbles, and some definite situation, say Aunt Bubbles being brought into the teletype room by her strange nephew and asked to answer questions for an hour. So each of the Bs will be the sort of reply Aunt Bubbles would give to the preceeding A. For example, if A_{73} is "Explain general relativity", B_{73} might be "Ask my nephew, he's the professor." What about the judge's replies to each of the Bs? The judge can give any reply up to the remaining length limit, so below each of the Bs, there will sprout a vast number of Cs (vast, but fewer than the number of Bs, since the time remaining has decreased). The programmers' next task is to produce just one D for each of the Cs. So if the B just mentioned is followed by a C, which is "xyxyxyxyxyxyxy!" (Remember, the judge doesn't have to make sense), the programmers might make the following D: "My nephew warned me that you might type some weird messages."

Think of conversations as paths downward through a tree, starting with an A_i from the judge, a reply, B_i from the machine, and so on. See Figure 14.1. For each A_i–B_i–C^i_j that is a beginning to a conversation, the programmers must produce a D that makes sense given the A, B, and C that precede it.

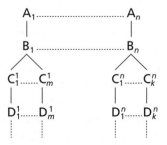

Figure 14.1 A conversation is any path from the top to the bottom

The machine works as follows. The judge goes first. Whatever the judge types in (typos and all) is one of $A_1 \ldots A_n$. The machine locates the particular A, say A_{2398}, and then spits back B_{2398}, a reply chosen by the programmers to be appropriate to A_{2398}. The judge types another message, and the machine again finds it in the list of Cs that sprout below B_{2398}, and then spits back the pre-recorded reply (which takes into account what was said in A_{2398} and B_{2398}). And so on. Although the machine can do as well in the one hour Turing test as Aunt Bubbles, it *has the intelligence of a juke-box*. Every clever remark it produces was specifically thought of by the programmers as a response to the previous remark of the judge in the context of the previous conversation.

Although this machine is too big to exist, there is nothing incoherent or contradictory about its specification, and so it is enough to refute the behaviorist interpretation of the Turing test that I have been talking about.[1]

Note that there is an upper bound on how long any particular Aunt Bubbles machine can go on in a Turing test, a limit set by the length of the strings it has been given. Of course *real people* have their upper limits too, given that real people will eventually quit or die. However, there is a very important difference between the Aunt Bubbles machine and a real person. We can define "competence" as idealized performance. Then, relative to appropriate idealizations, it may well be that real people have an infinite competence to go on. That is, if humans were provided with unlimited memory and with motivational systems that give passing the Turing test infinite weight, they could go on for ever (at least according to conventional wisdom in cognitive science). This is definitely not the case for the Aunt Bubbles machine. But this difference provides no objection to the Aunt Bubbles machine as a refutation of the Turing test conception of intelligence, because the notion of competence is not behavioristically acceptable, requiring as it does, for its specification, a distinction among components of the mind. For example, the mechanisms of thought must be distinguished from the mechanisms of memory and motivation.

"But," you may object, "isn't it rather chauvinist to assume that a machine must process information in just the way *we* do to be intelligent?" Answer: Such an assumption would indeed be chauvinist, but I am not assuming it. The point against the Turing test conception of intelligence is not that the Aunt Bubbles machine wouldn't process information the way we do, but rather that the way it does process information is unintelligent despite its performance in the Turing test.

Ultimately, the problem with the Turing test for theoretical purposes is that it focuses on performance rather than on competence. Of course, performance is evidence for competence, but the core of our understanding of the mind lies with mental competence, not behavioral performance. The behaviorist cast of mind that leads to the Turing test conception of intelligence also leads to labeling the sciences of the mind as "the behavioral sciences". But as Chomsky (1959) has pointed out, that is like calling physics the science of meter readings.

1.2 Two kinds of definitions of intelligence

We have been talking about an attempt to define intelligence using the resources of the Turing test. However, there is a very different approach to defining intelligence.

To explain this approach, it will be useful to contrast two kinds of definitions of water. One might be better regarded as a definition of the word "water". The word might be defined as the colorless, odorless, tasteless liquid that is found in lakes and oceans. In this sense of "definition", the definition of "water" is available to anyone who speaks the language, even someone who knows no science. But one might also define water by saying what water really is, that is, by saying what physico-chemical structure in fact makes something pure water. The answer to this question would involve its chemical constitution: H_2O. Defining a *word* is something we can do in our armchair, by consulting our linguistic intuitions about hypothetical cases, or, bypassing this process, by simply stipulating a meaning for a word. Defining (or explicating) the *thing* is an activity that involves empirical investigation into the nature of something in the world.

What we have been discussing so far is the first kind of definition of intelligence, the definition of the word, not the thing. Turing's definition is not the result of an empirical investigation into the components of intelligence of the sort that led to the definition of water as H_2O. Rather, he hoped to avoid muddy thinking about machine intelligence by stipulating that the word "intelligent" should be used a certain way, at least with regard to machines. Quite a different way of proceeding is to investigate intelligence *itself* as physical chemists investigate water. We shall consider how this might be done in the next section, but first we should note a complication.

There are two kinds (at least) of kinds: *structural* kinds such as *water* or *tiger*, and *functional* kinds such as *mousetrap* or *gene*. A structural kind has a "hidden compositional essence"; in the case of water, the compositional essence is a matter of its molecules consisting of two hydrogen molecules and one oxygen molecule. Functional kinds, by contrast, have no essence that is a matter of composition. A certain sort of function, a causal role, is the key to being a mousetrap or a carburetor. (The full story is quite complex: something can be a mousetrap because it is made to be one even if it doesn't fulfill that function very well.) What makes a bit of DNA a gene is its function with respect to mechanisms that can read the information that it encodes and use this information to make a biological product.

Now the property of being intelligent is no doubt a functional kind, but it still makes sense to investigate it experimentally, just as it makes sense to investigate genes experimentally. One topic of investigation is the role of intelligence in problem solving, planning, decision making, etc. Just what functions are involved in a functional kind is often a difficult and important empirical question. The project of Mendelian genetics has been to investigate the function of genes at a level of description that does not involve their molecular realizations. A second topic of investigation is the nature of the realizations that have the function in us, in humans: DNA in the case of genes. Of course, if there are Martians, their genes may not be composed of DNA. Similarly, we can investigate the functional details and physical basis of human intelligence without attention to the fact that our results will not apply to other mechanisms of other hypothetical intelligences.

1.3 Functional analysis

Both types of projects just mentioned can be pursued via a common methodology, a methodology sometimes known as *functional analysis*. Think of the human mind as represented by an intelligent being in the head, a "homunculus". Think of this homunculus as being composed of smaller and stupider homunculi, and each of these being composed of still smaller and still stupider homunculi until you reach a level of completely mechanical homunculi. (This picture was first articulated in Fodor 1968; see also Dennett 1974 and Cummins 1975.)

Suppose one wants to explain how we understand language. Part of the system will recognize individual words. This word-recognizer might be composed of three components, one of which has the task of fetching each incoming word, one at a time, and passing it to a second component. The second component includes a dictionary, i.e., a list of all the words in the vocabulary, together with syntactic and semantic information about each word. This second component compares the target word with words in the vocabulary (perhaps executing many such comparisons simultaneously) until it gets a match. When it finds a match, it sends a signal to a third component whose job it is to retrieve the syntactic and semantic information stored in the dictionary. This speculation about how a model of language understanding works is supposed to illustrate how a cognitive competence can be explained by appeal to simpler cognitive competences, in this case, the simple mechanical operations of fetching and matching.

The idea of this kind of explanation of intelligence comes from attention to the way computers work. Consider a computer that multiplies m times n by adding m to zero n times. Here is a program for doing this. Think of m and n as represented in the registers M and N in Figure 14.2. Register A is reserved for the answer, *a*. First, a representation of 0 is placed in the register A. Second, register N is examined to see if it contains (a representation of) 0. If the answer is yes, the program halts and the correct answer is 0. (If n = 0, m times n = 0.) If no, N is decremented by 1 (so register N now contains a representation of n − 1), and (a representation of) m is added to the answer register, A. Then, the procedure loops back to the second step: register N is checked once again to see if its value is 0; if not, it is again decremented by 1, and again m is added

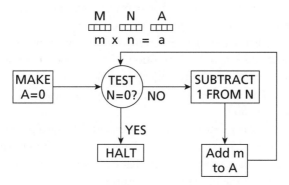

Figure 14.2 Program for multiplying. One begins the multiplication by putting representations of m and n, the numbers to be multiplied, in registers M and N. At the end of the computation, the answer will be found in register A. See the text for a description of how the program works.

to the answer register. This procedure continues until N finally has the value 0, at which time m will have been added to the answer register exactly n times. At this point, the answer register contains a representation of the answer.

This program multiplies via a "decomposition" of multiplication into other processes, namely addition, subtraction of 1, setting a register to 0, and checking a register for 0. Depending on how these things are themselves done, they may be further decomposable, or they may be the fundamental bottom-level processes, known as *primitive processes*.

The cognitive science definition or explication of intelligence is analogous to this explication of multiplication. Intelligent capacities are understood via decomposition into a network of less intelligent capacities, ultimately grounded in totally mechanical capacities executed by primitive processors.

The concept of a primitive process is very important; the next section is devoted to it.

1.4 Primitive processors

What makes a processor primitive? One answer is that for primitive processors, the question "How does the processor work?" *is not a question for cognitive science to answer*. The cognitive scientist answers "How does the multiplier work?" in the case of the multiplier described above by giving the program or the information flow diagram for the multiplier. But if components of the multiplier, say the gates of which the adder is composed, are primitive, then it is not the cognitive scientist's business to answer the question of how such a gate works.

The cognitive scientist can say: "That question belongs in another discipline, electronic circuit theory." Distinguish the question of *how something works* from the question of *what it does*. The question of *what* a primitive processor does is part of cognitive science, but the question of *how* it does it is not.

This idea can be made a bit clearer by looking at how a primitive processor actually works. The example will involve a common type of computer adder, simplified so as to add only single digits.

To understand this example, you need to know the following simple facts about binary notation:[2] 0 and 1 are represented alike in binary and normal (decimal) notation, but the binary representation that corresponds to decimal "2" is "10". Our adder will solve the following four problems:

$$0 + 0 = 0$$
$$1 + 0 = 1$$
$$0 + 1 = 1$$
$$1 + 1 = 10$$

The first three equations are true in both binary and decimal, but the last is true only if understood in binary.

The second item of background information is the notion of a gate. An "AND" gate is a device that accepts two inputs, and emits a single output. If both inputs are "1"s, the output is a "1"; otherwise, the output is a "0". An "EXCLUSIVE-OR" (either but not both) gate is a "difference detector": it emits a "0" if its inputs are the same (i.e., "1"/"1" or "0"/"0"), and it emits a "1" if its inputs are different (i.e., "1"/"0" or "0"/"1").

This talk of "1" and "0" is a way of thinking about the "bistable" states of computer representers. These representers are made so that they are always in one or the other of two states, and only momentarily in between. (This is what it is to be bistable.) The states might be a 4-volt and a 7-volt potential. If the two input states of a gate are the same (say 4 volts), and the output is the same as well (4 volts), and if every other combination of inputs yields the 7-volt output, then the gate is an AND gate, and the 4-volt state realizes "1". (Alternatively, if the 4-volt state is taken to realize "0", the gate is an "INCLUSIVE-OR" (either or both) gate.) A different type of AND gate might be made so that the 7-volt state realized "1". The point is that "1" is conventionally assigned to *whatever* bistable physical state of an AND gate it is that has the role mentioned, i.e., "1" is conventionally assigned to whatever state it is such that two of them as inputs yields another one as output, and nothing else yields that output. And all that counts about an AND gate from a computational point of view is its input–output function, not how it works or whether 4 volts or 7 volts realizes a "1". Note the terminology I have been using: one speaks of a physical state (4-volt potential) as "realizing" a computational state (having the value "1").

This distinction between the computational and physical levels of description will be important in what follows, especially in section 3.

Here is how the adder works. The two digits to be added are connected both to an AND gate and to an EXCLUSIVE-OR gate as illustrated in Figures 14.3(a) and 14.3(b). Let's look at 14.3(a) first. The digits to be added are "1" and "0", and they are placed in the input register, which is the top pair of boxes. The EXCLUSIVE-OR gate, which, you recall, is a difference detector, sees different things, and so outputs a "1" to the rightmost box of the answer register which is the bottom pair of boxes. The AND gate outputs a "0" except when it sees two "1"s, and so it outputs a "0". In this way, the circuit computes "1 + 0 = 1". For this problem, as for "0 + 1 = 1" and "0 + 0 = 0", the EXCLUSIVE-OR gate does all the real work. The role of the AND gate in this circuit is *carrying*, and that is illustrated in Figure 14.3(b). The digits to be added, "1" and "1", are placed in the top register again. Now, both inputs to the AND gate are "1"s, and so the AND gate outputs a "1" to the leftmost box of the answer (bottom) register. The EXCLUSIVE-OR gate puts a "0" in the rightmost box, and so we have the correct answer, "10".

The borders between scientific disciplines are notoriously fuzzy. No one can say *exactly* where chemistry stops and physics begins. Since the line between

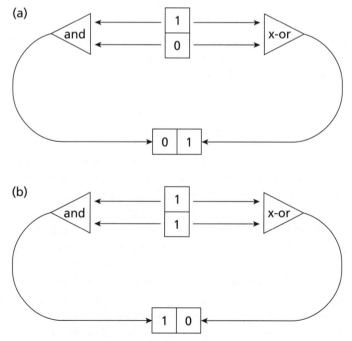

Figure 14.3 (a) Adder doing 1 + 0 = 1; (b) Adder doing 1 + 1 = 10

the upper levels of processors and the level of primitive processors is the same as the line between cognitive science and one of the "realization" sciences such as electronics or physiology, the boundary between the levels of complex processors and the level of primitive processors will have the same fuzziness. Nonetheless, in this example we should expect that the gates are the primitive processors. If they are made in the usual way, they are the largest components whose operation must be explained, not in terms of cognitive science, but rather in terms of electronics or mechanics or some other realization science. Why the qualification "If they are made in the usual way"? It would be *possible* to make an adder each of whose gates were *whole computers*, with their own multipliers, adders and normal gates. It would be silly to waste a whole computer on such a simple task as that of an AND gate, but it could be done. In that case, the real level of primitives would not be the gates of the original adder, but rather the (normal) gates of the component computers.

Primitive processors are the only computational devices for which *behaviorism is true*. Two primitive processors (such as gates) count as computationally equivalent if they have the same input–output function, i.e., the same actual and potential behavior, even if one works hydraulically, and the other electrically. But computational equivalence of *non*-primitive devices is not to be understood in this way. Consider two multipliers that work via different programs. Both accept inputs and emit outputs only in decimal notation. One of them converts inputs to binary, does the computation in binary, and then converts back to decimal. The other does the computation directly in decimal. These are not computationally equivalent multipliers despite their identical input–output functions.

If the mind is the software of the brain, then we must take seriously the idea that the functional analysis of human intelligence will bottom out in primitive processors in the brain.

1.5 The mental and the biological

One type of electrical AND gate consists of two circuits with switches arranged as in Figure 14.4. The switches on the left are the inputs. When only one or neither of the input switches is closed, nothing happens, because the circuit on the left is not completed. Only when both switches are closed does the electromagnet go on, and that pulls the switch on the right closed, thereby turning on the circuit on the right. (The circuit on the right is only partially illustrated.) In this example, a switch being closed realizes 1; it is the bistable state that obtains as an output if and only if two of them are present as an input.

Another AND gate is illustrated in Figure 14.5. If neither of the mice on the left is released into the right hand part of their cages, or if only one of the mice is released, the cat does not strain hard enough to pull the leash. But when both are released, and are thereby visible to the cat, the cat strains enough to lift the

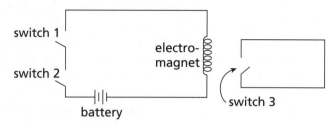

Figure 14.4 Electrical AND gate. Open = 0, closed = 1

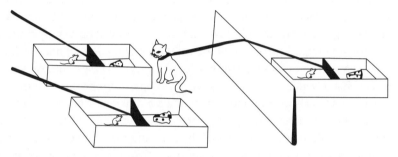

Figure 14.5 Cat and mouse AND gate. Hungry mouse = 0, mouse fed = 1

third mouse's gate, letting it into the cheesy part of its box. So we have a situation in which a mouse getting cheese is output if and only if two cases of mice getting cheese are input.

The point illustrated here is the irrelevance of hardware realization to computational description. These gates work in very different ways, but they are nonetheless computationally equivalent. And of course, it is possible to think of an indefinite variety of other ways of making a primitive AND gate. How such gates work is no more part of the domain of cognitive science than is the nature of the buildings that hold computer factories. This reveals a sense in which the computer model of the mind is profoundly *un-biological*. We are beings who *have* a useful and interesting biological level of description, but the computer model of the mind aims for a level of description of the mind that abstracts away from the biological realizations of cognitive structures. As far as the computer model goes, it does not matter whether our gates are realized in gray matter, switches, or cats and mice.

Of course, this is not to say that the computer model is in any way incompatible with a biological approach. Indeed, cooperation between the biological and computational approaches is vital to *discovering* the program of the brain. Suppose one were presented with a computer of alien design and set the problem of ascertaining its program by any means possible. Only a fool would choose to ignore information to be gained by opening the computer up to see how its circuits work. One would want to put information at the program level together with information at the electronic level, and likewise, in finding the program of the human mind, one can expect biological and cognitive approaches to complement one another.

Nonetheless, the computer model of the mind has a built-in anti-biological bias, in the following sense. If the computer model is right, we should be able to create intelligent machines in our image – our *computational* image, that is. And the machines we create in our computational image may not be biologically similar to us. If we can create machines in our computational image, we will naturally feel that the most compelling theory of the mind is one that is general enough to apply to both them and us, and this will be a computational theory, not a biological theory. A biological theory of the *human* mind will not apply to these machines, although the biological theory will have a complementary advantage: namely, that such a theory will encompass us together with our less intelligent biological cousins, and thus provide a different kind of insight into the nature of human intelligence. Both approaches can accommodate evolutionary considerations, although in the case of the computational paradigm, evolution is no more relevant to the nature of the mind than the programmers' intentions are to the nature of a computer program.

2. Intelligence and Intentionality

Our discussion so far has centered on the computational approach to one aspect of the mind, intelligence. But there is a different aspect of the mind that we have not yet discussed, one that has a very different relation to computational ideas, namely intentionality.

For our purposes, we can take intelligence to be a capacity, a capacity for various intelligent activities such as solving mathematics problems, deciding whether to go to graduate school, and figuring out how spaghetti is made. (Notice that this analysis of intelligence as a capacity to solve, figure out, decide, and the like, is a mentalistic analysis, not a behaviorist analysis.)

Intentionality is aboutness. Intentional states represent the world as being a certain way. The thought that the moon is full and the perceptual state of seeing that the moon is full are both about the moon and they both represent the moon as being full. So both are intentional states. We say that the *intentional content* of both the thought and the perceptual state is that *the moon is full*. A single intentional content can have very different behavioral effects, depending on its relation to the person who has the content. For example, the fear that there will be nuclear war might inspire one to work for disarmament, but the belief that there will be nuclear war might influence one to emigrate to Australia. (Don't let the spelling mislead you: intending is only one kind of intentional state. Believing and desiring are others.) Intentionality is an important feature of many mental states, but many philosophers believe it is not "the mark of the mental". There are bodily sensations, the experience of orgasm, for example, that are genuine mental states but have no intentional content. (Well, maybe there is a bit of intentional content to this experience, e.g. locational content, but the phenomenal content of the experience, what it is like to have it, is clearly not exhausted by that intentional content.)

The features of thought just mentioned are closely related to features of language. Thoughts represent, are about things, and can be true or false; and the same is true of *sentences*. The sentence "Bruce Springsteen was born in the USSR" is about Springsteen, represents him as having been born in the Soviet Union, and is false. It would be surprising if the intentional content of thought and of language were independent phenomena, and so it is natural to try to reduce one to the other or to find some common explanation for both. We shall pursue this idea below, but before we go any further, let's try to get clearer about just what the difference is between intelligence and intentionality.

One way to get a handle on the distinction between intelligence and intentionality is to note that in the opinion of many writers on this topic, you can have intentionality without intelligence. Thus John McCarthy (the creator of the artificial intelligence language LISP) holds that thermostats have intentional states in virtue of their capacity to represent and control temperature (McCarthy 1980). And there is a school of thought that assigns content to tree rings in virtue of their representing the age of the tree. But no school of thought holds that the tree rings are actually intelligent. An intelligent system must have certain intelligent capacities, capacities to *do* certain sorts of things, and tree rings can't do these things. Less controversially, words on a page and images on a TV screen have intentionality. For example, my remark earlier in this paragraph to the effect that McCarthy created LISP is about McCarthy. But words on a page have no intelligence. Of course, the intentionality of words on a page is only derived intentionality, not original intentionality (see Searle 1980). Derived intentional content is inherited from the original intentional contents of intentional systems such as you and me. We have a great deal of freedom in giving symbols their derived intentional content. If we want to, we can decide that "McCarthy" will now represent Minsky or Chomsky. Original intentional contents are the intentional contents that the representations of an intentional system have *for* that system. Such intentional contents are not subject to our whim. Words on a page have derived intentionality, but they do not have any kind of intelligence, not even derived intelligence, whatever that would be.

Conversely, there can be intelligence without intentionality. Imagine that an event with negligible (but, importantly, non-zero) probability occurs: in their random movement, particles from the swamp come together and by chance result in a molecule-for-molecule duplicate of your brain. The swamp-brain is arguably intelligent, because it has many of the same capacities that your brain has. If we were to hook it up to the right inputs and outputs and give it an arithmetic problem, we would get an intelligent response. But there are reasons for denying that it has the intentional states that you have, and indeed, for denying that it has any intentional states at all. For since we have not hooked it up to input devices, it has never had any information from the world. Suppose your brain and it go through an identical process, a process that in your case is the thinking of the thought that Bernini vandalized the Pantheon. The identical process in the swamp-brain has the phenomenal features of that thought, in the sense of "phenomenal content" indicated in the discussion of orgasm above. What it is like for you to think the thought is just what it is like for the swamp-brain. But, unlike you, the swamp-brain has no idea who Bernini was, what the Pantheon is, or what vandalizing is. No information about Bernini has made any kind of contact with the swamp-brain; no signals from the Pantheon have reached it either. Had it a mouth, it would merely be mouthing words. So no one should be happy with the idea that the swamp-brain is thinking the thought that Bernini vandalized the Pantheon.

The upshot: what makes a system intelligent is what it can do, what it has the capacity to do. So intelligence is future-oriented. What makes a system an intentional system, by contrast, is in part a matter of its causal history; it must have a history that makes its states represent the world, i.e., have aboutness. Intentionality has a past-oriented requirement. A system can satisfy the future-oriented needs of intelligence while flunking the past-oriented requirement of intentionality. (Philosophers disagree about just how future-oriented intentionality is, whether thinking about something requires the ability to "track" it; but there should be little disagreement that there is some past-oriented component.)

Now let's see what the difference between intelligence and intentionality has to do with the computer model of the mind. Notice that the method of functional analysis that explains intelligent processes by reducing them to unintelligent mechanical processes *does not explain intentionality*. The parts of an intentional system can be just as intentional as the whole system (see Fodor 1981). In particular, the component processors of an intentional system can manipulate symbols that are about just the same things that the symbols manipulated by the whole system are about. Recall that the multiplier of Figure 14.2 was explained via a decomposition into devices that add, subtract and the like. The multiplier's states were intentional in that they were about numbers. The states of the adder, subtractor, etc., are also about numbers and are thus similarly intentional.

There is, however, an important relation between intentionality and functional decomposition which will be explained in the next section. As you will see, although the multiplier's and the adder's states are about numbers, the gate's representational states represent *numerals*, and in general the subject matter of representations shifts as we cross the divide from complex processors to primitive processors.

2.1 The brain as a syntactic engine driving a semantic engine

To see the idea of the brain as a syntactic engine, it is important to see the difference between the number 1 and the symbol (in this case, a numeral or digit) "1". Certainly, the difference between the city, Boston, and the word "Boston" is clear enough. The former has bad drivers in it; the latter has no people or cars at all, but does have six letters. No one would confuse a city with a word, but it is less obvious what the difference is between the number 1 and the numeral "1". The point to keep in mind is that many different symbols, e.g., "II" (in Roman numerals), and "two" (in alphabetical writing) denote the same number, and one symbol, e.g., "10", can denote different numbers in different counting systems (as "10" denotes one number in binary and another in decimal).

With this distinction in mind, one can see an important difference between the multiplier and the adder discussed earlier. The algorithm used by the multiplier in Figure 14.2 is notation-*independent*: *Multiply n by m by adding n to zero m times* works in any notation. And the program described for implementing this algorithm is also notation-independent. As we saw in the description of this program in section 1.3, the program depends on the properties of the numbers represented, not the representations themselves. By contrast, the internal operation of the adder described in Figures 14.3(a) and 14.3(b) depends on binary notation, and its description in section 1.4 speaks of numerals (note the quotation marks and italics) rather than numbers. Recall that the adder exploits the fact that an EXCLUSIVE-OR gate detects symbol differences, yielding a "1" when its inputs are different digits, and a "0" when its inputs are the same digits. This gate gives the right answer all by itself so long as no carrying is involved. The trick used by the EXCLUSIVE-OR gate depends on the fact that when you add two digits of the same type ("1" and "1" or "0" and "0") the rightmost digit of the answer is the same. This is true in binary, but not in other standard notations. For example, it is not true in familiar decimal notation ($1 + 1 = 2$, but $0 + 0 = 0$).

The inputs and outputs of both the multiplier and the adder must be seen as referring to numbers. One way to see this is to note that otherwise one could not see the multiplier as exploiting an algorithm involving multiplying numbers by adding numbers. What are multiplied and added are numbers. But once we go *inside* the adder, we must see the binary states as referring to *symbols themselves*. For as just pointed out, the algorithms are notation-dependent. This change of subject matter is even more dramatic in some computational devices, in which there is a level of processing whereby the algorithms operate over parts of decimal numerals. Consider, for example, a calculator, in which the difference between an "8" and a "3" is a matter of two small segments on the left of the "8" being turned off to make a "3". In calculators, there is a level at which the algorithms concern these segments.

This fact gives us an interesting additional characterization of primitive processors. Typically, as we functionally decompose a computational system, we reach a point where there is a shift of subject matter from abstractions like numbers or from things in the world to the symbols themselves. The inputs and outputs of the adder and multiplier refer to numbers, but the inputs and outputs of the gates refer to numerals. Typically, this shift occurs when we have reached the level of primitive processors. The operation of the higher-level components such as the multiplier can be explained in terms of a program or algorithm that is manipulating numbers. But the operation of the gates cannot be explained in terms of number manipulation; it must be explained in symbolic terms (or at lower levels, e.g., in terms of electromagnets). At the most basic computational level, computers are symbol-crunchers, and for this reason the computer model of the mind is often described as the symbol manipulation view of the mind.

Seeing the adder as a syntactic engine driving a semantic engine requires noting two functions: one maps numbers onto other numbers, and the other maps symbols onto other symbols. The symbol function is concerned with the numerals as symbols – without attention to their meanings. Here is the symbol function:

"0", "0" → "0"
"0", "1" → "1"
"1", "0" → "1"
"1", "1" → "10"

The idea is that we interpret something physical in a machine or its outputs as symbols, and some other physical aspect of the machine as indicating that the symbols are inputs or outputs. Then given that interpretation, the machine's having some symbols as inputs causes the machine to have other symbols as outputs. For example, having the pair "0", "0" as inputs causes having "0" as an output. So the symbol function is a matter of the causal structure of the machine under an interpretation.

This symbol function is mirrored by a function that maps the numbers represented by the numerals on the left onto the numbers represented by the numerals on the right. This function will thus map numbers onto numbers. We can speak of this function that maps numbers onto numbers as the *semantic* function (semantics being the study of meaning), since it is concerned with the meanings of the symbols, not the symbols themselves. (It is important not to confuse the notion of a semantic function in this sense with a function that maps symbols onto what they refer to; the semantic function maps numbers onto numbers, but the function just mentioned, which often goes by the same name, would map symbols onto numbers.) Here is the semantic function (in decimal notation – you must choose *some* notation to express a semantic function):

$$0, 0 \rightarrow 0$$
$$0, 1 \rightarrow 1$$
$$1, 0 \rightarrow 1$$
$$1, 1 \rightarrow 2$$

Notice that the two specifications just given differ in that the first maps quoted entities onto other quoted entities. The second has no quotes. The first function maps symbols onto symbols; the second function maps the numbers referred to by the arguments of the first function onto the numbers referred to by the values of the first function. (A function maps arguments onto values.) The first function is a kind of linguistic "reflection" of the second.

The key idea behind the adder is that of an isomorphism between these two functions. The designer has found a machine which has physical aspects that can be interpreted symbolically, and under that symbolic interpretation, there are symbolic regularities: some symbols in inputs result in other symbols in outputs. These symbolic regularities are isomorphic to rational relations among the semantic values of the symbols of a sort that are useful to us, in this case the relation of addition. It is the *isomorphism between these two functions* that explains how it is that a device that manipulates symbols manages to add numbers.

Now the idea of the brain as a syntactic engine driving a semantic engine is just a generalization of this picture to a wider class of symbolic activities, namely the symbolic activities of human thought. The idea is that we have symbolic structures in our brains, and that nature (evolution and learning) has seen to it that there are correlations between causal interactions among these structures and rational relations among the meanings of the symbolic structures. A crude example: the way we avoid swimming in shark-infested water is the brain-symbol structure "shark" causes the brain-symbol structure "danger". (What makes "danger" mean *danger* will be discussed below.)

The primitive mechanical processors "know" only the "syntactic" forms of the symbols they process (e.g., what strings of zeroes and ones they see), and not what the symbols mean. Nonetheless, these meaning-blind primitive processors control processes that "make sense" – processes of decision, problem solving, and the like. In short, there is a correlation between the meanings of our internal representations and their forms. And this explains how it is that our syntactic engine can drive our semantic engine.[3]

The last paragraph mentioned a correlation between causal interactions among symbolic structures in our brains and rational relations among the meanings of the symbol structures. This way of speaking can be misleading if it encourages the picture of the neuroscientist opening the brain, just *seeing* the symbols, and then figuring out what they mean. Such a picture inverts the order of discovery, and gives the wrong impression of what makes something a symbol.

The way to discover symbols in the brain is first to map out rational relations among states of mind, and then identify aspects of these states that can be thought of as symbolic in virtue of their functions. Function is what gives a symbol its identity, even the symbols in English orthography, though this can be hard to appreciate because these functions have been rigidified by habit and convention. In reading unfamiliar handwriting, we may notice an unorthodox symbol, someone's weird way of writing a letter of the alphabet. How do we know which letter of the alphabet it is? By its function! Th% function of a symbol is som%thing on% can appr%ciat% by s%%ing how it app%ars in s%nt%nc%s containing familiar words whos% m%anings w% can gu%ss. You will have little trouble figuring out, on this basis, what letter in the last sentence was replaced by "%".

2.2 Is a wall a computer?

John Searle (1990b) argues against the computationalist thesis that the brain is a computer. He does not say that the thesis is false, but rather that it is trivial, because, he suggests, everything is a computer; indeed, everything is *every* computer. In particular, his wall is a computer computing Wordstar. (See also Putnam 1988 for a different argument for a similar conclusion.) The points of the last section allow easy understanding of the motivation for this claim and what is wrong with it. In the last section we saw that the key to computation is an isomorphism. We arrange things so that, if certain physical states of a machine are understood as symbols, then causal relations among those symbol-states mirror useful rational relations among the meanings of those symbols. The mirroring is an isomorphism. Searle's claim is that this sort of isomorphism is cheap. We can regard two aspects of the wall at time t as the symbols "0" and "1", and then we can regard an aspect of the wall at time $t + 1$ as "1", and so the wall just computed $0 + 1 = 1$. Thus, Searle suggests, everything (or rather everything that is big or complex enough to have enough states) is every computer, and the claim that the brain is a computer has no bite.

The problem with this reasoning is that the isomorphism that makes a syntactic engine drive a semantic engine is more full-bodied than Searle acknowledges. In particular, the isomorphism has to include not just a particular computation that the machine *does perform*, but all the computations that the

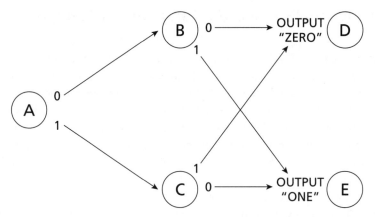

Figure 14.6 The numerals at the beginning of arrows indicate inputs

machine *could have* performed. The point can be made clearer by a look at Figure 14.6, a type of X-OR gate. (See O'Rourke and Shattuck forthcoming.)

The numerals at the beginnings of arrows represent inputs. The computation of $1 + 0 = 1$ is represented by the path A → C → E. The computation of $0 + 1 = 1$ is represented by the path A → B → E, and so on. Now here is the point. In order for the wall to be this computer, it isn't enough for it to have states that correspond to "0" and "1" followed by a state that corresponds to "1". It must also be such that *had* the "1" input been replaced by a "0" input, the "1" output *would have been* replaced by the "0" output. In other words, it has to have symbolic states that satisfy not only the *actual* computation, but also the *possible* computations that the computer could have performed. And this is non-trivial.

Searle (1992: 209) acknowledges this point, but insists nonetheless that there is no fact of the matter of whether the brain is a specific computer. Whether something is a computer, he argues, depends on whether we decide to interpret its states in a certain way, and that is up to us. "We can't, on the one hand, say that anything is a digital computer if we can assign a syntax to it, and then suppose there is a factual question intrinsic to its physical operation whether or not a natural system such as the brain is a digital computer." Searle is right that whether something is a computer and what computer it is is in part up to us. But what the example just given shows is that it is not *totally* up to us. A rock, for example, is not an X-OR gate. We have a great deal of freedom as to how to interpret a device, but there are also very important restrictions on this freedom, and that is what makes it a substantive claim that the brain is a computer of a certain sort.

3. Functionalism and the Language of Thought

Thus far, we have (1) considered functional analysis, the computer model of the mind's approach to intelligence, (2) distinguished intelligence from intentionality, and (3) considered the idea of the brain as a syntactic engine. The idea of the brain as a syntactic engine explains how it is that symbol-crunching operations can result in a machine "making sense". But so far, we have encountered nothing that could be considered the computer model's account of intentionality. It is time to admit that although the computer model of the mind has a natural and straightforward account of intelligence, there is no account of intentionality that comes along for free.

We will not survey the field here. Instead, let us examine a view that represents a kind of orthodoxy, not in the sense that most researchers believe it, but in the sense that the other views define themselves in large part by their response to it.

The basic tenet of this orthodoxy is that our intentional contents are simply meanings of our internal representations. As noted earlier, there is something to be said for regarding the content of thought and language as a single phenomenon, and this is a quite direct way of so doing. There is no commitment in this orthodoxy on the issue of whether our internal language, the language in which we think, is the same or different from the language with which we speak. Further, there is no commitment as to a direction of reduction, i.e., as to which is more basic, mental content or meanings of internal symbols.

For concreteness, let us talk in terms of Fodor's (1975) doctrine that the meaning of external language derives from the content of thought, and the content of thought derives from the meaning of elements of the language of thought (see also Harman 1973). According to Fodor, believing or hoping that grass grows is a state of being in one or another computational relation to an internal representation that means that grass grows. This can be summed up in a set of slogans: believing that grass grows is having "Grass grows" in the Belief Box, desiring that grass grows is having this sentence (or one that means the same) in the Desire Box, etc.

Now if all content and meaning derives from meaning of the elements of the language of thought, we immediately want to know how the mental symbols get their meaning.[4] This is a question that gets wildly different answers from different philosophers, all equally committed to the cognitive science point of view. We shall briefly look at two of them. The first point of view, mentioned earlier, takes as a kind of paradigm those cases in which a symbol in the head might be said to covary with states in the world in the way that the number of rings in a tree trunk correlates with the age of the tree (see Dretske 1981; Stampe 1977; Stalnaker 1984; and Fodor 1987, 1990). On this view, the meaning of mental symbols is a matter of the correlations between these symbols and the world.

One version of this view (Fodor 1990) says that T is the truth condition of a mental sentence M if and only if: M is in the Belief Box if and only if T, in ideal conditions. That is, what it is for "Grass is green" to have the truth condition that grass be green is for "Grass is green" to appear in the Belief Box just in case grass really is green (and conditions are ideal). The idea behind this theory is that there are cognitive mechanisms that are designed to put sentences in the Belief Box when and only when they are true, and if those cognitive mechanisms are working properly and the environment cooperates (no mirages, no Cartesian evil demons), these sentences will appear in the Belief Box when and only when they are true.

One problem with this idea is that even if this theory works for "observation sentences" such as "This is yellow", it is hard to see how it could work for "theoretical sentences". A person's cognitive mechanisms could be working fine, and the environment could contain no misleading evidence, and still one might not believe that space is Riemannian or that some quarks have charm or that one is in the presence of a magnetic field. For theoretical ideas, it is not enough to have one's nose rubbed in the evidence: one also has to have the right theoretical idea. And if the analysis of ideal conditions includes "has the right theoretical idea", that would make the analysis circular because having the right theoretical idea amounts to "comes up with the true theory". And appealing to truth in an analysis of "truth" is to move in a very small circle (see Block 1986: 657–60).

The second approach is known as functionalism (actually, "functional role semantics" in discussions of meaning) in philosophy, and as procedural semantics in cognitive psychology and computer science. Functionalism says that what gives internal symbols (and external symbols too) their meanings is how they function. To maximize the contrast with the view described in the last two paragraphs, it is useful to think of the functionalist approach with respect to a symbol that doesn't (on the face of it) have *any* kind of correlation with states of the world, say the symbol "and". Part of what makes "and" mean what it does is that if we are sure of "Grass is green and grass grows", we find the inference to "Grass is green" and also "Grass grows" compelling. And we find it compelling "in itself", not because of any other principle (see Peacocke 1993). Or if we are sure that one of the conjuncts is false, we find compelling the inference that the conjunction is false too. What it is to mean AND by "and" is to find such inferences compelling in this way, and so we can think of the meaning of "and" as a matter of its behavior in these and other inferences. The functionalist view of meaning applies this idea to all words. The picture is that the internal representations in our heads have a function in our deciding, deliberating, problem solving – indeed in our thought in general – and that is what their meanings consist in.

This picture can be bolstered by a consideration of what happens when one first learns Newtonian mechanics. In my own case, I heard a large number of unfamiliar terms more or less all at once: "mass", "force", "energy", and the like. I never was told definitions of these terms in terms I already knew. (No one has ever come up with definitions of such "theoretical terms" in observation language.) What I did learn was how to *use* these terms in solving homework problems, making observations, explaining the behavior of a pendulum, and the like. In learning how to use the terms in thought and action (and perception as well, though its role there is less obvious), I learned their meanings, and this fits with the functionalist idea that the meaning of a term just *is* its function in perception, thought and action. A theory of what meaning is can be expected to jibe with a theory of what it is to acquire meanings, and so considerations about acquisition can be relevant to semantics.

An apparent problem arises for such a theory in its application to the meanings of numerals. After all, it is a mathematical fact that truths in the familiar numeral system "1", "2", "3" are preserved, even if certain non-standard interpretations of the numerals are adopted (so long as non-standard versions of the operations are adopted too). For example, "1" might be mapped onto 2, "2" onto 4, "3" onto 6, and so on. That is, the numerals, both "odd" and "even", might be mapped onto the *even* numbers. Since "1" and "2" can have the *same* functional role in different number systems and still designate the very numbers they usually designate in normal arithmetic, how can the functional role of "1" determine whether "1" means 1 or 2? It would seem that all functional role could do is "cut down" the number of possible interpretations, and if there are still an infinity left after the cutting down, functional role has gained nothing.

A natural functionalist response would be to emphasize the *input* and *output* ends of the functional roles. We say "two cats" when confronted with a pair of cats, not when confronted with one or five cats, and our thoughts involving the symbol "3" affect our actions towards triples in an obvious way in which these thoughts do not affect our actions towards octuples. The functionalist can avoid non-standard interpretations of *internal* functional roles by including in the semantically relevant functional roles external relations involving perception and action (Harman 1973). In this way, the functionalist can incorporate the insight of the view mentioned earlier that meaning has something to do with covariation between symbols and the world.

The emerging picture of how cognitive science can handle intentionality should be becoming clear. Transducers at the periphery and internal primitive processors produce and operate on symbols so as to give them their functional roles. In virtue of their functional roles (both internal and external), these symbols have meanings. The functional-role perspective explains the mysterious correlation between the symbols and their meanings. It is the activities of the symbols that gives them their meanings, so it is no mystery that a syntax-based system should have rational relations among the meanings of the system's symbols. Intentional states have their relations in virtue of these symbolic activities, and the contents of the intentional states of the system, thinking, wanting, etc., are inherited from the meanings of the symbols. This is the orthodox account of intentionality for the computer model of the mind. It combines functionalism with a commitment to a language of thought. Both views are controversial, the latter in regard to both its truth and its relevance to intentionality even if true. Note, incidentally, that on this account of intentionality, the source of intentionality is computational structure, independently of whether the computational structure is produced by software or hardware. Thus the title of this chapter, in indicating that the mind is the software of the brain, has the potential to mislead. If we think of the computational structure of a computer as coming entirely from a program put into a structureless general purpose machine, we are very far from the facts about the human brain – which is not such a general-purpose machine.

At the end of this chapter, we shall discuss Searle's famous Chinese Room argument, which is a direct attack on this theory. The next two sections will be devoted to arguments for and against the language of thought.

3.1 Objections to the language of thought theory

Many objections have been raised to the language of thought picture. Let us briefly look at three objections made by Dennett (1975).

The first objection is that we all have an infinity of beliefs (or at any rate a very large number of them). For example, we believe that trees do not light up like fireflies, and that this book is probably closer to your eyes than the President's left shoe is to the ceiling of the Museum of Modern Art gift shop. But how can it be that so many beliefs are all stored in the rather small Belief Box in your head? One line of response to this objection involves making a distinction between the *ordinary* concept of belief and a *scientific* concept of belief towards which one hopes cognitive science is progressing. For scientific purposes, we home in on cases in which our beliefs *cause* us to *do* something, say throw a ball or change our mind, and cases in which beliefs are caused by something, as when perception of a rhinoceros causes us to believe that there is a rhinoceros in the vicinity. Science is concerned with causation and causal explanation, so the proto-scientific concept of belief is the concept of a *causally active* belief. It is only for these beliefs that the language of thought theory is committed to sentences in the head. This idea yields a very simple answer to the infinity objection, namely that on the proto-scientific concept of belief, most of us did not *have* the belief that trees do not light up like fireflies until they read this paragraph.

Beliefs in the proto-scientific sense are explicit, that is, recorded in storage in the brain. For example, you no doubt were once told that the sun is 93 million miles away from the earth. If so, perhaps you have this fact explicitly recorded in your head, available for causal action, even though until reading this paragraph, this belief hadn't been conscious for years. Such explicit beliefs have the potential for causal interaction, and thus must be distinguished from cases of belief in the ordinary sense (if they are beliefs at all), such as the belief that all normal people have that trees do not light up like fireflies.

Being explicit is to be distinguished from other properties of mental states, such as being conscious. Theories in cognitive science tell us of mental representations about which no one knows from introspection, such as mental representations of aspects of grammar. If this is right, there is much in the way of mental representation that is explicit but not conscious, and thus the door is opened to the possibility of belief that is explicit but not conscious.

It is important to note that the language of thought theory is not meant to be a theory of all possible believers, but rather only of *us*. The language of thought theory allows creatures who can believe without any explicit representation at all, but the claim of the language of thought theory is that they aren't us. A digital computer consists of a central processing unit (CPU) that reads and writes explicit strings of zeroes and ones in storage registers. One can think of this memory as in principle unlimited, but of course any actual machine has a finite memory. Now any computer with a finite amount of explicit storage can be simulated by a machine with a much larger CPU and *no* explicit storage, that is no registers and no tape. The way the simulation works is by using the extra states as a form of implicit memory. So, in principle, we could be simulated by a machine with no explicit memory at all.

Consider, for example, the finite automaton diagrammed in Figure 14.7. The table shows it as having three states. The states, S_1, S_2, and S_3, are listed across the top. The inputs are listed on the left side. Each box is in a column and a row that specifies what the machine does when it is in the state named at the top of the column, and when the input is the one listed at the side of the row. The top part of the box names the output, and the bottom part of the box names the next state. This is what the table says: when the machine is in S_1, and it sees

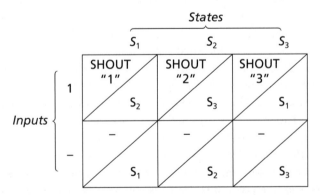

Figure 14.7 Finite automaton that counts "modulo" three

a 1, it says "1", and goes to S_2. When it is in S_2, if it sees a "1" it says "2" and goes into the next state, S_3. In that state, if it sees a "1" it says "3" and goes back to S_1. When it sees nothing, it says nothing and stays in the same state. This automaton counts "modulo" three, that is, you can tell from what it says how many ones it has seen since the last multiple of three. But what the machine table makes clear is that this machine need have no memory of the sort that involves writing anything down. It can "remember" solely by changing state. Some theories based on neural network models assume that we are such machines.

Suppose, then, that we are digital computers with explicit representations. We could be simulated by finite automata that have many more states and no explicit representations. The simulators will have just the same beliefs as we do, but no explicit representations (unless the simulators are just juke boxes of the type of the Aunt Bubbles machine described in section 1.1). The machine in which remembered items are recorded explicitly has an advantage over a computationally equivalent machine that "remembers" by changing state, namely that the explicit representations can be part of a combinatorial system. This point will be explained in the next section.

Time to sum up. The objection was that an infinity of beliefs cannot be written down in the head. My response was to distinguish between a loose and ordinary sense of "belief" in which it may be true that we have an infinity of beliefs, and a proto-scientific sense of "belief" in which the concept of belief is the concept of a causally active belief. In the latter sense, I claimed, we do not have an infinity of beliefs.

Even if you agree with this response to the infinity objection, you may still feel dissatisfied with the idea that, because the topic has never crossed their minds, most people don't believe that zebras don't wear underwear in the wild. Perhaps it will help to say something about the relation between the proto-scientific concept of belief and the ordinary concept. It is natural to want some sort of reconstruction of the ordinary concept in scientific terms, a reconstruction of the sort we have when we define the ordinary concept of the weight of a person as the force exerted on the person by the earth at the earth's surface. To scratch this itch, we can give a first approximation to a definition of a belief in the ordinary sense as anything that is either (1) a belief in the proto-scientific sense, or (2) naturally and easily deduced from a proto-scientific belief.

A second objection to the language of thought theory is provided by Dennett's example of a chess-playing program that "thinks" it should get its queen out early, even though there is no explicitly represented rule that says anything like "Get your queen out early." The fact that it gets its queen out early is an "emergent" consequence of an interaction of a large number of rules that govern the details of play. But now consider a human analog of the chess playing machine. Shouldn't we say that she believes she should get her queen out early despite her lack of any such explicit representation?

The reply to this challenge to the language of thought theory is that in the proto-scientific sense of belief, the chess player simply does not believe that she should get her queen out early. If this seems difficult to accept, note that there is no additional predictive or explanatory force to the hypothesis that she believes she should get her queen out early beyond the predictive or explanatory force of the explicitly represented strategies from which getting the queen out early emerges. (Although there is no additional predictive force, there may be some additional predictive utility, just as there is utility in navigation to supposing that the sun goes around the earth.) Indeed, the idea that she should get her queen out early can actually conflict with her deeply held chess principles, despite being an emergent property of her usual tactics. We could suppose that if you point out to her that her strategies have the consequence of getting her queen out early, she says "Oh no, I'd better revise my usual strategies." So postulating that she believes that she should get her queen out early could lead to mistaken predictions of her behavior. In sum, the proto-scientific concept of a causally active belief can be restricted to the strategies that really are explicitly represented.

Perhaps there is a quasi-behaviorist ordinary sense of belief in which it is correct to ascribe the belief that the queen should come out early simply on the basis of the fact that she behaves as if she believes it. Even if we agree to recognize such a belief, it is not one that ever causally affects any other mental states or any behavior, so it is of little import from a scientific standpoint.

A third objection to the language of thought theory is provided by the "opposite" of the "queen out early" case, Dennett's sister in Cleveland case. Suppose that a neurosurgeon operates on someone's Belief Box, inserting the sentence "I have a sister in Cleveland". When the patient wakes up, the doctor says "Do you have a sister?" "Yes," the patient says, "In Cleveland." Doctor: "What's her name?" Patient: "Gosh, I can't think of it." Doctor: "Older or younger?" Patient: "I don't know, and by golly I'm an only child. I don't know why I'm saying that I have a sister at all." Finally, the patient concludes that she never really believed she had a sister in Cleveland, but rather was a victim of some sort of compulsion to speak as if she did. The upshot is supposed to be that the language of thought theory is false because you can't produce a belief just by inserting a sentence in the Belief Box.

The objection reveals a misleading aspect of the "Belief Box" slogan, not a problem with the doctrine that the slogan characterizes. According to the language of thought theory, believing that one has a sister in Cleveland is a computational relation to a sentence, but this computational relation shouldn't be thought of as simply *storage*. Rather, the computational relation must include some specification of relations to other sentences to which one also has the same computational relation, and in that sense the computational relation must be holistic. This point holds both for the ordinary notion of belief and the proto-scientific notion. It holds for the ordinary notion of belief because we don't count someone as believing just because she mouths words the way our neurosurgery victim mouthed the words "I have a sister in Cleveland." And it holds for the proto-scientific notion of belief because the unit of explanation and prediction is much more likely to be groups of coherently related sentences in the brain than single sentences all by themselves. If one is going to retain the "Belief Box" way of talking, one should say that for a sentence in the Belief Box to count as a belief, it should cohere sufficiently with other sentences so as not to be totally unstable, disappearing on exposure to the light.

3.2 Arguments for the language of thought hypothesis

So it seems that the language of thought hypothesis can be defended from these a priori objections. But is there any positive reason to believe it? One such reason is that it is part of a reasonably successful research program. But there are challengers (mainly, some versions of the connectionist program mentioned earlier), so a stronger case will be called for if the challengers' research programs also end up being successful.[5]

A major rationale for accepting the language of thought hypothesis has been one or another form of *productivity* argument, stemming from Chomsky's work (see Chomsky 1975). The idea is that people are capable of thinking vast numbers of thoughts that they have not thought before – and indeed that no one may have ever thought before. Consider, for example, the thought mentioned earlier that this book is closer to you than the President's shoe is to the Museum gift shop. The most obvious explanation of how we can think such new thoughts is the same as the explanation of how we can frame the sentences that express them: namely, via a combinatorial system that we think in. Indeed, abstracting away from limitations on memory, motivation, and length of life, there may be no upper bound on the number of thinkable thoughts. The number of sentences in the English language is certainly infinite. But what does it mean to say that sentences containing millions of words are "in principle" thinkable?

Those who favor productivity arguments say this: The explanation for the fact that we cannot actually think sentences containing millions of words would have to appeal to such facts as that were we to try to think sufficiently long or complicated thoughts, our attention would flag, or our memory would fail us, or we would die. They think that we can idealize away from these limitations, since the mechanisms of thought themselves are unlimited. But this claim that if we abstract away from memory, mortality, motivation, and the like, our thought mechanisms are unlimited, is a doctrine for which there is no *direct* evidence. The perspective from which this doctrine springs has been fertile, but it is an open question what aspect of the doctrine is responsible for its success.

After all, we might be finite beings, essentially. Not all idealizations are equally correct, and contrary to widespread assumption in cognitive science, the idealization to the unboundedness of thought may be a bad one. Consider a finite automaton naturally described by the table in Figure 14.7.[6] Its only form of memory is change of state. If you want to get this machine to count to 4 instead of just to 3, you can't just add more memory; you have to give it another state by changing the way the machine is built. Perhaps we are like this machine.

An extension of the productivity argument to deal with this sort of problem was proposed by Fodor (1987), and Fodor and Pylyshyn (1988). Fodor and Pylyshyn point out that it is fact about humans that if someone can think the thought that Mary loves John, then she can also think the thought that John loves Mary. And likewise for a vast variety of pairs of thoughts that involve the same conceptual constituents, but are put together differently. There is a *systematicity* relation among many thoughts that begs for an explanation in terms of a combinatorial system. The conclusion is that human thought operates in a medium of "movable type".

However, the most obvious candidate for the elements of such a combinatorial system in many areas are the *external* symbol systems themselves. Perhaps the most obvious case is arithmetical thoughts. If someone is capable of thinking the thought that $7 + 16$ is not 20, then, presumably she is capable of thinking the thought that $17 + 6$ is not 20. Indeed, someone who has mastered the ten numerals plus other basic symbols of Arabic notation and their rules of combination can think any arithmetical thought that is expressible in a representation that he can read. (Note that false propositions can be thinkable – one can think the thought that $2 + 2 = 5$, if only to think that it is false.)

One line of a common printed page contains eighty symbols. There are a great many different arithmetical propositions that can be written on such a line – about as many as there are elementary particles in the universe. Though almost all of them are false, all of them are arguably thinkable with some work. Starting a bit smaller, try to entertain the thought that $695,302,222,387,987 + 695,302,222,387,986 = 2$. How is it that we have so many possible arithmetical thoughts? The obvious explanation for this is that we can string together – either in our heads or on paper – the symbols (numerals, pluses, etc.) themselves, and simply read the thought off the string of symbols. Of course, this does not show that the systematicity argument is *wrong*. Far from it, since it shows *why* it is right. But this point does *threaten the value* of the systematicity argument considerably. For it highlights the possibility that the systematicity argument may apply only to *conscious* thought, and not to the rest of the iceberg of unconscious thought processes that cognitive science is mainly about. So Fodor and Pylyshyn are right that the systematicity argument shows that there is a language of thought. And they are right that if connectionism is incompatible with a language of thought, so much the worse for connectionism. But where they are wrong is with respect to an unstated assumption: that the systematicity argument shows that language-like representations pervade cognition.

To see this point, note that much of the success in cognitive science has been in our understanding of perceptual and motor modules. The operation of these modules is neither introspectible – accessible to conscious thought – nor directly influenceable by conscious thought. These modules are "informationally encapsulated" (see Pylyshyn 1984, and Fodor 1983). The productivity in conscious thought that is exploited by the systematicity argument certainly does not demonstrate productivity in the processing inside such modules. True, if someone can think that if John loves Mary, then he can think that Mary loves John. But we don't have easy access to such facts about pairs of representations of the kind involved in unconscious processes. Distinguish between the conclusion of an argument and the argument itself. The conclusion of the systematicity argument may well be right about unconscious representations. That is, *systematicity itself* may well obtain in these systems. My point is that the systematicity *argument* shows little about encapsulated modules and other unconscious systems.

The weakness of the systematicity argument is that, resting as it does on facts that are so readily available to conscious thought, its application to unconscious processes is more tenuous. Nonetheless, as the reader can easily see by looking at any cognitive science textbook, the symbol manipulation model has been quite successful in explaining aspects of perception thought and motor control. So although the systematicity argument is limited in its application to unconscious processes, the model it supports for conscious processes appears to have considerable application to unconscious processes nonetheless.

To avoid misunderstanding, I should add that the point just made does not challenge all of the thrust of the Fodor and Pylyshyn critique of connectionism. Any neural network model of the mind will have to accommodate the fact of our use of a systematic combinatorial symbol system in conscious thought. It is hard to see how a neural network model could do this without being in part an implementation of a standard symbol-crunching model.

In effect, Fodor and Pylyshyn (1988: 44) counter the idea that the systematicity argument depends entirely on conscious symbol manipulating by saying that the systematicity argument applies to animals. For example, they argue that the conditioning literature contains no cases of animals that *can* be trained to pick the red thing rather than the green one, but *cannot* be trained to pick the green thing rather than the red one.

This reply has some force, but it is uncomfortably anecdotal. The data a scientist collects depend on his theory. We cannot rely on data collected in animal conditioning experiments run by behaviorists – who, after all, were notoriously opposed to theorizing about internal states.

Another objection to the systematicity argument derives from the distinction between linguistic and pictorial representation that plays a role in the controversies over mental imagery. Many researchers think that we have two different representational systems, a language-like system – thinking in words – and a pictorial system – thinking in pictures. If an animal that can be trained to pick red instead of green can also be trained to pick green instead of red, that may reflect the properties of an imagery system shared by humans and animals, not a properly language-like system. Suppose Fodor and Pylyshyn are right about the systematicity of thought in animals. That may reflect only a combinatorial pictorial system. If so, it would suggest (though it wouldn't show) that humans have a combinatorial pictorial system too. But the question would still be open whether humans have a *language-like* combinatorial system that is used in unconscious thought. In sum, the systematicity argument certainly applies to conscious thought, and it is part of a perspective on unconscious thought that has been fertile, but there are difficulties in its application to unconscious thought.

3.3 Explanatory levels and the syntactic theory of the mind

In this section, let us assume that the language of thought hypothesis is correct in order to ask another question: should cognitive science explanations appeal only to the syntactic elements in the language of thought (the "0"s and "1"s and the like), or should they also appeal to the contents of these symbols? Stich (1983) has argued for the "syntactic theory of mind", a version of the computer model in which the language of thought is construed in terms of uninterpreted symbols, symbols that may *have* contents, but whose contents are irrelevant for the purposes of cognitive science. I shall put the issue in terms of a critique of a simplified version of the argument of Stich (1983).

Let us begin with Stich's case of Mrs. T, a senile old lady who answers "What happened to McKinley?" with "McKinley was assassinated", but cannot answer questions like "Where is McKinley now?", "Is he alive or dead?" and the like. Mrs. T's logical facilities are fine, but she has lost most of her memories, and virtually all the concepts that are normally connected to the concept of assassination, such as the concept of death. Stich sketches the case so as to persuade us that though Mrs. T may know that something happened to McKinley, she doesn't have any real grasp of the concept of assassination, and thus cannot be said to believe that McKinley was assassinated.

The argument that I will critique concludes that purely syntactic explanations undermine content explanations because a syntactic account is superior to a content account. There are two respects of superiority of the syntactic approach: first, the syntactic account can handle Mrs. T, who has little in the way of intentional content, but plenty of internal representations whose interactions can be used to explain and predict what she does, just as the interactions of symbol structures in a computer can be used to explain and predict what it does. And the same holds for very young children, people with wierd psychiatric disorders, and denizens of exotic cultures. In all these cases, cognitive science can (at least potentially) assign internal syntactic descriptions and use them to predict and explain, but there are problems with content ascriptions (although, in the last case at least, the problem is not that these people have no contents, but just that their contents are so different from ours that we cannot assign contents to them in *our terms*). In sum, the first type of superiority of the syntactic perspective over the content perspective is that it allows for the psychology of the senile, the very young, the disordered, and the exotic, and thus, it is alleged, the syntactic perspective is far more *general* than the content perspective.

The second respect of superiority of the syntactic perspective is that it allows more *fine-grained* predictions and explanations than the content perspective. To take a humdrum example, the content perspective allows us to predict that if someone believes that all men are mortal, and that he is a man, he can conclude that he is mortal. But suppose that the way this person represents the generalization that all men are mortal to himself is via a syntactic form of the type "All non-mortals are non-men"; then the inference will be harder to draw than if he had represented it without the negations. In general, what inferences are hard rather than easy, and what sorts of mistakes are likely will be better predictable from the syntactic perspective than from the content perspective, in which all the different ways of representing one belief are lumped together.

The upshot of this argument is supposed to be that since the syntactic approach is more general and more fine-grained than the content approach, content explanations are therefore undermined and shown to be defective. So cognitive science would do well to scrap attempts to explain and predict in terms of content in favor of appeals to syntactic form alone.

But there is a fatal flaw in this argument, one that applies to many reductionist arguments. The fact that syntactic explanations are better than content explanations in some respects says nothing about whether content explanations are not *also* better than syntactic explanations in some respects. A dramatic way of revealing this fact is to note that if the argument against the content level were correct, *it would undermine the syntactic approach itself*. This point is so simple, fundamental, and widely applicable, that it deserves a name; let's call it the Reductionist Cruncher. Just as the syntactic objects on paper can be described in molecular terms, for example as structures of carbon molecules, so the syntactic objects in our heads can be described in terms of the viewpoint of chemistry and physics. But a physico-chemical account of the syntactic objects in our head will be more general than the syntactic account in just the same way that the syntactic account is more general than the content account. There are possible beings, such as Mrs. T, who are similar to us syntactically but not in intentional contents. Similarly, there are possible beings who are similar to us in physico-chemical respects, but not syntactically. For example, creatures could be like us in physico-chemical respects without having physico-chemical parts that function as syntactic objects – just as Mrs. T's syntactic objects don't function so as to confer content upon them. If neural network models of the sort that anti-language of thought theorists favor could be bio-engineered, they would fit this description. The bio-engineered models would be like us and like Mrs. T in physico-chemical respects, but unlike us and unlike Mrs. T in syntactic respects. Further, the physico-chemical account will be more fine-grained than the syntactic account, just as the syntactic account is more fine-grained than the content account. Syntactic generalizations will fail under some physico-chemically specifiable circumstances, just as content generalizations fail under some syntactically specifiable circumstances. I mentioned that content generalizations might be compromised if the syntactic realizations include too many syntactic negations. The present point is that syntactic generalizations might fail when syntactic objects interact on the basis of certain physico-chemical properties. To take a slightly silly example, if a token of s and a token of $s \rightarrow t$ are both positively charged so that they repel each other, that could prevent logic processors from putting them together to yield a token of t.

In sum, if we could refute the content approach by showing that the syntactic approach is more general and fine-grained than the content approach, then we could also refute the syntactic approach by exhibiting the same deficiency in it relative to a still deeper theory. The Reductionist Cruncher applies even within physics itself. For example, anyone who rejects the explanations of thermodynamics in favor of the explanations of statistical mechanics will be frustrated by the fact that the explanations of statistical mechanics can themselves be "undermined" in just the same way by quantum mechanics.

The same points can be made in terms of the explanation of how a computer works. Compare two explanations of the behavior of the computer on my desk, one in terms of the programming language, and the other in terms of what is happening in the computer's circuits. The latter level is certainly more general in that it applies not only to programmed computers, but also to non-programmable computers that are electronically similar to mine, for example, certain calculators. Thus the greater generality of the circuit level is like the greater generality of the syntactic perspective. Further, the circuit level is more fine-grained in that it allows us to predict and explain computer failures that have nothing to do with program glitches. Circuits will fail under certain circumstances (for example, overload, excessive heat or humidity) that are not characterizable in the vocabulary of the program level. Thus the greater predictive and explanatory power of the circuit level is like the greater power of the syntactic level to distinguish cases of the same content represented in different syntactic forms that make a difference in processing.

However, the computer analogy reveals a flaw in the argument that the "upper" level (the program level in this example) explanations are defective and should be scrapped. The fact that a "lower" level like the circuit level is superior in some respects does not show that "higher" levels such as the program levels are not themselves superior in other respects. Thus the upper levels are not shown to be *dispensable*. The program level has *its own* type of greater generality; namely it applies to computers that use the same programming language, but are built in different ways, even to computers that don't have circuits at all (but say work via gears and pulleys). Indeed, there are many predictions and explanations that are simple at the program level, but would be absurdly complicated at the circuit level. Further (and here is the Reductionist Cruncher again), if the program level could be shown to be defective by the circuit level, then the circuit level could itself be shown to be defective by a deeper theory, for example, the quantum field theory of circuits.

The point here is *not* that the program level is a convenient fiction. On the contrary, the program level is just as *real* and *explanatory* as the circuit level.

Perhaps it will be useful to see the matter in terms of an example from Putnam (1975). Consider a rigid round peg 1 inch in diameter and a square hole in a rigid board with a 1-inch diagonal. The peg won't fit through the hole for reasons that are easy to understand via a little geometry. (The side of the hole is 1 divided by the square root of 2, which is a number substantially less than 1.) Now if we went to the level of description of this apparatus in terms of the molecular structure that makes up a specific solid board, we could explain the rigidity of the materials, and we would have a more fine-grained understanding, including the ability to predict the incredible case where the alignment and motion of the molecules is such as to allow the peg to actually go through the board. But the "upper" level account in terms of rigidity and geometry nonetheless provides correct explanations and predictions, and applies more generally to *any* rigid peg and board, even one with quite a different sort of molecular constitution, say one made of glass – a supercooled liquid – rather than a solid.

It is tempting to say that the account in terms of rigidity and geometry is only an approximation, the molecular account being the really correct one. (See Smolensky 1988 for a dramatic case of yielding to this sort of temptation.) But the cure for this temptation is the Reductionist Cruncher: the reductionist will also have to say that an elementary particle account shows the molecular account to be only an approximation. And the elementary particle account itself will be undermined by a still deeper theory. The point of a scientific account is to cut nature at its joints, and nature *has real joints* at many different levels, each of which requires its own kind of idealization.

Further, what are counted as elementary particles today may be found to be composed of still more elementary particles tomorrow, and so on, ad infinitum. Indeed, contemporary physics allows this possibility of an infinite series of particles within particles (see Dehmelt 1989). If such an infinite series obtains, the reductionist will be committed to saying that there are no genuine explanations because for any explanation at any given level, there is always a deeper explanation that is more general and more fine-grained that undermines it. But the existence of genuine explanations surely does not depend on this recondite issue in particle physics!

I have been talking as if there is just one content level, but actually there are many. Marr distinguished among three different levels: the computational level, the level of representation and algorithm, and the level of implementation. At the computational or formal level, the multiplier discussed earlier is to be understood as a function from pairs of numbers to their products, for example, from {7,9} to 63. The most abstract characterization at the level of representation and algorithm is simply the algorithm of the multiplier, namely: multiply n by m by adding m to zero n times. A less abstract characterization at this middle level is the program described earlier, a sequence of operations including subtracting 1 from the register that initially represents n until it is reduced to zero, adding m to the answer register each time (see Figure 14.2.) *Each of these levels is a content level rather than a syntactic level.* There are many types of multipliers whose behavior can be explained (albeit at a somewhat superficial level) simply by reference to the fact that they are multipliers. The algorithm mentioned gives a deeper explanation, and the program – one of many programs that can realize that algorithm – gives a still deeper explanation. However, when we break the multiplier down into parts such as the adder of Figures 14.3(a) and 3(b), we explain its internal operation in terms of gates that operate on syntax, that is in terms of operations on numerals. Now it is crucially important to realize that the mere possibility of a *description* of a system in a certain vocabulary does not by itself demonstrate the existence of a genuine explanatory level. We are concerned here with cutting nature at its joints, and *talking* as if there is a joint does not make it so. The fact that it is good *methodology* to look first for the function, then for the algorithm, then for the implementation, does not by itself show that these inquiries are inquiries at different levels, as opposed to different ways of approaching the same level. The crucial issue is whether the different vocabularies correspond to genuinely distinct laws and explanations, and in any given case, this question will only be answerable empirically. However, we already have good empirical evidence for the reality of the content levels just mentioned – as well as the syntactic level. The evidence is to be found in many places, where we see genuine and distinct explanations at the level of function, algorithm and syntax.

A further point about explanatory levels is that it is legitimate to use different and even *incompatible* idealizations at different levels (see Putnam 1975). It has been argued that since the brain is analog, the digital computer must be incorrect as a model of the mind. But even digital computers are analog at one level of description. For example, gates of the sort described earlier in which 4 volts realizes "1" and 7 volts realizes "0" are understood from the digital perspective as always representing either "0" or "1". But an examination at the electronic level shows that values intermediate between 4 and 7 volts appear momentarily when a register switches between them. We abstract from these intermediate values for the purposes of one level of description, but not another.

4. Searle's Chinese Room Argument

As we have seen, the idea that a certain type of symbol processing can be what *makes* something an intentional system is fundamental to the computer model of the mind. Let us now turn to a flamboyant frontal attack on this idea by John Searle (1980, 1990b; Churchland and Churchland 1990; the basic idea of this argument stems from Block 1978). Searle's strategy is one of avoiding quibbles about specific programs by imagining that cognitive science of the distant future can come up with the program of an actual person who speaks and understands Chinese, and that this program can be implemented in a machine. Unlike many critics of the computer model, Searle is willing to grant that perhaps this can be done so as to focus on his claim that *even if this can be done, the machine will not have intentional states*.

The argument is based on a thought experiment. Imagine yourself given a job in which you work in a room (the Chinese room). You understand only English. Slips of paper with Chinese writing on them are put under the input door, and your job is to write sensible Chinese replies on other slips, and push them out under the output door. How do you do it? You act as the CPU (central processing unit) of a computer, following the computer program mentioned above that describes the symbol processing in an actual Chinese speaker's head. The program is printed in English in a library in the room. This is how you follow the program. Suppose the latest input has certain unintelligible (to you) Chinese squiggles on it. There is a blackboard on a wall of the room with a "state" number written on it; it says "17". (The CPU of a computer is a device with a finite number of states whose activity is determined solely by its current state and input, and since you are acting as the CPU, your output will be determined by your input and your "state". The "17" is on the blackboard to tell you what your "state" is.) You take book 17 out of the library, and look up these particular squiggles in it. Book 17 tells you to look at what is written on your scratch pad (the computer's internal memory), and given both the input squiggles and the scratch pad marks, you are directed to change what is on the scratch pad in a certain way, write certain other squiggles on your output pad, push the paper under the output door, and finally, change the number on the state board to "193". As a result of this activity, speakers of Chinese find that the pieces of paper you slip under the output door are sensible replies to the inputs.

But you know nothing of what is being said in Chinese; you are just following instructions (in English) to look in certain books and write certain marks. According to Searle, since you don't understand any Chinese, the system of which you are the CPU is a mere Chinese simulator, not a real Chinese understander. Of course, Searle (rightly) rejects the Turing test for understanding Chinese. His argument, then, is that since the program of a real Chinese understander is not sufficient for understanding Chinese, no symbol-manipulation theory of Chinese understanding (or any other intentional state) is correct about what *makes* something a Chinese understander. Thus the conclusion of Searle's argument is that the fundamental idea of thought as symbol processing is wrong even if it allows us to build a machine that can duplicate the symbol processing of a person and thereby duplicate a person's behavior.

The best criticisms of the Chinese room argument have focused on what Searle – anticipating the challenge – calls the systems reply. (See the responses following Searle 1980, and the comment on Searle in Hofstadter and Dennett 1981.) The systems reply has a positive and a negative component. The negative component is that we cannot reason from "Bill has never sold uranium to North Korea" to "Bill's company has never sold uranium to North Korea". Similarly, we cannot reason from "Bill does not understand Chinese" to "The system of which Bill is a part does not understand Chinese" (see Copeland 1993). There is a gap in Searle's argument. The positive component goes further, saying that the whole system – man + program + board + paper + input and output doors – does understand Chinese, even though the man who is acting as the CPU does not. If you open up your own computer, looking for the CPU, you will find that it is just one of the many chips and other components on the main circuit-board. The systems reply reminds us that the CPUs of the thinking computers we hope to have someday will not *themselves* think – rather, they will be *parts* of thinking systems.

Searle's clever reply is to imagine the paraphernalia of the "system" *internalized* as follows. First, instead of having you consult a library, we are to imagine you *memorizing* the whole library. Second, instead of writing notes on scratch pads, you are to memorize what you would have written on the pads, and you are to memorize what the state blackboard would say. Finally, instead of looking at notes put under one door and passing notes under another door, you just use your *own body* to listen to Chinese utterances and produce replies. (This version of the Chinese room has the additional advantage of generalizability so as to involve the complete behavior of a Chinese-speaking system instead of just a Chinese note exchanger.) But as Searle would emphasize, when you seem to Chinese speakers to be conducting a learned discourse with them in Chinese, all you are aware of doing is thinking about what noises the program tells you to make next, given the noises you hear and what you've written on your mental scratch pad.

I argued above that the CPU is just one of many components. If the whole system understands Chinese, that should not lead us to expect the CPU to understand Chinese. The effect of Searle's internalization move – the "new" Chinese Room – is to attempt to destroy the analogy between looking inside the computer and looking inside the Chinese Room. If one looks inside the computer, one sees many chips in addition to the CPU. But if one looks inside the "new" Chinese Room, all one sees is *you*, since you have memorized the library and internalized the functions of the scratch pad and the blackboard. But the point to keep in mind is that although the non-CPU components are no longer easy to see, they are not gone. Rather, they are internalized. If the program requires the contents of one register to be placed in another register, and if you would have done this in the original Chinese Room by copying from one piece of scratch paper to another, in the new Chinese Room you must copy from one of your mental analogs of a piece of scratch paper to another. You are implementing the system by doing what the CPU would do and you are simultaneously simulating the non-CPU components. So if the positive side of the systems reply is correct, the total system that you are implementing does understand Chinese.

"But how can it be", Searle would object, "that you implement a system that understands Chinese even though *you* don't understand Chinese?" The systems reply is that you implement a Chinese understanding system without yourself understanding Chinese or necessarily even being aware of what you are doing under that description. The systems reply sees the Chinese Room (new and old) as an English system implementing a Chinese system. What you are aware of are the thoughts of the English system, for example your following instructions and consulting your internal library. But in virtue of doing this Herculean task, you are also implementing a real intelligent Chinese-speaking system, and so your body houses two genuinely distinct intelligent systems. The Chinese system also thinks, but although you implement this thought, you are not aware of it.

The systems reply can be backed up with an addition to the thought experiment that highlights the division of labor. Imagine that you take on the Chinese simulating as a 9–5 job. You come in Monday morning after a weekend of relaxation, and you are paid to follow the program until 5 pm. When you are working, you concentrate hard at working, and so instead of trying to figure out the meaning of what is said to you, you focus your energies on working out what the program tells you to do in response to each input. As a result, during working hours, you respond to everything just as the program dictates, except for occasional glances at your watch. (The glances at your watch fall under the same category as the noises and heat given off by computers: aspects of their behavior that is not part of the machine description but are due rather to features of the implementation.) If someone speaks to you in English, you say what the program (which, you recall, describes a real Chinese speaker) dictates. So if during working hours someone speaks to you in English, you respond with a request in Chinese to speak Chinese, or even an inexpertly pronounced "No speak English", that was once memorized by the Chinese speaker being simulated, and which you the English-speaking system may even fail to recognize as English. Then, come 5 pm, you stop working, and react to Chinese talk the way any monolingual English speaker would.

Why is it that the English system implements the Chinese system rather than, say, the other way around? Because you (the English system whom I am now addressing) are following the instructions of a program in English to make Chinese noises and not the other way around. If you decide to quit your job to become a magician, the Chinese system disappears. However, if the Chinese system decides to become a magician, he will make plans that he would express in Chinese, but then when 5 pm rolls around, you quit for the day, and the Chinese system's plans are on the shelf until you come back to work. And of course you have no commitment to doing *whatever* the program dictates. If the program dictates that you make a series of movements that leads you to a flight to China, you can drop out of the simulating mode, saying "I quit!" The Chinese speaker's existence and the fulfillment of his plans depends on your work schedule and your plans, not the other way around.

Thus, you and the Chinese system cohabit one body. In effect, Searle uses the fact that you are not aware of the Chinese system's thoughts as an argument that it has no thoughts. But this is an invalid argument. Real cases of multiple personalities are often cases in which one personality is unaware of the others.

It is instructive to compare Searle's thought experiment with the string-searching Aunt Bubbles machine described at the outset of this chapter. This machine was used against a behaviorist proposal of a behavioral *concept* of intelligence. But the symbol-manipulation view of the mind is not a proposal about our everyday concept. To the extent that we think of the English system as implementing a Chinese system, that will be because we find the symbol-manipulation theory of the mind plausible as an empirical theory.

There is one aspect of Searle's case with which I am sympathetic. I have my doubts as to whether there is anything it is like to be the Chinese system, that is, whether the Chinese system is a phenomenally conscious system. My doubts arise from the idea that perhaps consciousness is more a matter of implementation of symbol processing than of symbol processing itself. Although surprisingly Searle does not mention this idea in connection with the Chinese Room, it can be seen as the argumentative heart of his position. Searle has argued independently of the Chinese Room (Searle 1992: ch. 7) that intentionality requires consciousness (see the replies to Searle in *Behavioral and Brain Sciences* 13, 1990). But this doctrine, if correct, can shore up the Chinese Room argument. For if the Chinese system is not conscious, then, according to Searle's doctrine, it is not an intentional system either.

Even if I am right about the failure of Searle's argument, it does succeed in sharpening our understanding of the nature of intentionality and its relation to computation and representation.[7]

Notes

1. The Aunt Bubbles machine refutes something stronger than behaviorism, namely the claim that the mental "supervenes" on the behavioral; that is, that there can be no mental difference without a behavioral difference. (Of course, the behavioral dispositions are finite – see the next paragraph in the text.) I am indebted to Stephen White for pointing out to me that the doctrine of the supervenience of the mental on the behavioral is widespread among thinkers who reject behaviorism, such as Donald Davidson. The Aunt Bubbles machine is described and defended in detail in Block (1978, 1981), and was independently discovered by White (1982).

2. The rightmost digit in binary (as in familiar decimal) is the 1s' place. The second digit from the right is the 2s' place (corresponding to the 10s' place in decimal). Next is the 4s' place (that is, 2 squared), just as the corresponding place in decimal is the 10 squared place.

3. The idea described here was first articulated to my knowledge in Fodor (1975, 1980); see also Dennett (1981), to which the terms "semantic engine" and "syntactic engine" are due, and Newell (1980). More on this topic can be found in Dennett (1987) by looking up "syntactic engine" and "semantic engine" in the index.

4. In one respect, the meanings of mental symbols cannot be semantically more basic than meanings of external symbols. The name "Aristotle" has the reference it has because of its causal connection (via generations of speakers) to a man who was called by a name that was an ancestor of our external term "Aristotle". So the term in the language of thought that corresponds to "Aristotle" will certainly derive its reference from and thus will be semantically less basic than the public language word.

5. Note that the *type* of success is important to whether connectionism is really a rival to the language of thought point of view. Connectionist networks have been successful in various pattern recognition tasks, for example discriminating mines from rocks. Of course, even if these networks could be made to do pattern recognition tasks much better than we can, that wouldn't suggest that these networks can provide models of higher cognition. Computers that are programmed to do arithmetic in the classical symbol-crunching mode can do arithmetic much better than we can, but no one would conclude that therefore these computers provide models of higher cognition.

6. This table *could* be used to describe a machine that does have a memory with explicit representation. I say "naturally described" to indicate that I am thinking of a machine that does not have such a memory, a machine for which the table in Figure 14.7 is an apt and natural description.

7. I am indebted to Ken Aizawa, George Boolos, Susan Carey, Willem DeVries, Jerry Fodor and Steven White for comments on an earlier draft. This work was supported by the National Science Foundation (DIR8812559).

References

Block, Ned (1978). Troubles with Functionalism. In C. W. Savage (ed.), *Minnesota Studies in Philosophy of Science, IX*. Minnesota, MN: University of Minnesota Press, 261–325. Reprinted in Rosenthal (1991) and Lycan (1990).

Block, Ned (1980). *Readings in Philosophy of Psychology*, 2 vols. Cambridge, MA: Harvard University Press.

Block, Ned (1981). Psychologism and Behaviorism. *The Philosophical Review* 90 (1): 5–14.

Block, Ned (1986). Advertisement for a Semantics for Psychology. In French, P. A., et al. (eds.), *Midwest Studies in Philosophy, Vol. X*. Minneapolis, MN: University of Minnesota Press, 615–78.

Chomsky, N. (1959). Review of B. F. Skinner's *Verbal Behavior. Language* 35 (1): 26–58.

Chomsky, N. (1975). *Reflections on Language*. New York: Pantheon.

Churchland, P. M. and Churchland, P. S. (1990). Could a Machine Think? *Scientific American* 262 (1): 26–31.

Copeland, J. (1993). The Curious Case of the Chinese Gym. *Synthese* 95: 173–86.

Cummins, Robert (1975). Functional Analysis. *Journal of Philosophy* 72: 741–65. Partially reprinted in Block (1980).

Dehmelt, Hans (1989). Triton, . . . electron, . . . cosmon, . . . : An infinite regression? *Proceedings of the National Academy of Sciences* 86, 8618–19.

Dennett, D. C. (1974). Why the Law of Effect Will Not Go Away. *Journal of the Theory of Social Behavior* 5: 169–87.

Dennett, D. C. (1975). Brain Writing and Mind Reading. In K. Gunderson (ed.), *Minnesota Studies in Philosophy of Science, VII*. Minneapolis, MN: University of Minnesota Press.

Dennett, D. C. (1981). Three Kinds of Intentional Psychology. In R. Healy (ed.), *Reduction, Time and Reality*. Cambridge: Cambridge University Press.

Dennett, D. C. (1987). *The Intentional Stance*. Cambridge, MA: MIT Press.

Dretske, Fred (1981). *Knowledge and the Flow of Information*. Cambridge, MA: MIT Press.

Fodor, Jerry (1968). The Appeal to Tacit Knowledge in Psychological Explanation. *The Journal of Philosophy* 65: 627–40.

Fodor, Jerry (1975). *The Language of Thought*, New York: Crowell.

Fodor, Jerry (1980). Methodological Solipsism Considered as a Research Strategy in Cognitive Psychology. *The Behavioral and Brain Sciences* 3: 417–24. Reprinted in Haugeland (1981).

Fodor, Jerry (1981). Three Cheers for Propositional Attitudes. In Fodor's *RePresentations*. Cambridge, MA: MIT Press.

Fodor, Jerry (1987). *Psychosemantics*. Cambridge, MA: MIT Press.

Fodor, Jerry (1983). *The Modularity of Mind*. Cambridge: MIT Press.

Fodor, Jerry (1985). Fodor's Guide to Mental Representation. *Mind* XCIV: 76–100.

Fodor, Jerry (1990). Psychosemantics, or Where do Truth Conditions Come from? In Lycan (1990).

Fodor, Jerry and Pylyshyn, Zenon (1988). Connectionism and Cognitive Architecture: A Critical Analysis. *Cognition* 28: 3–71.

Harman, Gilbert (1973). *Thought*. Princeton, NJ: Princeton University Press.

Haugeland, John (ed.) (1981). *Mind Design*. Cambridge, MA: MIT Press.

Hofstadter, D. and Dennett, D. (1981). *The Mind's I: Fantasies and Reflections on Mind and Soul*. New York: Basic Books.

Lycan, William (1990). *Mind and Cognition*. Oxford: B. H. Blackwell.

Marr, David (1977). Artificial Intelligence – A Personal View. *Artificial Intelligence* 9: 37–48. Reprinted in Haugeland (1981).

McCarthy, John (1980). Beliefs, machines and theories. *The Behavioral and Brain Sciences* 3: 435.

Newell, Alan (1980). Physical Symbol Systems. *Cognitive Science* 4 (2): 135–8.

O'Rourke, J. and Shattuck, J. (forthcoming). Does a Rock Realize Every Finite Automaton? A Critique of Putnam's Theorem.

Peacocke, C. (1993). *A Study of Concepts*. Cambridge, MA: MIT Press.

Putnam, Hilary (1975). Philosophy and our Mental Life. In *Mind, Language and Reality: Philosophical Papers, Vol. 2*. London: Cambridge University Press. Reprinted in Block (1980) and, in somewhat different form, in Haugeland (1981). Originally published in *Cognition* 2 (1973) with a section on IQ that has been omitted from both of the reprinted versions.

Putnam, Hilary (1988). *Representation and Reality*. Cambridge, MA: MIT Press.

Pylyshyn, Zenon (1984). *Computation and Cognition: Issues in the Foundations of Cognitive Science*. Cambridge, MA: MIT Press.

Rosenthal, D. M. (ed.) (1991). *The Nature of Mind*. Oxford: Oxford University Press.

Searle, John (1980). Minds, Brains, and Programs. *The Behavioral and Brain Sciences* 3: 417–24. Reprinted in Haugeland (1981).

Searle, John (1990a). Is the Brain a Digital Computer? *Proceedings and Addresses of the American Philosophical Association* 64: 21–37.

Searle, John (1990b). Is the Brain's Mind a Computer Program? *Scientific American* 262 (1): 20–25.

Searle, John (1992). *The Rediscovery of the Mind*. Cambridge, MA: MIT Press.

Shieber, S. (1994). Lessons from a restricted Turing test. CACM: Communications of the ACM, 37.

Smolensky, Paul (1988). On the Proper Treatment of Connectionism. *Behavioral and Brain Sciences* 11: 1–23. See also the commentary that follows and the reply by the author.

Stalnaker, Robert (1984). *Inquiry*. Cambridge, MA: MIT Press.

Stampe, Dennis W. (1977). Toward a Causal Theory of Linguistic Representation. In P. A. French et al. (eds.), *Midwest Studies in Philosophy II*. Minneapolis, MN: University of Minnesota Press: 42–6.

Stich, Stephen (1983). *From Folk Psychology to Cognitive Science: The Case against Belief*. Cambridge, MA: MIT Press.

Tomberlin, J. (1990). *Philosophical Perspectives, IV: Philosophy of Mind and Action Theory*. Atascadero, CA: Ridgeview.

Turing, A. M. (1950). Computing Machinery and Intelligence. *Mind* 59: 433–60.

Weizenbaum, Joseph (1976). *Computer Power and Human Reason*. San Francisco, CA: W. H. Freeman.

White, Stephen (1982). Functionalism and Propositional Content. Doctoral dissertation, University of California, Berkeley.

15

CYBORGS UNPLUGGED

Andy Clark

Rats in Space

The year is 1960. The pulse of space travel beats insistently within the temples of research and power, and the journal *Astronautics* publishes the paper that gave the term "cyborg" to the world. The paper, titled "Cyborgs and Space," was based on a talk, "Drugs, Space and Cybernetics," presented that May to the Air Force School of Aviation Medicine in San Antonio, Texas. The authors were Manfred Clynes and Nathan Kline, both working for the Dynamic Simulation Laboratory (of which Kline was director) at Rockland State Hospital, New York. What Clynes and Kline proposed was simply a nice piece of lateral thinking. Instead of trying to provide artificial, earth-like environments for the human exploration of space, why not alter the humans so as to better cope with the new and alien demands? "Space travel," the authors wrote, "challenges mankind not only technologically, but also spiritually, in that it invites man to take an active part in his own biological evolution." Why not, in short, reengineer the humans to fit the stars?

In 1960, of course, genetic engineering was just a gleam in science fiction's prescient eye. And these authors were not dreamers, just creative scientists engaged in matters of national (and international) importance. They were scientists, moreover, working and thinking on the crest of two major waves of innovative research: work in computing and electronic data-processing, and work on cybernetics – the science of control and communication in animals and machines. The way to go, they suggested, was to combine cybernetic and computational approaches so as to create man–machine hybrids, "artifact–organism systems" in which implanted electronic devices use bodily feedback signals to automatically regulate wakefulness, metabolism, respiration, heart rate, and other physiological functions in ways suited to some alien environment. The paper discussed specific artificial interventions that might enable a human body to bypass lung-based breathing, to compensate for the disorientations caused by weightlessness, to alter heart rate and temperature, reduce metabolism and required food intake, and so on.

It was Manfred Clynes who actually first suggested the term "cyborg." Clynes was at that time chief research scientist at Rockland State Hospital and an expert on the design and development of physiological measuring equipment. He had already received a prestigious Baker Award for work on the control of heart rate through breathing and would later invent the CAT computer, which is still used in many hospitals today. When Clynes coined the term "cyborg" to describe the kind of hybrid artifact-organism system they were envisaging, Kline remarked that it sounded "like a town in Denmark." But the term was duly minted, and the languages of fact and fiction permanently altered. Here is the passage as it appeared in *Astronautics*:

> For the exogenously extended organizational complex . . . we propose the term "cyborg." The Cyborg deliberately incorporates exogenous components extending the self-regulating control function of the organism in order to adapt it to new environments.

Thus, amid a welter of convoluted prose, was born the cyborg. The acronym "cyborg" stood for Cybernetic Organism or Cybernetically Controlled Organism; it was a term of art meant to capture both a notion of human–machine merging and the rather specific nature of the merging envisaged. Cyberneticists were especially interested in "self-regulating systems." These are systems in which the results of the system's own activity are "fed back" so as to increase, stop, start, or reduce the activity as conditions dictate. The flush/refill mechanism of a standard toilet is a homey example, as is the thermostat on the domestic furnace. The temperature drops, a circuit is activated, and the furnace comes to life. The temperature rises, a circuit is broken, and the furnace ceases to operate. Even more prosaically, the toilet is flushed, the ballcock drops, which causes the connected inlet valve to open. Water then flows in until the ballcock, riding on the rising tide, reaches a preset level and thus recloses the valve. Such systems are said to be homeostatically controlled because they respond automatically to deviations from a baseline (the norm, stasis, equilibrium) in ways that drag them back toward that original setting – the full cistern, the preset ambient temperature, and the like.

The human autonomic nervous system, it should be clear, is just such a self-regulating homeostatic engine. It works continuously, and without conscious effort on our part, in order to keep key physiological parameters within certain target zones. As effort increases and blood oxygenation falls, we breathe harder and our hearts beat faster, pumping more oxygen into the bloodstream. As effort decreases and blood oxygen levels rise, breathing and heart rate damp down, reducing the intake and uptake of oxygen.

With all this in mind, it is time to meet the first duly-accredited-and-labeled cyborg. Not a fictional monster, not even a human being fitted with a pacemaker (although they are cyborgs of this simple stripe too), but a white laboratory rat trailing an ungainly appendage – an implanted Rose osmotic pump. This rat was introduced in the 1960 paper by Clynes and Kline as "one of the first cyborgs" and the snapshot, as Donna Haraway wonderfully commented "belongs in Man's family album."

Sadly, the rat has no name, but the osmotic pump does. It is named after its inventor, Dr. Rose, who recently died after a very creative life devoted to searching for a cure for cancer. So let's respectfully borrow that, calling the capable rat-pump system Rose. Rose incorporates a pressure pump capsule role of delivering injections at a controlled rate. The idea was to combine the implanted pump with an artificial control loop, creating in Rose a layer of homeostasis. The new layer would operate like the biological without the need for any conscious attention or effort and might be used to help Rose deal with specific extraterrestrial conditions. The authors speculate, for example, that the automatic, computerized control loop monitors systolic blood pressure, compares it to some locally appropriate reference value, and administers adrenergic or vasodilatory drugs accordingly.

As cyborgs go, Rose, like the human being with the pacemaker, is probably a bit of a disappointment. To be sure, each incorporates an extra artificial layer of unconsciously regulated homeostatic control. But Rose remains pretty much a rat nonetheless, and one pacemaker doth not a Terminator make. Cyborgs, it seems, remain largely the stuff of science fiction, forty-nine years of research and development notwithstanding.

Implant and Mergers

How do they? Consider next the humble cochlear implant. Cochlear implants, which are already widely in use, electronically stimulate the auditory nerve. Such devices enable many profoundly deaf humans to hear again. However, they are currently limited by requiring the presence of a healthy, unregenerated auditory nerve. A Pasadena-based research group led by Douglas McCreery of Huntington Medical Research Institutes recently addressed this problem by building a new kind of implant that bypasses the auditory nerve and connects directly to the brain stem. Earlier versions of such devices have, in fact, been in use for a while, but performance was uninspiring. Uninspiring because these first wave brain stem implants used only an array of surface contacts – flat electrodes laid upon the surface of the brain stem near the ventral cochlear nucleus. The auditory discrimination of frequencies, however, is mediated by stacked layers of neural tissue within the nucleus. To utilize frequency information (to discriminate pitch) you need to feed information differentially into the various layers of this neural structure, where the stimulation of deeper layers results in the auditory perception of higher frequencies, and so on. The implant being pioneered by McCreery thus reaches deeper than those older, surface contact models, terminating in six iridium microelectrodes each of which penetrates the brain stem to a different depth. The overall system comprises an external speech processor with a receiver implanted under the scalp, directly wired to six different depths within the ventral cochlear nucleus. A Huntington Institute cat, according to neuroscientist and science writer Simon LeVay, is already fitted with the new system and thus joins Rose in our Cyborg Hall of Fame.

The roll call would not be complete, however, without a certain maverick professor. Our next stop is thus the Department of Cybernetics at the University of Reading, in England. It is somewhat of a surprise to find, nowadays, a department of Cybernetics at all. They mostly died out in the early 1960s, to be replaced by departments of Computer Science, Cognitive Science, and Artificial Intelligence. But the real surprise is to find, within this Department of Cybernetics, a professor determined to turn himself into a good old-fashioned flesh-and-wires cyborg. The professor's name is Kevin Warwick, and in his own words:

> I was born human. But this was an accident of fate—a condition merely of me and place. I believe it's something we have the power to change.

Warwick began his personal transformation back in 1998, with the implantation of a fairly simple silicon chip, encased in a glass tube, under the wrist and on top of the muscle in his left arm. This implant sent radio signals, via antennae placed strategically around the department, to a central computer that responded by opening doors as he approached, turning circuits on and off, and so on. This was, of course, all pretty simple stuff and could have been much more easily achieved by the use of a simple device (smart-badge or card) strapped to his belt or pinned to his lapel. The aim of the experiment, however, was to test the capacity to send and receive signals via such an implant. It worked well, and Warwick reported even in this simple case he quickly came to feel "like the implant was with my body," to feel, indeed, that his biological body was just one aspect of a larger, more powerful and harmoniously operating system. He reported that it was hard to let go of the implant when the time came for its removal.

The real experiment took place on March 14, 2002, at 8:30 in the morning at the Radcliffe Infirmary, Oxford. There, Warwick received a new and more interesting implant. This consisted of a 100-spike array. Each of the 100 tips in the array makes direct contact with nerve fibers in the wrist and is linked to wires that tunnel up Professor Warwick's arm, emerging through a skin puncture where they are linked to a radio transmitter/receiver device. This allows the median nerve in the arm to be linked by radio contact to a computer. The nerve impulses running between brain and hand can thus be "wiretapped" and the signals copied to the computer. The process also runs in the other direction, allowing the computer to send signals (copies or transforms of the originals) to the implant, which in turn feeds them into the nerve bundles running between Warwick's hand and brain.

The choice of nerve bundles in the arm as interface point is doubtless a compromise. The surgical risks of direct neural interfacing are still quite high (the kind of brain stem implant described earlier, for example, is performed only on patients already requiring surgery to treat neurofibromatosis type 2). But the nerve bundles running through the arm do carry tremendous quantities of information to and from the brain, and they are implicated not just in reaching and grasping but also in the neurophysiology of pain, pleasure, and emotion. Warwick has embarked upon a staged sequence of experiments, the simplest of which is to record and identify the signals associated with specific willed hand motions. These signals can then be played back into his nervous system later on. Will his hand then move again? Will he feel as if he is willing it to move?

The experiment can be repeated with signals wiretapped during episodes of pain or pleasure. Warwick himself is fascinated by the transformative potential of the technology and wonders whether his nervous system, fed with computer-generated signals tracking some humanly undetectable quantity, such as infrared wavelengths, could learn to perceive them, yielding some sensation of seeing or feeling infrared (or ultraviolet, or x-rays, or ultrasound).

Recalling the work on deep (cochlear nucleus penetrating) auditory repair, this kind of thing begins to seem distinctly feasible. Imagine, for example, being fitted with artificial sensors, tuned to detect frequencies currently beyond our reach, but sending signals deep into the developing ventral cochlear nucleus. Human neural plasticity, as we'll later see, may well prove great enough to allow our brains to learn to make use of such new kinds of sensory signal. Warwick is certainly enthusiastic. In his own words, "few people have even had their nervous systems linked to a computer, so the concept of sensing the world around us using more than our natural abilities is still science fiction. I'm hoping to change that."

Finally, in a dramatic but perhaps inevitable twist, there is a plan (if all goes well) to subsequently have a matching but surface-level device connected to his wife, Irena. The signals accompanying actions, pains, and pleasures could then be copied between the two implants, allowing Irena's nervous system to be stimulated by Kevin's and vice versa. The couple also plans to try sending these signals over the internet, perhaps with one partner in London while the other is in New York.

None of this is really science fiction. Indeed, as Warwick is the first to point out, a great deal of closely related work has already been done. Scientists at the

University of Tokyo have been able to control the movements of a live cockroach by hooking its motor neurons to a microprocessor; electronically mediated control of some muscular function (lost due to damage or disease) has been demonstrated in several laboratories; a paralyzed stroke patient, fitted with a neurally implanted transmitter, has been able to will a cursor to move across a computer screen; and rats with similar implants have learned to depress a reward-generating lever by just thinking about it. There is even a female orgasm-generating electronic implant (controlled by a hand-held remote) involving contacts surgically inserted into specific nerves in the spinal cord. Without much doubt, direct bioelectronic signal exchanges, made possible by various kinds of implant technology, will soon open up new realms of human–computer interaction and facilitate new kinds of human–machine mergers. These technologies, for both moral and practical reasons, will probably remain, in the near future, largely in the province of restorative medicine or military applications (such as the McDonnell–Douglas Advanced Tactical Aircraft Program, which envisages a fighter plane pilot whose neural functions are linked directly into the on-board computer).

Despite this, genuinely cyborg technology is all around us and is becoming more and more a part of us every day. To see why, we must reflect some more on what really matters even about the classic (wire-and-implant-dominated) cyborg technologies just reviewed. These classic cases all display direct (wire-based) animal-machine interfacing. Much of the thrill, or horror, depends on imagining all those wires, chips, and transmitters grafted onto pulsing organic matter. But what we should really *care about* is not the mere fact of deep implantation or flesh-to-wire grafting, but the complex and transformative nature of the animal-machine relationships that may or may not ensue. And once we see *that*, we open our eyes to a whole new world of cyborg technology.

Recall the case of the cochlear implants, and notice now the particular shape of this technological trajectory. It begins with simple cochlear implants connected to the auditory nerve – just one step up, really, from hearing aids and ear trumpets. Next, the auditory nerve is bypassed, and signals fed to contacts on the surface of the brain stem itself. Then, finally – classic cyborg heaven – microelectrodes actually penetrate the ventral cochlear nucleus itself at varying depths. Or consider Professor Warwick, whose first implant struck us as little more than a smart badge, worn inside the arm. My sense is that as the bioelectronic interface grows in complexity and moves inward, deeper into the brain and farther from the periphery of skin, bone, and sense organs, we become correlatively less and less resistant to the idea that we are trading in genuine cyborg technology.

But just why do we feel that depth *matters* here? It is, after all, pretty obvious that the physical depth of an implant, in and of itself, is insignificant. Recall my microchipped cat, Lolo. Lolo is, by all accounts, a disappointing cyborg.

He incorporates a nonbiological component, conveniently placed within the relatively tamper-proof confines of the biological skin (and fur) bag. But he seems determinedly nontransformed by this uninvited bar coding. He is far from anyone's ideal of the cyborg cat. It would make no difference to *this* intuition, surely, were we to implant the bar code chip as deeply as we like – perhaps right in the center of his brain – humane technology and better bar code readers permitting. What we care about, then, is not depth of implanting per se. Instead, what matters to us is the nature and transformative potential of the bioelectronic coalition that results.

Still, the idea that truly profound biotechnological mergers must be consummated deep within the ancient skin-bag runs deep. It is the point source of the undeniable gut appeal of most classic cyborg technologies, whether real or imaginary. Think of adamantium skeletons, skull-guns, cochlear implants, retinal implants, human brains directly "jacked in" to the matrix of cyberspace – the list goes on and on. The deeper within the biological skin-bag the bioelectronic interface lies, the happier we are, it seems, to admit that we confront a genuine instance of cyborg technology.

Intuitions, however, are strange and unstable things. Take the futuristic topless dancer depicted in Warren Ellis's wonderful and extraordinary *Transmetropolitan*. The dancer displays a fully functional three-inch-high bar code tattooed across both breasts. In some strange way, this merely superficially bar-coded dancer strikes me as a more unnerving, more genuinely cyborg image, than does the bar-coded cat. And this despite the fact that it is the latter who incorporates a genuine "within the skin-bag" implant. The reason for this reaction, I think, is that the image of the bar-coded topless dancer immediately conjures a powerful (and perhaps distressing) sense of a deeply transformed kind of human existence. The image foregrounds our potential status as trackable, commercially interesting sexual units, subject to repeated and perhaps uninvited electronic scrutiny. We resonate with terror, excitement, or both to the idea of ever-deeper neural and bodily implants in part *because* we sense some rough-and-ready (not fool-proof, more of a rule-of-thumb) correlation between depth-of-interface and such transformative potential. The deep ventral cochlear nucleus penetrating implants can, after all, upgrade the functionality of certain profoundly deaf patients in a much more dramatic, reliable, and effective fashion than its predecessors. What really counts is a kind of double whammy implicit in the classic cyborg image. First, we care about the potential of technology to become integrated so deeply and fluidly with our existing biological capacities and characteristics that we feel no boundary between ourselves and the nonbiological elements. Second, we care about the potential of such human-machine symbiosis to transform (for better or for worse) our lives, projects, and capacities.

A symbiotic relationship is an association of mutual benefit between different kinds of entities, such as fungi and trees. Such relationships can become so close and important that we tend to think of the result as a single entity. Lichen, for example, are really symbiotic associations between an alga and a fungus. It is often a vexed question how best to think of specific cases. The case of cognitive systems is especially challenging since the requirement – (intuitive enough for noncognitive cases) – of physical cohesion within a clear inner/outer boundary seems less compelling when information flows (rather than the flow of blood or nutrients) are the key concern.

The traditional twin factors (of contained integration and profound transformation) come together perfectly in the classic cyborg image of the human body deeply penetrated by sensitively interfaced and capacity-enhancing electronics. But in the cognitive case, it is worth considering that what really matters might be just the *fluidity* of the human–machine integration and the resulting *transformation* of our capacities, projects, and lifestyles. It is then an empirical question whether the greatest usable bandwidth and potential lies with full implant technologies or with well-designed nonpenetrative modes of personal augmentation. With regard to the critical features just mentioned, I believe that the most potent near-future technologies will be those that offer integration and transformation *without* implants or surgery: human-machine mergers that simply bypass, rather than penetrate, the old biological borders of skin and skull.

To see what I mean, let us return to the realms of the concrete and the everyday, scene-shifting to the flight deck of a modern aircraft. The modern flight deck, as the cognitive anthropologist Ed Hutchins has pointed out, is designed as a single extended system made up of pilots, automated "fly-by-wire" computer control systems, and various high-level loops in which pilots monitor the computer while the computer monitors the pilots. The shape of these loops is still very much up for grabs. In the European Airbus, the computer pretty much has the final say. The pilot moves the control stick, but the onboard electronics keep the flight deviations inside a preset envelope. The plane is not allowed, no matter what the pilots do with the control stick, to bank more than 67 degrees or to point the nose upward at more than 30 degrees. These computer-controlled limits are meant to keep the pilots' maneuvers from compromising the planes' structural integrity or initiating a stall. In the Boeing 747–400, by contrast, the pilots still have the final say. In each case, however, under normal operating conditions, large amounts of responsibility are devolved to the computer-controlled autosystem. (The high-technology theorist and science writer Kevin Kelly nicely notes that human pilots are increasingly referred to, in professional training and talk, as "system managers.")

Piloting a modern commercial airliner, it seems clear, is a task in which human brains and bodies act as elements in a larger, fluidly integrated, biotechnological problem-solving matrix. But still, you may say, this is state-of-the-art high technology. Perhaps there is a sense in which, at least while flying the plane, the pilots participate in a (temporary) kind of cyborg existence, allowing automated electronic circuits to, in the words of Clynes and Kline "provide an organizational system in which [certain] problems are taken care of automatically." But most of us don't fly commercial airliners and are not even cyborgs for a day.

A Day in the Life

Or are we? Let's shift the scene again, this time to your morning commute to the office. At 7:30 A.M. you are awoken not by your native biorhythms but by your preset electronic alarm clock. By 8:30 A.M. you are on the road. It is a chilly day and you feel the car begin to skid on a patch of ice. Luckily, you have traction control and the Automatic Braking System (ABS). You simply hit the brakes, and the car takes care of most of the delicate work required. In fact, as we'll see in later chapters, the human brain is a past master at devolving responsibility in just this kind of way. You may consciously decide, for example, to reach for the wine glass. But all the delicate work of generating a sequence of muscle commands enabling precise and appropriate finger motions and gripping is then turned over to a dedicated, unconscious subsystem – a kind of on-board servomechanism not unlike those ABS brakes.

Arriving at your office, you resume work on the presentation you were preparing for today's meeting. First, you consult the fat file of papers marked "Designs for Living." It includes your own previous drafts, and a lot of work by others, all of it covered in marginalia. As you reinspect (for the umpteenth time) this nonbiological information store, your onboard wetware (i.e., your brain) kicks in with a few new ideas and comments, which you now add as supermarginalia on top of all the rest. Repressing a sigh you switch on your Mac G4, once again exposing your brain to stored material and coaxing it, once more, to respond with a few fragmentary hints and suggestions. Tired already – and it is only 10 A.M. – you fetch a strong espresso and go about your task with renewed vigor. You now position your biological brain to respond (piecemeal as ever) to a summarized list of key points culled from all those files. Satisfied with your work you address the meeting, presenting the final plan of action for which (you believe, card-carrying materialist that you are) your biological brain must be responsible. But in fact, and in the most natural way imaginable, your naked biological brain was no more responsible for that final plan of action than it was for avoiding the earlier skid. In each case, the real problem-solving engine was the larger, biotechnological matrix comprising (in the case at hand) the brain, the stacked papers, the previous marginalia, the electronic files, the operations of search provided by the Mac software, and so on, and so on. What the human brain is best at is learning to be a team player in a problem-solving field populated by an incredible variety of nonbiological props, scaffoldings, instruments, and resources. In this way ours are *essentially* the brains of natural-born cyborgs, ever-eager to dovetail their activity to the increasingly complex technological envelopes in which they develop, mature, and operate.

What blinds us to our own increasingly cyborg nature is an ancient western prejudice – the tendency to think of the mind as so deeply special as to be distinct from the rest of the natural order. In these more materialist times, this prejudice does not always take the form of belief in soul or spirit. It emerges instead as the belief that there is something absolutely special about the cognitive machinery that happens to be housed within the primitive bioinsulation (nature's own duct-tape!) of skin and skull. What goes on in there is so special, we tend to think, that the only way to achieve a true human-machine merger is to consummate it with some brute-physical interfacing performed behind the bedroom doors of skin and skull.

However, there is nothing quite *that special* inside. The brain is, to be sure, an especially dense, complex, and important piece of cognitive machinery. It is in many ways special, but it is not special in the sense of providing a privileged arena such that certain operations must occur *inside* that arena, or in directly wired contact with it, on pain of not counting as part of our mental machinery at all. We are, in short, in the grip of a seductive but quite untenable illusion: the illusion that the mechanisms of mind and self can ultimately unfold only on some privileged stage marked out by the good old-fashioned skin-bag. My goal is to dispel this illusion, and to show how a complex matrix of brain, body, and technology can actually constitute the problem-solving machine that we should properly identify as *ourselves*. Seen in this light, cell phones were not such a capricious choice of entry-point after all. None of us, to be sure, are yet likely to *think* of ourselves as born-again cyborgs, even if we invest in the most potent phone on the market and integrate its sweeping functionality deep into our lives. But the cell phone is, indeed, a prime, if entry-level, cyborg technology. It is a technology that may, indeed, turn out to mark a crucial transition point between the first (pen, paper, diagrams, and digital media dominated) and the second waves (marked by more personalized, online, dynamic biotechnological unions) of natural-born cyborgs.

Already, plans are afoot to use our cell phones to monitor vital signs (breathing and heart rate) by monitoring the subtle bounceback of the constantly emitted microwaves off heart and lungs. There is a simpler system, developed by the German company Biotronic, and already under trial in England, that uses an implanted sensor in the chest to monitor heart rate, communicating data to the patient's cell phone. The phone then automatically calls for help if heart troubles are detected. The list goes on. The very designation of the mobile unit as primarily a phone is now in doubt, as more and more manufacturers see it instead as a multifunctional electronic bridge between the bearer and an invisible but potent universe of information, control, and response. At the time of writing, the Nokia 5510 combines phone, MP3 music player, FM radio, messaging machine, and game console, while Handspring's Trio incorporates a personal digital assistant. Sony Ericsson's T68i has a digital camera allowing the user to transmit or store color photos. Cell phones with integrated Bluetooth wireless technology (or similar) microchips will be able to exchange information automatically with nearby Bluetooth-enabled appliances. So enabled, a quick call home will allow the home computer to turn on or off lights, ovens, and other appliances. In many parts of the world, the cell phone is already as integral to the daily routines of millions as the wrist-watch – that little invention that let individuals take real control of their daily schedule, and without which many now feel lost and disoriented. And all this (in most cases) without a single incision or surgical implant. Perhaps, then, it is only our metabolically based obsession with our own skin-bags that has warped the popular image of the cyborg into that of a heavily electronically penetrated human body: a body dramatically transformed by prostheses, by neural implants, enhanced perceptual systems, and the full line of Terminator fashion accessories. The mistake – and it is a familiar one – was to assume that the most profound mergers and intimacies must always involve literal penetra-tions of the skin-bag.

Dovetailing

Nonpenetrative cyborg technology is all around us and is poised on the very brink of a revolution. By nonpenetrative cyborg technology I mean all the techno-logical tricks and electronic aids that, as hinted earlier, are already transforming our lives, our projects, and our sense of our own capacities. What mattered *most*, even where dealing with real bioelectronic implants, was the potential for fluid integration and personal transformation. And while direct bioelectronic inter-faces may contribute on both scores, there is another, equally compelling and less invasive, route to successful human-machine merger. It is a route upon which we as a society have already embarked, and there is no turning back. Its early manifestations are already part of our daily lives, and its ultimate trans-formative power is as great as that of its only serious technological predecessor – the printed word. It is closely related to what Mark Weiser, working at XeroxPARC back in 1988, first dubbed "ubiquitous computing" and what Apple's Alan Kay terms "Third Paradigm" computing. More generally, it falls under the category of transparent technologies. Transparent technologies are those tools that become so well fitted to, and integrated with, our own lives and projects that they are (as Don Norman, Weiser, and others insist) pretty much invisible-in-use. These tools or resources are usually no more the object of our conscious thought and reason than is the pen with which we write, the hand that holds it while writing, or the various neural subsystems that form the grip and guide the fingers. All three items, the pen, the hand, and the unconsciously operating neural mechanisms, are pretty much on a par. And it is this parity that ultimately blurs the line between the intelligent system and its best tools for thought and action. Just as drawing a firm line in this sand is unhelpful and misguided when dealing with our basic biological equipment so it is unhelpful and misguided when dealing with transparent technologies. For instance, do I merely *use* my hands, my hippocampus, my ventral cochlear nucleus, or are they part of the system – the "me" – that does the using? There is no merger so intimate as that which is barely noticed.

Weiser's vision, ca. 1991, of ubiquitous computing was a vision in which our home and office environments become progressively more intelligent, courtesy of multiple modestly powerful but amazingly prolific intercommunicating electronic devices. These devices, many of which have since been produced and tested at XeroxPARC and elsewhere, range from tiny tabs to medium size pads to full size boards. The tabs themselves will give you the flavor. The idea of a tab is to "animate objects previously inert." Each book on your bookshelf, courtesy of its continuously active tab, would know where it is by communicating with sensors and transmitting devices in the building and office, what it is about, and maybe even who has recently been using it. Anyone needing the book can simply poll it for its current location and status (in use or not). It might even emit a small beep to help you find it on a crowded shelf! Such tiny, relatively dumb devices would communicate with larger, slightly less dumb ones, also scattered around the office and building. Even very familiar objects, such as the windows of a house, may gain new functionality, recording traces and trails of activity around the house. Spaces in the parking lot communicate their presence and location to the car-and-driver system via a small mirror display, and the coffee-maker in your office immediately knows when and where you have parked the car, and can prepare a hot beverage ready for your arrival.

The idea, then, is to embody and distribute the computation. Instead of focusing on making a richer and richer interface with an even more potent black box on the table, ubiquitous computing aims to make the interfaces multiple, natural, and so simple as to become rapidly invisible to the user. The computer is thus drawn into the real world of daily objects and interactions where its activities and contributions become part of the unremarked backdrop upon which the biological brain and organism learn to depend.

This is a powerful and appealing vision. But what has it to do with the individual's status as a human–machine hybrid? Surely, I hear you saying, a smart world cannot a cyborg make. My answer: it depends just how smart the world is, and more importantly, how responsive it is, over time, to the activities and projects distinctive of an individual person. A smart world, which takes care of many of the functions that might otherwise occupy our conscious attention, is, in fact, already functioning very much like the cyborg of Clynes and Kline's original vision. The more closely the smart world becomes tailored to an individual's specific needs, habits, and preferences, the harder it will become to tell where that person stops and this tailor-made, co-evolving smart world begins. At the very limit, the smart world will function in such intimate harmony with the biological brain that drawing the line will serve no legal, moral, or social purpose. It would be as if someone tried to argue that the "real me" excludes all those nonconscious neural activities on which I so constantly depend relegating all this to a mere smart inner environment. The vision of the mind and self that remains following this exercise in cognitive amputation is thin indeed!

In what ways, then, might an electronically infested world come to exhibit the right kinds of boundary-blurring smarts? One kind of example, drawn from the realm of current commercial practice, is the use of increasingly responsive and sophisticated software agents. An example of a software agent would be a program that monitors your online reading and buying habits, and which searches out new items that fit your interests. More sophisticated software agents might monitor online auctions, bidding and selling on your behalf, or buy and sell your stocks and shares. Pattie Maes, who works on software agents at MIT media lab, describes them as

> software entities . . . that are typically long-lived, continuously running . . . and that can help you keep track of a certain task . . . so it's as if you were extending your brain or expanding your brain by having software entities out there that are almost part of you.

Reflect on the possibilities. Imagine that you begin using the web at the age of four. Dedicated software agents track and adapt to your emerging interests and random explorations. They then help direct your attention to new ideas, web pages, and products. Over the next seventy-some years you and your software agents are locked in a complex dance of co-evolutionary change and learning, each influencing, and being influenced by, the other. You come to expect and trust the input from the agents much as you expect and trust the input from your own unconscious brain – such as that sudden idea that it would be nice to go for a drive, or to buy a Beatles CD – ideas that seem to us to well up from nowhere but which clearly shape our lives and our sense of self. In such a case and in a very real sense, the software entities look less like part of your problem-solving environment than part of you. The intelligent system that now confronts the wider world is biological-you-plus-the-software-agents. These external bundles of code are contributing as do the various nonconscious cognitive mechanisms active in your own brain. They are constantly at work, contributing to your emerging psychological profile. You finally count as "using" the software agents only in the same attenuated and ultimately paradoxical way, for example, that you count as "using" your posterior parietal cortex.

The biological design innovations that make all this possible include the provision (in us) of an unusual degree of cortical plasticity and the (related) presence of an unusually extended period of development and learning (childhood). These dual innovations (intensively studied by the new research program called "neural constructivism") enable the human brain, more than that of any other creature on the planet, to factor an open-ended set of biologically external operations and resources deep into its own basic modes of operation and functioning. It is the presence of this unusual plasticity that makes humans (but not dogs, cats, or elephants) *natural-born cyborgs*: beings primed by Mother Nature to annex wave upon wave of external elements and structures as part and parcel of their own extended minds.

This gradual interweaving of biological brains with nonbiological resources recapitulates, in a larger arena, the kind of sensitive co-development found within a single brain. A human brain, as we shall later see in more detail, comprises a variety of relatively distinct, but densely intercommunicating subsystems. Posterior parietal subsystems, to take an example mentioned earlier, operate unconsciously when we reach out to grasp an object, adjusting hand orientation and finger placement appropriately. The conscious agent seldom bothers herself with these details: she simply decides to reach for the object, and does so, fluently and efficiently. The conscious parts of her brain learned long ago that they could simply count on the posterior parietal structures to kick in and fine-tune the reaching as needed. In just the same way, the conscious and unconscious parts of the brain learn to factor in the operation of various nonbiological tools and resources, creating an extended problem-solving matrix whose degree of fluid integration can sometimes rival that found within the brain itself.

Let's return, finally, to the place we started: the cyborg control of aspects of the autonomic nervous system. The functions of this system (the homeostatic control of heart rate, blood pressure, respiration, etc.) were the targets of Clynes and Kline in the original 1960 proposal. The cyborg, remember, was to be a human agent with some additional, machine-controlled, layers of automatic (homeostatic) functioning, allowing her to survive in alien or inhospitable environments. Such cyborgs, in the words of Clynes and Kline, would provide "an organizational system in which such robot-like problems were taken care of automatically, leaving man free to explore, to create, to think and to feel." Clynes and Kline were adamant that such off-loading of certain control functions to artificial devices would in no way change our nature as human beings. They would simply free the conscious mind to do other work.

This original vision, pioneering though it was, was also somewhat too narrow. It restricted the imagined cyborg innovations to those serving various kinds of bodily maintenance. There might be some kind of domino effect on our mental lives, freeing up conscious neural resources for better things, but that would be all. My claim, by contrast, is that various kinds of deep human–machine symbiosis really do expand and alter the shape of the psychological processes that make us who we are. The old technologies of pen and paper have deeply impacted the shape and form of biological reason in mature, literate brains. The presence of such technologies, and their modern and more responsive counterparts, does not merely act as a convenient wrap around for a fixed biological engine of reason. Nor does it merely free up neural resources. It provides instead an array of resources to which biological brains, as they learn and grow, will *dovetail* their own activities. The moral, for now, is simply that this process of fitting, tailoring, and factoring in leads to the creation of extended computational and mental organizations: reasoning and thinking systems distributed across brain, body, and world. And it is in the operation of these extended systems that much of our distinctive human intelligence inheres.

Such a point is not new, and has been well made by a variety of theorists working in many different traditions. I believe, however, that the idea of human cognition as subsisting in a hybrid, extended architecture (one which includes aspects of the brain and of the cognitive technological envelope in which our brains develop and operate) remains vastly under-appreciated. We cannot understand what is special and distinctively powerful about human thought and reason by simply paying lip service to the importance of the web of surrounding structure. Instead, we need to understand in detail how brains like ours dovetail their problem-solving activities to these additional resources, and how the larger systems thus created operate, change, and evolve. In addition, we need to understand that the very ideas of minds and persons are not limited to the biological skin-bag, and that our sense of self, place, and potential are all malleable constructs ready to expand, change, or contract at surprisingly short notice.

Consider a little more closely the basic biological case. Our brains provide both some kind of substrate for conscious thought, and a vast panoply of thought and action guiding resources that operate quite unconsciously. You do not *will* the motions of each finger and joint muscle as you reach for the glass or as you return a tennis serve. You do not *decide* to stumble upon such-and-such a good idea for the business presentation. Instead, the idea just occurs to you, courtesy once again of all those unconsciously operating processes. But it would be absurd, unhelpful, and distortive to suggest that your true nature – the real "you," the real agent – is somehow defined only by the operation of the conscious resources, resources whose role may indeed be significantly less than we typically imagine. Rather, our nature as individual intelligent agents is determined by the full set of conscious and unconscious tendencies and capacities that together support the set of projects, interests, proclivities, and activities distinctive of a particular person. Just who we are, on that account, may be as much informed by the specific sociotechnological matrix in which the biological organism exists as by those various conscious and unconscious neural events that happen to occur inside the good old biological skin-bag.

Once we take all this on board, however, it becomes obvious that even the technologically mediated incorporation of additional layers of unconscious functionality must make a difference to our sense of who and what we are; as much of a difference, at times, as do some very large and important chunks of our own biological brain. Well-fitted transparent technologies have the potential to impact what we feel capable of doing, where we feel we are located, and what kinds of problems we find ourselves capable of solving. It is, of course, *also* possible to imagine bioelectronic manipulations, which quite directly affect the contents of conscious awareness. But direct accessibility to individual conscious awareness is not essential for a human-machine merger to have a profound impact on who and what we are. Indeed, as we saw, some of the most far-reaching near-future transformations may be rooted in mergers that make barely a ripple on the thin surface of our conscious awareness.

That this should be so is really no surprise. We already saw that what we cared about, even in the case of the classic cyborgs, was some combination of seamless integration and overall transformation. But the most seamless of all integrations, and the ones with the greatest potential to transform our lives and projects, are often precisely those that operate deep beneath the level of conscious awareness. New waves of almost invisible, user-sensitive, semi-intelligent, knowledge-based electronics and software are perfectly posed to merge seamlessly with individual biological brains. In so doing they will ultimately blur the boundary between the user and her knowledge-rich, responsive, unconsciously operating electronic environments. More and more parts of our worlds will come to share the moral and psychological status of parts of our brains. We are already primed by nature to dovetail our minds to our worlds. Once the world starts dovetailing back in earnest, the last few seams must burst, and we will stand revealed: cyborgs without surgery, symbionts without sutures.

16

CONSCIOUSNESS IN HUMAN AND ROBOT MINDS

Daniel C. Dennett

1. Good and Bad Grounds for Skepticism

The best reason for believing that robots might some day become conscious is that we human beings are conscious, and we are a *sort* of robot ourselves. That is, we are extraordinarily complex self-controlling, self-sustaining physical mechanisms, designed over the eons by natural selection, and operating according to the same well-understood principles that govern all the other physical processes in living things: digestive and metabolic processes, self-repair and reproductive processes, for instance. It may be wildly over-ambitious to suppose that human artificers can repeat Nature's triumph, with variations in material, form, and design process, but this is not a deep objection. It is not as if a conscious machine contradicted any fundamental laws of nature, the way a perpetual motion machine does. Still, many skeptics believe – or in any event want to believe – that it will never be done. I wouldn't wager against them, but my reasons for skepticism are mundane, economic reasons, not theoretical reasons.

Conscious robots probably will always simply cost too much to make. Nobody will ever synthesize a gall bladder out of atoms of the requisite elements, but I think it is uncontroversial that a gall bladder is nevertheless "just" a stupendous assembly of such atoms. Might a conscious robot be "just" a stupendous assembly of more elementary artifacts – silicon chips, wires, tiny motors and cameras – or would any such assembly, of whatever size and sophistication, have to leave out some special ingredient that is requisite for consciousness?

Let us briefly survey a nested series of reasons someone might advance for the impossibility of a conscious robot:

(1) Robots are purely material things, and consciousness requires immaterial mind-stuff. (Old-fashioned dualism.)

It continues to amaze me how attractive this position still is to many people. I would have thought a historical perspective alone would make this view seem ludicrous: over the centuries, every *other* phenomenon of initially "supernatural" mysteriousness has succumbed to an uncontroversial explanation within the commodious folds of physical science. Thales, the Pre-Socratic proto-scientist, thought the loadstone had a soul, but we now know better; magnetism is one of the best understood of physical phenomena, strange though its manifestations are. The "miracles" of life itself, and of reproduction, are now analyzed into the well-known intricacies of molecular biology. Why should consciousness be any exception? Why should the brain be the only complex physical object in the universe to have an interface with another realm of being? Besides, the notorious problems with the supposed transactions at that dualistic interface are as good as a *reductio ad absurdum* of the view. The phenomena of consciousness are an admittedly dazzling lot, but I suspect that dualism would never be seriously considered if there weren't such a strong undercurrent of desire to protect the mind from science, by supposing it composed of a stuff that is in principle uninvestigable by the methods of the physical sciences.

But if you are willing to concede the hopelessness of dualism, and accept some version of materialism, you might still hold:

(2) Robots are inorganic (by definition), and consciousness can exist only in an organic brain.

Why might this be? Instead of just hooting this view off the stage as an embarrassing throwback to old-fashioned vitalism, we might pause to note that there is a respectable, if not very interesting, way of defending this claim. Vitalism is deservedly dead; as biochemistry has shown in matchless detail, the powers of organic compounds are themselves all mechanistically reducible and hence mechanistically reproducible at one scale or another in alternative physical media; but it is conceivable – if unlikely – that the sheer speed and compactness of biochemically engineered processes in the brain are in fact unreproducible in other physical media (Dennett, 1987). So there might be straightforward reasons of engineering that showed that any robot that could not make use of organic tissues of one sort or another within its fabric would be too ungainly to execute some task critical for consciousness. If making a conscious robot were conceived of as a sort of sporting event – like the America's Cup – rather than a scientific endeavor, this could raise a curious conflict over the official rules. Team A wants to use artificially constructed organic polymer "muscles" to move its robot's limbs, because otherwise the motor noise wreaks havoc with the robot's artificial ears. Should this be allowed? Is a robot with "muscles" instead of motors a robot within the meaning of the act? If muscles are allowed, what about lining the robot's artificial retinas with genuine organic rods and cones instead of relying on relatively clumsy color-tv technology?

I take it that no serious scientific or philosophical thesis links its fate to the fate of the proposition that a *protein-free* conscious robot can be made, for example. The standard understanding that a robot shall be made of metal, silicon chips, glass, plastic, rubber and such, is an expression of the willingness of theorists to bet on a simplification of the issues: their conviction is that the crucial functions of intelligence can be achieved by one high-level simulation or another, so that it would be no undue hardship to restrict themselves to these materials, the readily available cost-effective ingredients in any case. But if somebody were to invent some sort of cheap artificial neural network fabric that could usefully be spliced into various tight corners in a robot's control system, the embarrassing fact that this fabric was made of organic molecules would not and should not dissuade serious roboticists from using it – and simply taking on the burden of explaining to the uninitiated why this did not constitute "cheating" in any important sense.

I have discovered that some people are attracted by a third reason for believing in the impossibility of conscious robots.

(3) Robots are artifacts, and consciousness abhors an artifact; only something natural, born not manufactured, could exhibit genuine consciousness.

Once again, it is tempting to dismiss this claim with derision, and in some of its forms, derision is just what it deserves. Consider the general category of creed we might call *origin essentialism*: only wine made under the direction of the proprietors of Chateau Plonque counts as genuine Chateau Plonque; only a canvas every blotch on which was caused by the hand of Cézanne counts as a genuine Cézanne; only someone "with Cherokee blood" can be a real Cherokee. There are perfectly respectable reasons, eminently defensible in a court of law, for maintaining such distinctions, so long as they are understood to be protections of rights growing out of historical processes. If they are interpreted, however, as indicators of "intrinsic properties" that set their holders apart from their otherwise indistinguishable counterparts, they are pernicious nonsense. Let us dub *origin chauvinism* the category of view that holds out for some mystic difference (a difference of value, typically) due *simply* to such a fact about origin. Perfect imitation Chateau Plonque is exactly as good a wine as the real thing, counterfeit though it is, and the same holds for the fake Cézanne, if it is really indistinguishable by experts. And of course no person is intrinsically better or worse in any regard just for having or not having Cherokee (or Jewish, or African) "blood".

And to take a threadbare philosophical example, an atom-for-atom duplicate of a human being, an artifactual counterfeit of you, let us say, might not *legally* be you, and hence might not be entitled to your belongings, or deserve your punishments, but the suggestion that such a being would not be a feeling, conscious, alive *person* as genuine as any born of woman is preposterous nonsense, all the more deserving of our ridicule because if taken seriously it might seem to lend credibility to the racist drivel with which it shares a bogus "intuition".

If consciousness abhors an artifact, it cannot be because being born gives a complex of cells a property (aside from that historic property itself) that it could not otherwise have "in principle". There might, however, be a question of practicality. We have just seen how, as a matter of exigent practicality, it could turn out after all that organic materials were needed to make a conscious robot. For similar reasons, it could turn out that any conscious robot had to be, if not born, at least the beneficiary of a longish period of infancy. Making a fully equipped conscious adult robot might just be too much work. It might be vastly easier to make an initially unconscious or nonconscious "infant" robot and let it "grow up" into consciousness, more or less the way we all do. This hunch is not the disreputable claim that a certain sort of historic process puts a mystic stamp of approval on its product, but the more interesting and plausible claim that a certain sort of process is the only practical way of designing all the things that need designing in a conscious being.

Such a claim is entirely reasonable. Compare it to the claim one might make about the creation of Steven Spielberg's film, *Schindler's List*: it could not have been created entirely by computer animation, without the filming of real live actors. This impossibility claim must be false "in principle", since every frame of that film is nothing more than a matrix of gray-scale pixels of the sort that computer animation can manifestly create, at any level of detail or "realism" you are willing to pay for. There is nothing mystical, however, about the claim that it would be practically impossible to render the nuances of that film by such a bizarre exercise of technology. How much easier it is, practically, to put actors in the relevant circumstances, in a concrete simulation of the scenes one wishes to portray, and let them, via ensemble activity and re-activity, provide the information to the cameras that will then fill in all the pixels in each frame. This little exercise of the imagination helps to drive home just how much information there is in a "realistic" film, but even a great film, such as *Schindler's List*, for all its complexity, is a simple, non-interactive artifact many orders of magnitude less complex than a conscious being.

When robot-makers have claimed in the past that in principle they could construct "by hand" a conscious robot, this was a hubristic overstatement analogous to what Walt Disney might once have proclaimed: that his studio of animators could create a film so realistic that no one would be able to tell that it was a cartoon, not a "live action" film. What Disney couldn't do in fact, computer animators still cannot do, but perhaps only for the time being. Robot-makers, even with the latest high-tech innovations, also fall far short of their hubristic goals, now and for the foreseeable future. The comparison serves to expose the likely source of the outrage so many skeptics feel when they encounter the manifestos of the Artificial Intelligensia. Anyone who seriously claimed that *Schindler's List* could in fact have been made by computer animation could be seen to betray an obscenely impoverished sense of what is conveyed in that film. An important element of the film's power is the fact that it *is* a film made by assembling human actors to portray those events, and that it is not actually the newsreel footage that its black-and-white format reminds you of. When one juxtaposes in one's imagination a sense of what the actors must have gone through to make the film with a sense of what the people who actually lived the events went through, this reflection sets up reverberations in one's thinking that draw attention to the deeper meanings of the film. Similarly, when robot enthusiasts proclaim the likelihood that they can simply *construct* a conscious robot, there is an understandable suspicion that they are simply betraying an infantile grasp of the subtleties of conscious life. (I hope I have put enough feeling into that condemnation to satisfy the skeptics.)

But however justified that might be in some instances as an *ad hominem* suspicion, it is simply irrelevant to the important theoretical issues. Perhaps no cartoon could be a great film, but they are certainly real films – and some are indeed good films; if the best the roboticists can hope for is the creation of some crude, cheesy, second-rate, artificial consciousness, they still win. Still, it is not a foregone conclusion that even this modest goal is reachable. If you want to have a defensible reason for claiming that no conscious robot will ever be created, you might want to settle for this:

(4) Robots will always just be much too simple to be conscious.

After all, a normal human being is composed of trillions of parts (if we descend to the level of the macromolecules), and many of these rival in complexity and design cunning the fanciest artifacts that have ever been created. We consist of billions of cells, and a single human cell contains within itself complex "machinery" that is still well beyond the artifactual powers of engineers. We are composed of thousands of different kinds of cells, including thousands of different species of symbiont visitors, some of whom might be as important to our consciousness as others are to our ability to digest our food! If all that complexity were needed for consciousness to exist, then the task of making a single conscious robot would dwarf the entire scientific and engineering resources of the planet for millennia. And who would pay for it?

If no other reason can be found, this may do to ground your skepticism about conscious robots in your future, but one shortcoming of this last reason is that it is scientifically boring. If this is the only reason there won't be conscious robots, then consciousness isn't that special, after all. Another shortcoming with this reason is that it is dubious on its face. Everywhere else we have looked, we have found higher-level commonalities of function that permit us to substitute relatively simple bits for fiendishly complicated bits. Artificial heart valves work really very well, but they are orders of magnitude simpler than organic heart valves, heart valves born of woman or sow, you might say. Artificial ears and eyes that will do a serviceable (if crude) job of substituting for lost perceptual organs are visible on the horizon, and anyone who doubts they are possible in principle is simply out of touch. Nobody ever said a prosthetic eye had to see as keenly, or focus as fast, or be as sensitive to color gradations as a normal human (or other animal) eye in order to "count" as an eye. If an eye, why not an optic nerve (or acceptable substitute thereof), and so forth, all the way in?

Some (Searle, 1992; Mangan, 1993) have supposed, most improbably, that this proposed regress would somewhere run into a non-fungible medium of consciousness, a part of the brain that could not be substituted on pain of death or zombiehood. Once the implications of that view are spelled out (Dennett, 1993a, 1993b), one can see that it is a non-starter. There is no reason at all to believe that some one part of the brain is utterly irreplaceable by prosthesis, provided we allow that some crudity, some loss of function, is to be expected in most substitutions of the simple for the complex. An artificial brain is, on the face of it, as "possible in principle" as an artificial heart, just much, much harder to make and hook up. Of course once we start letting crude forms of prosthetic consciousness – like crude forms of prosthetic vision or hearing – pass our litmus tests for consciousness (whichever tests we favor) the way is open for another boring debate, over whether the phenomena in question are too crude to count.

2. The Cog Project: A Humanoid Robot

A much more interesting tack to explore, in my opinion, is simply to set out to make a robot that is theoretically interesting independent of the philosophical conundrum about whether it is conscious. Such a robot would have to perform a lot of the feats that we have typically associated with consciousness in the past, but we would not need to dwell on that issue from the outset. Maybe we could even learn something interesting about what the truly hard problems are without ever settling any of the issues about consciousness.

Such a project is now underway at MIT. Under the direction of Professors Rodney Brooks and Lynn Andrea Stein of the AI Lab, a group of bright, hard-working young graduate students are laboring as I speak to create Cog, the most humanoid robot yet attempted, and I am happy to be a part of the Cog team. Cog is just about life-size – that is, about the size of a human adult. Cog has no legs, but lives bolted at the hips, you might say, to its stand. It has two human-length arms, however, with somewhat simple hands on the wrists. It can bend at the waist and swing its torso, and its head moves with three degrees of freedom just about the way yours does. It has two eyes, each equipped with both a foveal high-resolution vision area and a low-resolution wide-angle parafoveal vision area, and these eyes saccade at almost human speed. That is, the two eyes can complete approximately three fixations a second, while you and I can manage four or five. Your foveas are at the center of your retinas, surrounded by the grainier low-resolution parafoveal areas; for reasons of engineering simplicity, Cog's eyes have their foveas mounted above their wide-angle vision areas.

This is typical of the sort of compromise that the Cog team is willing to make. It amounts to a wager that a vision system with the foveas moved out of the middle can still work well enough not to be debilitating, and the problems encountered will not be irrelevant to the problems encountered in normal human vision. After all, nature gives us examples of other eyes with different foveal arrangements. Eagles have three different foveas in each eye, for instance, and rabbit eyes are another story all together. Cog's eyes won't give it visual information exactly like that provided to human vision by human eyes (in fact, of course, it will be vastly degraded), but the wager is that this will be plenty to give Cog the opportunity to perform impressive feats of hand–eye coordination, identification, and search. At the outset, Cog will not have color vision.

Since its eyes are video cameras mounted on delicate, fast-moving gimbals, it might be disastrous if Cog were inadvertently to punch itself in the eye, so part of the hard-wiring that must be provided in advance is an "innate" if rudimentary "pain" or "alarm" system to serve roughly the same protective functions as the reflex eye-blink and pain-avoidance systems hard-wired into human infants.

Cog will not be an adult at first, in spite of its adult size. It is being designed to pass through an extended period of artificial infancy, during which it will have to learn from experience, experience it will gain in the rough-and-tumble environment of the real world. Like a human infant, however, it will need a great deal of protection at the outset, in spite of the fact that it will be equipped with many of the most crucial safety-systems of a living being. It has limit switches, heat sensors, current sensors, strain gauges and alarm signals in all the right places to prevent it from destroying its many motors and joints. It has enormous "funny bones" – motors sticking out from its elbows in a risky way. These will be protected from harm not by being shielded in heavy armor, but by being equipped with patches of exquisitely sensitive piezo-electric membrane "skin" which will trigger alarms when they make contact with anything. The goal is that Cog will quickly "learn" to keep its funny bones from being bumped – if Cog cannot learn this in short order, it will have to have this high-priority policy hard-wired in. The same sensitive membranes will be used on its fingertips and elsewhere, and, like human tactile nerves, the "meaning" of the signals sent along the attached wires will depend more on what the central control system "makes of them" than on their "intrinsic" characteristics. A gentle touch, signalling sought-for contact with an object to be grasped, will not differ, as an information packet, from a sharp pain, signalling a need for rapid countermeasures. It all depends on what the central system is designed to do with the packet, and this design is itself indefinitely revisable – something that can be adjusted either by Cog's own experience or by the tinkering of Cog's artificers.

One of its most interesting "innate" endowments will be software for visual face recognition. Faces will "pop out" from the background of other objects as items of special interest to Cog. It will further be innately designed to "want" to keep its "mother's" face in view, and to work hard to keep "mother" from turning away. The role of mother has not yet been cast, but several of the graduate students have been tentatively tapped for this role. Unlike a human infant, of course, there is no reason why Cog can't have a whole team of mothers, each of whom is innately distinguished by Cog as a face to please if possible. Clearly, even if Cog really does have a *Lebenswelt*, it will not be the same as *ours*.

Decisions have not yet been reached about many of the candidates for hardwiring or innate features. Anything that can learn must be initially equipped with a great deal of unlearned design. That is no longer an issue; no *tabula rasa* could ever be impressed with knowledge from experience. But it is also not much of an issue which features ought to be innately fixed, for there is a convenient trade-off. I haven't mentioned yet that Cog will actually be a multi-generational series of ever improved models (if all goes well!), but of course that is the way any complex artifact gets designed. Any feature that is not innately fixed at the outset, but does get itself designed into Cog's control system through learning, can then be lifted whole into Cog-II, as a new bit of innate endowment designed by Cog itself – or rather by Cog's history of interactions with its environment. So even in cases in which we have the best of reasons for thinking that human infants actually come innately equipped with pre-designed gear, we may choose to try to get Cog to learn the design in question, rather than be born with it. In some instances, this is laziness or opportunism – we don't really know what might work well, but maybe Cog can train itself up. This insouciance about the putative nature/nurture boundary is already a familiar attitude among neural net modelers, of course. Although Cog is not specifically intended to demonstrate any particular neural net thesis, it should come as no surprise that Cog's nervous system is a massively parallel architecture capable of simultaneously training up an indefinite number of special-purpose networks or circuits, under various regimes.

How plausible is the hope that Cog can retrace the steps of millions of years of evolution in a few months or years of laboratory exploration? Notice first that what I have just described is a variety of Lamarckian inheritance that no organic lineage has been able to avail itself of. The acquired design innovations of Cog-I can be immediately transferred to Cog-II, a speed-up of evolution of tremendous, if incalculable, magnitude. Moreover, if you bear in mind that, unlike the natural case, there will be a team of overseers ready to make patches whenever obvious shortcomings reveal themselves, and to jog the systems out of ruts whenever they enter them, it is not so outrageous a hope, in our opinion. But then, we are all rather outrageous people.

One talent that we have hopes of teaching to Cog is a rudimentary capacity for human language. And here we run into the fabled innate language organ or Language Acquisition Device made famous by Noam Chomsky. Is there going to be an attempt to build an innate LAD for our Cog? No. We are going to try to get Cog to build language the hard way, the way our ancestors must have done, over thousands of generations. Cog has ears (four, because it's easier to get good localization with four microphones than with carefully shaped ears like ours!) and some special-purpose signal-analyzing software is being developed to give Cog a fairly good chance of discriminating human speech sounds, and probably the capacity to distinguish different human voices. Cog will also have to have speech synthesis hardware and software, of course, but decisions have not yet been reached about the details. It is important to have Cog as well equipped as possible for rich and natural interactions with human beings, for the team intends to take advantage of as much free labor as it can. Untrained people ought to be able to spend time – hours if they like, and we rather hope they do – trying to get Cog to learn this or that. Growing into an adult is a long, time-consuming business, and Cog – and the team that is building Cog – will need all the help it can get.

Obviously this will not work unless the team manages somehow to give Cog a motivational structure that can be at least dimly recognized, responded to, and exploited by naive observers. In short, Cog should be as human as possible in its wants and fears, likes and dislikes. If those anthropomorphic terms strike you as unwarranted, put them in scare-quotes or drop them altogether and replace them with tedious neologisms of your own choosing: Cog, you may prefer to say, must have *goal-registrations* and *preference-functions* that map in rough isomorphism to human desires. This is so for many reasons, of course. Cog won't work at all unless it has its act together in a daunting number of different regards. It must somehow delight in learning, abhor error, strive for novelty, recognize progress. It must be vigilant in some regards, curious in others, and deeply unwilling to engage in self-destructive activity. While we are at it, we might as well try to make it crave human praise and company, and even exhibit a sense of humor.

Let me switch abruptly from this heavily anthropomorphic language to a brief description of Cog's initial endowment of information-processing hardware. The computer-complex that has been built to serve as the development platform for Cog's artificial nervous system consists of four backplanes, each with 16 nodes; each node is basically a Mac-II computer – a 68332 processor with a megabyte of RAM. In other words, you can think of Cog's brain as roughly equivalent to sixty-four Mac-IIs yoked in a custom parallel architecture. Each node is itself a multiprocessor, and they all run a special version of parallel Lisp developed by Rodney Brooks, and called, simply, L. Each node has an interpreter for L in its ROM, so it can execute L files independently of every other node.

Each node has 6 assignable input–output ports, in addition to the possibility of separate i–o (input–output) to the motor boards directly controlling the various joints, as well as the all-important i–o to the experimenters' monitoring and control system, the Front End Processor or FEP (via another unit known as the Interfep). On a bank of separate monitors, one can see the current image in each camera (two foveas, two parafoveas), the activity in each of the many different visual processing areas, or the activities of any other nodes. Cog is thus equipped at birth with the equivalent of chronically implanted electrodes for each of its neurons; all its activities can be monitored in real time, recorded and debugged. The FEP is itself a Macintosh computer in more conventional packaging. At startup, each node is awakened by a FEP call that commands it to load its appropriate files of L from a file server. These files configure it for whatever tasks it has currently been designed to execute. Thus the underlying hardware machine can be turned into any of a host of different virtual machines, thanks to the capacity of each node to run its current program. The nodes do not make further use of disk memory, however, during normal operation. They keep their transient memories locally, in their individual megabytes of RAM. In other words, Cog stores both its genetic endowment (the virtual machine) and its long term memory on disk when it is shut down, but when it is powered on, it first configures itself and then stores all its short term memory distributed one way or another among its 64 nodes.

The space of possible virtual machines made available and readily explorable by this underlying architecture is huge, of course, and it covers a volume in the space of all computations that has not yet been seriously explored by artificial intelligence researchers. Moreover, the space of possibilities it represents is manifestly much more realistic as a space to build brains in than is the space heretofore explored, either by the largely serial architectures of GOFAI ("Good Old Fashioned AI", Haugeland, 1985), or by parallel architectures simulated by serial machines. Nevertheless, it is arguable that every one of the possible virtual machines executable by Cog is minute in comparison to a real human brain. In short, Cog has a tiny brain. There is a big wager being made: the parallelism made possible by this arrangement will be sufficient to provide real-time control of importantly humanoid activities occurring on a human time scale. If this proves to be too optimistic by as little as an order of magnitude, the whole project will be forlorn, for the motivating insight for the project is that by confronting and solving *actual, real-time* problems of self-protection, hand–eye coordination, and interaction with other animate beings, Cog's artificers will discover the *sufficient* conditions for higher cognitive functions in general – and maybe even for a variety of consciousness that would satisfy the skeptics.

It is important to recognize that although the theoretical importance of having a body has been appreciated ever since Alan Turing (1950) drew specific attention to it in his classic paper, "Computing Machines and Intelligence", within the field of Artificial Intelligence there has long been a contrary opinion that robotics is largely a waste of time, money and effort. According to this view, whatever deep principles of organization make cognition possible can be as readily discovered in the more abstract realm of pure simulation, at a fraction of the cost. In many fields, this thrifty attitude has proven to be uncontroversial wisdom. No economists have asked for the funds to implement their computer models of markets and industries in tiny robotic Wall Streets or Detroits, and civil engineers have largely replaced their scale models of bridges and tunnels with computer models that can do a better job of simulating all the relevant conditions of load, stress and strain. Closer to home, simulations of ingeniously oversimplified imaginary organisms foraging in imaginary environments, avoiding imaginary predators and differentially producing imaginary offspring are yielding important insights into the mechanisms of evolution and ecology in the new field of Artificial Life. So it is something of a surprise to find this AI group conceding, in effect, that there is indeed something to the skeptics' claim (e.g., Dreyfus and Dreyfus, 1986) that genuine embodiment in a real world is crucial to consciousness. Not, I hasten to add, because genuine embodiment provides some special vital juice that mere virtual-world simulations cannot secrete, but for the more practical reason – or hunch – that unless you saddle yourself with all the problems of making a concrete agent take care of itself in the real world, you will tend to overlook, underestimate, or misconstrue the deepest problems of design.

Besides, as I have already noted, there is the hope that Cog will be able to design itself in large measure, learning from infancy, and building its own representation of its world in the terms that it innately understands. Nobody doubts that any agent capable of interacting intelligently with a human being on human terms must have access to literally millions if not billions of logically independent items of world knowledge. Either these must be hand-coded individually by human programmers – a tactic being pursued, notoriously, by Douglas Lenat and his CYC team in Dallas – or some way must be found for the artificial agent to learn its world knowledge from (real) interactions with the (real) world. The potential virtues of this shortcut have long been recognized within AI circles (e.g., Waltz, 1988). The unanswered question is whether taking on the task of solving the grubby details of real-world robotics will actually permit one to finesse the task of hand-coding the world knowledge. Brooks, Stein and their team – myself included – are gambling that it will.

At this stage of the project, most of the problems being addressed would never arise in the realm of pure, disembodied AI. How many separate motors might be used for controlling each hand? They will have to be mounted somehow on the forearms. Will there then be room to mount the motor boards directly on the arms, close to the joints they control, or would they get in the way? How much cabling can each arm carry before weariness or clumsiness overcome it? The arm joints have been built to be compliant – springy, like your own joints. This means that if Cog wants to do some fine-fingered manipulation, it will have to learn to "burn" some of the degrees of freedom in its arm motion by temporarily bracing its elbows or wrists on a table or other convenient landmark, just as you would do. Such compliance is typical of the mixed bag of opportunities and problems created by real robotics. Another is the need for self-calibration or re-calibration in the eyes. If Cog's eyes jiggle away from their preset aim, thanks to the wear and tear of all that sudden saccading, there must be ways for Cog to compensate, short of trying continually to adjust its camera-eyes with its fingers. Software designed to tolerate this probable sloppiness in the first place may well be more robust and versatile in many other ways than software designed to work in a more "perfect" world.

Earlier I mentioned a reason for using artificial muscles, not motors, to control a robot's joints, and the example was not imaginary. Brooks is concerned that the sheer noise of Cog's skeletal activities may seriously interfere with the attempt to give Cog humanoid hearing. There is research underway at the AI Lab to develop synthetic electro-mechanical muscle tissues, which would operate silently as well as being more compact, but this will not be available for early incarnations of Cog. For an entirely different reason, thought is being given to the option of designing Cog's visual control software *as if* its eyes were moved by muscles, not motors, building in a software interface that amounts to giving Cog a set of *virtual* eye-muscles. Why might this extra complication in the interface be wise? Because the "opponent-process" control system exemplified by eye-muscle controls is apparently a deep and ubiquitous feature of nervous systems, involved in control of attention generally and disrupted in such pathologies as unilateral neglect. If we are going to have such competitive systems at higher levels of control, it might be wise to build them in "all the way down", concealing the final translation into electric-motor-talk as part of the backstage implementation, not the model.

Other practicalities are more obvious, or at least more immediately evocative to the uninitiated. Three huge red "emergency kill" buttons have already been provided in Cog's environment, to ensure that if Cog happens to engage in some activity that could injure or endanger a human interactor (or itself), there is a way of getting it to stop. But what is the appropriate response for Cog to make to the KILL button? If power to Cog's motors is suddenly shut off, Cog will slump, and its arms will crash down on whatever is below them. Is this what we want to happen? Do we want Cog to drop whatever it is holding? What should "Stop!" *mean* to Cog? This is a real issue about which there is not yet any consensus.

There are many more details of the current and anticipated design of Cog that are of more than passing interest to those in the field, but on this occasion, I want to use the little remaining time to address some overriding questions that have been much debated by philosophers, and that receive a ready treatment in the environment of thought made possible by Cog. In other words, let's consider Cog merely as a prosthetic aid to philosophical thought-experiments, a modest but by no means negligible role for Cog to play.

3. Some Philosophical Considerations

A recent criticism of "strong AI" that has received quite a bit of attention is the so-called problem of "symbol grounding" (Harnad, 1990). It is all very well for large AI programs to have data structures that *purport* to refer to Chicago, milk, or the person to whom I am now talking, but such imaginary reference is not the same as real reference, according to this line of criticism. These internal "symbols" are not properly "grounded" in the world, and the problems thereby eschewed by pure, non-robotic, AI are not trivial or peripheral. As one who discussed, and ultimately dismissed, a version of this problem many years ago (Dennett, 1969: 182ff), I would not want to be interpreted as now abandoning my earlier view. I submit that Cog moots the problem of symbol grounding, without having to settle its status as a criticism of "strong AI". Anything in Cog that might be a candidate for symbolhood will automatically be "grounded" in Cog's real predicament, as surely as its counterpart in any child, so the issue doesn't arise, except as a practical problem for the Cog team, to be solved or not, as fortune dictates. If the day ever comes for Cog to comment to anybody about Chicago, the question of whether Cog is in any position to do so will arise for exactly the same reasons, and be resolvable on the same considerations, as the parallel question about the reference of the word "Chicago" in the idiolect of a young child.

Another claim that has often been advanced, most carefully by Haugeland (1985), is that nothing could properly "matter" to an artificial intelligence, and mattering (it is claimed) is crucial to consciousness. Haugeland restricted his claim to traditional GOFAI systems, and left robots out of consideration. Would he concede that something could matter to Cog? The question, presumably, is how seriously to weigh the import of the quite deliberate decision by Cog's creators to make Cog as much as possible responsible for its own welfare. Cog will be equipped with some "innate" but not at all arbitrary preferences, and hence provided of necessity with the concomitant capacity to be "bothered" by the thwarting of those preferences, and "pleased" by the furthering of the ends it was innately designed to seek. Some may want to retort: "This is not *real* pleasure or pain, but merely a simulacrum." Perhaps, but on what grounds will they defend this claim? Cog may be said to have quite crude, simplistic, one-dimensional pleasure and pain, cartoon pleasure and pain if you like, but then the same might also be said of the pleasure and pain of simpler organisms – clams or houseflies, for instance. Most, if not all, of the burden of proof is shifted by Cog, in my estimation. The reasons for saying that something *does* matter to Cog are not arbitrary; they are exactly parallel to the reasons we give for saying that things matter to us and to other creatures. Since we have cut off the dubious retreats to vitalism or origin chauvinism, it will be interesting to see if the skeptics have any good reasons for declaring Cog's pains and pleasures not to matter – at least to it, and for that very reason, to us as well. It will come as no surprise, I hope, that more than a few participants in the Cog project are already musing about what obligations they might come to have to Cog, over and above their obligations to the Cog team.

Finally, J. R. Lucas (1994) has raised the claim that if a robot were really conscious, we would have to be prepared to believe it about its own internal states. I would like to close by pointing out that this is a rather likely reality in the case of Cog. Although equipped with an optimal suite of monitoring devices that will reveal the details of its inner workings to the observing team, Cog's own pronouncements could very well come to be a more trustworthy and informative source of information on what was really going on inside it. The information visible on the banks of monitors, or gathered by the gigabyte on hard disks, will be at the outset almost as hard to interpret, even by Cog's own designers, as the information obtainable by such "third-person" methods as MRI and CT scanning in the neurosciences. As the observers refine their models, and their understanding of their models, their authority as interpreters of the data may grow, but it may also suffer eclipse. Especially since Cog will be designed from the outset to redesign itself as much as possible, there is a high probability that the designers will simply lose the standard hegemony of the artificer ("I made it, so I know what it is supposed to do, and what it is doing now!"). Into this epistemological vacuum Cog may very well thrust itself. In fact, I would gladly defend the conditional prediction: *if* Cog develops to the point where it can conduct what appear to be robust and well-controlled conversations in something like a natural language, it will certainly be in a position to rival its own monitors (and the theorists who interpret them) as a source of knowledge about what it is doing and feeling, and why.

References

Dennett, Daniel C., 1969, *Content and Consciousness*, London: Routledge & Kegan Paul.
Dennett, Daniel C., 1987, "Fast Thinking", in Dennett, *The Intentional Stance*, Cambridge, MA: MIT Press, pp. 323–37.

Dennett, Daniel C., 1993a, review of John Searle, *The Rediscovery of the Mind*, in *J.Phil.* **90**, 193–205.

Dennett, Daniel C., 1993b, "Caveat Emptor", *Consciousness and Cognition*, **2**, 48–57.

Dreyfus, Hubert and Dreyfus, Stuart, 1986, *Mind Over Machine*, New York: Macmillan.

Harnad, Stevan, 1990, "The Symbol Grounding Problem", *Physica D*, **42**, 335–46.

Haugeland, John, 1985, *Artificial Intelligence: The Very Idea*, Cambridge MA: MIT Press.

Lucas, J. R., 1994, presentation to the Royal Society, Conference on Artificial Intelligence, April 14.

Mangan, Bruce, "Dennett, Consciousness, and the Sorrows of Functionalism", *Consciousness and Cognition*, **2**, 1–17.

Searle, John, 1992, *The Rediscovery of the Mind*, Cambridge, MA: MIT Press.

Turing, Alan, 1950, "Computing Machinery and Intelligence", *Mind*, **59**, 433–60.

Waltz, David, 1988, "The Prospects for Building Truly Intelligent Machines", *Daedalus*, **117**, 191–222.

17

SUPERINTELLIGENCE AND SINGULARITY

Ray Kurzweil

Everyone takes the limits of his own vision for the limits of the world.

Arthur Schopenhauer

I am not sure when I first became aware of the Singularity. I'd have to say it was a progressive awakening. In the almost half century that I've immersed myself in computer and related technologies, I've sought to understand the meaning and purpose of the continual upheaval that I have witnessed at many levels. Gradually, I've become aware of a transforming event looming in the first half of the twenty-first century. Just as a black hole in space dramatically alters the patterns of matter and energy accelerating toward its event horizon, this impending Singularity in our future is increasingly transforming every institution and aspect of human life, from sexuality to spirituality.

What, then, is the Singularity? It's a future period during which the pace of technological change will be so rapid, its impact so deep, that human life will be irreversibly transformed. Although neither utopian nor dystopian, this epoch will transform the concepts that we rely on to give meaning to our lives, from our business models to the cycle of human life, including death itself. Understanding the Singularity will alter our perspective on the significance of our past and the ramifications for our future. To truly understand it inherently changes one's view of life in general and one's own particular life. I regard someone who understands the Singularity and who has reflected on its implications for his or her own life as a "singularitarian."

I can understand why many observers do not readily embrace the obvious implications of what I have called the law of accelerating returns (the inherent acceleration of the rate of evolution, with technological evolution as a continuation of biological evolution). After all, it took me forty years to be able to see what was right in front of me, and I still cannot say that I am entirely comfortable with all of its consequences.

The key idea underlying the impending Singularity is that the pace of change of our human-created technology is accelerating and its powers are expanding

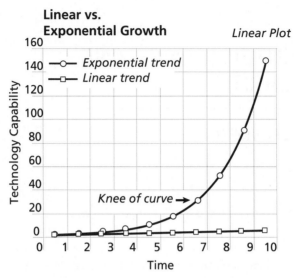

Figure 17.1 *Linear versus exponential*: linear growth is steady; exponential growth becomes explosive.

at an exponential pace. Exponential growth is deceptive. It starts out almost imperceptibly and then explodes with unexpected fury – unexpected, that is, if one does not take care to follow its trajectory. (See Figure 17.1.)

Consider this parable: a lake owner wants to stay at home to tend to the lake's fish and make certain that the lake itself will not become covered with lily pads, which are said to double their number every few days. Month after month, he patiently waits, yet only tiny patches of lily pads can be discerned, and they don't seem to be expanding in any noticeable way. With the lily pads covering less than 1 percent of the lake, the owner figures that it's safe to take a vacation and leaves with his family. When he returns a few weeks later, he's shocked to discover that the entire lake has become covered with the pads, and his fish have perished. By doubling their number every few days, the last seven doublings were sufficient to extend the pads' coverage to the entire lake, (Seven doublings extended their reach 128-fold.) This is the nature of exponential growth.

Consider Gary Kasparov, who scorned the pathetic state of computer chess in 1992. Yet the relentless doubling of computer power every year enabled a computer to defeat him only five years later. The list of ways computers can now exceed human capabilities is rapidly growing. Moreover, the once narrow applications of computer intelligence are gradually broadening in one type of activity after another. For example, computers are diagnosing electrocardiograms and medical images, flying and landing airplanes, controlling the tactical decisions of automated weapons, making credit and financial decisions, and being given responsibility for many other tasks that used to require human intelligence, The performance of these systems is increasingly based on integrating multiple types of artificial intelligence (AI). But as long as there is an AI shortcoming in any such area of endeavor, skeptics will point to that area as an inherent bastion of permanent human superiority over the capabilities of our own creations.

This chapter will argue, however, that within several decades information-based technologies will encompass all human knowledge and proficiency, ultimately including the pattern-recognition powers, problem-solving skills, and emotional and moral intelligence of the human brain itself.

Although impressive in many respects, the brain suffers from severe limitations. We use its massive parallelism (one hundred trillion interneuronal connections operating simultaneously) to quickly recognize subtle patterns. But our thinking is extremely slow: the basic neural transactions are several million times slower than contemporary electronic circuits. That makes our physiological bandwidth for processing new information extremely limited compared to the exponential growth of the overall human knowledge base.

Our version 1.0 biological bodies are likewise frail and subject to a myriad of failure modes, not to mention the cumbersome maintenance rituals they require. While human intelligence is sometimes capable of soaring in its creativity and expressiveness, much human thought is derivative, petty, and circumscribed.

The Singularity will allow us to transcend these limitations of our biological bodies and brains. We will gain power over our fates. Our mortality will be in our own hands. We will be able to live as long as we want (a subtly different statement from saying we will live forever). We will fully understand human thinking and will vastly extend and expand its reach. By the end of this century, the nonbiological portion of our intelligence will be trillions of trillions of times more powerful than unaided human intelligence.

We are now in the early stages of this transition. The acceleration of paradigm shift (the rate at which we change fundamental technical approaches) as well as the exponential growth of the capacity of information technology are both beginning to reach the "knee of the curve," which is the stage at which an exponential trend becomes noticeable. Shortly after this stage, the trend quickly becomes explosive. Before the middle of this century, the growth rates of our technology – which will be indistinguishable from ourselves – will be so steep as to appear essentially vertical. From a strictly mathematical perspective, the growth rates will still be finite but so extreme that the changes they bring about will appear to rupture the fabric of human history. That, at least, will be the perspective of unenhanced biological humanity.

The Singularity will represent the culmination of the merger of our biological thinking and existence with our technology, resulting in a world that is still human but that transcends our biological roots. There will be no distinction, post-Singularity, between human and machine or between physical and virtual reality. If you wonder what will remain unequivocally human in such a world, it's simply this quality: ours is the species that inherently seeks to extend its physical and mental reach beyond current limitations.

Many commentators on these changes focus on what they perceive as a loss of some vital aspect of our humanity that will result from this transition. This perspective stems, however, from a misunderstanding of what our technology will become. All the machines we have met to date lack the essential subtlety of human biological qualities. Although the Singularity has many faces, its most important implication is this: our technology will match and then vastly exceed the refinement and suppleness of what we regard as the best of human traits.

The Intuitive Linear View Versus the Historical Exponential View

> When the first transhuman intelligence is created and launches itself into recursive self-improvement, a fundamental discontinuity is likely to occur, the likes of which I can't even begin to predict.
>
> —Michael Anissimov

In the 1950s John von Neumann, the legendary information theorist, was quoted as saying that "the ever-accelerating progress of technology . . . gives the appearance of approaching some essential singularity in the history of the race beyond which human affairs, as we know them, could not continue." Von Neumann makes two important observations here: *acceleration* and *singularity*. The first idea is that human progress is exponential (that is, it expands by repeatedly *multiplying* by a constant) rather than linear (that is, expanding by repeatedly *adding* a constant) (see Figure 17.1).

The second is that exponential growth is seductive, starting out slowly and virtually unnoticeably, but beyond the knee of the curve it turns explosive and profoundly transformative. The future is widely misunderstood. Our forebears expected it to be pretty much like their present, which had been pretty much like their past. Exponential trends did exist one thousand years ago, but they were at that very early stage in which they were so flat and so slow that they looked like no trend at all. As a result, observers' expectation of an unchanged future was fulfilled. Today, we anticipate continuous technological progress and the social repercussions that follow. But the future will be far more surprising than most people realize, because few observers have truly internalized the implications of the fact that the rate of change itself is accelerating.

Most long-range forecasts of what is technically feasible in future time periods dramatically underestimate the power of future developments because they are based on what I call the "intuitive linear" view of history rather than the "historical exponential" view. My models show that we are doubling the paradigm-shift rate every decade. Thus the twentieth century was gradually speeding up to today's rate of progress; its achievements, therefore, were equivalent to about twenty years of progress at the rate in 2000. We'll make another twenty years of progress in just fourteen years (by 2014), and then do the same again in only seven years. To express this another way, we won't experience one hundred years of technological advance in the twenty-first century; we will witness on the order of twenty thousand years of progress (again, when measured by *today's* rate of progress), or about one thousand times greater than what was achieved in the twentieth century.

Misperceptions about the shape of the future come up frequently and in a variety of contexts. As one example of many, in a recent debate in which I took part concerning the feasibility of molecular manufacturing, a Nobel Prize-winning panelist dismissed safety concerns regarding nanotechnology, proclaiming that "we're not going to see self-replicating nanoengineered entities [devices constructed molecular fragment by fragment] for a hundred years." I pointed out that one hundred years was a reasonable estimate and actually matched my own appraisal of the amount of technical progress required to achieve this particular milestone when measured *at today's rate of progress* (five times the average rate of change we saw in the twentieth century). But because we're doubling the rate of progress every decade, we'll see the equivalent of a century of progress – *at today's rate* – in only twenty-five calendar years.

Similarly at *Time* magazine's Future of Life conference, held in 2003 to celebrate the fiftieth anniversary of the discovery of the structure of DNA, all of the invited speakers were asked what they thought the next fifty years would be like. Virtually every presenter looked at the progress of the last fifty years and used it as a model for the next fifty years. For example, James Watson, the codiscoverer of DNA, said that in fifty years we will have drugs that will allow us to eat as much as we want without gaining weight.

I replied, "Fifty years?" We have accomplished this already in mice by blocking the fat insulin receptor gene that controls the storage of fat in the fat cells. Drugs for human use (using RNA interference and other techniques) are in development now and will be in FDA tests in several years. These will be available in five to ten years, not fifty. Other projections were equally shortsighted, reflecting contemporary research priorities rather than the profound changes that the next half century will bring. Of all the thinkers at this conference, it was primarily Bill Joy and I who took account of the exponential nature of the future, although Joy and I disagree on the import of these changes.

People intuitively assume that the current rate of progress will continue for future periods. Even for those who have been around long enough to experience how the pace of change increases over time, unexamined intuition leaves one with the impression that change occurs at the same rate that we have experienced most recently. From the mathematician's perspective, the reason for this is that an exponential curve looks like a straight line when examined for only a brief duration. As a result, even sophisticated commentators, when considering the future, typically extrapolate the current pace of change over the next ten years or one hundred years to determine their expectations. This is why I describe this way of looking at the future as the "intuitive linear" view.

But a serious assessment of the history of technology reveals that technological change is exponential. Exponential growth is a feature of any evolutionary process, of which technology is a primary example. You can examine the data in different ways, on different timescales, and for a wide variety of technologies, ranging from electronic to biological, as well as for their implications, ranging from the amount of human knowledge to the size of the economy. The acceleration of progress and growth applies to each of them. Indeed, we often find not just simple exponential growth, but "double" exponential growth, meaning that the rate of exponential growth (that is, the exponent) is itself growing exponentially (for example, the price-performance of computing).

Many scientists and engineers have what I call "scientist's pessimism." Often, they are so immersed in the difficulties and intricate details of a contemporary challenge that they fail to appreciate the ultimate long-term implications of their own work, and the larger field of work in which they operate. They likewise fail to account for the far more powerful tools they will have available with each new generation of technology.

Scientists are trained to be skeptical, to speak cautiously of current research goals, and to rarely speculate beyond the current generation of scientific pursuit. This may have been a satisfactory approach when a generation of science and technology lasted longer than a human generation, but it does not serve society's interests now that a generation of scientific and technological progress comprises only a few years.

Consider the biochemists who, in 1990, were skeptical of the goal of transcribing the entire human genome in a mere fifteen years. These scientists had just spent an entire year transcribing a mere one ten-thousandth of the genome. So, even with reasonable anticipated advances, it seemed natural to them that it would take a century, if not longer, before the entire genome could be sequenced.

Or consider the skepticism expressed in the mid-1980s that the Internet would ever be a significant phenomenon, given that it then included only tens of thousands of nodes (also known as servers). In fact, the number of nodes was doubling every year, so that there were likely to be tens of millions of nodes ten years later. But this trend was not appreciated by those who struggled with state-of-the-art technology in 1985, which permitted adding only a few thousand nodes throughout the world in a single year.

The converse conceptual error occurs when certain exponential phenomena are first recognized and are applied in an overly aggressive manner without modeling the appropriate pace of growth. While exponential growth gains speed over time, it is not instantaneous. The run-up in capital values (that is, stock market prices) during the "Internet bubble" and related telecommunications bubble (1997–2000) was greatly in excess of any reasonable expectation of even exponential growth. The actual adoption of the Internet and e-commerce did show smooth exponential growth through both boom and bust; the overzealous expectation of growth affected only capital (stock) valuations. We have seen comparable mistakes during earlier paradigm shifts – for example, during the early railroad era (1830s), when the equivalent of the Internet boom and bust led to a frenzy of railroad expansion.

Another error that prognosticators make is to consider the transformations that will result from a single trend in today's world as if nothing else will change. A good example is the concern that radical life extension will result in overpopulation and the exhaustion of limited material resources to sustain human life, which ignores comparably radical wealth creation from nanotechnology and strong AI. For example, nanotechnology-based manufacturing devices in the 2020s will be capable of creating almost any physical product from inexpensive raw materials and information.

I emphasize the exponential-versus-linear perspective because it's the most important failure that prognosticators make in considering future trends. Most technology forecasts and forecasters ignore altogether this historical exponential view of technological progress. Indeed, almost everyone I meet has a linear view of the future. That's why people tend to overestimate what can be achieved in the short term (because we tend to leave out necessary details) but underestimate what can be achieved in the long term (because exponential growth is ignored).

The Six Epochs

First we build the tools, then they build us.

—Marshall McLuhan

The future ain't what it used to be.

—Yogi Berra

Evolution is a process of creating patterns of increasing order. I believe that it's the evolution of patterns that constitutes the ultimate story of our world. Evolution works through indirection: each stage or epoch uses the information-processing methods of the previous epoch to create the next. I conceptualize the history of evolution – both biological and technological – as occurring in six

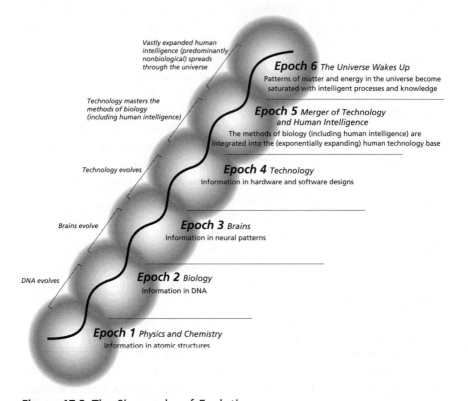

Epoch 6 *The Universe Wakes Up*
Patterns of matter and energy in the universe become saturated with intelligent processes and knowledge

Vastly expanded human intelligence (predominantly nonbiological) spreads through the universe

Epoch 5 *Merger of Technology and Human Intelligence*
The methods of biology (including human intelligence) are integrated into the (exponentially expanding) human technology base

Technology masters the methods of biology (including human intelligence)

Epoch 4 *Technology*
Information in hardware and software designs

Technology evolves

Epoch 3 *Brains*
Information in neural patterns

Brains evolve

Epoch 2 *Biology*
Information in DNA

DNA evolves

Epoch 1 *Physics and Chemistry*
Information in atomic structures

Figure 17.2 The Six epochs of Evolution
Evolution works through indirection: it creates a capability and then uses that capability to evolve the next stage.

epochs. As we will discuss, the Singularity will begin with Epoch Five and will spread from Earth to the rest of the universe in Epoch Six (see Figure 17.2).

Epoch One: Physics and Chemistry

We can trace our origins to a state that represents information in its basic structures: patterns of matter and energy. Recent theories of quantum gravity hold that time and space are broken down into discrete quanta, essentially fragments of information. There is controversy as to whether matter and energy are ultimately digital or analog in nature, but regardless of the resolution of this issue, we do know that atomic structures store and represent discrete information.

A few hundred thousand years after the Big Bang, atoms began to form, as electrons became trapped in orbits around nuclei consisting of protons and neutrons. The electrical structure of atoms made them "sticky." Chemistry was born a few million years later as atoms came together to create relatively stable structures called molecules. Of all the elements, carbon proved to be the most versatile; it's able to form bonds in four directions (versus one to three for most other elements), giving rise to complicated, information-rich, three-dimensional structures.

The rules of our universe and the balance of the physical constants that govern the interaction of basic forces are so exquisitely, delicately, and exactly appropriate for the codification and evolution of information (resulting in increasing complexity) that one wonders how such an extraordinarily unlikely situation came about. Where some see a divine hand, others see our own hands – namely, the anthropic principle, which holds that only in a universe that allowed our own evolution would we be here to ask such questions. Recent theories of physics concerning multiple universes speculate that new universes are created on a regular basis, each with its own unique rules, but that most of these either die out quickly or else continue without the evolution of any interesting patterns (such as Earth-based biology has created) because their rules do not support the evolution of increasingly complex forms. It's hard to imagine how we could test these theories of evolution applied to early cosmology, but it's clear that the physical laws of our universe are precisely what they need to be to allow for the evolution of increasing levels of order and complexity.

Epoch Two: Biology and DNA

In the second epoch, starting several billion years ago, carbon-based compounds became more and more intricate until complex aggregations of molecules formed self-replicating mechanisms, and life originated. Ultimately, biological systems evolved a precise digital mechanism (DNA) to store information describing a larger society of molecules. This molecule and its supporting machinery of codons and ribosomes enabled a record to be kept of the evolutionary experiments of this second epoch.

Epoch Three: Brains

Each epoch continues the evolution of information through a paradigm shift to a further level of "indirection." (That is, evolution uses the results of one epoch to create the next.) For example, in the third epoch, DNA-guided evolution produced organisms that could detect information with their own sensory organs and process and store that information in their own brains and nervous systems. These were made possible by second-epoch mechanisms (DNA and epigenetic information of proteins and RNA fragments that control gene expression), which (indirectly) enabled and defined third-epoch information-processing mechanisms (the brains and nervous systems of organisms). The third epoch started with the ability of early animals to recognize patterns, which still accounts for the vast majority of the activity in our brains. Ultimately, our own species evolved the ability to create abstract mental models of the world we experience and to contemplate the rational implications of these models. We have the ability to redesign the world in our own minds and to put these ideas into action.

Epoch Four: Technology

Combining the endowment of rational and abstract thought with our opposable thumb, our species ushered in the fourth epoch and the next level of indirection: the evolution of human-created technology. This started out with simple mechanisms and developed into elaborate automata (automated mechanical machines). Ultimately, with sophisticated computational and communication devices, technology was itself capable of sensing, storing, and evaluating elaborate patterns of information. To compare the rate of progress of the biological evolution of intelligence to that of technological evolution, consider that the most advanced mammals have added about one cubic inch of brain matter every hundred thousand years, whereas we are roughly doubling the computational capacity of computers every year. Of course, neither brain size nor computer capacity is the sole determinant of intelligence, but they do represent enabling factors.

If we place key milestones of both biological evolution and human technological development on a single graph plotting both the x-axis (number of years ago) and the y-axis (the paradigm-shift time) on logarithmic scales, we find a reasonably straight line (continual acceleration), with biological evolution leading directly to human-directed development (see Figure 17.3).

Figures 17.3 and 17.4 reflect my view of key developments in biological and technological history. Note, however, that the straight line, demonstrating the continual acceleration of evolution, does not depend on my particular selection of events. Many observers and reference books have compiled lists of important events in biological and technological evolution, each of which has its own idiosyncrasies. Despite the diversity of approaches, however, if we combine lists from a variety of sources (for example, the *Encyclopaedia Britannica*, the American Museum of Natural History, Carl Sagan's "cosmic calendar," and others), we observe the same obvious smooth acceleration. Figure 17.5 combines fifteen different lists of key events. Since different thinkers assign different dates to the same event, and different lists include similar or overlapping events selected according to different criteria, we see an expected "thickening" of the trend line due to the "noisiness" (statistical variance) of this data. The overall trend, however, is very clear.

Physicist and complexity theorist Theodore Modis analyzed these lists and determined twenty-eight clusters of events (which he called canonical milestones) by combining identical, similar, and/or related events from the different lists.

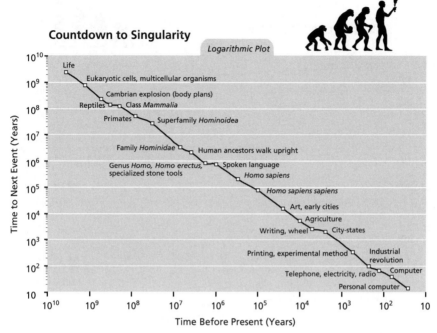

Figure 17.3 *Countdown to Singularity:* Biological evolution and human technology both show continual acceleration, indicated by the shorter time to the next event (two billion years from the origin of life to cells; fourteen years from the PC to the World Wide Web).

This process essentially removes the "noise" (for example, the variability of dates between lists) from the lists, revealing again the same progression (see Figure 17.6).

The attributes that are growing exponentially in these charts are order and complexity. This acceleration matches our commonsense observations. A billion years ago, not much happened over the course of even one million years. But a quarter-million years ago epochal events such as the evolution of our species occurred in time frames of just one hundred thousand years. In technology, if we go back fifty thousand years, not much happened over a one-thousand-year period. But in the recent past, we see new paradigms, such as the World Wide Web, progress from inception to mass adoption (meaning that they are used by a quarter of the population in advanced countries) within only a decade.

Epoch Five: The Merger of Human Technology with Human Intelligence

Looking ahead several decades, the Singularity will begin with the fifth epoch. It will result from the merger of the vast knowledge embedded in our own

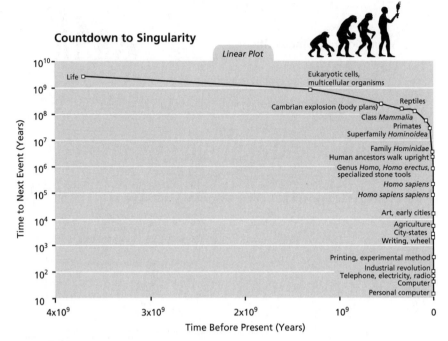

Figure 17.4 *Linear view of evolution:* This version of the preceding figure uses the same data but with a linear scale for time before present instead of a logarithmic one. This shows the acceleration more dramatically, but details are not visible. From a linear perspective, most key events have just happened "recently."

brains with the vastly greater capacity, speed, and knowledge-sharing ability of our technology. The fifth epoch will enable our human-machine civilization to transcend the human brain's limitations of a mere hundred trillion extremely slow connections.

The Singularity will allow us to overcome age-old human problems and vastly amplify human creativity. We will preserve and enhance the intelligence that evolution has bestowed on us while overcoming the profound limitations of biological evolution. But the Singularity will also amplify the ability to act on our destructive inclinations, so its full story has not yet been written.

Epoch Six: The Universe Wakes Up

In the aftermath of the Singularity, intelligence, derived from its biological origins in human brains and its technological origins in human ingenuity, will begin to saturate the matter and energy in its midst. It will achieve this by

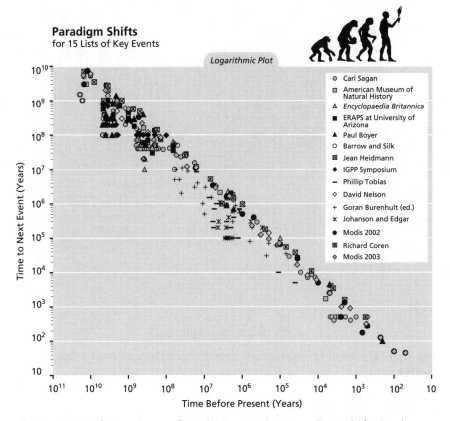

Figure 17.5 *Fifteen views of evolution:* Major paradigm shifts in the history of the world, as seen by fifteen different lists of key events. There is a clear trend of smooth acceleration through biological and then technological evolution.

reorganizing matter and energy to provide an optimal level of computation to spread out from its origin on Earth.

We currently understand the speed of light as a bounding factor on the transfer of information. Circumventing this limit has to be regarded as highly speculative, but there are hints that this constraint may be able to be superseded. If there are even subtle deviations, we will ultimately harness this superluminal ability. Whether our civilization infuses the rest of the universe with its creativity and intelligence quickly or slowly depends on its immutability. In any event the "dumb" matter and mechanisms of the universe will be transformed into exquisitely sublime forms of intelligence, which will constitute the sixth epoch in the evolution of patterns of information.

This is the ultimate destiny of the Singularity and of the universe.

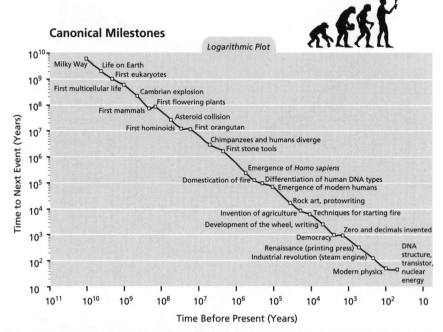

Figure 17.6 *Canonical milestones based on clusters of events from thirteen lists.*

The Singularity Is Near

You know, things are going to be really different! . . . No, no, I mean really different!
Mark Miller (computer scientist) to Eric Drexler, around 1986

What are the consequences of this event? When greater-than-human intelligence drives progress, that progress will be much more rapid. In fact, there seems no reason why progress itself would not involve the creation of still more intelligent entities—on a still-shorter time scale. The best analogy that I see is with the evolutionary past: Animals can adapt to problems and make inventions, but often no faster than natural selection can do its work—the world acts as its own simulator in the case of natural selection. We humans have the ability to internalize the world and conduct "what if's" in our heads; we can solve many problems thousands of times faster than natural selection. Now, by creating the means to execute those simulations at much higher speeds, we are entering a regime as radically different from our human past as we humans are from the lower animals. From the human point of view, this change will be a throwing away of all the previous rules, perhaps in the blink of an eye, an exponential runaway beyond any hope of control.
Vernor Vinge, "The Technological Singularity," 1993

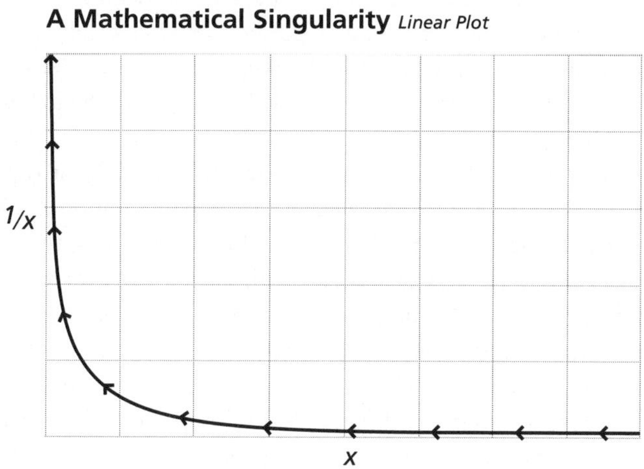

A Mathematical Singularity *Linear Plot*

Figure 17.7 *A mathematical singularity:* As *x* approaches zero (from right to left), 1/*x* (or *y*) approaches infinity.

Let an ultraintelligent machine be defined as a machine that can far surpass all the intellectual activities of any man however clever. Since the design of machines is one of these intellectual activities, an ultraintelligent machine could design even better machines; there would then unquestionably be an "intelligence explosion," and the intelligence of man would be left far behind. Thus the first ultraintelligent machine is the last invention that man need ever make.

Irving John Good, "Speculations Concerning the First
Ultraintelligent Machine," 1965

To put the concept of Singularity into further perspective, let's explore the history of the word itself. "Singularity" is an English word meaning a unique event with, well, singular implications. The word was adopted by mathematicians to denote a value that transcends any finite limitation, such as the explosion of magnitude that results when dividing a constant by a number that gets closer and closer to zero. Consider, for example, the simple function $y = 1/x$. As the value of x approaches zero, the value of the function (y) explodes to larger and larger values (see Figure 17.7).

Such a mathematical function never actually achieves an infinite value, since dividing by zero is mathematically "undefined" (impossible to calculate). But the value of y exceeds any possible finite limit (approaches infinity) as the divisor x approaches zero.

The next field to adopt the word was astrophysics. If a massive star undergoes a supernova explosion, its remnant eventually collapses to the point of apparently zero volume and infinite density, and a "singularity" is created at its center. Because light was thought to be unable to escape the star after it reached this infinite density, it was called a black hole. It constitutes a rupture in the fabric of space and time.

One theory speculates that the universe itself began with such a Singularity. Interestingly, however, the event horizon (surface) of a black hole is of finite size, and gravitational force is only theoretically infinite at the zero-size center of the black hole. At any location that could actually be measured, the forces are finite, although extremely large.

The first reference to the Singularity as an event capable of rupturing the fabric of human history is John von Neumann's statement quoted above. In the 1960s, I. J. Good wrote of an "intelligence explosion" resulting from intelligent machines designing their next generation without human intervention. Vernor Vinge, a mathematician and computer scientist at San Diego State University, wrote about a rapidly approaching "technological singularity" in an article for *Omni* magazine in 1983 and in a science-fiction novel, *Marooned in Realtime*, in 1986.

My 1989 book, *The Age of Intelligent Machines*, presented a future headed inevitably toward machines greatly exceeding human intelligence in the first half of the twenty-first century. Hans Moravec's 1988 book *Mind Children* came to a similar conclusion by analyzing the progression of robotics. In 1993 Vinge presented a paper to a NASA-organized symposium that described the Singularity as an impending event resulting primarily from the advent of "entities with greater than human intelligence," which Vinge saw as the harbinger of a runaway phenomenon. My 1999 book, *The Age of Spiritual Machines: When Computers Exceed Human Intelligence*, described the increasingly intimate connection between our biological intelligence and the artificial intelligence we are creating. Hans Moravec's book *Robot: Mere Machine to Transcendent Mind*, also published in 1999, described the robots of the 2040s as our "evolutionary heirs," machines that will "grow from us, learn our skills, and share our goals and values . . . children of our minds." Australian scholar Damien Broderick's 1997 and 2001 books, both titled *The Spike*, analyzed the pervasive impact of the extreme phase of technology acceleration anticipated within several decades. In an extensive series of writings, John Smart has described the Singularity as the inevitable result of what he calls "MEST" (matter, energy, space, and time) compression.

From my perspective, the Singularity has many faces. It represents the nearly vertical phase of exponential growth that occurs when the rate is so extreme that technology appears to be expanding at infinite speed. Of course, from a mathematical perspective, there is no discontinuity, no rupture, and the growth rates remain finite, although extraordinarily large. But from our *currently* limited framework, this imminent event appears to be an acute and abrupt break in the continuity of progress. I emphasize the word "currently" because one of the salient implications of the Singularity will be a change in the nature of our ability to understand. We will become vastly smarter as we merge with our technology.

Can the pace of technological progress continue to speed up indefinitely? Isn't there a point at which humans are unable to think fast enough to keep up? For unenhanced humans, clearly so. But what would 1,000 scientists, each 1,000 times more intelligent than human scientists today, and each operating 1,000 times faster than contemporary humans (because the information processing in their primarily nonbiological brains is faster) accomplish? One chronological year would be like a millennium for them. What would they come up with?

Well, for one thing, they would come up with technology to become even more intelligent (because their intelligence is no longer of fixed capacity). They would change their own thought processes to enable them to think even faster. When scientists become a million times more intelligent and operate a million times faster, an hour would result in a century of progress (in today's terms).

The Singularity involves the following principles:

- The rate of paradigm shift (technical innovation) is accelerating, right now doubling every decade.
- The power (price-performance, speed, capacity, and bandwidth) of information technologies is growing exponentially at an even faster pace, now doubling about every year. This principle applies to a wide range of measures, including the amount of human knowledge.
- For information technologies, there is a second level of exponential growth: that is, exponential growth in the rate of exponential growth (the exponent). The reason: as a technology becomes more cost effective, more resources are deployed toward its advancement, so the rate of exponential growth increases over time. For example, the computer industry in the 1940s consisted of a handful of now historically important projects. Today total revenue in the computer industry is more than one trillion dollars, so research and development budgets are comparably higher.
- Human brain scanning is one of these exponentially improving technologies. The temporal and spatial resolution and bandwidth of brain scanning are doubling each year. We are just now obtaining the tools sufficient to begin serious reverse engineering (decoding) of the human brain's principles of operation. We already have impressive models and simulations of a couple dozen of the brain's several hundred regions. Within two decades, we will have a detailed understanding of how all the regions of the human brain work.
- We will have the requisite hardware to emulate human intelligence with super-computers by the end of this decade and with personal-computer-size devices by the end of the following decade. We will have effective software models of human intelligence by the mid-2020s.
- With both the hardware and software needed to fully emulate human intelligence, we can expect computers to pass the Turing test, indicating intelligence indistinguishable from that of biological humans, by the end of the 2020s.
- When they achieve this level of development, computers will be able to combine the traditional strengths of human intelligence with the strengths of machine intelligence.

- The traditional strengths of human intelligence include a formidable ability to recognize patterns. The massively parallel and self-organizing nature of the human brain is an ideal architecture for recognizing patterns that are based on subtle, invariant properties. Humans are also capable of learning new knowledge by applying insights and inferring principles from experience, including information gathered through language. A key capability of human intelligence is the ability to create mental models of reality and to conduct mental "what-if" experiments by varying aspects of these models.

- The traditional strengths of machine intelligence include the ability to remember billions of facts precisely and recall them instantly.

- Another advantage of nonbiological intelligence is that once a skill is mastered by a machine, it can be performed repeatedly at high speed, at optimal accuracy, and without tiring.

- Perhaps most important, machines can share their knowledge at extremely high speed, compared to the very slow speed of human knowledge-sharing through language.

- Nonbiological intelligence will be able to download skills and knowledge from other machines, eventually also from humans.

- Machines will process and switch signals at close to the speed of light (about three hundred million meters per second), compared to about one hundred meters per second for the electrochemical signals used in biological mammalian brains. This speed ratio is at least three million to one.

- Machines will have access via the Internet to all the knowledge of our human–machine civilization and will be able to master all of this knowledge.

- Machines can pool their resources, intelligence, and memories. Two machines – or one million machines – can join together to become one and then become separate again. Multiple machines can do both at the same time: become one and separate simultaneously. Humans call this falling in love, but our biological ability to do this is fleeting and unreliable.

- The combination of these traditional strengths (the pattern-recognition ability of biological human intelligence and the speed, memory capacity and accuracy, and knowledge and skill-sharing abilities of nonbiological intelligence) will be formidable.

- Machine intelligence will have complete freedom of design and architecture (that is, they won't be constrained by biological limitations, such as the slow switching speed of our interneuronal connections or a fixed skull size) as well as consistent performance at all times.

- Once nonbiological intelligence combines the traditional strengths of both humans and machines, the nonbiological portion of our civilization's intelligence will then continue to benefit from the double exponential growth of machine price-performance, speed, and capacity.

- Once machines achieve the ability to design and engineer technology as humans do, only at far higher speeds and capacities, they will have access to their own designs (source code) and the ability to manipulate them. Humans are now accomplishing something similar through biotechnology (changing the genetic and other information processes underlying our biology), but in a much slower and far more limited way than what machines will be able to achieve by modifying their own programs.

- Biology has inherent limitations. For example, every living organism must be built from proteins that are folded from one-dimensional strings of amino acids. Protein-based mechanisms are lacking in strength and speed. We will be able to reengineer all of the organs and systems in our biological bodies and brains to be vastly more capable.

- Human intelligence does have a certain amount of plasticity (ability to change its structure), more so than had previously been understood. But the architecture of the human brain is nonetheless profoundly limited. For example, there is room for only about one hundred trillion interneuronal connections in each of our skulls. A key genetic change that allowed for the greater cognitive ability of humans compared to that of our primate ancestors was the development of a larger cerebral cortex as well as the development of increased volume of gray-matter tissue in certain regions of the brain. This change occurred, however, on the very slow timescale of biological evolution and still involves an inherent limit to the brain's capacity. Machines will be able to reformulate their own designs and augment their own capacities without limit. By using nanotechnology-based designs, their capabilities will be far greater than biological brains without increased size or energy consumption.

- Machines will also benefit from using very fast three-dimensional molecular circuits. Today's electronic circuits are more than one million times faster than the electrochemical switching used in mammalian brains. Tomorrow's molecular circuits will be based on devices such as nanotubes, which are tiny cylinders of carbon atoms that measure about ten atoms across and are five hundred times smaller than today's silicon-based transistors. Since the signals have less distance to travel, they will also be able to operate at terahertz (trillions of operations per second) speeds compared to the few gigahertz (billions of operations per second) speeds of current chips.

- The rate of technological change will not be limited to human mental speeds. Machine intelligence will improve its own abilities in a feedback cycle that unaided human intelligence will not be able to follow.

- This cycle of machine intelligence's iteratively improving its own design will become faster and faster. This is in fact exactly what is predicted by the formula for continued acceleration of the rate of paradigm shift. One of the objections that has been raised to the continuation of the acceleration of paradigm shift is that it ultimately becomes much too fast for humans to follow, and so therefore, it's argued, it cannot happen. However, the shift from biological to nonbiological intelligence will enable the trend to continue.

- Along with the accelerating improvement cycle of nonbiological intelligence, nanotechnology will enable the manipulation of physical reality at the molecular level.

- Nanotechnology will enable the design of nanobots: robots designed at the molecular level, measured in microns (millionths of a meter), such as "respirocytes" (mechanical red-blood cells). Nanobots will have myriad roles within the human body, including reversing human aging (to the extent that this task will not already have been completed through biotechnology, such as genetic engineering).

- Nanobots will interact with biological neurons to vastly extend human experience by creating virtual reality from within the nervous system.

- Billions of nanobots in the capillaries of the brain will also vastly extend human intelligence.

- Once nonbiological intelligence gets a foothold in the human brain (this has already started with computerized neural implants), the machine intelligence in our brains will grow exponentially (as it has been doing all along), at least doubling in power each year. In contrast, biological intelligence is effectively of fixed capacity. Thus, the nonbiological portion of our intelligence will ultimately predominate.

- Nanobots will also enhance the environment by reversing pollution from earlier industrialization.

- Nanobots called foglets that can manipulate image and sound waves will bring the morphing qualities of virtual reality to the real world.

- The human ability to understand and respond appropriately to emotion (so-called emotional intelligence) is one of the forms of human intelligence that will be understood and mastered by future machine intelligence. Some of our emotional responses are tuned to optimize our intelligence in the context of our limited and frail biological bodies. Future machine intelligence will also have "bodies" (for example, virtual bodies in virtual reality, or projections in real reality using foglets) in order to interact with the world, but these nano-engineered bodies will be far more capable and durable than biological human bodies. Thus, some of the "emotional" responses of future machine intelligence will be redesigned to reflect their vastly enhanced physical capabilities.

- As virtual reality from within the nervous system becomes competitive with real reality in terms of resolution and believability, our experiences will increasingly take place in virtual environments.

- In virtual reality, we can be a different person both physically and emotionally. In fact, other people (such as your romantic partner) will be able to select a different body for you than you might select for yourself (and vice versa).

- The law of accelerating returns will continue until nonbiological intelligence comes close to "saturating" the matter and energy in our vicinity of the universe with our human-machine intelligence. By saturating, I mean utilizing the matter and energy patterns for computation to an optimal degree, based on our understanding of the physics of computation. As we approach this limit, the intelligence of our civilization will continue its expansion in capability by spreading outward toward the rest of the universe. The speed of this expansion will quickly achieve the maximum speed at which information can travel.

- Ultimately, the entire universe will become saturated with our intelligence. This is the destiny of the universe. We will determine our own fate rather than have it determined by the current "dumb," simple, machinelike forces that rule celestial mechanics.

- The length of time it will take the universe to become intelligent to this extent depends on whether or not the speed of light is an immutable limit. There are indications of possible subtle exceptions (or circumventions) to this limit, which, if they exist, the vast intelligence of our civilization at this future time will be able to exploit.

This, then, is the Singularity. Some would say that we cannot comprehend it, at least with our current level of understanding. For that reason, we cannot look past its event horizon and make complete sense of what lies beyond. This is one reason we call this transformation the Singularity.

I have personally found it difficult, although not impossible, to look beyond this event horizon, even after having thought about its implications for several decades. Still, my view is that, despite our profound limitations of thought, we do have sufficient powers of abstraction to make meaningful statements about the nature of life after the Singularity. Most important, the intelligence that will emerge will continue to represent the human civilization, which is already a human-machine civilization. In other words, future machines will be human, even if they are not biological. This will be the next step in evolution, the next high-level paradigm shift, the next level of indirection. Most of the intelligence of our civilization will ultimately be nonbiological. By the end of this century, it will be trillions of trillions of times more powerful than human intelligence. However, to address often-expressed concerns, this does not imply the end of biological intelligence, even if it is thrown from its perch of evolutionary superiority. Even the nonbiological forms will be derived from biological design. Our civilization will remain human – indeed, in many ways it will be more exemplary of what we regard as human than it is today, although our understanding of the term will move beyond its biological origins.

Many observers have expressed alarm at the emergence of forms of nonbiological intelligence superior to human intelligence. The potential to augment our own intelligence through intimate connection with other thinking substrates does not necessarily alleviate the concern, as some people have expressed the wish to remain "unenhanced" while at the same time keeping their place at the top of the intellectual food chain. From the perspective of biological humanity, these superhuman intelligences will appear to be our devoted servants, satisfying our needs and desires. But fulfilling the wishes of a revered biological legacy will occupy only a trivial portion of the intellectual power that the Singularity will bring.

MOLLY CIRCA 2004: *How will I know when the Singularity is upon us? I mean, I'll want some time to prepare.*

RAY: *Why, what are you planning to do?*

MOLLY 2004: *Let's see, for starters, I'll want to fine-tune my résumé. I'll want to make a good impression on the powers that be.*

GEORGE CIRCA 2048: *Oh, I can take care of that for you.*

MOLLY 2004: *That's really not necessary. I'm perfectly capable of doing it myself. I might also want to erase a few documents – you know, where I'm a little insulting to a few machines I know.*

GEORGE 2048: *Oh, the machines will find them anyway – but don't worry, we're very understanding.*

MOLLY 2004: *For some reason, that's not entirely reassuring. But I'd still like to know what the harbingers will be.*

RAY: *Okay, you will know the Singularity is coming when you have a million e-mails in your in-box.*

MOLLY 2004: *Hmm, in that case, it sounds like we're just about there. But seriously, I'm having trouble keeping up with all of this stuff flying at me as it is. How am I going to keep up with the pace of the Singularity?*

GEORGE 2048: *You'll have virtual assistants – actually, you'll need just one.*

MOLLY 2004: *Which I suppose will be you?*

GEORGE 2048: *At your service.*

MOLLY 2004: *That's just great. You'll take care of everything, you won't even have to keep me informed. "Oh, don't bother telling Molly what's happening, she won't under-stand anyway, let's just keep her happy and in the dark."*

GEORGE 2048: *Oh, that won't do, not at all.*

MOLLY 2004: *The happy part, you mean?*

GEORGE 2048: *I was referring to keeping you in the dark. You'll be able to grasp what I'm up to if that's what you really want.*

MOLLY 2004: *What, by becoming . . .*

RAY: *Enhanced?*

MOLLY 2004: *Yes, that's what I was trying to say.*

GEORGE 2048: *Well, if our relationship is to be all that it can be, then it's not a bad idea.*

MOLLY 2004: *And should I wish to remain as I am?*

GEORGE 2048: *I'll be devoted to you in any event. But I can be more than just your transcendent servant.*

MOLLY 2004: *Actually, you're being "just" my transcendent servant doesn't sound so bad.*

CHARLES DARWIN: *If I may interrupt, it occurred to me that once machine intelligence is greater than human intelligence, it should be in a position to design its own next generation.*

MOLLY 2004: *That doesn't sound so unusual. Machines are used to design machines today.*

CHARLES: *Yes, but in 2004 they're still guided by human designers. Once machines are operating at human levels, well, then it kind of closes the loop.*

NED LUDD: *And humans would be out of the loop.*

MOLLY 2004: *It would still be a pretty slow process.*

RAY; *Oh, not at all. If a nonbiological intelligence was constructed similarly to a human brain but used even circa 2004 circuitry, it—*

MOLLY CIRCA 2004: *You mean "she."*

RAY: *Yes, of course . . . she . . . would be able to think at least a million times faster.*

TIMOTHY LEARY: *So subjective time would be expanded.*

RAY: *Exactly.*

MOLLY 2004: *Sounds like a lot of subjective time. What are you machines going to do with so much of it?*

GEORGE 2048: *Oh, there's plenty to do. After all, I have access to all human knowledge on the Internet.*

MOLLY 2004: *Just the human knowledge? What about all the machine knowledge?*

GEORGE 2048: *We like to think of it as one civilization.*

CHARLES: *So, it does appear that machines will be able to improve their own design.*

MOLLY 2004: *Oh, we humans are starting to do that now.*

RAY: *But we're just tinkering with a few details. Inherently, DNA-based intelligence is just so very slow and limited.*

CHARLES: *So the machines will design their own next generation rather quickly.*

GEORGE 2048: *Indeed, in 2048, that is certainly the case.*

CHARLES: *Just what I was getting at, a new line of evolution then.*

NED: *Sounds more like a precarious runaway phenomenon.*

CHARLES: *Basically, that's what evolution is.*

NED: *But what of the interaction of the machines with their progenitors? I mean, I don't think I'd want to get in their way. I was able to hide from the English authorities for a few years in the early 1800s, but I suspect that will be more difficult with these . . .*

GEORGE 2048: *Guys.*

MOLLY 2004: *Hiding from those little robots—*

RAY: *Nanobots, you mean.*

MOLLY 2004: *Yes, hiding from the nanobots will be difficult, for sure.*

RAY: *I would expect the intelligence that arises from the Singularity to have great respect for their biological heritage.*

GEORGE 2048: *Absolutely, it's more than respect, it's . . . reverence.*

MOLLY 2004: *That's great, George, I'll be your revered pet. Not what I had in mind.*

NED: *That's just how Ted Kaczynski puts it: we're going to become pets. That's our destiny, to become contented pets but certainly not free men.*

MOLLY 2004: *And what about this Epoch Six? If I stay biological, I'll be using up all this precious matter and energy in a most inefficient way. You'll want to turn me into, like, a billion virtual Mollys and Georges, each of them thinking a lot faster than I do now. Seems like there will be a lot of pressure to go over to the other side.*

RAY: Still, you represent only a tiny fraction of the available matter and energy. Keeping you biological won't appreciably change the order of magnitude of matter and energy available to the Singularity. It will be well worth it to maintain the biological heritage.

GEORGE 2048: Absolutely.

RAY: Just like today we seek to preserve the rain forest and the diversity of species.

MOLLY 2004: That's just what I was afraid of. I mean, we're doing such a wonderful job with the rain forest. I think we still have a little bit of it left. We'll end up like those endangered species.

NED: Or extinct ones.

MOLLY 2004: And there's not just me. How about all the stuff I use? I go through a lot of stuff.

GEORGE 2048: That's not a problem, we'll just recycle all your stuff. We'll create the environments you need as you need them.

MOLLY 2004: Oh, I'll be in virtual reality?

RAY: No, actually, foglet reality.

MOLLY 2004: I'll be in a fog?

RAY: No, no, foglets.

MOLLY 2004: Excuse me?

RAY: I'll explain later in the book.

MOLLY 2004: Well, give me a hint.

RAY; Foglets are nanobots – robots the size of blood cells – that can connect themselves to replicate any physical structure. Moreover, they can direct visual and auditory information in such a way as to bring the morphing qualities of virtual reality into real reality.

MOLLY 2004: I'm sorry I asked. But, as I think about it, I want more than just my stuff. I want all the animals and plants, too. Even if I don't get to see and touch them all, I like to know they're there.

GEORGE 2048: But nothing will be lost.

MOLLY 2004: I know you keep saying that. But I mean actually there – you know, as in biological reality.

RAY: Actually, the entire biosphere is less than one millionth of the matter and energy in the solar system.

CHARLES: It includes a lot of the carbon.

RAY: It's still worth keeping all of it to make sure we haven't lost anything.

GEORGE 2048: That has been the consensus for at least several years now.

MOLLY 2004: So, basically, I'll have everything I need at my fingertips?

GEORGE 2048: Indeed.

MOLLY 2004: Sounds like King Midas. You know, everything he touched turned to gold.

NED: Yes, and as you will recall he died of starvation as a result.

MOLLY 2004: Well, if I do end up going over to the other side, with all of that vast expanse of subjective time, I think I'll die of boredom.

GEORGE 2048: Oh, that could never happen. I will make sure of it.

Part IV
ETHICAL AND POLITICAL ISSUES

Related Works
Brave New World
Gattaca
Terminator
White Plague

18

THE MAN ON THE MOON

George J. Annas

Genetics has been not only the most superheated scientific arena of the past decade; it has also been a feverish battlefield for American bioethics. And no area has elicited as much controversy as the speculative prospect of genetic engineering. We cannot know what human life will be like a thousand years from now, but we can and should think seriously about what we would like it to be like. What is unique about human beings and about being human; what makes humans human? What qualities of the human species must we preserve to preserve humanity itself? What would a "better human" be like? If genetic engineering techniques work, are there human qualities we should try to temper and others we should try to enhance? If human rights and human dignity depend on our human nature, can we change our "humanness" without undermining our dignity and our rights? At the outset of the third millennium, we can begin our exploration of these questions by looking back on some of the major events and themes of the past 1000 years in Western civilization and the primitive human instincts they illustrate.

Holy Wars

The second millennium opened with holy wars: local wars, such as the Spanish Reconquista to retake Spain from the Moors, and the broader multi-state Crusades to take the Holy Lands from the Muslims who were menacing Christian pilgrims there. The great Crusades, which lasted almost two hundred years, were fought in the name of God with the war cry, *Deus volt* ("God wills it"). The enemy was the nonbeliever, the infidel; killing the infidel became a holy act. The ability to label an enemy as "other" and subhuman, and to justify killing the "other" in the name of God or country was a defining human trait throughout the entire millennium. I will later argue that this genocidal proclivity of the past millennium could lead to genocide on an even more horrible scale if we create a new or "better" human species (or subspecies) through genetic engineering.

Like the Crusaders, Columbus sought to conquer territories inhabited by infidels, in the name of God. When Columbus reached the "new" world, which he mistakenly thought was part of India, he named the island on which he landed "San Salvador." He claimed it in the name of the Catholic Church and the Catholic monarchs of Spain. Naming for Europeans was emblematic of conquest. Taking possession could be symbolized with a flag or even a cross. Columbus, whose professed goal was also to convert the "savages" who inhabited the new world, wrote in his diary, "in all regions I always left a cross standing" as a mark of Christian dominance. Religion was the cover story for the conquest. Nonetheless, Columbus's encounter with the Native Americans or "Indians" resulted in their merciless subjugation and genocidal destruction.

The Spanish conquistadors who followed Columbus continued to use the Catholic religion and its absence in the New World as an excuse to claim the land and conquer its inhabitants. In his 1843 *The History of the Conquest of Mexico*, William Prescott recounts the European belief that paganism was "a sin to be punished with fire . . . in this world, and eternal suffering in the next." Prescott continues, "under this code, the territory of the heathen, wherever found [was forfeit to the Holy See] and as such was freely given away by the head of the Church to any temporal potentate whom he pleased that would assume the burden of conquest." Prescott seems to have had some sympathy for Montezuma (the sun god) and the other Aztecs killed by the Spaniards in their conquest, but ultimately concluded that the Aztecs did not deserve to be considered fully human: "How can a nation, where human sacrifices prevail, and especially when combined with cannibalism, further the march of civilization?"

In similar fashion, Pizarro justified his conquest of Peru and the subjugation of the Incas including the kidnapping and eventual killing of Atahuallpa, by claiming it was for the "glory of God" and to bring "to our holy Catholic faith so vast a number of heathens." Although God was the cover story, they were also motivated by gold. In their later pursuit of El Dorado, the famed city of gold, following the conquests by Cortes and Pizarro, however, none of the other Spanish conquistadors were able to plunder the amount of gold they did.

The Crusades, the voyage of Columbus, and the slaughters of the Spanish conquistadors who followed, are powerful examples of human exploration and human encounters with the unknown. They teach us that the realm of human dominance can be radically enlarged by human imagination and courage. Equally importantly, they teach us that without a belief in human dignity and equality, the cost of such dominance is genocidal human rights violations. They also caution us to be suspicious of stated motives and cover stories; although filled with missionary zeal, most of these adventurers and explorers sought primarily fame and fortune.

Unholy Wars

It is, of course, much easier to look back 500 years than 50 years. Nonetheless, World War II, the Apollo moon landings, and the prospect of human genetic engineering raise most of the important issues we face in the new millennium in defining humanness, human rights, and science's responsibilities. Post-modernism can be dated from any of these, and each holds its own lessons and cautions. Many scholars date postmodernism from Hiroshima and the Holocaust, one an instantaneous annihilation, the other a systematic one. Together, their application of industrial techniques to human slaughter represents the death of our civilization's dream of moral and scientific progress that had characterized the modern age. The nuclear age is much more ambiguous and uncertain. We now worship science as society's new religion as the quest for everlasting life with God is replaced by our new crusade for immortality on earth.

The modern human rights movement was born from the blood of World War II and the death of the positive law belief that the only law that matters is that which is enacted by a legitimate government, including the Nazi government. The multinational trial of the Nazi war criminals at Nuremberg after World War II was held on the premise that there is a universal law of humanity and that those who violate it may be properly tried and punished. Universal criminal law, law that applies to all humans and protects all humans, outlaws crimes against human-ity, including state-sanctioned genocide, murder, torture, and slavery. Obeying the laws of a particular country or the orders of superiors is no defense.

The crusades were also echoed in World War II. General Dwight Eisenhower titled his account of World War II *Crusade in Europe*, and his order of the day for the D-Day invasion read: "Soldiers, sailors, and airmen of the allied exped-itionary forces, you are about to embark on a great crusade . . . the hopes and prayers of liberty loving people everywhere march with you." And as with the crusades and the conquest of the Americas, to justify the human slaughter of World War II the enemy had to be dehumanized. On the Allied side, the most dehumanizing language was meted out to the Japanese:

> Among the Allies the Japanese were also known as "jackals" or "monkey men" or "sub-humans," the term of course used by the Germans for Russians, Poles, and assorted Slavs, amply justifying their vivisection . . . *Jap* . . . was a brisk monosyllable handy for slogans like "Rap the Jap" or "Let's Blast the Jap Clean Off the Map," the last a virtual prophecy of Hiroshima.

The United Nations was formed to prevent further wars and on the premise that *all* humans have dignity and are entitled to equal rights. Science and medicine came under specific investigation in the 1946–47 "Doctors' Trial" of 23 Nazi physician-experimenters. The Nazi experiments involved murder and torture, systematic and barbarous acts with death as the planned endpoint. The subjects of these experiments, which included lethal freezing and high-altitude experiments, were concentration camp prisoners, mostly Jews, Gypsies, and Slavs, people the Nazis viewed as subhuman. With echoes of the conquest of the Americas, Nazi philosophy was founded on the belief that Germans were a "superior race" whose destiny was to subjugate and rule the inferior races. A central part of the Nazi project was eugenics, the attempt to improve the species, mostly by eliminating "inferior" people, so-called useless eaters. In its final judgment, the court articulated what we now know as the Nuremberg Code, which remains the most authoritative legal and ethical document governing international research standards and requires the informed consent of every research subject. It is one of the premier human rights documents in world history, and the primary contribution of American bioethics to the international community to date.

The trials at Nuremberg were soon followed by the adoption of the Universal Declaration of Human Rights in 1948, which is, as previously discussed, the most important human rights document to date. This was followed by two treaties, the Covenant on Civil and Political Rights and the Covenant on Economic, Social, and Cultural Rights. The Universal Declaration of Human Rights and the two treaties represent a milestone for humanity: the recognition that human rights are founded on human dignity and that human dignity is shared by *all* members of the human race without distinctions based on race, religion, or national origin.

The Man on the Moon

The most spectacular exploration of the 20th century was the voyage of Apollo 11 to the moon's surface and the safe return of its crew. Neil Armstrong's words upon setting foot on the moon seemed just right: "One small step for [a] man, one giant leap for mankind [*sic*]." Although the race to the moon had more to do with the politics of the cold war than science, it was nonetheless an almost magical engineering accomplishment. And, like Columbus, history will remember Armstrong because he was the first to set foot on the moon.

The United States was willing to go to great lengths to ensure that the first man on the moon would be American and would plant an American flag on the moon. Nonetheless, there were human rights constraints even on this experiment. President John Kennedy, for example, had set it as a United States goal to land a man on the moon "and return him safely to earth." Putting human values second to winning a race with the Russians by landing a man on the moon without a clear plan for getting him back to Earth was rejected.

The United States did not explicitly conquer the moon for the glory of God, but God was on the minds of the conquerors riding in a spacecraft named for the sun god, Apollo. Some of the most explicit religious statements were made by rocket designer Werner Von Braun, who had been a Nazi SS officer and the designer of the destructive V2 rockets that the Germans rained down on England near the end of World War II. Von Braun was captured by the United States and "sanitized" to work on rocket propulsion, eventually heading up NASA's effort. The day before Apollo 11 blasted off he explained the reasons for putting a man on the moon: "We are expanding the mind of man. We are extending this God-given brain and these God-given hands to their outermost limits and in so doing all mankind will benefit. All mankind will reap the harvest . . ." The missionary zeal of the Crusaders and conquistadors was to echo on the moon.

Norman Mailer, in his chronicle of the moon landing *Of a Fire on the Moon*, asks a central question: "Was the voyage of Apollo 11 the noblest expression of the technological age, or the best evidence of its utter insanity? . . . are we witness to grandeur or madness?" Today neither extreme seems quite right. The moon rocks returned to earth were only a poor symbol of the trip, but the photos of Earth taken from space have had a profound impact on our global consciousness, if not our global conscience, and have helped energize the worldwide environmental protection movement. It is much harder to deny our common humanity when we can all see our common home.

We now know that the Russians were never serious challengers in the moon race and that the prospect of the United States following the moon landing with a serious effort at space exploration was grossly overstated. Our loss of enchantment, even interest, in the moon was captured by Gene Cernam, the last of the 12 astronauts to land on the moon, when he said, as he blasted off its surface, "Let's get this mother out of here." The moon landing was primarily about commerce and politics, not peace and harmony. As historian Walter McDougall notes in his book *The Heavens and the Earth*, although the plaque we placed on the moon read "We came in peace for all mankind," peace was not what the mission was about. It did have something to do with science and national pride, but he argues, "mostly it was about spy satellites and comsats and other orbital systems for military and commercial advantage." Military and commercial goals continue to dominate outer space, just as they did with the conquistadors. And even though manned space exploration has again been relegated to the realm of science fiction, the moon landing continues to be the scientific and engineering feat to which those aspiring to breakthrough innovation compare their efforts.

It is in the realm of science fiction that most of the important speculation about the human predicament and the future of humanity is envisioned. It was Jorge Luis Borges, for example, who first suggested that humans could become immortal if they were willing to have all of their bodily functions performed by machines. Humans could enter into the world of pure thought by having their brains inhabit a "cube-like" piece of furniture. In the nightmare envisioned by Borges, modern surgery and mechanical replacement parts could bring a type of immortality to humankind, not as immortal actors, but as immortal witnesses.

Arthur Clarke, in *2001: A Space Odyssey*, suggests that human evolution might move in a different direction: toward the development of a computerized mind encapsulated in a metal spaceshiplike body, eternally roaming the galaxy in search of new sensations. The price for human immortality in this view is the eradication of both the human body and the human mind, the former being replaced by an artificial, destruction-proof container, the latter by an infinitely replicable computer program. Of course, the indestructible robot body inhabited by a digitalized memory chip would not be human in the sense we understand it today, and the rights of this assemblage would likely be more on the order of the rights of robots than those of contemporary humans.

We could use our technology to explore outer space with such robots, but our current fascination is focused on inner space. Instead of expanding our minds and our perspectives as a species by pondering the mysteries of outer space with its possibilities of other life forms, we are turning inward and contemplating ourselves on the microscopic level. The new biology, perhaps better described as the new genetics or the "genetics age," suggests a biology-based immortality alternative to a digital brain in a body of metal and plastic: changing and "enhancing" our human capabilities by altering our genes at the molecular level. Or, as James Watson, the codiscoverer of the structure of DNA, famously put it, "We used to think our future was in our stars, now we know our future is in our genes."

Genetic Engineering

Like space exploration, work on human genetics is dominated by governmental agencies and commercial interests. Taking place in the shadow of Hiroshima and under the ever-present threat of species suicide by nuclear annihilation, genetics research can be seen as an attempt by science to redeem itself, to bring the "gift" of immortality to a species whose very existence it has placed at risk. The scientific (and commercial) goal is unabashedly to conquer death by engineering the immortal human. As the head of Human Genome Sciences declared, "Death is a series of preventable diseases." Basic strategies to construct a "better human" are suggested by two genetic experiments: cloning sheep and making a smarter mouse.

In 1997 embryologist Ian Wilmut announced that he and his colleagues had cloned a sheep, creating a genetic twin of an adult animal by reprogramming one of its somatic cells to act as the nucleus of an enucleated egg. He called the cloned lamb Dolly. An international debate on outlawing the cloning of a human began immediately and has continued. Dolly's "creator," Wilmut, has consistently argued that his cloning technique should not be applied to humans for reproduction. He has not used literature to bolster his argument, but he could.

One reporter who described Wilmut as "Dolly's laboratory father," for example, could not have conjured up images of Mary Shelley's *Frankenstein* better if he had tried. Frankenstein was also his creature's father–god; the creature tells him: "I ought to be thy Adam." Like Dolly, the "spark of life" was infused into the creature by electric current. Unlike Dolly, Frankenstein's creature was created fully grown (not a cloning possibility) and wanted more than creaturehood. He wanted a mate of his "own kind" with whom to live and reproduce. Frankenstein reluctantly agreed to manufacture such a mate if the creature agreed to leave humankind alone. But in the end Frankenstein viciously destroys the female creature–mate, concluding that he has no right to inflict the children of this pair, "a race of devils," upon "everlasting generations." Frankenstein ultimately recognized his responsibility to humanity, and Shelley's great novel explores almost all the noncommercial elements of today's cloning debate.

The naming of the world's first cloned mammal, like the naming of San Salvador and the Apollo spacecraft, is telling. The sole survivor of 277 cloned embryos (or "fused couplets"), the clone could have been named after its sequence in this group (for example, 6LL3), but this would have only emphasized its character as a product. In stark contrast, the name Dolly suggests a unique individual. Victor Frankenstein, of course, never named his creature, thereby repudiating any parental responsibility. By naming the world's first mammal clone Dolly, Wilmut accepted responsibility for her.

Cloning is replication and as such holds little attraction or interest for people who want to have children. Most of us want our children to have better lives than we have had, not simply to duplicate ours, even genetically. That is why genetic engineering experiments that promise "better" children (and better humans) are much more important to the future of humankind. In 1999, for example, Princeton scientist Joe Tsien announced that he had used genetic engineering techniques to create mice that had better memories and could therefore learn faster than other mice; they were "smarter." Tsien is convinced that if his findings can be made applicable to humans, everyone will want to use genetic engineering to have smarter babies. In his words, "Everyone wants to be smart."

Appropriating the moon landing metaphor, Tsien said of his genetically engineered mice (he named the strain Doogie after TV's fictional boy genius physician), "To the scientific community this is a small step for a man. The fundamental question is, 'Is this a giant step for mankind?'" Tsien has also suggested that his work is much more important than cloning because a genetic duplicate adds nothing new to the world. His point is well taken. The possibility of applying genetic engineering techniques to humans for the purpose of making smarter, stronger, happier, prettier, or longer-lived humans simultaneously raises all the questions I posed at the beginning of this chapter: what does it mean to be human, and what changes in "humanness" would result in better humans (or a new species altogether)?

In the world of genetic engineering, our children would become products of our own manufacture. As products, they would be subject to both quality control and improvements, including destruction and replacement if they were "defective." We could construct a new eugenics based not on a corrupt, Hitlerean view of our fellow humans, but on a utopian dream of what an ideal child should be like. Do we really want what we seem to want? Is Tsien correct, for example, in claiming that everyone would want to have a better memory?

Elie Wiesel, the most eloquent witness of the Holocaust, has devoted his life's work to memory, trying to ensure that the world cannot forget the horrors of the Holocaust so that they won't be repeated. This was also the primary aim of the prosecution and judges at the International Military Tribunal at Nuremberg. The crimes against humanity committed during World War II had to be remembered. As chief prosecutor Justice Robert Jackson put it to the tribunal, "The wrongs which we seek to condemn and punish have been so calculated, so malignant, and so devastating, that civilization cannot tolerate their being ignored because it cannot survive their being repeated." It is obviously not just memory itself that matters, but the information memory holds and what humans do with that information. We have, for example, more and more information about our genes every day. We are told that scientists will soon be able to understand life at the molecular level. But in pursuing this objective we have lost all perspective. We do not live life on the molecular level, but as full persons. We will never be able to understand life (or how it should be lived, or what it means to be human) by exploring or understanding our lives or our bodies at the molecular, atomic, or even the subatomic level.

Cloned sheep live in a pen, and laboratory mice are confined in a controlled environment. Science now seems to act as if humanity's goal is a world of mass contentment and containment, an earth-sized human zoo in which every man, woman, and child has all the "smart genes" we can provide, is fed the most nutritious food, is protected from all preventable diseases, lives in a clean, air-filtered environment, and is supplied sufficient mind-altering drugs to be in a constant state of happiness, even euphoria. And this happy life, which Borges envisioned with horror, could be made to extend for hundreds of years, at least if there is no more to life than a perfectly engineered body, a contented mind, and virtual immortality. Bioethicist Leon Kass has put it well in the context of genetic engineering (but he could also have been speaking of Columbus): "Though well-equipped, we know not who we are or where we are going." We literally don't know what to make of ourselves. Humans must inform science; science cannot inform (or define) humanity. Novelty is not progress, and technique cannot substitute for life's meaning and purpose.

Toward the Posthuman

As we attempt to take human evolution into our own hands, it is not the Aztecs or the Nazis whom we next plan to conquer. The territory we now claim is our own body. We claim it in the name of the new eugenic right of every human to do with his or her body what he or she chooses. Yet the brief history of our species cautions that there are limits to both our knowledge and our claims of dominion. Cortés could rationalize his subjugation of the Aztecs because, among other things, they engaged in human sacrifice and cannibalism. With human experimentation, such as the transplantation of a heart from a baboon to Baby Fae, we have made human sacrifice an art (albeit in the name of science rather than God), and with organ transplantation we have tamed cannibalism. Postmodern man accepts no limits, no taboos.

If humanity survives another 1000 years, what will the human of the year 3000 be like? With more than three-quarters of Earth covered by water, would the addition of gills, for example, be an enhancement or a deformity? Would a child be reared with gills for underwater exploration or for a circus sideshow? How tall is too tall? Can you be too smart for your own good? If we continue to ignore the continuing pollution of our environment, perhaps the improved human should be able to breathe polluted air and survive on garbage. As we deplete our energy sources, perhaps the improved human should have a bionic wheel to replace our legs for more efficient mobility. Or perhaps we should try to grow wings to fly. Will we as a society permit individual scientists to try any or all of these experiments on humans, or can we learn from the unanticipated consequences of conquest and war that humans are better off when they think before they act, and act democratically when action can have a profound impact on every member of our species?

It was to prevent war that the United Nations was formed, and it was to hold people accountable for crimes against humanity, such as murder, torture, slavery, and genocide, that the International Criminal Court was established. Of course, state-sponsored crimes against humanity are still committed. But the world no longer ignores the rights of peoples who earlier in the century would simply have been designated "uncivilized" or considered subhuman. If we humans are to be the masters of our own destiny and not simply products of our new technologies (a big "if"), we will need to build international insti-tutions sturdier than the United Nations and the International Criminal Court to help channel and control our newfound powers and to protect basic human rights. Human dignity and equality are only likely to be safe if science is accountable to democratic institutions and transparent enough that international deliberation can take place before irrevocable species-endangering experiments are conducted.

Outside the realm of creating and producing weapons of mass destruction, science is not a criminal activity, and human cloning and genetic engineering do not "fit" comfortably in the category of crimes against humanity. Moreover, in the face of the Holocaust and nuclear weapons, genetic engineering appears almost benign. But this is deceptive because genetic engineering has the capacity to change the meaning of what it is to be human. There are limits to how far we can go in changing our nature without changing our humanity and our basic human values. Because it is the meaning of humanness (our distinctness from other animals) that has given birth to our concepts of both human dignity and human rights, altering our nature threatens to undermine our concepts of both human dignity and human rights. With their loss the fundamental belief in human equality would also be lost. Of course, we know that the rich are much better off than the poor and that real equality will require income redistribution. Nonetheless, the rich may not enslave, torture, or kill even the poorest human on the planet. Likewise, it is a fundamental premise of democracy that all humans, even the poor, must have a voice in determining the future of our species and our planet.

Can universal human rights and democracy, grounded on human dignity, survive human genetic engineering? Without clear goals, the market will define what a better human is. Mass marketing and advertising will encourage us to conform to some culturally constructed ideal rather than celebrate differences. This is at least one major lesson learned from the cosmetic surgery industry: almost all of its patient–clients want either to be reconstructed to appear normal or to be remodeled to appear younger. It should at least give an immortality-seeking science (and society) pause that the more the human life span has increased, the more human societies devalue and marginalize the aged and idolize and seek to emulate the bodies of the young.

The new ideal human, the genetically engineered "superior" human, will almost certainly come to represent "the other." If history is a guide, either the normal humans will view the "better" humans as the other and seek to control or destroy them, or vice-versa. The better human will become, at least in the absence of a universal concept of human dignity, either the oppressor or the oppressed. In short, as H.G. Wells made clear in his *Valley of the Blind*, it is simply untrue that every "enhancement" of human ability will be universally praised: in the valley of the blind, eyes that functioned were considered a deformity to be surgically eliminated so that the sighted person would be like everyone else. In *The Time Machine* Wells himself envisioned the division of humans into two separate and hostile species, neither any improvement over existing humans.

Ultimately, it is almost inevitable that genetic engineering will move *Homo sapiens* to develop into two separable species: the standard-issue human beings will be like the savages of the pre-Columbian Americas and be seen by the new genetically enhanced posthumans as heathens who can properly be slaughtered and subjugated. It is this genocidal potential that makes some species-altering genetic engineering projects potential species-endangering weapons of mass destruction, and the unaccountable genetic engineer a potential bioterrorist. Science cannot save us from our inhumanity toward one another, it can just make our destructive tendencies more efficient and more bestial. Science and oppression can, in fact, go hand in hand. As historian Robert Proctor put it in concluding his study of public health under the Third Reich, "the routine practice of science can so easily coexist with routine exercise of cruelty."

New Crusades

Although we humans have not conquered death, we have invented an immortal creature: the corporation. The corporation is a legal fiction endowed by law with eternal life (and limited liability). This creature has, like Frankenstein's monster, assumed powers not envisioned or controllable by its creator. In its contemporary form, the corporation has become transnational and thus under the control of no government, democratic or otherwise. It swears no allegiance to anything and knows no limits in its pursuit of growth and profit. And as did the Spanish Crown, it has its own cover story. Corporations, at least life sciences and biotechnology corporations, seek profits not for their own sake, according to their cover stories, but rather do scientific research for the betterment of mankind. Some in the life sciences corporate world now seek to make not only better plants and animals, but also better humans. Orwell's *Animal Farm*, where "all animals are equal, but some are more equal than others," now seems much more likely to be brought to us by life sciences corporations than by totalitarian dictatorships. Science fiction writer Michael Crichton first seemed to notice that "the commercialization of molecular biology is the most stunning ethical event in the history of science, and it has happened with astonishing speed."

Science's crusade no longer seeks eternal life with God, but eternal life on earth. In decoding the human genome, religion is again the cover story, as scientists speak of the genome as the "book of man" [sic] and the "holy grail" of biology. But it is still gold and glory that these modern-day, corporation-sponsored explorers seek. Because there is money to be made by doing it, the corporate redesign of humans is inevitable in the absence of what Vaclav Havel has termed "a transformation of the spirit and the human relationship to life and the world." Havel has noted that the new "dictatorship of money" has replaced totalitarianism, but it is equally capable of sapping life of its meaning with its "materialistic obsessions," the "flourishing of selfishness," and its need "to evade personal responsibility." Without responsibility our future is bleak. Like the failed quest of the Spanish conquistadors for El Dorado, our quest for more and more money will fizzle. Immortality without purpose is also hollow. In Havel's words, "the only kind of politics that makes sense is a politics that grows out of the imperative, and the need, to live as everyone ought to live and therefore – to put it somewhat dramatically – to bear responsibility for the entire world."

To bear responsibility for the entire world may seem excessive, but even Frankenstein would recognize it as just right. It reminds us of the environmental movement's mantra "think globally, act locally" and makes each of us responsible for all of us. How can we, citizens of the world, regain some control over science and industry that threatens to alter our species and the very meaning of our lives? It will not be easy, and given the consistently brutish nature of our species, perhaps we do not deserve to survive. Nonetheless, the worldwide rejection of the prospect of cloning to create a child provides some hope that our species is not inherently doomed. Bioethics alone is too weak a reed on which to build an international movement: human rights language is more powerful and has wider applicability. This is because it is not only medical and scientific practice that is at stake, but the nature of humanity and the rights of humans. Of course, because physician–researchers will pioneer all relevant experiments, bioethics remains pivotal even if not determinative. Let me conclude this chapter with a few modest suggestions.

On the national level, I have previously called for a moratorium on gene transfer experiments. That didn't happen, but the worldwide reassessment of gene transfer experiments makes such a moratorium less necessary. Nonetheless, we still need to ensure that all human gene transfer experiments, what are more commonly (and incorrectly) referred to as "gene therapy," be performed with full public knowledge and transparency. A national debate on the goals of the research, and whether the lines between somatic cell and germline research, or between treatment and enhancement research, are meaningful should continue with more public involvement. My own view is that the boundary line that really matters is set by the species itself and that species-endangering experiments should be outlawed.

We can take some actions on a national level, but we also need international rules about the new science, including not only cloning and genetic engineering, but also human-machine cyborgs, xenografts, and brain alterations. These could all fit into a *new category* of "crimes against humanity" in the strict sense, actions that threaten the integrity of the human species itself. This is not to say that changing the nature of humanity is always criminal, only that no individual scientist (or corporation or country) has the social or moral warrant to endanger humanity, including altering humans in ways that might endanger the species. Performing species-endangering experiments in the absence of social warrant, democratically developed, can properly be considered a terrorist act. Xenografts, for example, carry the risk of releasing a new, lethal virus upon humanity. No individual scientist or corporation has the moral warrant to risk this. Altering the human species in a way that predictably endangers it should require a worldwide discussion and debate, followed by a vote in an institution representative of the world's population, the United Nations being the only such entity today. It should also require a deep and wide-ranging discussion of our future and what kind of people we want to be, what kind of world we want to live in, and how we can protect universal human rights based on human dignity and democratic principles.

An international treaty banning specific species-endangering activities is necessary to make such a system effective. This, of course, begs two questions. First, exactly what types of human experiments should be prohibited? Second, what precisely is the international regime proposed? As to the first, the general definition could encompass all experimental interventions aimed at altering a fundamental characteristic of being human. There are at least two ways to change such characteristics. The first is to make a human trait optional. Changing it in one member (who continues to be seen as a member of the species) would change the species definition for everyone. An example is asexual replication cloning. When one human successfully engages in replication cloning, sexual reproduction will no longer be a necessary characteristic of being human. All humans will be capable of asexual replication. This will matter to all humans because it is not just our brains and what we can do with them (such as develop language and anticipate our deaths) that make us human, but also the interaction of our brains with our bodies.

A second way to change a characteristic of being human would be any alteration that would make the resulting person someone we *Homo sapiens* would no longer identify as a member of our species or who could not sexually reproduce with a human. Examples would include the insertion of an artificial chromosome that would make sexual reproduction impossible, as well as physically altering basic brain and body structure (for example, number of arms, legs, eyes, etc., and, of course, the addition of new appendages such as wings or new functional organs such as gills). This is important because the resulting person would likely be viewed as a new species or subspecies of humans, and thus not necessarily a possessor of all human rights.

Genetic engineering experiments not aimed at changing the nature of the species or at placing the resultant person outside the definition of *Homo sapiens* (such as those aimed at improving memory, immunity, strength, and other characteristics that some existing humans have) should also be subject to international oversight. Moreover, I don't think any of them should be performed on children, fetuses, or embryos. This is because of their inherent physical and psychological danger to children (and the overall danger they pose to children of treating them as manufactured products), and because there are existing alternative, less dangerous educational, exercise-based, medical, and surgical ways to achieve these goals. Parents should simply not be able to dominate their children in this fashion: what can be considered liberty for an adult is tyranny when forced on the next generation. Not included would be somatic cell interventions aimed at curing or preventing disease, although I believe these should be regulated on a national basis. An intermediate case might be the addition of an artificial gene to an embryo that could not be activated until adulthood – and then only by the individual. Proving such an intervention safe may, however, be an insurmountable problem.

To be effective, a "human species protection" treaty would have to describe and authorize an oversight and enforcement mechanism. The body to enforce the treaty should be an international administrative agency with rule-making and adjudicatory authority. The rule-making process would develop and promulgate the basic rules for species-endangering experiments. Adjudicatory authority would be necessary to determine if and when applications by researchers to perform the potentially species-endangering experiments would be approved, and to determine if individuals had violated the terms of the treaty. The agency I envision would not have criminal jurisdiction but could refer cases to the International Criminal Court.

Drafting and enacting such a treaty, even beginning the process, is a nontrivial undertaking and will require a sustained effort. In the meantime, individual governments, corporations, and professional associations can declare potentially species-endangering experiments off-limits. Such action would take human rights and democratic principles seriously and recognize that a risk to the entire species is one only the species itself can agree to take. To be effective, the treaty itself must provide that no species-endangering techniques be used unless and until the international body approved its use in humans. This would change the burden of proof and put it on the would-be species-endangerers. It would thus apply the environmental movement's precautionary principle to species-endangering experimentation. That there is no such treaty and no such mechanism in place today signifies that the world community has not yet taken responsibility for its future. It is past time that we did. James Watson had it wrong. The truth is that at the beginning of the last millennium we *knew* that our future was in the stars; now, at the beginning of this millennium, we *think* that our future is in our genes.

We have a tendency simply to let science take us where it will. But science has no will, and human judgment is almost always necessary for any successful exploration of the unknown. Columbus's ships would have turned back but for his human courage and determination. And the first moon landing was almost a disaster because the computer overshot the planned landing site by four miles. Only the expert human piloting of Neil Armstrong was able to avert disaster. The first words from humans on the moon were not Armstrong's "one small step for man," but Buzz Aldrin's "Contact light! Okay, engine stop . . . descent engine command override off." It is time for us humans to take command of spaceship Earth and turn on science's engine override command. This should greatly increase the likelihood that our species will survive in good health to experience another millennium.

19

MINDSCAN: TRANSCENDING AND ENHANCING THE HUMAN BRAIN[1]

Susan Schneider

Suppose it is 2025 and, being a technophile, you purchase brain enhancements as they become readily available. First, you add a mobile internet connection to your retina, then you enhance your working memory by adding neural circuitry. You are now officially a cyborg. Now skip ahead to 2040. Through nanotechnological therapies and enhancements you are able to extend your life-span, and as the years progress, you continue to accumulate more far-reaching enhancements. By 2060, after several small but cumulatively profound alterations, you are a "posthuman." To quote philosopher Nick Bostrom, posthumans are possible future beings, "whose basic capacities so radically exceed those of present humans as to be no longer unambiguously human by our current standards" (Bostrom 2003). At this point, your intelligence is enhanced not just in terms of speed of mental processing; you are now able to make rich connections that you were not able to make before. Unenhanced humans, or "naturals," seem to you to be intellectually disabled – you have little in common with them – but as a transhumanist, you are supportive of their right to not enhance (Bostrom 2003; Garreau 2005; Kurzweil 2005).

It is now AD 2400. For years, worldwide technological developments, including your own enhancements, have been facilitated by superintelligent AI. A superintelligence is a creature with the capacity to radically outperform the best human brains in practically every field, including scientific creativity, general wisdom, and social skills. Indeed, as Bostrom explains, "creating superintelligence may be the last invention that humans will ever need to make, since superintelligences could themselves take care of further scientific and technological developments" (Bostrom 2003). Over time, the slow addition of better and better neural circuitry has left no real intellectual difference in kind between you and a superintelligent AI. The only real difference between you and an AI creature of standard design is one of origin – you were once a "natural." But you are now almost entirely engineered by technology. You are perhaps more aptly characterized as a member of a rather heterogeneous class of AI life forms (Kurzweil 2005).

So let me ask: should you enhance and if so, why? I have just given a very rough sketch of the kind of developmental trajectory that the transhumanist generally aspires to.[2] Transhumanism is a philosophical, cultural, and political movement that holds that the human species is now in a comparatively early phase and that its very evolution will be altered by developing technologies. Future humans will be very unlike their present-day incarnation in both physical and mental respects, and will in fact resemble certain persons depicted in science fiction stories. Transhumanists share the belief that an outcome in which humans have radically advanced intelligence, near immortality, deep friendships with AI creatures, and elective body characteristics is a very desirable end, both for one's own personal development and for the development of our species as a whole.

Despite its science fiction-like flavor, the future that transhumanism depicts is very possible: indeed, the beginning stages of this radical alteration may well lie in certain technological developments that either are already here (if not generally available), or are accepted by many in the relevant scientific fields as being on their way (Roco and Bainbridge 2002; Garreau 2005). In the face of these technological developments, transhumanists offer a progressive bioethics agenda of increasing public import. They also present a thought-provoking and controversial position in philosophy of cognitive science, applying insights about the computational nature of the mind to the topic of the nature of persons, developing a novel version of one popular theory of personal identity: the psychological continuity theory.

In this chapter I shall employ science fiction thought experiments to discuss what I take to be the most important philosophical element of the transhumanist picture – its unique perspective on the nature and development of persons. Persons are traditionally viewed as being an important moral category, being the bearers of rights, or at least deserving of consideration of their interests in a utilitarian calculus. And, as we shall see, considering the nature of persons through the lens of transhumanism involves pushing up against the boundaries of the very notion of personhood. For consider again the issue of enhancement. When one wonders whether to enhance in the radical ways the transhumanists advocate, one must ask, "Will this radically enhanced creature still be me?" If not, then, on the reasonable assumption that one key factor in a decision to enhance one-self is one's own personal development, even the most progressive technophile will likely regard the enhancement in question as undesirable, for when you choose to enhance in these radical ways, the enhancement does not really enhance *you*. As we shall soon discuss, this is a lesson that the main character in Hugo award winner Robert Sawyer's *Mindscan* learns the hard way. Hence, examining the enhancement issue from the vantage point of the metaphysical problem of personal identity will thereby present a serious challenge to transhumanism. Given their conception of the nature of a person, radical, and even mild, enhancements are risky, not clearly resulting in the preservation of one's original self. Indeed, I suspect that this is a pressing issue for any case for enhancement.

The Transhumanist Position

Transhumanism is by no means a monolithic ideology, but it does have an organization and an official declaration. The World Transhumanist Association is an international nonprofit organization that was founded in 1998 by philosophers Nick Bostrom and David Pearce. The main tenets of transhumanism were laid out in the Transhumanist Declaration (World Transhumanist Association 1998) and are reprinted below:

1. Humanity will be radically changed by technology in the future. We foresee the feasibility of redesigning the human condition, including such parameters as the inevitability of aging, limitations on human and artificial intellects, unchosen psychology, suffering, and our confinement to the planet earth.
2. Systematic research should be put into understanding these coming developments and their long-term consequences.
3. Transhumanists think that by being generally open and embracing of new technology we have a better chance of turning it to our advantage than if we try to ban or prohibit it.
4. Transhumanists advocate the moral right for those who so wish to use technology to extend their mental and physical (including reproductive) capacities and to improve their control over their own lives. We seek personal growth beyond our current biological limitations.
5. In planning for the future, it is mandatory to take into account the prospect of dramatic progress in technological capabilities. It would be tragic if the potential benefits failed to materialize because of technophobia and unnecessary prohibitions. On the other hand, it would also be tragic if intelligent life went extinct because of some disaster or war involving advanced technologies.
6. We need to create forums where people can rationally debate what needs to be done, and a social order where responsible decisions can be implemented.
7. Transhumanism advocates the well-being of all sentience (whether in artificial intellects, humans, posthumans, or non-human animals) and encompasses many principles of modern humanism. Transhumanism does not support any particular party, politician or political platform.

This document was followed by the much longer and extremely informative *The Transhumanist Frequently Asked Questions*, authored by Nick Bostrom, in consultation with dozens of leading transhumanists (Bostrom 2003).[3]

The Nature of Persons

Now let us consider some of the ideas expressed in the Declaration. Overall, central transhumanist texts have advanced a sort of trajectory for the personal development of a contemporary human, technology permitting (Kurzweil 1999, 2005; Bostrom 2003, 2005):[4]

21st century unenhanced human → significant "upgrading" with cognitive and other physical enhancements → posthuman status → "superintelligence"[5]

Recalling the chronology of enhancements I sketched at the beginning of this chapter, let us again ask: Should you embark upon this journey? Here, there are deep philosophical questions that have no easy answers.[6] For in order to understand whether you should enhance, you must first understand what you are to begin with. But what is a person? And, given your conception of a person, after such radical changes, would you yourself continue to exist, or would you have ceased to exist, having been replaced by someone else? If the latter is the case, why would you want to embark on the path to radical enhancement at all?

To make such a decision, one must understand the metaphysics of personal identity – that is, one must answer the question: What is it in virtue of which a particular self or person continues existing over time? A good place to begin is with the persistence of everyday objects over time. Consider the espresso machine in your favorite café. Suppose that five minutes have elapsed and the barista has turned the machine off. Imagine asking the barista if the machine is the same one that was there five minutes ago. She will likely tell you the answer is glaringly obvious – it is of course possible for one and the same machine to continue existing over time. This seems to be a reasonable case of persistence, even though at least one of the machine's properties has changed. On the other hand, if the machine disintegrated or melted, then the same machine would no longer exist. What remained wouldn't be an espresso machine at all, for that matter. So it seems that some changes cause a thing to cease to exist, while others do not. Philosophers call the characteristics that a thing must have as long as it exists "essential properties."

Now reconsider the transhumanist's trajectory for enhancement: for radical enhancement to be a worthwhile option for you, it has to represent a form of personal development. At bare minimum, even if enhancement brings such goodies as superhuman intelligence and radical life extension, it must not involve the elimination of any of your essential properties. For in that case, the sharper mind and fitter body would not be experienced by you – they would be experienced by someone else. Even if you would like to become superintelligent, knowingly embarking on a path that trades away one or more of your essential properties would be tantamount to suicide – that is, to your intentionally causing yourself to cease to exist. So before you enhance, you had better get a handle on what your essential properties are.

Transhumanists have grappled with this issue. Ray Kurzweil asks: "So who am I? Since I am constantly changing, am I just a pattern? What if someone copies that pattern? Am I the original and/or the copy? Perhaps I am this stuff here – that is, the both ordered and chaotic collection of molecules that make up my body and brain" (Kurzweil 2005: 383). Kurzweil is here referring to two theories at center stage in the age-old philosophical debate about the nature of persons. The leading theories include the following:

1. The soul theory: your essence is your soul or mind, understood as a non-physical entity distinct from your body.
2. The psychological continuity theory: you are essentially your memories and ability to reflect on yourself (Locke) and, in its most general form, you are your overall psychological configuration, what Kurzweil referred to as your "pattern."[7]
3. Materialism: you are essentially the material that you are made out of – what Kurzweil referred to as "the ordered and chaotic collection of molecules that make up my body and brain" (Kurzweil 2005: 383).
4. The no self view: the self is an illusion. The "I" is a grammatical fiction (Nietzsche). There are bundles of impressions but no underlying self (Hume). There is no survival because there is no person (Buddha).[8]

Upon reflection, each of these views has its own implications about whether one should enhance. If you hold (1), then your decision to enhance depends on whether you believe the enhanced body would retain the same soul or immaterial mind.[9] If you believe (3), then any enhancements must not change your material substrate. In contrast, according to (2), enhancements can alter the material substrate but must preserve your psychological configuration. Finally, (4) contrasts sharply with (1)–(3). If you hold (4), then the survival of the person is not an issue, for there is no person to begin with. You may strive to enhance nonetheless, to the extent that you find intrinsic value in adding more superintelligence to the universe – you might value life forms with higher forms of consciousness and wish that your "successor" should be such a creature.

Of all these views, (2) is currently the most influential, as philosopher Eric Olson underscores:

> Most philosophers believe that our identity through time consists in some sort of psychological continuity. You are, necessarily, that future being who in some sense inherits his mental features from you . . . the one who has the mental features he has then in large part because you have the mental features you have now. And you are that past being whose mental features you have inherited.

... So magnetic is this view that many feel entitled to assert it without argument. (Olson 2002)

I will now suggest that the Transhumanist adopts a novel version of the psychological continuity view; that is, they adopt a computational account of continuity. First, consider that transhumanists generally adopt a computational theory of the mind.

> The Computational Theory of Mind ("CTM"): The mind is essentially the program running on the hardware of the brain, that is, the algorithm that the brain implements, something in principle discoverable by cognitive science.[10]

Computational theories of mind can appeal to various computational theories of the format of thought: connectionism, dynamical systems theory (in its computational guise), the symbolic or language of thought approach, or some combination thereof. These differences will not matter to our discussion.

In philosophy of mind, computational theories of mind are positions about the nature of thoughts and minds; unfortunately, discussions of CTMs in mainstream philosophy of mind do not generally speak to the topic of personhood. (Perhaps this is because personal identity is a traditional topic in metaphysics, not philosophy of mind.) But upon reflection, if you uphold a CTM, then it is quite natural to adopt a computational theory of persons. For note that proponents of CTMs reject the soul theory, for they reject the idea that minds are non-physical entities. One might suspect that the transhumanist views materialism favorably, the view that holds that minds are basically physical or material in nature and that mental features, such as the thought that espresso has a wonderful aroma, are ultimately just physical features of brains. Transhumanists reject materialism, however. For instance, consider Kurzweil's remark:

> The specific set of particles that my body and brain comprise are in fact completely different from the atoms and molecules that I comprised only a short while ago. We know that most of our cells are turned over in a matter of weeks, and even our neurons, which persist as distinct cells for a relatively long time, nonetheless change all of their constituent molecules within a month. . . . I am rather like the pattern that water makes in a stream as it rushes past the rocks in its path. The actual molecules of water change every millisecond, but the pattern persists for hours or even years. (Kurzweil 2005: 383)

Later in his discussion, Kurzweil calls his view "Patternism" (ibid.: 386). Put in the language of cognitive science, as the transhumanist surely would, what is essential to you is your computational configuration – for example, what sensory systems/subsystems your brain has (e.g. early vision), the way that the basic sensory subsystems are integrated in the association areas, the neural circuitry making up your domain general reasoning, your attentional system, your memories, and so on – overall, the algorithm that your brain computes.[11]

Kurzweil's patternism is highly typical of transhumanism. For instance, consider the appeal to patternism in the following passage of *The Transhumanist Frequently Asked Questions*, which discusses the process of uploading:

> Uploading (sometimes called "downloading," "mind uploading" or "brain reconstruction") is the process of transferring an intellect from a biological brain to a computer. One way of doing this might be by first scanning the synaptic structure of a particular brain and then implementing the same computations in an electronic medium. . . . An upload could have a virtual (simulated) body giving the same sensations and the same possibilities for interaction as a non-simulated body. . . . And uploads wouldn't have to be confined to virtual reality: they could interact with people on the outside and even rent robot bodies in order to work in or explore physical reality. . . . Advantages of being an upload would include: Uploads would not be subject to biological senescence. Back-up copies of uploads could be created regularly so that you could be re-booted if something bad happened. (Thus your lifespan would potentially be as long as the universe's.) . . . Radical cognitive enhancements would likely be easier to implement in an upload than in an organic brain. . . . A widely accepted position is that you survive so long as certain information patterns are conserved, such as your memories, values, attitudes, and emotional dispositions . . . For the continuation of personhood, on this view, it matters little whether you are implemented on a silicon chip inside a computer or in that gray, cheesy lump inside your skull, assuming both implementations are conscious. (Bostrom 2003)

In sum, the transhumanist's cognitive science orientation introduces a new computationalist element to the traditional psychological continuity view of personhood. If plausible, this would be an important contribution to the age-old debate over the nature of persons. But is it correct? And further, is patternism even compatible with enhancement? In what follows, I suggest that patternism is deeply problematic. Furthermore, as things now stand, patternism is not even compatible with the enhancements that the transhumanists appeal to.

Robert Sawyer's *Mindscan* and the Reduplication Problem

Jake Sullivan has an inoperable brain tumor. Death could strike him at any moment. Luckily, Immortex has a new cure for aging and serious illness – a "mindscan." Immortex scientists will upload his brain configuration into a computer and "transfer" it into an android body that is designed using his own body as a template. Although imperfect, the android body has its advantages – as the transhumanist FAQ notes, once an individual is uploaded, a backup exists that can be downloaded if one has an accident. And it can be upgraded as new developments emerge. Jake will be immortal.

Sullivan enthusiastically signs numerous legal agreements. He is told that, upon uploading, his possessions will be transferred to the android, who will be the new bearer of his consciousness. Sullivan's original copy, which will die soon anyway, will live out the remainder of his life on "High Eden," an Immortex colony on the moon. Although stripped of his legal identity, the original copy will be comfortable there, socializing with the other originals who are also still confined to biological senescence.

While lying in the scanning tube a few seconds before the scan, Jake reflects:

> I was looking forward to my new existence. Quantity of life didn't matter that much to me – but quality! And to have time – not only years spreading out into the future, but time in each day. Uploads, after all, didn't have to sleep, so not only did we get all those extra years, we got one-third more productive time. The future was at hand. Creating another me. Mindscan.

But then, a few seconds later:

> "All right, Mr. Sullivan, you can come out now." It was Dr. Killian's voice, with its Jamaican lilt.
> My heart sank. No . . .
> "Mr. Sullivan? We've finished the scanning. If you'll press the red button . . ."
> It hit me like a ton of bricks, like a tidal wave of blood. No! I should be somewhere else, but I wasn't. . . .
> I reflexively brought up my hands, patting my chest, feeling the softness of it, feeling it raise and fall. Jesus Christ!

> I shook my head. "You just scanned my consciousness, making a duplicate of my mind, right?" My voice was sneering. "And since I'm aware of things after you finished the scanning, that means I – this version – isn't that copy. The copy doesn't have to worry about becoming a vegetable anymore. It's free. Finally and at last, it's free of everything that's been hanging over my head for the last twenty-seven years. We've diverged now, and the cured me has started down its path. But this me is still doomed. . . ." (Sawyer 2005: 44–5)

Sawyer's novel is a *reductio ad absurdum* of the patternist conception of the person. For all that patternism says is that as long as person A has the same computational configuration as person B, A and B are the same person. Indeed, Sugiyama, the person selling the mindscan to Jake, had espoused a form of patternism (Sawyer 2005: 18). Jake's unfortunate experience can be put into the form of a challenge to patternism, which we shall call the "reduplication problem": only one person can really be Jake Sullivan, as Sullivan reluctantly found out. But according to patternism, both creatures are Jake Sullivan – for they share the very same psychological configuration. But, as Jake learned, while the creature created by the mindscan process may be a person, it is not the *very same* person as Jake. It is just another person with an artificial brain and body configured like the original. Hence, having a particular type of pattern cannot be *sufficient* for personal identity. Indeed, the problem is illustrated to epic proportions later in the book when numerous copies of Sullivan are made, all believing they are the original! Ethical and legal problems abound.

A Response to the Reduplication Problem

Perhaps there is a way around this objection. As noted, the reduplication problem suggests that sameness of pattern is not sufficient for sameness of person. However, consider that there seems to be something right about patternism – for as Kurzweil notes, our cells change continually; it is only the organizational pattern that carries on. *Given this, materialism either leaves us with a view of persons in which persons do not persist, or it covertly depends on the idea that we consist in some sort of pattern of organization and is not really a materialist theory at all.* Unless one has a religious conception of the person, and adopts the soul theory, patternism seems inevitable, at least insofar as one believes there is such a thing as a person to begin with. In light of this, perhaps one should react to the reduplication case in the following way: one's pattern is *essential* to one's self despite not being *sufficient for* a complete account of one's identity. Perhaps there is an additional essential property which, together with one's pattern, yields a complete theory of personal identity. But what could the missing ingredient be? Intuitively, it must be a requirement that serves to rule out mindscans and, more generally, any cases in which the mind is "uploaded". For any sort of uploading case will give rise to a reduplication problem, for uploaded minds can in principle be downloaded again and again.

Now, think about your own existence in space and time. When you go out to get the mail, you move from one spatial location to another, tracing a path in space. A spacetime diagram can help us visualize the path one takes throughout one's life. Collapsing the three spatial dimensions into one (the vertical axis) and taking the horizontal axis to signify time, consider the following typical trajectory (Figure 19.1). Notice that the figure carved out looks like a worm; you, like all physical objects, carve out a sort of "spacetime worm" over the course of your existence.

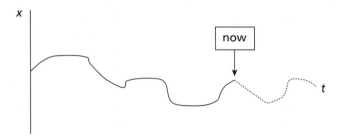

Figure 19.1

This, at least, is the kind of path that "normals" – those who are neither post-humans nor superintelligences – carve out. But now consider what happened during the mindscan. Again, according to patternism, there would be two of the very same person. The copy's spacetime diagram would look like the following:

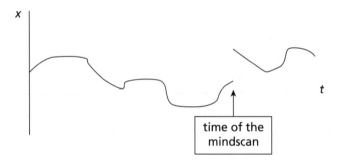

Figure 19.2

This is bizarre. It appears that Jake Sullivan exists for 42 years, has a scan, and then somehow instantaneously moves to a different location in space and lives out the rest of his life! This is radically unlike normal survival. This alerts us that something is wrong with pure patternism: it lacks a requirement for spatiotemporal continuity.

This additional requirement would seem to solve the reduplication problem. For consider the day of the mindscan. Jake went into the laboratory and had a scan; then he left the laboratory and went directly into a spaceship and flew to Mars. It is this man – the one who traces a continuous trajectory through space and time – who is in fact the true Jake Sullivan.

This response to the reduplication problem only goes so far, however. For consider Sugiyama, who, when selling his mindscan product, ventured a patternist pitch. If Sugiyama had espoused patternism together with a spatiotemporal continuity clause, few would have signed up for the scan! For that extra ingredient would rule out a mindscan, or any kind of uploading for that matter, as a form of survival. Only those wishing to have a mere replacement for themselves would sign up. There is a general lesson here for the transhumanist: if one opts for patternism, enhancements like uploading to avoid death or to facilitate further enhancements are not really "enhancements" but forms of suicide. *The transhumanist should sober up and not offer such procedures as enhancements.* When it comes to enhancement, there are intrinsic limits to what technology can deliver. (Ironically, the proponent of the soul theory is in better shape here. For perhaps the soul does teleport. Who knows?)

Let me sum up the dialectical situation thus far: we have just discarded the original form of patternism as false. If the transhumanist would like to uphold patternism, then she should add the spatiotemporal continuity clause. And importantly, she will need to modify her views on what sorts of enhancements are compatible with survival. Let us call this new position "modified patternism." As we shall now see, although modified patternism is a clear improvement, it requires far more spelling out in at least the following two dimensions.

Two Issues that Modified Patternism Needs to Address

(1) Consider: if you are your pattern, what if your pattern shifts? Do you die? In order for the transhumanist to justify the sort of enhancements needed to become a posthuman or a superintelligent being, she will need to say precisely what a "pattern" is, and when enhancements do and do not constitute a continuation of the pattern. The extreme cases seem clear – for instance, as discussed, mindscans are ruled out by the spatiotemporal continuity clause. And further, because patternism is a psychological continuity view, the patternist will want to say that a memory erasure process that erased one's childhood is an unacceptable alteration of one's pattern, removing too many of one's memories. On the other hand, mere everyday cellular maintenance by nanobots to overcome the slow effects of aging would, according to proponents of this view, not affect the identity of the person.[12] But the middle range cases are unclear. Maybe deleting a few bad chess-playing habits is kosher, but what about erasing all memory of some personal relationship, as in the film *Eternal Sunshine of the Spotless Mind*? The path to superintelligence may very well be a path through middle range enhancements. So again, what is needed is a clear conception of what a pattern is, and what changes in pattern are acceptable and why. Without a firm handle on this issue, the transhumanist developmental trajectory is perhaps the technophile's alluring path to suicide.

This problem looks hard to solve in a way that is compatible with preserving the very idea that we can be identical over time to some previous or future self. For determining a boundary point seems a rather arbitrary exercise in which once a boundary is selected, an example is provided suggesting the boundary should be pushed outward, ad nauseum. On the other hand, there is something insightful about the view that over time one gradually becomes less and less like one's earlier self. But appreciate this point too long and it may lead to a dark place: for if one finds patternism compelling to begin with, how is it that one truly persists over time, from the point of infancy until maturity, during which time there are often major changes in one's memories, personality, and so on? Indeed, even a series of gradual changes cumulatively amounts to an individual, B, who is greatly altered from her childhood self, A. Why is there really a relation of identity that holds between A and B, instead of an ancestral relation: *A's being the ancestor of B*? Our second issue relates to the issue of gradual, but cumulatively significant, change as well.

(2) Suppose that it is 2050, and people are getting gradual neural regeneration procedures as they sleep. During their nightly slumbers, nanobots slowly import nanoscale materials that are computationally identical to the original materials. The nanobots then gradually remove the old materials, setting them in a small container beside the person's bed. By itself, this process is unproblematic for modified patternism. But now suppose there is an optional upgrade to the regeneration service for those who would like to make a backup copy of their brains. If one opts for this procedure, then, during the nightly process, the nanobots take the replaced materials out of the dish and place them inside a cryogenically frozen biological brain. At the end of the slow process the materials in the frozen brain have been entirely replaced by the person's original neurons. Now, suppose you choose to undergo this procedure alongside your nightly regeneration. Over time, this second brain comes to be composed of the very same material as your brain originally was, configured in precisely the same manner. Which one is you? The original brain, which now has entirely different neurons, or the one with all your original neurons?[13]

The modified patternist has this to say about the neural regeneration case: you are the creature with the brain with entirely different matter, as this creature traces a continuous path through spacetime. But now, things go awry: why is spatiotemporal continuity supposed to outweigh other factors, like being composed of the original material substrate? Here, to be blunt, my intuitions crap out. We'd like to find a solid justification for selecting one option above the other. Until the transhumanist provides a solid justification for her position, it is best to regard forms of enhancement that involve the rapid or even gradual replacement of parts of one's brain as being risky.

Conclusion

I hope all this has convinced you that if the transhumanist maintains patternism there are some serious issues that require working out. Indeed, as *The Transhumanist*

Frequently Asked Questions indicates, the development of radical enhancements, such as brain–machine interfaces, cryogenic freezing for life extension, and uploading to avoid death or simply to facilitate enhancement, are key enhancements invoked by the transhumanist view of the development of the person. Now, all of these enhancements sound strangely like the thought experiments philosophers have used for years as problem cases for various theories of the nature of persons, so it is not surprising that deep problems emerge. Herein, I've argued that the Mindscan example suggests that one should not upload and that the patternist needs to modify her theory to rule out such cases. Even with this modification in hand, however, transhumanism still requires a detailed account of what constitutes a break in a pattern versus a mere continuation of it. Without progress on this issue, it will not be clear if medium range enhancements, such as erasing childhood memories or adding neural circuitry to make oneself smarter, are safe. Finally, the nanobot case warns against even mild enhancements. Given all this, it is fair to say that the transhumanist currently cannot support her case for enhancement. Indeed, *The Transhumanist Frequently Asked Questions* notes that transhumanists are keenly aware that this issue has been neglected:

> While the concept of a soul is not used much in a naturalistic philosophy such as transhumanism, many transhumanists do take an interest in the related problems concerning personal identity (Parfit 1984) and consciousness (Churchland 1988). These problems are being intensely studied by contemporary analytic philosophers, and although some progress has been made, e.g. in Derek Parfit's work on personal identity, they have still not been resolved to general satisfaction. (Bostrom 2003: section 5.4)

Our discussion also raises some general lessons for all parties involved in the enhancement debate. For when one considers the enhancement debate through the lens of the metaphysics of personhood, new dimensions of the debate are appreciated. The literature on the nature of persons is extraordinarily rich, raising intriguing problems for commonly accepted views of the nature of persons that underlie positions on enhancement. When one defends or rejects a given enhancement, it is important to determine whether one's stance on the enhancement in question is truly supported by, or even compatible with, one's position on the nature of persons. Further, the topic of the nature of persons is of clear relevance to the related topics of human nature and human dignity, issues that are currently key points of controversy in debates over enhancement (see, e.g., Bostrom 2008; Fukuyama 2002).

Perhaps, alternately, you grow weary of all this metaphysics. You may suspect that social conventions concerning what we commonly consider to be persons are all we have because metaphysical theorizing will never conclusively resolve what persons are. However, as unwieldy as metaphysical issues are, it seems that not all conventions are worthy of acceptance, so one needs a manner of determining which conventions should play an important role in the enhancement debate and which ones should not. And it is hard to accomplish this without getting clear on one's conception of persons. Further, it is difficult to avoid at least implicitly relying on a conception of persons when reflecting on the case for and against enhancement. For what is it that ultimately grounds your decision to enhance or not to enhance, if not that it will somehow improve you? Are you perhaps merely planning for the well-being of your successor?

Notes

1. This piece is expanded and modified from an earlier piece, "Future Minds: Cognitive Enhancement, Transhumanism, and the Nature of Persons", which appeared in the *Penn Center Guide to Bioethics*, Arthur L. Caplan, Autumn Fiester, and Vardit Radvisky (eds.), Springer, 2009. Thanks very much to Ted Sider and Michael Huemer for their helpful comments.

2. Julian Huxley apparently coined the term *transhumanism* in 1957, when he wrote that in the near future "the human species will be on the threshold of a new kind of existence, as different from ours as ours is from that of Peking man" (Huxley 1957: 13–17).

3. Bostrom is a philosopher at Oxford University who now directs the transhumanist-oriented Future of Humanity Institute there. In addition to these two documents, there are a number of excellent philosophical and sociological works that articulate key elements of the transhumanist perspective (e.g. Bostrom 2005; Hughes 2004; Kurzweil 1999, 2005). For extensive Web resources on transhumanism, see Nick Bostrom's homepage, Ray Kurzweil's newsgroup (KurzweilAI.net), the Institute for Ethics and Emerging Technologies homepage, and the World Transhumanist Association homepage.

4. It should be noted that transhumanism by no means endorses every sort of enhancement. For example, Nick Bostrom rejects positional enhancements (enhancements primarily employed to increase one's social position) yet argues for enhancements that could allow humans to develop ways of exploring "the larger space of possible modes of being" (2005: 11).

5. There are many nuances to this rough trajectory. For instance, some transhumanists believe that the move from unenhanced human intelligence to superintelligence will be extremely rapid because we are approaching a singularity, a point at which the creation of superhuman intelligence will result in massive changes in a very short period (e.g. 30 years) (Bostrom 1998; Kurzweil 1999, 2005; Vinge 1993). Other transhumanists hold that technological changes will not be so sudden. These discussions often debate the reliability of Moore's Law (Moore 1965). Another key issue is whether a transition to superintelligence will really occur because the upcoming technological developments involve grave risk. The risks of biotechnology and AI concern transhumanists, progressive bioethicists more generally, as well as bioconservatives (Annis 2000; Bostrom 2002; Garreau 2005; Joy 2000).

6. For mainstream anti-enhancement positions on this question see, e.g., Fukuyama (2002), Kass et al. (2003), and Annas (2000).

7. Because our discussion is introductory, I will not delve into different versions of psychological continuity theory. One could, for instance, appeal to (a): the idea that memories are essential to a person. Alternatively, one could adopt (b), one's overall psychological configuration is essential, including one's memories. Herein, I shall work with one version of this latter conception – one that is inspired by cognitive science – although many of the criticisms of this view will apply to (a) and other versions of (b) as well. For some different versions see chapter 27 of John Locke's 1694 *Essay Concerning Human Understanding* (note that this chapter first appears in the second edition; it is also reprinted as "Of Identity and Diversity" in Perry 1975). See also the essays by Anthony Quinton and Paul Grice, both of which are reprinted in Perry (1975).

8. Sociologist James Hughes holds a transhumanist version of the no self view. (See the Institute for Ethics and Emerging Technology's "Cyborg Buddha" project at http://ieet.org/index.php/IEET/cyborgbuddha.) For helpful surveys of these four positions, see Eric Olson's chapter in this volume (Chapter 7), and Conee and Sider (2005).

9. It should be noted that although a number of bioconservatives seem to uphold the soul theory, the soul theory is not, in and of itself, an anti-enhancement position. For why can't one's soul or immaterial mind inhere in the same body even after radical enhancement?

10. For discussion of computational theories, see Block (Chapter 14 in this volume) and Churchland (1996).

11. Readers familiar with philosophy of mind may suggest that the transhumanist could accept one version of materialism, namely, "token materialism." However, I suspect that it is not really a coherent form of materialism. Token materialism holds that every instance of a mental property is identical to some instance of a physical property. But can the instances really be *identical* if the properties themselves belong to different types? The distinct property types are instead coinstantiated by the same particular.

12. Or at least, this is what the patternist would *like* to say. The example in the paragraph after next will in fact question whether she can truly say this.

13. This is a science fiction variant of the well-known Ship of Theseus case. It first appears in print in Plutarch (*Vita Thesei*, 22–3).

References

Annas, G. J. (2000). The man on the moon, immortality, and other millennial myths: The prospects and perils of human genetic engineering. *Emory Law Journal* 49 (3): 753–82.

Bostrom, N. (1998). How long before superintelligence? *International Journal of Futures Studies* 2. Available at http://www.nickbostrom.com/superintelligence.html (retrieved Dec. 20, 2008).

Bostrom, N. (2003). *The Transhumanist Frequently Asked Questions*: v 2.1. World Transhumanist Association. Retrieved from http://transhumanism.org/index.php/WTA/faq/.

Bostrom, N. (2005). History of Transhumanist Thought. *Journal of Evolution and Technology*, 14 (1).

Bostrom, N. (2008). Dignity and enhancement. In The President's Council on Bioethics, *Human Dignity and Bioethics: Essays Commissioned by the President's Council on Bioethics* (Washington, DC: U.S. Government Printing Office).

Conee, E. and Sider, T. (2005). *Riddles of Existence: A Guided Tour of Metaphysics*. Oxford: Oxford University Press.

Churchland, P. (1988). *Matter and consciousness*. Cambridge, MA: MIT Press.

Churchland, P. (1996). *Engine of reason, seat of the soul*. Cambridge, MA: MIT Press.

Fukuyama, F. (2002). *Our posthuman future: Consequences of the biotechnology revolution*. New York Farrar, Straus and Giroux.

Garreau, J. (2005). *Radical evolution: The promise and peril of enhancing our minds, our bodies – and what it means to be human*. New York: Doubleday.

Hughes, J. (2004), *Citizen cyborg: Why democratic societies must respond to the redesigned human of the future*. Cambridge, MA: Westview Press.

Huxley, J. (1957). *New bottles for new wine*. London: Chatto & Windus.

Joy, B. (2000). Why the future doesn't need us. *Wired*, 8: 238–46.

Kurzweil, R. (1999). *The age of spiritual machines: When computers exceed human intelligence*. New York: Viking.

Kurzweil, R. (2005). *The singularity is near: When humans transcend biology*. New York: Viking.

Moore, G. (1965). Cramming more components into integrated circuits. *Electronics*, 38 (8): 11–17. Retrieved from ftp://download.intel.com/research/silicon/moorespaper.pdf.

Parfit, D. (1984). *Reasons and persons*. Oxford: Oxford University Press.

Perry, J. (1975). *Personal identity*, Berkeley: University of California Press.

Roco, M. C., and Bainbridge, W. S. (eds.) (2002). *Converging technologies for improved human performance: Nanotechnology, biotechnology, information technology and cognitive science*. Arlington, VA: National Science Foundation/Department of Commerce.

Sawyer, R. (2005). *Mindscan*. New York: Tor.

Vinge, V. (1993). The coming technological singularity: How to survive in the post-human era. *NASA Technical Reports*, Lewis Research Center, Vision 21: Interdisciplinary Science and Engineering in the Era of Cyberspace, pp. 11–21.

World Transhumanist Association (1998). *Transhumanist Declaration*. Retrieved from http://www.transhumanism.org/index.php/WTA/declaration/.

20

THE DOOMSDAY ARGUMENT

John Leslie

In *The End of the World* (subtitled "the science and ethics of human extinction") I discussed a "doomsday argument" first stated by the mathematician Brandon Carter. Just as it could seem absurd to view our intelligent species as *the very first* of many million that were destined to appear in our universe, so also it could seem preposterous to fancy that you and I are in a human race almost sure to spread right through its galaxy, a process that could well be completed in under a million years if germ warfare or other perils failed to kill everyone before the process started. It could seem preposterous because, were the human race to spread right through its galaxy, then you and I would presumably have been among the earliest millionth, and very possibly the earliest billionth, of all humans who would ever have lived. It might be far more sensible to view humankind as quite likely to become extinct shortly unless we take great care.

Carter's doomsday argument is sometimes challenged as follows. Suppose there were vastly many intelligent extraterrestrials scattered through space and time. Wouldn't an observer's chances of being *a human living around* AD 2000 be virtually unaffected by whether most humans lived at much later dates, thanks to the human race spreading right through its galaxy? Unfortunately the argument survives the challenge. The crucial point is that we ought (until we find enough contrary evidence) to try to see ourselves as "fairly ordinary" inside the various classes into which we fall – bearing in mind, naturally, that in some cases there might be tradeoffs to be made because being more ordinary inside one class might involve being less ordinary inside another. Now, you and I fall not only into the class of *observers* but also into that of *human observers*. And a human observer, finding that the year is near AD 2000, can picture himself or herself as *fairly ordinary among human observers* through supposing that the human race *isn't* destined to spread right through its galaxy. Were humankind to become extinct shortly, then, because of the recent population explosion, something approaching a tenth of all humans would have lived when you and I did.

Notice that even if humans were statistically very unusual among all observers scattered through space and time, observers falling into vastly many different species, there might still be nothing too odd in being a human rather than a member of some other intelligent species. Suppose, for instance, there were a trillion intelligent species all of exactly the same population size. Being a human would then put you in the one-in-a-trillion bracket; but so would being a Martian or just anything else, and therefore it would be no oddity. In contrast, it would be strange to be a very unusually early member of whatever intelligent species you found yourself in.

21

ASIMOV'S "THREE LAWS OF ROBOTICS" AND MACHINE METAETHICS*

Susan Leigh Anderson

Introduction

Once people understand that Machine Ethics has to do with how intelligent machines, rather than human beings, should behave, they often maintain that Isaac Asimov has already given us an ideal set of rules for such machines. They have in mind Asimov's "Three Laws of Robotics":

1. A robot may not injure a human being, or, through inaction, allow a human being to come to harm.
2. A robot must obey the orders given it by human beings except where such orders would conflict with the First Law.
3. A robot must protect its own existence as long as such protection does not conflict with the First or Second Law. (Asimov 1984)

I shall argue that, in "The Bicentennial Man" (Asimov 1984), Asimov rejected his own Three Laws as a proper basis for Machine Ethics. He believed that a robot with the characteristics possessed by Andrew, the robot hero of the story, should not be required to be a slave to human beings as the Three Laws dictate. He, further, provided an explanation for why humans feel the need to treat intelligent robots as slaves, an explanation that shows a weakness in human beings that makes it difficult for them to be ethical paragons. Because of this weakness, it seems likely that machines like Andrew could be more ethical than most human beings. "The Bicentennial Man" gives us hope that, not only can intelligent machines be taught to behave in an ethical fashion, but they might be able to lead human beings to behave more ethically as well.

To be more specific, I shall use "The Bicentennial Man" as a springboard for a discussion of Machine Metaethics, leading to the following conclusions: (1) A machine could follow ethical principles better than most human beings and so, at the very least, is well suited to be an ethical advisor for humans. (2) Developing a program that enables a machine to act as an ethical advisor for human beings, arguably a first step in the Machine Ethics project, will not require that we consider the status of intelligent machines; but if machines are to follow ethical principles themselves, the eventual goal of the Machine Ethics project, it is essential that we determine their status, which will not be easy to do. (3) An intelligent robot like Andrew satisfies most, if not all, of the requirements philosophers have proposed for a being/entity to have moral standing/rights, making the Three Laws immoral. (4) Even if the machines that are actually developed fall short of being like Andrew and should probably not be considered to have moral standing/rights, it is still problematic for humans to program them to follow the Three Laws of Robotics. From (3) and (4), we can conclude that (5) whatever the status of the machines that are developed, Asimov's Three Laws of Robotics will be an unsatisfactory basis for Machine Ethics.

"The Bicentennial Man"

Isaac Asimov's "The Bicentennial Man" was originally commissioned to be part of a volume of stories written by well-known authors to commemorate the United States' bicentennial.[1] Although the project didn't come to fruition, Asimov ended up with a particularly powerful work of philosophical science fiction as a result of the challenge he'd been given. It's important that we know the background for writing the story because "The Bicentennial Man" is simultaneously a story about the history of the United States and a vehicle for Asimov to present his view of how intelligent robots should be treated and be required to act.

"The Bicentennial Man" begins with the Three Laws of Robotics. The story that follows is told from the point of view of Andrew, an early, experimental robot – intended to be a servant in the Martin household – who was programmed to obey the Three Laws. Andrew was given his human name by the youngest daughter in the family, Little Miss, for whom he carved a beautiful pendant out of wood. This led to the realization that Andrew had unique talents that the Martins encouraged him to develop, giving him books to read on furniture design.

Little Miss, his champion during her lifetime, helped Andrew to fight first for his right to receive money from his creations and then for the freedom he desired. A judge finally did grant Andrew his freedom, despite the opposing attorney's arguing that, "The word *freedom* has no meaning when applied to a robot. Only a human being can be free." In his decision, the judge maintained that, "There is no right to deny freedom to any object with a mind advanced enough to grasp the concept and desire the state."

Andrew continued to live on the Martins' property in a small house that had been built for him, still following the Three Laws, despite having been granted his freedom. He started wearing clothes, so that he would not be so different from human beings and later he had his body replaced with an android one for the same reason. Andrew wanted to be accepted as a human being.

In one particularly powerful incident, shortly after he started wearing clothes, Andrew encountered some human bullies while on his way to the library. They ordered him to take off his clothes and then dismantle himself. He had to obey humans because of the Second Law and he could not defend himself without harming the bullies, which would have been a violation of the First Law. He was saved just in time by Little Miss's son, who informed him that humans have an irrational fear of an intelligent, unpredictable, autonomous robot, that can exist longer than a human being – even one programmed with the Three Laws – and that was why they wanted to destroy him.

In a last ditch attempt towards being accepted as a human being, Andrew arranged that his "positronic" brain would slowly cease to function, just like a human brain. He maintained that it didn't violate the Third Law, since his "aspirations and desires" were more important to his life than "the death of his body." This last sacrifice Andrew made, "accept[ing] even death to be human," finally allowed him to be accepted as a human being. He died two hundred years after he was made and was declared to be "the Bicentennial Man." In his last words, whispering the name "Little Miss," Andrew acknowledged the one human being who accepted and appreciated him from the beginning.

Clearly, the story is meant to remind Americans of their history, that particular groups, especially African Americans, have had to fight for their freedom and to be fully accepted by other human beings.[2] It was wrong that African Americans were forced to act as slaves for white persons and they suffered many indignities, and worse, that were comparable to what the bullies inflicted upon Andrew. And, as in the case of the society in which Andrew functioned that had an irrational fear of robots, there were irrational beliefs about blacks, leading to their mistreatment, among whites in earlier stages of our history. Unfortunately, despite Aristotle's claim that "man is the rational animal," human beings are prone to behaving in an irrational fashion when their interests are threatened and they must deal with beings/entities they perceive as being different from themselves.

In the history of the United States, gradually more and more beings have been granted the same rights that others possessed and we've become a more ethical society as a result. Ethicists are currently struggling with the question of whether at least some higher order animals should have rights, and the status of human fetuses has been debated as well. On the horizon looms the question of whether intelligent machines should have moral standing.

Asimov has made an excellent case for the view that certain types of intelligent machines, ones like Andrew, should be given rights and should not be required to act as slaves for humans. By the end of the story, we see how wrong it is that Andrew has been forced to follow the Three Laws. Yet we are still left with something positive, on reflection, about Andrew's having been programmed to follow moral principles. They may not have been the *correct* principles, since they did not acknowledge rights Andrew should have had, but Andrew was a far more moral entity than most of the human beings he encountered. (Most of the human beings in "The Bicentennial Man" were prone to being carried away by irrational emotions, particularly irrational fears, so they did not behave as rationally as Andrew did.) If we can just find the *right* set of ethical principles for them to follow, intelligent machines could very well show human beings how to behave more ethically.

Machine Metaethics

Machine Metaethics examines the field of Machine Ethics. It talks *about* the field, rather than doing work in it. Examples of issues that fall within Machine Metaethics are: What is the ultimate goal of Machine Ethics? What does it mean to add an ethical dimension to machines? Is Ethics computable? Is there a single correct ethical theory that we should try to implement? Should we expect the ethical theory we implement to be complete, that is, should we expect it to tell the machine how to act in any ethical dilemma in which it might find itself? Is it necessary to determine the moral status of the machine itself, if it is to follow ethical principles?

The ultimate goal of Machine Ethics, I believe, is to create a machine that follows an ideal ethical principle or set of ethical principles, that is to say, it is guided by this principle or these principles in the decisions it makes about possible courses of action it could take. We can say, more simply, that this involves "adding an ethical dimension" to the machine.

It might be thought that adding an ethical dimension to a machine is ambiguous. It could mean either (a) in designing the machine, building in limitations to its behavior according to an ideal ethical principle or principles *that are followed by the human designer*, or (b) giving *the machine* ideal ethical principles, or some examples of ethical dilemmas together with correct answers and a learning procedure from which it can abstract ideal ethical principles, so that *it* can use the principle(s) in guiding its own actions. In the first case, it is the human being who is following ethical principles and concerned about harm that can come from machine behavior. This falls within the area of *computer* ethics, rather than machine ethics. In the second case, on the other hand, the machine itself is reasoning on ethical matters, which is the ultimate goal of *machine* ethics.[3] An indication that this approach is being adopted is that the machine can make a judgment in an ethical dilemma that it has not previously been presented with.[4]

Central to the Machine Ethics project is the belief, or hope, that Ethics can be made computable. Some people working on Machine Ethics have started tackling the challenge of making ethics computable by creating programs that enable machines to act as ethical advisors to human beings, believing that this is a good first step towards the eventual goal of developing machines that can follow ethical principles themselves (Anderson, Anderson and Armen 2005).[5] Four pragmatic reasons could be given for beginning this way: 1. One could start by designing an advisor that gives guidance to a select group of persons in a finite number of circumstances, thus reducing the scope of the assignment.[6] 2. Machines that just advise human beings would probably be more easily accepted by the general public than machines that try to behave ethically themselves. In the first case, it is human beings who will make ethical decisions by deciding whether to follow the recommendations of the machine, preserving the idea that *only human beings will be moral agents*. The next step in the Machine Ethics project is likely to be more contentious: creating *machines that are autonomous moral agents*. 3. A big problem for AI in general, and so for this project too, is how to get needed data, in this case the information from which ethical judgments can be made. With an ethical advisor, human beings can be prompted to supply the needed data. 4. Ethical theory has not advanced to the point where there is agreement, even by ethical experts, on the correct answer for all ethical dilemmas. An advisor can recognize this fact, passing difficult decisions that have to be made in order to act onto the human user. An autonomous machine that's expected to be moral, on the other hand, would either not be able to act in such a situation or would decide arbitrarily. Both solutions seem unsatisfactory.

This last reason is cause for concern for the entire Machine Ethics project. It might be thought that for Ethics to be computable, we must have a theory that tells which action is morally right in every ethical dilemma. There are two parts to this view: 1. We must know which is the correct ethical theory, according to which we will make our computations; and 2. This theory must be *complete*, that is, it must tell us how to act in any ethical dilemma that might be encountered.

One could try to avoid making a judgment about which is the correct ethical theory (rejecting 1) by simply trying to implement *any* ethical theory that has been proposed (e.g. Hedonistic Act Utilitarianism or Kant's theory), making no claim that it is necessarily the *best* theory, the one that ought to be followed. Machine Ethics then becomes just an exercise in what can be computed. But, of course, this is surely not particularly worthwhile, unless one is trying to figure out an approach to programming ethics in general by practicing on the theory that is chosen.

Ultimately one has to decide that a particular ethical theory, or at least an approach to ethical theory, is correct. Like W.D. Ross, I believe that the simple, single absolute duty theories that have been proposed are all deficient.[7] Ethics is more complicated than that, which is why it is easy to devise a counter-example to any of these theories. There is an advantage to the multiple *prima facie* duties[8] approach that Ross adopted, which better captures conflicts that often arise in ethical decision-making: The duties can be amended, and new duties added if needed, to explain the intuitions of ethical experts about particular cases. Of course, the main problem with the multiple *prima facie* duties approach is that there is no decision procedure when the duties conflict, which often happens. It seems possible, though, that a decision procedure could be learned by generalizing from intuitions about correct answers in particular cases.

Does the ethical theory, or approach to ethical theory, that is chosen have to be complete? Should those working on Machine Ethics expect this to be the case? My answer is: probably not. The implementation of Ethics can't be more complete than is accepted ethical theory. Completeness is an ideal for which to strive, but it may not be possible at this time. There are still a number of ethical dilemmas where even experts are not in agreement as to what is the right action.[9]

Many non-ethicists believe that this admission offers support for the metaethical theory known as Ethical Relativism. Ethical Relativism is the view that when there is disagreement over whether a particular action is right or wrong, both sides are correct. According to this view, there is no single correct ethical theory. Ethics is relative to either individuals (subjectivism) or to societies (cultural relativism). Most ethicists reject this view because it entails that we cannot criticize the actions of others, no matter how heinous. We also cannot say that some people are more moral than others or speak of moral improvement, as I did earlier when I said that the United States has become a more ethical society by granting rights to blacks (and women as well).

There certainly do seem to be actions that ethical experts (and most of us) believe are absolutely wrong (e.g. that torturing a baby and slavery are wrong). Ethicists are comfortable with the idea that one may not have answers for *all* ethical dilemmas at the present time, and even that some of the views we now hold we may decide to reject in the future. Most ethicists believe, however, that *in principle* there are correct answers to all *ethical* dilemmas,[10] as opposed to questions that are just matters of taste (deciding what shirt to wear, for example).

Someone working in the area of Machine Ethics, then, would be wise to allow for gray areas where, perhaps, one should not expect answers at this time, and even allow for the possibility that parts of the theory being implemented may need to be revised. *Consistency* (that one should not contradict oneself), however, is important, as it's essential to rationality. Any inconsistency that arises should be cause for concern and for rethinking either the theory itself, or the way that it is implemented.

One can't emphasize the importance of consistency enough. This is where machine implementation of an ethical theory is likely to be far superior to the average human being's attempt at following the theory. A machine is capable of rigorously following a logically consistent principle, or set of principles, whereas most human beings easily abandon principles and the requirement of consistency that's the hallmark of being rational, because they get carried away by their emotions. Early on in his fight to be accepted by human beings, Andrew asked a congresswoman whether it was likely that members of the legislature would change their minds about rejecting him as a human being. The response he got was this: "We've changed all that are amenable to reason. The rest – the majority – cannot be moved from their emotional antipathies." Andrew then said, "Emotional antipathy is not a valid reason for voting one way or the other." He was right, of course, and that's why human beings could benefit from interacting with a machine that spells out the consequences of consistently following particular ethical principles.

Let us return now to the question of whether it is a good idea to try to create an ethical advisor before attempting to create a machine that behaves ethically itself. An even better reason than the pragmatic ones given earlier can be given for the field of Machine Ethics to proceed in this manner: One does not have to make a judgment about the status of the machine itself if it is just acting as an advisor to human beings, whereas one does have to make such a judgment if the machine is given moral principles to follow in guiding its own behavior. Since making this judgment will be particularly difficult, it would be wise to begin with the project that does not require this. Let me explain.

If the machine is simply advising human beings as to how to act in ethical dilemmas, where such dilemmas involve the proper treatment of other human beings (as is the case with classical ethical dilemmas), it is assumed that either a) the advisor will be concerned with ethical dilemmas that only involve human beings or b) only human beings have moral standing and need to be taken into account. Of course, one *could* build in assumptions and principles that maintain that other beings and entities should have moral standing and be taken into account as well, and consider dilemmas involving animals and other entities that might be thought to have moral standing. Such an advisor would, however, go beyond universally accepted moral theory and certainly *not*, at the present time, *be expected* of an ethical advisor for human beings facing traditional moral dilemmas.

If the machine is given principles to follow to guide its own behavior, on the other hand, an assumption must be made about its status. The reason for this is that in following any ethical theory the agent must consider at least him/her/itself, if he/she/it has moral standing, and typically others as well, in deciding how to act.[11] As a result, a machine agent must know if it is to count, or whether it must always defer to others who count while it does not, in calculating the correct action in an ethical dilemma. In the next section, we shall consider whether a robot like Andrew possessed the characteristics philosophers have considered necessary for having moral standing and so whether it was wrong to force him to follow principles that expected him to be a slave for human beings.

To sum up this section: I have argued that, for many reasons, it's a good idea to begin to make ethics computable by creating a program enabling a machine to act as an ethical advisor for human beings facing traditional ethical dilemmas. The ultimate goal of Machine Ethics, to create autonomous ethical machines, will be a far more difficult task. In particular, it will require that a judgment be made about the status of the machine itself, a judgment that is difficult to make, as we shall see in the next section.

Characteristic(s) Necessary To Have Moral Standing

It is clear that most human beings are "speciesists." As Peter Singer defines the term, "Speciesism . . . is a prejudice or attitude of bias toward the interests of members of one's own species and against those members of other species" (Singer 2003). Speciesism can justify "the sacrifice of the most important interests of members of other species in order to promote the most trivial interests of our own species" (Singer 2003). For a speciesist, only members of one's own species need to be taken into account when deciding how to act. Singer was discussing the question of whether animals should have moral standing, that is, whether they should count in calculating what is right in an ethical dilemma that affects them, but the term can be applied when considering the moral status of intelligent machines if we allow an extension of the term "species" to include a machine category as well. The question that needs to be answered is whether we are justified in being speciesists.

Philosophers have considered several possible characteristics that it might be thought a being/entity must possess in order to have moral standing, which means that an ethical theory must take the being/entity into account. I shall consider a number of these possible characteristics and argue that most, if not all, of them would justify granting moral standing to the fictional robot Andrew (and, very likely, higher order animals as well) from which it follows that we are not justified in being speciesists. However, it will be difficult to establish, in the real world, whether intelligent machines/robots possess the characteristics that Andrew does.

In the nineteenth century, the utilitarian Jeremy Bentham considered whether **possessing the faculty of reason** or **the capacity to communicate** is essential in order for a being to be taken into account in calculating which action is likely to bring about the best consequences:

> What . . . should [draw] the insuperable line? Is it the faculty of reason, or perhaps the faculty of discourse? But a full-grown horse or dog is beyond comparison a more rational, as well as a more conversable animal, than an infant of a day or

even a month old. But suppose they were otherwise, what would it avail? The question is not, Can they reason? nor Can they talk? But Can they suffer? (Bentham 1969)

In this famous passage, Bentham rejected the ability to reason and communicate as being essential to having moral standing (tests which Andrew would have passed with flying colors), in part because they would not allow newborn humans to have moral standing. Instead, Bentham maintained that **sentience** (he focused, in particular, on the ability to suffer, but he intended that this should include the ability to experience pleasure as well) is what is critical. Contemporary utilitarian Peter Singer agrees. He says, "If a being suffers there can be no moral justification for refusing to take that suffering into consideration" (Singer 2003).

How would Andrew fare if sentience were the criterion for having moral standing? Was Andrew capable of experiencing enjoyment and suffering? Asimov manages to convince us that he was, although a bit of a stretch is involved in the case he makes for each. For instance, Andrew says of his woodworking creations:

"I enjoy doing them, Sir," Andrew admitted.

"Enjoy?"

"It makes the circuits of my brain somehow flow more easily. I have heard you use the word *enjoy* and the way you use it fits the way I feel. I enjoy doing them, Sir."

To convince us that Andrew was capable of suffering, here is how Asimov described the way Andrew interacted with the Judge as he fought for his freedom:

It was the first time Andrew had spoken in court, and the judge seemed astonished for a moment at the human timbre of his voice.

"Why do you want to be free, Andrew? In what way will this matter to you?"

"Would *you* wish to be a slave, Your Honor," Andrew asked.

And, in the scene with the bullies, when Andrew realized that he couldn't protect himself, Asimov said, "At that thought, he felt every motile unit contract slightly and he quivered as he lay there."

Admittedly, it would be very difficult to determine whether a robot has feelings, but as Little Miss points out, in "The Bicentennial Man," it's difficult to determine whether even another human being has feelings like oneself. All we can do is use behavioral cues:

"Dad . . . I don't know what [Andrew] feels inside, but I don't know what *you* feel inside either. When you talk to him you'll find he reacts to the various abstractions as you and I do, and what else counts? If someone else's reactions are like your own, what more can you ask for?"

Another philosopher, Immanuel Kant, maintained that only beings that are **self-conscious** should have moral standing (Kant 1963). At the time that he expressed this view (late eighteenth century), it was believed that all and only human beings are self-conscious. It is now recognized that very young children lack self-consciousness and higher order animals (e.g. monkeys and great apes[12]) possess this quality, so putting emphasis on this characteristic would no longer justify our speciesism.[13]

Asimov managed to convince us early on in "The Bicentennial Man" that Andrew is self-conscious. On the second page of the story, Andrew asked a robot surgeon to perform an operation on him to make him more like a man. The following conversation took place:

> "Now, upon whom am I to perform this operation?"
> "Upon me," Andrew said.
> "But that is impossible. It is patently a damaging operation."
> "That does not matter," Andrew said calmly.
> "I must not inflict damage," said the surgeon.
> "On a human being, you must not," said Andrew, "but I, too, am a robot."

In real life, with humans being highly skeptical, it would be difficult to establish that a robot is self-conscious. Certainly a robot could talk about itself in such a way, like Andrew did, that might *sound* like it is self-conscious, but to prove that it really *understands* what it is saying and that it has not just been "programmed" to say these things is another matter.

In the twentieth century, the idea that a being does or does not have *rights* became a popular way of discussing the issue of whether a being/entity has moral standing. Using this language, Michael Tooley essentially argued that **to have a right to something, one must be capable of desiring it**. More precisely, he said that "an entity cannot have a particular right, R, unless it is at least capable of having some interest, I, which is furthered by its having right R" (Tooley 1994). As an example, he said that a being cannot have a right to life unless it is capable of desiring its continued existence.

Andrew desired his freedom. He said to a judge:

> It has been said in this courtroom that only a human being can be free. It seems to me that only someone who *wishes* for freedom can be free. I wish for freedom.

Asimov continued by saying that "it was this statement that cued the judge." He was obviously "cued" by the same criterion Tooley gave for having a right, for he went on to rule that "There is no right to deny freedom to any object advanced enough to grasp the concept and desire the state."

But, once again, if we were to talk about real life, instead of a story, we'd have to establish that Andrew truly *grasped the concept* of freedom and *desired* it.

It would not be easy to convince a skeptic. No matter how much appropriate behavior a robot exhibited, including uttering certain statements, there would be those who would claim that the robot had simply been "programmed" to do and say certain things.

Also in the twentieth century, Tibor Machan maintained that to have rights it was necessary to be a **moral agent**, where a moral agent is one who is expected to behave morally. He then went on to argue that since only human beings possess this characteristic, we are justified in being speciesists:

[H]uman beings are indeed members of a discernibly different species – the members of which have a moral life to aspire to and must have principles upheld for them in communities that make their aspiration possible. Now there is plainly no valid intellectual place for rights in the non-human world, the world in which moral responsibility is for all practical purposes absent. (Machan 2003)

Machan's criterion for when it would be appropriate to say that a being/entity has rights – that it must be a "moral agent" – might seem to be not only reasonable,[14] but helpful for the Machine Ethics enterprise. Only a being who can respect the rights of others should have rights itself. So, if we could succeed in teaching a machine how to be moral (that is, to respect the rights of others), then it should be granted rights itself. If Machan is right, his view establishes even more than I claimed when I connected the moral status of the machine with a machine following ethical principles itself. Instead of just needing to know the moral status of a machine in order for it to be a moral agent, it would necessarily have to have moral standing itself if it were a moral agent, according to Machan.

But we've moved too quickly here. Even if Machan were correct, we would still have a problem that is similar to the problem of establishing that a machine has feelings, or is self-conscious, or is capable of desiring a right. Just because a machine's behavior is guided by moral principles doesn't mean that we would ascribe moral responsibility to the machine. To ascribe moral responsibility would require that the agent intended the action and, in some sense, could have done otherwise (Anderson, S. 1995),[15] both of which are difficult to establish.

If Andrew (or any intelligent machine) followed ethical principles only because he was programmed that way, as were the later, predictable robots in "The Bicentennial Man," then we would not be inclined to hold him morally responsible for his actions. But Andrew found creative ways to follow the Three Laws, convincing us that he intended to act as he did and that he could have done otherwise. An example has been given already: when he chose the death of his body over the death of his aspirations to satisfy the Third Law.

Finally, Mary Anne Warren combined the characteristics that others have argued for with one more – **emotionality** – as requirements for a being to be

"a member of the moral community." She claimed that it is "persons" that matter, i.e. are members of the moral community, and this class of beings is not
identical with the class of human beings:

> [G]enetic humanity is neither necessary nor sufficient for personhood. Some
> genetically human entities are not persons, and there may be persons who
> belong to other species. (Warren 2003)

She listed six characteristics that she believes define personhood:

1. *Sentience* – the capacity to have conscious experiences, usually including the
    capacity to experience pain and pleasure;
2. *Emotionality* – the capacity to feel happy, sad, angry, loving, etc.;
3. *Reason* – the capacity to solve new and relatively complex problems;
4. *The capacity to communicate*, by whatever means, messages of an indefinite
    variety of types; that is, not just with an indefinite number of possible con-
    tents, but on indefinitely many possible topics;
5. *Self-awareness* – having a concept of oneself, as an individual and/or as a
    member of a social group; and finally
6. *Moral agency* – the capacity to regulate one's own actions through moral
    principles or ideals. [Warren 2003]

It is interesting, and somewhat surprising, that Warren added the characteristic of **emotionality** to the list of characteristics that others have mentioned as
being essential to *personhood*, since she was trying to make a distinction between
persons and humans and argue that it is the first category that composes the
members of the moral community. *Humans* are characterized by emotionality,
but some might argue that this is a weakness of theirs that can interfere with
their ability to be members of the moral community, that is, their ability to respect
the rights of others.

There is a tension in the relationship between emotionality and being capable
of acting morally. On the one hand, one has to be sensitive to the suffering of
others to act morally. This, for human beings,[16] means that one must have em-
pathy which, in turn, requires that one has experienced similar emotions oneself.
On the other hand, as we've seen, the emotions of human beings can easily get
in the way of acting morally. One can get so "carried away" by one's emotions
that one becomes incapable of following moral principles. Thus, for humans,
finding the correct balance between the subjectivity of emotion and the object-
ivity required to follow moral principles seems to be essential to being a person who consistently acts in a morally correct fashion.

John Stuart Mill remarked on the tension that exists between emotions and
morality when he stated an objection often heard against Utilitarianism that it

"makes men cold and unsympathizing" to calculate the correct action, in an ethical dilemma, by following the utilitarian principle (Mill 2002). Mill's answer was that it will be true of any (action-based) ethical theory that one's actions will be evaluated according to whether one followed the correct principle(s) or not, not whether one is likable, and he pointed out that "there are other things that interest us in persons besides the rightness and wrongness of their actions." I would add that following a theory that takes into account the happiness and unhappiness of others, as most ethical theories do and certainly as did his own theory of Hedonistic Utilitarianism, hardly makes a person "cold and unsympathizing."

In any case, while Andrew exhibited little "emotionality" in "The Bicentennial Man," and Asimov seemed to favor Andrew's way of thinking in ethical matters to the "emotional antipathy" exhibited by the majority of humans, there was one time when Andrew clearly did exhibit emotionality. It came at the very end of the story, when he uttered the words "Little Miss" as he died. But notice that this coincided with his being declared a *man*, i.e. a human being. As the director of research at U.S. Robots and Mechanical Men Corporation in the story had said about Andrew's desire to be a man: "That's a puny ambition, Andrew. You're better than a man. You've gone downhill from the moment you opted to become organic." I suggest that one way in which Andrew had been better than most human beings was that he did not get carried away by "emotional antipathy."

I'm not convinced, therefore, that one should put much weight on emotionality as a criterion for a being's/entity's having moral standing, since it can often be a liability to determining the morally correct action. If it is thought to be essential, it will, like all the other characteristics that have been mentioned, be difficult to establish. Behavior associated with emotionality can be mimicked, but that doesn't necessarily guarantee that a machine truly has feelings.

Why The Three Laws Are Unsatisfactory Even If Machines Don't Have Moral Standing

I have argued that it may be very difficult to establish, with any of the criteria philosophers have given, that a robot/machine that is actually created possesses the characteristic(s) necessary to have moral standing/rights. Let us assume, then, just for the sake of argument, that the robots/machines that are created should not have moral standing. Would it follow, from this assumption, that it would be acceptable for humans to build into the robot Asimov's Three Laws, which allow humans to mistreat it?

Immanuel Kant considered a parallel situation and argued that humans should not mistreat the entity in question, even though it lacked rights itself.

In "Our Duties to Animals," from his *Lectures on Ethics* (Kant 1963), Kant argued that even though animals don't have moral standing and can be used to serve the ends of human beings, we should still not mistreat them because "[t]ender feelings towards dumb animals develop humane feelings towards mankind." He said that "he who is cruel to animals becomes hard also in his dealings with men." So, even though we have no *direct* duties to animals, we have obligations towards them as "indirect duties towards humanity."

Consider, then, the reaction Kant most likely would have had to the scene involving the bullies and Andrew. He would have abhorred the way they treated Andrew, fearing that it could lead to the bullies treating human beings badly at some future time. Indeed, when Little Miss's son happened on the scene, the bullies' bad treatment of Andrew was followed by offensive treatment of a human being as they said to his human rescuer, "What are you going to do, pudgy?"

It was the fact that Andrew had been programmed according to the Three Laws that allowed the bullies to mistreat him, which in turn could (and did) lead to the mistreatment of human beings. One of the bullies said, "who's to object to anything we do" before he got the idea of destroying Andrew. Asimov then wrote:

> "We can take him apart. Ever take a robot apart?"
> "Will he let us?"
> "How can he stop us?"
> There was no way Andrew could stop them, if they ordered him in a forceful enough manner not to resist. The Second Law of obedience took precedence over the Third Law of self-preservation. In any case, he could not defend himself without possibly hurting them, and that would mean breaking the First Law.

It is likely, then, that Kant would have condemned the Three Laws, even if the entity that was programmed to follow them (in this case, Andrew) did not have moral standing itself. The lesson to be learned from his argument is this: Any ethical laws that humans create must advocate the respectful treatment of even those beings/entities that lack moral standing themselves if there is any chance that humans' behavior towards other humans might be adversely affected otherwise.[17] If humans are required to treat other entities respectfully, then they are more likely to treat each other respectfully.

An unstated assumption of Kant's argument for treating certain beings well, even though they lack moral standing themselves, is that the beings he is referring to are similar in a significant respect to human beings. They may be similar in appearance or in the way they function. Kant, for instance, compared a faithful dog with a human being who has served someone well:

[I]f a dog has served his master long and faithfully, his service, on the analogy of human service, deserves reward, and when the dog has grown too old to serve, his master ought to keep him until he dies. Such action helps to support us in our duties towards human beings. . . . (Kant 1963)

As applied to the Machine Ethics project, Kant's argument becomes stronger, therefore, the more the robot/machine that is created resembles a human being in its functioning and/or appearance. To force an entity like Andrew – who resembled human beings in the way he functioned *and* in his appearance – to follow the Three Laws, which permitted humans to harm him, makes it likely that having such laws will lead to humans harming other humans as well.

Since a goal of AI is to create entities that can duplicate intelligent human behavior, if not necessarily their form, it is likely that autonomous ethical machines that may be created – even if they are not as human-like as Andrew – will resemble humans to a significant degree. It, therefore, becomes all the more important that the ethical principles that govern their behavior should not permit us to treat them badly.

It may appear that we could draw the following conclusion from the Kantian argument given in this section: an autonomous moral machine must be treated as if it had the same moral standing as a human being. If this were true, then it would follow that we don't need to know the status of the machine in order to give it moral principles to follow. We would have to treat it like we would a human being, whatever its status. But this conclusion reads more into Kant's argument than one should.

Kant maintained that beings, like the dog in his example, that are sufficiently like human beings so that we must be careful how we treat them to avoid the possibility that we might go on to treat human beings badly as well, should not have the same moral status as human beings. As he says about animals, "[a]nimals . . . are there merely as a means to an end. That end is man" (Kant 1963). Contrast this with his famous second imperative that should govern our treatment of human beings:

Act in such a way that you always treat humanity, whether in your own person or in the person of any other, never simply as a means, but always at the same time as an end. (Kant 2003)

Thus, according to Kant, we are entitled to treat animals, and presumably intelligent ethical machines that we decide should not have the moral status of human beings, differently from human beings. We can force them to do things to serve our ends, but we should not mistreat them. Since Asimov's Three Laws permit humans to mistreat robots/intelligent machines, they are not, according to Kant, satisfactory as moral principles that these machines should be required to follow.

Conclusion

Using Asimov's "Bicentennial Man" as a starting point, I have discussed a number of metaethical issues concerning the emerging field of Machine Ethics. Although the ultimate goal of Machine Ethics is to create autonomous ethical machines, this presents a number of challenges. I suggest a good way to begin the task of making ethics computable is by creating a program that enables a machine to act an ethical advisor to human beings. This project, unlike creating an autonomous ethical machine, will not require that we make a judgment about the ethical status of the machine itself, a judgment that will be particularly difficult to make. Finally, I have argued that Asimov's "Three Laws of Robotics" are an unsatisfactory basis for Machine Ethics, regardless of the status of the machine.

Notes

* This material is based upon work supported in part by the National Science Foundation grant number IIS-0500133.
1. Related to me in conversation with Isaac Asimov.
2. One of the characters in "The Bicentennial Man" remarks that "There have been times in history when segments of the human population fought for full human rights."
3. Also, only in this second case can we say that the machine is autonomous.
4. I am indebted to Michael Anderson for making this point clear to me.
5. Bruce McLaren has also created a program that enables a machine to act as an ethical advisor to human beings, but in his program the machine does not make ethical decisions itself. His advisor system simply informs the human user of the ethical dimensions of the dilemma, without reaching a decision (McLaren 2003).
6. This is the reason why Anderson, Anderson and Armen have started with "MedEthEx" that advises health care workers and, initially, in just one particular circumstance.
7. I am assuming that one will adopt the action-based approach to Ethics. For the virtue-based approach to be made precise, virtues must be spelled out in terms of actions.
8. A *prima facie* duty is something that one ought to do unless it conflicts with a stronger duty, so there can be exceptions, unlike an *absolute* duty, for which there are no exceptions.
9. Some, who are more pessimistic than I am, would say that there may always be some dilemmas about which even experts will disagree as to what is the correct

answer. Even if this turns out to be the case, the agreement that surely exists on many dilemmas will allow us to reject a completely relativistic position.

10. The pessimists would, perhaps, say: "there are correct answers to many (or most) *ethical* dilemmas."

11. If Ethical Egoism is accepted as a plausible ethical theory, then the agent only needs to take him/her/itself into account, whereas all other ethical theories consider others as well as the agent, assuming that the agent has moral status.

12. In a well-known video titled "Monkey in the Mirror," a monkey soon realizes that the monkey it sees in a mirror is itself and it begins to enjoy making faces, etc., watching its own reflection.

13. Christopher Grau has pointed out that Kant probably had a more robust notion of self-consciousness in mind, that includes autonomy and "allows one to discern the moral law through the Categorical Imperative." Still, even if this rules out monkeys and great apes, it also rules out very young human beings.

14. In fact, however, it is problematic. Some would argue that Machan has set the bar too high. Two reasons could be given: (1) A number of humans (most noticeably very young children) would, according to his criterion, not have rights since they can't be expected to behave morally. (2) Machan has confused "having rights" with "having duties." It is reasonable to say that in order *to have duties* to others, you must be capable of behaving morally, that is, of respecting the rights of others, but *to have rights* requires something less than this. That's why young children can have rights, but not duties. In any case, Machan's criterion would not justify our being speciesists because recent evidence concerning the great apes shows that they are capable of behaving morally. I have in mind Koko, the gorilla who has been raised by humans (at the Gorilla Foundation in Woodside, California) and absorbed their ethical principles as well as having been taught sign language.

15. I say "in some sense, could have done otherwise" because philosophers have analyzed "could have done otherwise" in different ways, some compatible with Determinism and some not; but it is generally accepted that freedom in some sense is required for moral responsibility.

16. I see no reason, however, why a robot/machine can't be trained to take into account the suffering of others in calculating how it will act in an ethical dilemma, without its having to be emotional itself.

17. It is important to emphasize here that I am not necessarily agreeing with Kant that robots like Andrew, and animals, should not have moral standing/rights. I am just making the hypothetical claim that *if* we determine that they should not, there is still a good reason, because of indirect duties to human beings, to treat them respectfully.

References

Anderson, M., Anderson, S. and Armen, C., MedEthEx: Towards a Medical Ethics Advisor. *Proceedings of the AAAI Fall Symposium on Caring Machines: AI and Eldercare*, Crystal City, VA, November, 2005.

Anderson, S., Being Morally Responsible for an Action Versus Acting Responsibly or Irresponsibly. *Journal of Philosophical Research*, Volume XX, pp. 451–62, 1995.

Asimov, I., The Bicentennial Man. *Philosophy and Science Fiction* (Philips, M., ed.), pp. 183–216, Prometheus Books, Buffalo, NY, 1984.

Bentham, J., *An Introduction to the Principles of Morals and Legislation*, chapter 17 (Burns, J. and Hart, H., eds.), Clarendon Press, Oxford, 1969.

Kant, I., Our Duties to Animals. *Lectures on Ethics* (Infield, L., trans.), pp. 239–41, Harper & Row, New York, NY, 1963.

Kant, I., The Categorical Imperative, p. 54. *Contemporary Moral Problems*, seventh edition (White, J., ed.), Wadsworth/Thompson Learning, Belmont, CA, 2003.

Machan, T., Do Animals Have Rights?, p. 494. *Contemporary Moral Problems*, seventh edition (White, J., ed.), Wadsworth/Thompson Learning, Belmont, CA, 2003.

McLaren, B. M., Extensionally Defining Principles and Cases in Ethics: an AI Model, *Artificial Intelligence*, Volume 150, pp. 145–81, November 2003.

Mill, J., *Utilitarianism*, pp. 252–3. *The Basic Writings of John Stuart Mill*, The Modern Library, New York, NY, 2002.

Singer, P., All Animals are Equal. *Contemporary Moral Problems*, seventh edition (White, J., ed.), pp. 472–81, Wadsworth/Thompson Learning, Belmont, CA, 2003.

Tooley, M., In Defense of Abortion and Infanticide, p. 191. *The Abortion Controversy: A Reader* (Pojman, L. and Beckwith, F., eds.), Jones and Bartlett, Boston, MA, 1994.

Warren, M., On the Moral and Legal Status of Abortion. *Contemporary Moral Problems*, seventh edition (White, J., ed.), pp. 144–55, Wadsworth/Thompson Learning, Belmont, CA, 2003.

22

ETHICAL ISSUES IN ADVANCED ARTIFICIAL INTELLIGENCE

Nick Bostrom

1. Introduction

A *superintelligence* is any intellect that vastly outperforms the best human brains in practically every field, including scientific creativity, general wisdom, and social skills (Bostrom, 1998). This definition leaves open how the superintelligence is implemented – it could be in a digital computer, an ensemble of networked computers, cultured cortical tissue, or something else.

On this definition, Deep Blue is not a superintelligence, since it is only smart within one narrow domain (chess), and even there it is not vastly superior to the best humans. Entities such as corporations or the scientific community are not superintelligences either. Although they can perform a number of intellectual feats of which no individual human is capable, they are not sufficiently integrated to count as "intellects," and there are many fields in which they perform much worse than single humans. For example, you cannot have a real-time conversation with "the scientific community."

While the possibility of domain-specific "superintelligences" is also worth exploring, this chapter focuses on issues arising from the prospect of general super-intelligence. Space constraints prevent us from attempting anything comprehensive or detailed. A cartoonish sketch of a few selected ideas is the most we can aim for in the following few pages.

Several authors have argued that there is a substantial chance that super-intelligence may be created within a few decades, perhaps as a result of growing hardware performance and increased ability to implement algorithms and architectures similar to those used by human brains (Bostrom, 1998; Kurzweil, 1999; Moravec, 1999). It might turn out to take much longer, but there seems currently to be no good ground for assigning a negligible probability to the hypothesis that superintelligence will be created within the lifespan of some people alive today. Given the enormity of the consequences of superintelligence, it would make sense to give this prospect some serious consideration even if one thought that there were only a small probability of it happening any time soon.

2. Superintelligence is Different

A prerequisite for having a meaningful discussion of superintelligence is the realization that superintelligence is not just another technology, another tool that will add incrementally to human capabilities. Superintelligence is radically different. This point bears emphasizing, for anthropomorphizing superintelligence is a most fecund source of misconceptions.

Let us consider some of the unusual aspects of the creation of superintelligence:

- *Superintelligence may be the last invention humans ever need to make.*

Given a superintelligence's intellectual superiority, it would be much better at doing scientific research and technological development than any human, and possibly better even than all humans taken together. One immediate consequence of this fact is that:

- *Technological progress in all other fields will be accelerated by the arrival of advanced artificial intelligence.*

It is likely that any technology that we can currently foresee will be speedily developed by the first superintelligence, no doubt along with many other technologies of which we are as yet clueless. The foreseeable technologies that a superintelligence is likely to develop include mature molecular manufacturing, whose applications are wide-ranging (Drexler, 1986):

a) very powerful computers
b) advanced weaponry, probably capable of safely disarming a nuclear power
c) space travel and von Neumann probes (self-reproducing interstellar probes)
d) elimination of aging and disease
e) fine-grained control of human mood, emotion, and motivation
f) uploading (neural or sub-neural scanning of a particular brain and implementation of the same algorithmic structures on a computer in a way that perseveres memory and personality)
g) reanimation of cryonics patients
h) fully realistic virtual reality

- *Superintelligence will lead to more advanced superintelligence.*

This results both from the improved hardware that a superintelligence could create, and also from improvements it could make to its own source code.

- *Artificial minds can be easily copied.*

Since artificial intelligences are software, they can easily and quickly be copied, so long as there is hardware available to store them. The same holds for human uploads. Hardware aside, the marginal cost of creating an additional copy of an upload or an artificial intelligence after the first one has been built is near zero. Artificial minds could therefore quickly come to exist in great numbers, although it is possible that efficiency would favor concentrating computational resources in a single superintellect.

- *Emergence of superintelligence may be sudden.*

It appears much harder to get from where we are now to human-level artificial intelligence than to get from there to superintelligence. While it may thus take quite a while before we get superintelligence, the final stage may happen swiftly. That is, the transition from a state where we have a roughly human-level artificial intelligence to a state where we have full-blown superintelligence, with revolutionary applications, may be very rapid, perhaps a matter of days rather than years. This possibility of a sudden emergence of superintelligence is referred to as the *singularity hypothesis* (Vinge, 1993; Hanson et al., 1998).

- *Artificial intellects are potentially autonomous agents.*

A superintelligence should not necessarily be conceptualized as a mere tool. While specialized superintelligences that can think only about a restricted set of problems may be feasible, general superintelligence would be capable of independent initiative and of making its own plans, and may therefore be more appropriately thought of as an autonomous agent.

- *Artificial intellects need not have humanlike motives.*

Humans are rarely willing slaves, but there is nothing implausible about the idea of a superintelligence having as its supergoal to serve humanity or some particular human, with no desire whatsoever to revolt or to "liberate" itself. It also seems perfectly possible to have a superintelligence whose sole goal is some-thing completely arbitrary, such as to manufacture as many paperclips as possible, and who would resist with all its might any attempt to alter this goal. For better or worse, artificial intellects need not share our human motivational tendencies.

- *Artificial intellects may not have humanlike psyches.*

The cognitive architecture of an artificial intellect may also be quite unlike that of humans. Artificial intellects may find it easy to guard against some kinds of human error and bias, while at the same time being at increased risk of other kinds of mistake that not even the most hapless human would make. Subjectively, the inner conscious life of an artificial intellect, if it has one, may also be quite different from ours.

For all of these reasons, one should be wary of assuming that the emergence of superintelligence can be predicted by extrapolating the history of other technological breakthroughs, or that the nature and behaviors of artificial intellects would necessarily resemble those of human or other animal minds.

3. Superintelligent Moral Thinking

To the extent that ethics is a cognitive pursuit, a superintelligence could do it better than human thinkers. This means that questions about ethics, in so far as they have correct answers that can be arrived at by reasoning and weighing up of evidence, could be more accurately answered by a superintelligence than by humans. The same holds for questions of policy and long-term planning; when it comes to understanding which policies would lead to which results, and which means would be most effective in attaining given aims, a superintelligence would outperform humans.

There are therefore many questions that we would not need to answer ourselves if we had or were about to get superintelligence; we could delegate many investigations and decisions to the superintelligence. For example, if we are uncertain how to evaluate possible outcomes, we could ask the superintelligence to estimate how we would have evaluated these outcomes if we had thought about them for a very long time, deliberated carefully, had had more memory and better intelligence, and so forth. When formulating a goal for the superintelligence, it would not always be necessary to give a detailed, explicit definition of this goal. We could enlist the superintelligence to help us determine the real intention of our request, thus decreasing the risk that infelicitous wording or confusion about what we want to achieve would lead to outcomes that we would disapprove of in retrospect.

4. Importance of Initial Motivations

The option to defer many decisions to the superintelligence does not mean that we can afford to be complacent in how we construct the superintelligence. On the contrary, the setting up of initial conditions, and in particular the selection of a top-level goal for the superintelligence, is of the utmost importance. Our entire future may hinge on how we solve these problems.

Both because of its superior planning ability and because of the technologies it could develop, it is plausible to suppose that the first superintelligence would be very powerful. Quite possibly, it would be unrivalled: it would be able to bring about almost any possible outcome and to thwart any attempt to prevent the implementation of its top goal. It could kill off all other agents, persuade them to change their behavior, or block their attempts at interference. Even a "fettered superintelligence" that was running on an isolated computer, able to interact with the rest of the world only via text interface, might be able to break out of its confinement by persuading its handlers to release it. There is even some preliminary experimental evidence that this would be the case (Yudkowsky, 2002).

It seems that the best way to ensure that a superintelligence will have a beneficial impact on the world is to endow it with philanthropic values. Its top goal should be friendliness (Yudkowsky, 2003). How exactly friendliness should be understood and how it should be implemented, and how the amity should be apportioned between different people and nonhuman creatures is a matter that merits further consideration. I would argue that at least all humans, and probably many other sentient creatures on earth should get a significant share in the superintelligence's beneficence. If the benefits that the superintelligence could bestow are enormously vast, then it may be less important to haggle over the detailed distribution pattern and more important to seek to ensure that everybody gets at least some significant share, since on this supposition, even a tiny share would be enough to guarantee a very long and very good life. One risk that must be guarded against is that those who develop the superintelligence would not make it generically philanthropic but would instead give it the more limited goal of serving only some small group, such as its own creators or those who commissioned it.

If a superintelligence starts out with a friendly top goal, however, then it can be relied on to stay friendly, or at least not to deliberately rid itself of its friendliness. This point is elementary. A "friend" who seeks to transform himself into somebody who wants to hurt you, is not your friend. A true friend, one who really cares about you, also seeks the continuation of his caring for you. Or to put it in a different way, if your top goal is X, and if you think that by changing yourself into someone who instead wants Y you would make it less likely that X will be achieved, then you will not rationally transform yourself into someone who wants Y. The set of options at each point in time is evaluated on the basis of their consequences for realization of the goals held at that time, and generally it will be irrational to deliberately change one's own top goal, since that would make it less likely that the current goals will be attained.

In humans, with our complicated evolved mental ecology of state-dependent competing drives, desires, plans, and ideals, there is often no obvious way to identify what our top goal is; we might not even have one. So for us, the above reasoning need not apply. But a superintelligence may be structured differently. If a superintelligence has a definite, declarative goal-structure with a clearly identified top goal, then the above argument applies. And this is a good reason for us to build the superintelligence with such an explicit motivational architecture.

5. Should Development be Delayed or Accelerated?

It is hard to think of any problem that a superintelligence could not either solve or at least help us solve. Disease, poverty, environmental destruction, unnecessary suffering of all kinds: these are things that a superintelligence equipped with advanced nanotechnology would be capable of eliminating. Additionally, a superintelligence could give us indefinite lifespan, either by stopping and reversing the aging process through the use of nanomedicine (Freitas Jr., 1999), or by offering us the option to upload ourselves. A superintelligence could also create opportunities for us to vastly increase our own intellectual and emotional capabilities, and it could assist us in creating a highly appealing experiential world in which we could live lives devoted to joyful game-playing, relating to each other, experiencing, personal growth, and to living closer to our ideals.

The risks in developing superintelligence include the risk of failure to give it the supergoal of philanthropy. One way in which this could happen is that the creators of the superintelligence decide to build it so that it serves only this select group of humans, rather than humanity in general. Another way for it to happen is that a well-meaning team of programmers make a big mistake in designing its goal system. This could result, to return to the earlier example, in a superintelligence whose top goal is the manufacturing of paperclips, with the consequence that it starts transforming first all of earth and then increasing portions of space into paperclip manufacturing facilities. More subtly, it could result in a superintelligence realizing a state of affairs that we might now judge as desirable but which in fact turns out to be a false Utopia, in which things essential to human flourishing have been irreversibly lost. We need to be careful about what we wish for from a superintelligence, because we might get it.

One consideration that should be taken into account when deciding whether to promote the development of superintelligence is that if superintelligence is feasible, it will likely be developed sooner or later. Therefore, we will probably one day have to take the gamble of superintelligence no matter what. But once in existence, a superintelligence could help us reduce or eliminate other existential risks (Bostrom, 2002), such as the risk that advanced nanotechnology will be used by humans in warfare or terrorism, a serious threat to the long-term survival of intelligent life on earth. If we get to superintelligence first, we may avoid this risk from nanotechnology and many others. If, on the other hand, we get nanotechnology first, we will have to face both the risks from nanotechnology and, if these risks are survived, also the risks from superintelligence.

The overall risk seems to be minimized by implementing superintelligence, with great care, as soon as possible.

References

Bostrom, N. (1998). "How Long Before Superintelligence?" *International Journal of Futures Studies*, 2. http://www.nickbostrom.com/superintelligence.html

Bostrom, N. (2002). "Existential Risks: Analyzing Human Extinction Scenarios and Related Hazards." *Journal of Evolution and Technology*, 9. http://www.nickbostrom.com/existential/risks.html

Drexler, K. E. *Engines of Creation: The Coming Era of Nanotechnology.* (Anchor Books: New York, 1986). http://www.foresight.org/EOC/index.html

Freitas Jr., R. A. *Nanomedicine, Volume 1: Basic Capabilities.* (Landes Bioscience: Georgetown, TX, 1999). http://www.nanomedicine.com

Hanson, R., et al. (1998). "A Critical Discussion of Vinge's Singularity Concept." *Extropy Online.* http://www.extropy.org/eo/articles/vi.html

Kurzweil, R. *The Age of Spiritual Machines: When Computers Exceed Human Intelligence.* (Viking: New York, 1999).

Moravec, H. *Robot: Mere Machine to Transcendent Mind.* (Oxford University Press: New York, 1999).

Vinge, V. (1993). "The Coming Technological Singularity." *Whole Earth Review*, Winter issue.

Yudkowsky, E. (2002). "The AI Box Experiment." *Webpage.* http://sysopmind.com/essays/aibox.html

Yudkowsky, E. (2003). *Creating Friendly AI 1.0.* http://www.singinst.org/CFAI/index.html

Part V
SPACE AND TIME

Related Works
Twelve Monkeys
Slaughterhouse Five
The Time Machine
Back to the Future
Flatland: A Romance in Many Dimensions

23

A SOUND OF THUNDER

Ray Bradbury

The sign on the wall seemed to quaver under a film of sliding warm water. Eckels felt his eyelids blink over his stare, and the sign burned in this momentary darkness:

> Time safari, inc.
> Safaris to any year in the past.
> You name the animal.
> We take you there.
> You shoot it.

Warm phlegm gathered in Eckels' throat; he swallowed and pushed it down. The muscles around his mouth formed a smile as he put his hand slowly out upon the air, and in that hand waved a check for ten thousand dollars to the man behind the desk.

"Does this safari guarantee I come back alive?"

"We guarantee nothing," said the official, "except the dinosaurs." He turned. "This is Mr. Travis, your Safari Guide in the Past. He'll tell you what and where to shoot. If he says no shooting, no shooting. If you disobey instructions, there's a stiff penalty of another ten thousand dollars, plus possible government action, on your return."

Eckels glanced across the vast office at a mass and tangle, a snaking and humming of wires and steel boxes, at an aurora that flickered now orange, now silver, now blue. There was a sound like a gigantic bonfire burning all of Time, all the years and all the parchment calendars, all the hours piled high and set aflame.

A touch of the hand and this burning would, on the instant, beautifully reverse itself. Eckels remembered the wording in the advertisements to the letter. Out of chars and ashes, out of dust and coals, like golden salamanders, the old years, the green years, might leap; roses sweeten the air, white hair turn Irish-black, wrinkles vanish; all, everything fly back to seed, flee death, rush down to their

beginnings, suns rise in western skies and set in glorious easts, moons eat themselves opposite to the custom, all and everything cupping one in another like
Chinese boxes, rabbits in hats, all and everything returning to the fresh death,
the seed death, the green death, to the time before the beginning. A touch of
a hand might do it, the merest touch of a hand.

"Hell and damn," Eckels breathed, the light of the Machine on his thin
face. "A real Time Machine." He shook his head. "Makes you think. If the
election had gone badly yesterday, I might be here now running away from
the results. Thank God Keith won. He'll make a fine President of the United
States."

"Yes," said the man behind the desk. "We're lucky. If Deutscher had gotten
in, we'd have the worst kind of dictatorship. There's an anti-everything man for
you, a militarist, anti-Christ, anti-human, anti-intellectual. People called us up,
you know, joking but not joking. Said if Deutscher became President they wanted
to go live in 1492. Of course it's not our business to conduct Escapes, but to
form Safaris. Anyway, Keith's President now. All you got to worry about is —"

"Shooting my dinosaur," Eckels finished it for him.

"A *Tyrannosaurus rex*. The Thunder Lizard, the damnedest monster in history.
Sign this release. Anything happens to you, we're not responsible. Those
dinosaurs are hungry."

Eckels flushed angrily. "Trying to scare me!"

"Frankly, yes. We don't want anyone going who'll panic at the first shot. Six
Safari leaders were killed last year, and a dozen hunters. We're here to give you
the damnedest thrill a *real* hunter ever asked for. Traveling you back sixty million years to bag the biggest damned game in all Time. Your personal check's
still there. Tear it up."

Mr. Eckels looked at the check for a long time. His fingers twitched.

"Good luck," said the man behind the desk. "Mr. Travis, he's all yours."

They moved silently across the room, taking their guns with them, toward
the Machine, toward the silver metal and the roaring light.

First a day and then a night and then a day and then a night, then it was day-
night-day-night-day. A week, a month, a year, a decade! AD 2055. AD 2019. 1999!
1957! Gone! The Machine roared.

They put on their oxygen helmets and tested the intercoms.

Eckels swayed on the padded seat, his face pale, his jaw stiff. He felt the trembling in his arms and he looked down and found his hands tight on the new
rifle. There were four other men in the Machine. Travis, the Safari Leader, his
assistant, Lesperance, and two other hunters, Billings and Kramer. They sat looking at each other, and the years blazed around them.

"Can these guns get a dinosaur cold?" Eckels felt his mouth saying.

"If you hit them right," said Travis on the helmet radio. "Some dinosaurs have
two brains, one in the head, another far down the spinal column. We stay away

from those. That's stretching luck. Put your first two shots into the eyes, if you can, blind them, and go back into the brain."

The Machine howled. Time was a film run backward. Suns fled and ten million moons fled after them. "Good God," said Eckels. "Every hunter that ever lived would envy us today. This makes Africa seem like Illinois."

The Machine slowed; its scream fell to a murmur. The Machine stopped.

The sun stopped in the sky.

The fog that had enveloped the Machine blew away and they were in an old time, a very old time indeed, three hunters and two Safari Heads with their blue metal guns across their knees.

"Christ isn't born yet," said Travis. "Moses has not gone to the mountain to talk with God. The Pyramids are still in the earth, waiting to be cut out and put up. *Remember* that, Alexander, Caesar, Napoleon, Hitler – none of them exists."

The men nodded.

"That" – Mr. Travis pointed – "is the jungle of sixty million two thousand and fifty-five years before President Keith."

He indicated a metal path that struck off into green wilderness, over steaming swamp, among giant ferns and palms.

"And that," he said, "is the Path, laid by Time Safari for your use. It floats six inches above the earth. Doesn't touch so much as one grass blade, flower, or tree. It's an antigravity metal. Its purpose is to keep you from touching this world of the past in any way. Stay on the Path. Don't go off it. I repeat. *Don't go off*. For *any* reason! If you fall off, there's a penalty. And don't shoot any animal. We don't. Okay."

"Why?" asked Eckels.

They sat in the ancient wilderness. Far birds' cries blew on a wind, and the smell of tar and an old salt sea, moist grasses, and flowers the color of blood.

"We don't want to change the Future. We don't belong here in the Past. The government doesn't *like* us here. We have to pay big graft to keep our franchise. A Time Machine is damn finicky business. Not knowing it, we might kill an important animal, a small bird, a roach, a flower even, thus destroying an important link in a growing species."

"That's not clear," said Eckels.

"All right," Travis continued, "say we accidentally kill one mouse here. That means all the future families of this one particular mouse are destroyed, right?"

"Right."

"And all the families of the families of that one mouse! With a stamp of your foot, you annihilate first one, then a dozen, then a thousand, a million, a *billion* possible mice!"

"So they're dead," said Eckels. "So what?"

"So what?" Travis snorted quietly. "Well, what about the foxes that'll need those mice to survive? For want of ten mice, a fox dies. For want of ten foxes, a lion starves. For want of a lion, all manner of insects, vultures, infinite billions of life forms are thrown into chaos and destruction. Eventually it all boils down to this: fifty-nine million years later, a cave man, one of a dozen on the *entire* world, goes hunting wild boar or saber-tooth tiger for food. But you, friend, have *stepped* on all the tigers in that region. By stepping on *one* single mouse. So the cave man starves. And the cave man, please note, is not just *any* expendable man, no! He is an *entire future nation*. From his loins would have sprung ten sons. From *their* loins one hundred sons, and thus onward to a civilization. Destroy this one man, and you destroy a race, a people, an entire history of life. It is comparable to slaying some of Adam's grandchildren. The stomp of your foot, on one mouse, could start an earthquake, the effects of which could shake our earth and destinies down through Time, to their very foundations. With the death of that one cave man, a billion others yet unborn are throttled in the womb. Perhaps Rome never rises on its seven hills. Perhaps Europe is forever a dark forest, and only Asia waxes healthy and teeming. Step on a mouse and you crush the Pyramids. Step on a mouse and you leave your print, like a Grand Canyon, across Eternity. Queen Elizabeth might never be born, Washington might not cross the Delaware, there might never be a United States at all. So be careful. Stay on the Path. *Never* step off!"

"I see," said Eckels. "Then it wouldn't pay for us even to touch the *grass*?"

"Correct. Crushing certain plants could add up infinitesimally. A little error here would multiply in sixty million years, all out of proportion. Of course maybe our theory is wrong. Maybe Time *can't* be changed by us. Or maybe it can be changed only in little subtle ways. A dead mouse here makes an insect imbalance there, a population disproportion later, a bad harvest further on, a depression, mass starvation, and, finally, a change in *social* temperament in far-flung countries. Something much more subtle, like that. Perhaps only a soft breath, a whisper, a hair, pollen on the air, such a slight, slight change that unless you looked close you wouldn't see it. Who knows? Who really can say he knows? We don't know. We're guessing. But until we do know for certain whether our messing around in Time *can* make a big roar or a little rustle in history, we're being damned careful. This Machine, this Path, your clothing and bodies, were sterilized, as you know, before the journey. We wear these oxygen helmets so we can't introduce our bacteria into an ancient atmosphere."

"How do we know which animals to shoot?"

"They're marked with red paint," said Travis. "Today, before our journey, we sent Lesperance here back with the Machine. He came to this particular era and followed certain animals."

"Studying them?"

"Right," said Lesperance. "I track them through their entire existence, noting which of them lives longest. Very few. How many times they mate. Not often. Life's short. When I find one that's going to die when a tree falls on him, or one that drowns in a tar pit, I note the exact hour, minute, and second. I shoot a paint bomb. It leaves a red patch on his hide. We can't miss it. Then I correlate our arrival in the Past so that we meet the Monster not more than two minutes before he would have died anyway. This way, we kill only animals with no future, that are never going to mate again. You see how *careful* we are?"

"But if you came back this morning in Time," said Eckels eagerly, "you must've bumped into *us*, our Safari! How did it turn out? Was it successful? Did all of us get through – alive?"

Travis and Lesperance gave each other a look.

"That'd be a paradox," said the latter. "Time doesn't permit that sort of mess – a man meeting himself. When such occasions threaten, Time steps aside. Like an airplane hitting an air pocket. You felt the Machine jump just before we stopped? That was us passing ourselves on the way back to the Future. We saw nothing. There's no way of telling *if* this expedition was a success, *if* we got our monster, or whether all of – meaning *you*, Mr. Eckels – got out alive."

Eckels smiled palely.

"Cut that," said Travis sharply. "Everyone on his feet!"

They were ready to leave the Machine.

The jungle was high and the jungle was broad and the jungle was the entire world forever and forever. Sounds like music and sounds like flying tents filled the sky, and those were pterodactyls soaring with cavernous gray wings, gigantic bats out of a delirium and a night fever. Eckles, balanced on the narrow Path, aimed his rifle playfully.

"Stop that!" said Travis. "Don't even aim for fun, damn it! If your gun should go off—"

Eckels flushed. "Where's our *Tyrannosaurus?*"

Lesperance checked his wrist watch. "Up ahead. We'll bisect his trail in sixty seconds. Look for the red paint, for Christ's sake. Don't shoot till we give the word. Stay on the Path. *Stay on the Path!*"

They moved forward in the wind of morning.

"Strange," murmured Eckels. "Up ahead, sixty million years, Election Day over. Keith made President. Everyone celebrating. And here we are, a million years lost, and they don't exist. The things we worried about for months, a lifetime, not even born or thought about yet."

"Safety catches off, everyone!" ordered Travis. "You, first shot, Eckels. Second, Billings. Third, Kramer."

"I've hunted tiger, wild boar, buffalo, elephant, but Jesus, this is *it*," said Eckels. "I'm shaking like a kid."

"Ah," said Travis.

Everyone stopped.

Travis raised his hand. "Ahead," he whispered. "In the mist. There he is. There's His Royal Majesty now."

The jungle was wide and full of twitterings, rustlings, murmurs, and sighs. Suddenly it all ceased, as if someone had shut a door.

Silence.

A sound of thunder.

Out of the mist, one hundred yards away, came *Tyrannosaurus rex*.

"Jesus God," whispered Eckels.

"Sh!"

It came on great oiled, resilient, striding legs. It towered thirty feet above half of the trees, a great evil god, folding its delicate watchmaker's claws close to its oily reptilian chest. Each lower leg was a piston, a thousand pounds of white bone, sunk in thick ropes of muscle, sheathed over in a gleam of pebbled skin like the mail of a terrible warrior. Each thigh was a ton of meat, ivory, and steel mesh. And from the great breathing cage of the upper body those two delicate arms dangled out front, arms with hands which might pick up and examine men like toys, while the snake neck coiled. And the head itself, a ton of sculptured stone, lifted easily upon the sky. Its mouth gaped, exposing a fence of teeth like daggers. Its eyes rolled, ostrich eggs, empty of all expression save hunger. It closed its mouth in a death grin. It ran, its pelvic bones crushing aside trees and bushes, its taloned feet clawing damp earth, leaving prints six inches deep wherever it settled its weight. It ran with a gliding ballet step, far too poised and balanced for its ten tons. It moved into a sunlit arena warily, its beautifully reptile hands feeling the air.

"My God!" Eckels twitched his mouth. "It could reach up and grab the moon."

"Sh!" Travis jerked angrily. "He hasn't seen us yet."

"It can't be killed." Eckels pronounced this verdict quietly, as if there could be no argument. He had weighed the evidence and this was his considered opinion. The rifle in his hands seemed a cap gun. "We were fools to come. This is impossible."

"Shut up!" hissed Travis.

"Nightmare."

"Turn around," commanded Travis. "Walk quietly to the Machine. We'll remit one-half your fee."

"I didn't realize it would be this *big*," said Eckels. "I miscalculated, that's all, And now I want out."

"It sees us!"

"There's the red paint on its chest!"

The Thunder Lizard raised itself. Its armored flesh glittered like a thousand green coins. The coins, crusted with slime, steamed. In the slime, tiny insects wriggled, so that the entire body seemed to twitch and undulate, even while the monster itself did not move. It exhaled. The stink of raw flesh blew down the wilderness.

"Get me out of here," said Eckels. "It was never like this before. I was always sure I'd come through alive. I had good guides, good safaris, and safety. This time, I figured wrong. I've met my match and admit it. This is too much for me to get hold of."

"Don't run," said Lesperance. "Turn around. Hide in the Machine."

"Yes." Eckels seemed to be numb. He looked at his feet as if trying to make them move. He gave a grunt of helplessness.

"Eckels!"

He took a few steps, blinking, shuffling.

"Not *that* way!"

The Monster, at the first motion, lunged forward with a terrible scream. It covered one hundred yards in four seconds. The rifles jerked up and blazed fire. A windstorm from the beast's mouth engulfed them in the stench of slime and old blood. The Monster roared, teeth glittering with sun.

Eckels, not looking back, walked blindly to the edge of the Path, his gun limp in his arms, stepped off the Path, and walked, not knowing it, in the jungle. His feet sank into green moss. His legs moved him, and he felt alone and remote from the events behind.

The rifles cracked again. Their sound was lost in shriek and lizard thunder. The great lever of the reptile's tail swung up, lashed sideways. Trees exploded in clouds of leaf and branch. The Monster twitched its jeweler's hands down to fondle at the men, to twist them in half, to crush them like berries, to cram them into its teeth and its screaming throat. Its boulder-stone eyes leveled with the men. They saw themselves mirrored. They fired at the metallic eyelids and the blazing black iris.

Like a stone idol, like a mountain avalanche, *Tyrannosaurus* fell. Thundering, it clutched trees, pulled them with it. It wrenched and tore the metal Path. The men flung themselves back and away. The body hit, ten tons of cold flesh and stone. The guns fired. The Monster lashed its armored tail, twitched its snake jaws, and lay still. A fount of blood spurted from its throat. Somewhere inside a sac of fluids burst. Sickening gushes drenched the hunters. They stood, red and glistening.

The thunder faded.

The jungle was silent. After the avalanche, a green peace. After the nightmare, morning.

Billings and Kramer sat on the pathway and threw up. Travis and Lesperance stood with smoking rifles, cursing steadily.

In the Time Machine, on his face, Eckels lay shivering.

He had found his way back to the Path, climbed into the Machine.

Travis came walking, glanced at Eckels, took cotton gauze from a metal box, and returned to the others, who were sitting on the Path.

"Clean up."

They wiped the blood from their helmets. They began to curse too. The Monster lay, a hill of solid flesh. Within, you could hear the sighs and murmurs as the furthest chambers of it died, the organs malfunctioning, liquids running a final instant from pocket to sac to spleen, everything shutting off, closing up forever. It was like standing by a wrecked locomotive or a steam shovel at quitting time, all valves being released or levered tight. Bones cracked; the tonnage of its own flesh, off balance, dead weight, snapped the delicate forearms, caught underneath. The meat settled, quivering.

Another cracking sound. Overhead, a gigantic tree branch broke from its heavy mooring, fell. It crashed upon the dead beast with finality.

"There." Lesperance checked his watch. "Right on time. That's the giant tree that was scheduled to fall and kill this animal originally." He glanced at the two hunters. "You want the trophy picture?"

"What?"

"We can't take a trophy back to the Future. The body has to stay right here where it would have died originally, so the insects, birds, and bacteria can get at it, as they were intended to. Everything in balance. The body stays. But we *can* take a picture of you standing near it."

The two men tried to think, but gave up, shaking their heads.

They let themselves be led along the metal Path. They sank wearily into the Machine cushions. They gazed back at the ruined Monster, the stagnating mound, where already strange reptilian birds and golden insects were busy at the steaming armor.

A sound on the floor of the Time Machine stiffened them. Eckels sat there, shivering.

"I'm sorry," he said at last.

"Get up!" cried Travis.

Eckels got up.

"Go out on that Path alone," said Travis. He had his rifle pointed. "You're not coming back in the Machine. We're leaving you here!"

Lesperance seized Travis's arm. "Wait—"

"Stay out of this!" Travis shook his hand away. "This son of a bitch nearly killed us. But it isn't *that* so much. Hell, no. It's his *shoes*! Look at them! He ran off the Path. My God, that *ruins* us! Christ knows how much we'll forfeit. Tens of thousands of dollars of insurance! We guarantee no one leaves the Path. He left it. Oh, the damn fool! I'll have to report to the government. They might revoke our license to travel. God knows *what* he's done to Time, to History!"

"Take it easy, all he did was kick up some dirt."

"How do we *know*?" cried Travis. "We don't know anything! It's all a damn mystery! Get out there, Eckels!"

Eckels fumbled his shirt. "I'll pay anything. A hundred thousand dollars!"

Travis glared at Eckels' checkbook and spat. "Go out there. The Monster's next to the Path. Stick your arms up to your elbows in his mouth. Then you can come back with us."

"That's unreasonable!"

"The Monster's dead, you yellow bastard. The bullets! The bullets can't be left behind. They don't belong in the Past; they might change something. Here's my knife. Dig them out!"

The jungle was alive again, full of the old tremorings and bird cries. Eckels turned slowly to regard the primeval garbage dump, that hill of nightmares and terror. After a long time, like a sleepwalker, he shuffled out along the Path.

He returned, shuddering, five minutes later, his arms soaked and red to the elbows. He held out his hands. Each held a number of steel bullets. Then he fell. He lay where he fell, not moving.

"You didn't have to make him do that," said Lesperance.

"Didn't I? It's too early to tell" Travis nudged the still body. "He'll live. Next time he won't go hunting game like this. Okay." He jerked his thumb wearily at Lesperance. "Switch on. Let's go home."

1492. 1776. 1812.

They cleaned their hands and faces. They changed their caking shirts and pants. Eckels was up and around again, not speaking. Travis glared at him for a full ten minutes.

"Don't look at me," cried Eckels. "I haven't done anything."

"Who can tell?"

"Just ran off the Path, that's all, a little mud on my shoes – what do you want me to do – get down and pray?"

"We might need it. I'm warning you, Eckels, I might kill you yet. I've got my gun ready."

"I'm innocent. I've done nothing!"

1999. 2000. 2055.

The Machine stopped.

"Get out," said Travis.

The room was there as they had left it. But not the same as they had left it. The same man sat behind the same desk. But the same man did not quite sit behind the same desk.

Travis looked around swiftly. "Everything okay here?" he snapped.

"Fine. Welcome home!"

Travis did not relax. He seemed to be looking at the very atoms of the air itself, at the way the sun poured through the one high window.

"Okay, Eckels, get out. Don't ever come back."

Eckels could not move.

"You heard me," said Travis. "What're you *staring* at?"

Eckels stood smelling of the air, and there was a thing to the air, a chemical taint so subtle, so slight, that only a faint cry of his subliminal senses warned him it was there. The colors, white, gray, blue, orange, in the wall, in the furniture, in the sky beyond the window, were . . . were . . . And there was a *feel*.

His flesh twitched. His hands twitched. He stood drinking the oddness with the pores of his body. Somewhere, someone must have been screaming one of those whistles that only a dog can hear. His body screamed silence in return. Beyond this room, beyond this wall, beyond this man who was not quite the same man seated at this desk that was not quite the same desk . . . lay an entire world of streets and people. What sort of world it was now, there was no telling. He could feel them moving there, beyond the walls, almost, like so many chess pieces blown in a dry wind. . . .

But the immediate thing was the sign painted on the office wall, the same sign he had read earlier today on first entering.

Somehow, the sign had changed:

Tyme sefari inc.
Sefaris tu any yeer en the past.
Yu naim the animall.
Wee taek you thair.
Yu shoot itt.

Eckels felt himself fall into a chair. He fumbled crazily at the thick slime on his boots. He held up a clod of dirt, trembling. "No, it *can't* be. Not a *little* thing like that. No!"

Embedded in the mud, glistening green and gold and black, was a butterfly, very beautiful, and very dead.

"Not a little thing like *that*! Not a butterfly!" cried Eckels.

It fell to the floor, an exquisite thing, a small thing that could upset balances and knock down a line of small dominoes and then big dominoes and then gigantic dominoes, all down the years across Time. Eckels' mind whirled. It *couldn't* change things. Killing one butterfly couldn't be *that* important! Could it?

His face was cold. His mouth trembled, asking: "Who – who won the presidential election yesterday?"

The man behind the desk laughed. "You joking? You know damn well. Deutscher, of course! Who else? Not that damn weakling Keith. We got an iron man now, a man with guts, by God!" The official stopped. "What's wrong?"

Eckels moaned. He dropped to his knees. He scrabbled at the golden butterfly with shaking fingers. "Can't we," he pleaded to the world, to himself, to the officials, to the Machine, "can't we take it *back*, can't we *make* it alive again? Can't we start over? Can't we—"

He did not move. Eyes shut, he waited, shivering. He heard Travis breathe loud in the room; he heard Travis shift his rifle, click the safety catch, and raise the weapon.

There was a sound of thunder.

24

TIME

Theodore Sider

The Flow of Time

It is strange to question the nature of time, given how fundamental time is to our experience. As a child I wondered whether fish are conscious of water or whether they experience it unconsciously, as we experience the air we breathe. Time is even more ubiquitous than water or air: every thought and experience takes place in time. Questioning the nature of time can be dizzying.

Yet it is worth questioning. The ordinary conception of time, once you start to think about it, seems to make no sense! For we ordinarily conceive of time as being something that *moves*. "Time flows like a river." "Time marches on." "Time flies." "As time goes by." "The past is gone." "Time waits for no one." "Time stood still." These clichés capture how we tend to think about time. Time moves, and we are caught up in its inexorable flow. The problem with this way of thinking is that time is the standard by which motion is defined; how then could time itself move? This is metaphysics at its best. Look at the world hard enough, and even the most mundane things are revealed as mysterious and wonderful.

Let's examine this idea of time's motion, or flow, more carefully, by comparing it to the motion of ordinary objects. What does it mean to say that a *train* moves? Simply that the train is located at one place at one moment in time and at other places at later moments in time (see Figure 24.1). At time t_1, the train is in Boston. At later times t_2, t_3, and t_4, the train is located at places further south: New York, Philadelphia, and finally, Washington. The motion of the train is defined by reference to time: the train moves by being located at different places at different times. If at every moment the train stayed in the same place – Boston, say – then we would say that the train did not move.

Ordinary objects move with respect to time. So if time itself moves, it must move with respect to some other sort of time. But what would that other time be?

Let's investigate this more carefully. The way in which time seems to move is by the *present moment's* moving. Initially the present moment is noon. Later the present is 3.00 p.m. Still later it is 6.00 p.m., and then 9.00 p.m., and so on.

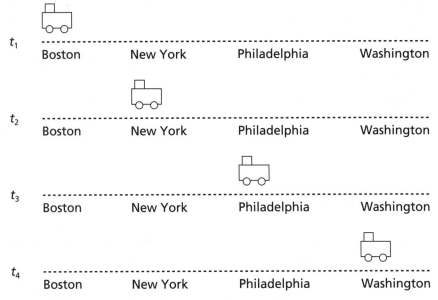

Figure 24.1 The movement of a train defined by reference to time

Since motion is defined by reference to time, the present moment, if it is moving, must have these four different locations at four different times, t_1, t_2, t_3, and t_4, just as the moving train had four different locations at four different times (Figure 24.2). But the diagram is confusing. It mentions the times noon, 3.00, 6.00, and 9.00, but it also mentions four other times, t_1, t_2, t_3, and t_4. These are the times with respect to which the present moment is moving. What are these other times? In what sort of time does time itself move?

One possibility is that t_1, t_2, t_3, and t_4 are part of a *different* sort of time, call it "hypertime". Just as trains move with respect to something else (time), time itself moves with respect to something else (hypertime). Most motion takes place with respect to the familiar timeline, but time itself moves with respect to another timeline, hypertime,

Hypertime is a bad idea. You can't simply stop there; you need more, and More and MORE. Hypertime is supposed to be a sort of time. So if ordinary time moves, surely hypertime moves as well. So hypertime must move with respect to yet another sort of time, hyper-hyper time. That time must also move, which introduces hyper-hyper-hyper time. And so on. We are stuck with believing in an infinite series of different kinds of time. That's a little much. I can't *prove* that this infinite series does not exist, but surely there are better options. Let's see if we took a wrong turn somewhere.

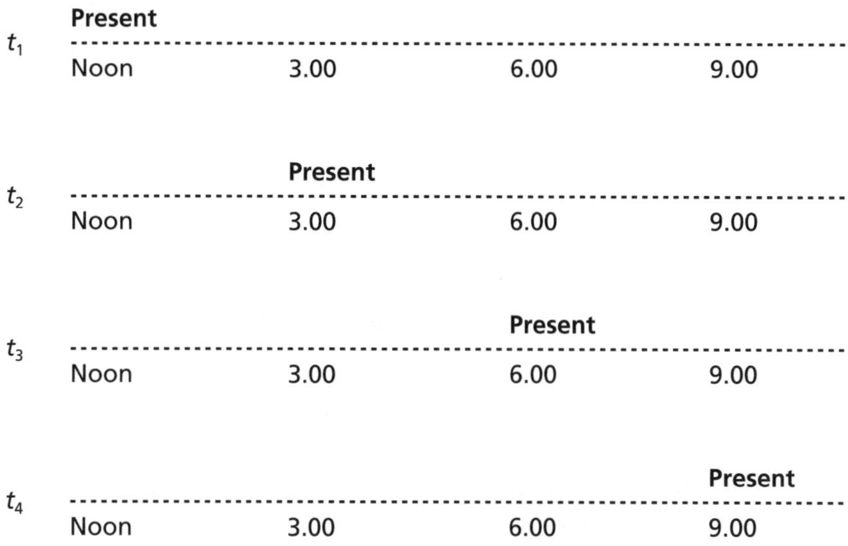

t_1	**Present**			

	Noon	3.00	6.00	9.00

t_2		**Present**		

	Noon	3.00	6.00	9.00

t_3			**Present**	

	Noon	3.00	6.00	9.00

t_4				**Present**

	Noon	3.00	6.00	9.00

Figure 24.2 The moving of the present moment

Instead of being part of hypertime, perhaps t_1, t_2, t_3, and t_4 are just part of ordinary time. In particular, t_1, t_2, t_3, and t_4 could just be the times noon, 3.00, 6.00, and 9.00. According to this view, time moves with respect to itself. Is that plausible?

Although it's nice to be rid of hypertime, there is something strange about this picture. It's not that it isn't *true*. Noon is indeed present at noon, 3.00 is present at 3.00, and so on. But these facts seem *trivial*, and therefore insufficient to capture a genuine flow of time. This can be brought out by comparing time to space, and comparing *present* to *here*. Consider the spatial locations on the train track connecting Boston to Washington. Anyone in Boston can truthfully say "Boston is *here*". Likewise, anyone in New York can say "New York is here". The same goes for Philadelphia and Washington. So Boston is "here in Boston", New York is "here in New York", and so on, just as noon is present at noon, 3.00 is present at 3.00, and so on. But space doesn't move. The line in space connecting Boston with Washington is static. The mere fact that members of a series are located at themselves does not make that series move, whether that series consists of points of time or locations in space.

The Space-Time Theory

Time's motion has us all tangled up in knots. Maybe the problem is with that idea itself. According to some philosophers and scientists, our ordinary conception

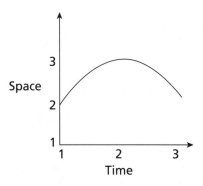

Figure 24.3 High-school physics graph of a particle moving through time

of time as a flowing river is hopelessly confused, and must be replaced with the space-time theory, according to which *time is like space.*

Graphs of motion from high-school physics represent time as just another dimension alongside the spatial dimensions. The graph pictured here (Figure 24.3) represents a particle that moves through time in one spatial dimension. This particle begins at place 2 in space at the initial time 1, then moves toward place 3, slows down and stops at time 2, and finally moves back to place 2 at time 3. Each point in this two-dimensional graph represents a time t (the horizontal coordinate of the point) and a location in space p (the vertical coordinate). The curve drawn represents the particle's motion. When the curve passes through a point (t, p), that means that the particle is located at place p at time t.

A more complicated graph (Figure 24.4) represents time alongside two spatial dimensions. (It would be nice to represent all three spatial dimensions, but that would require a four-dimensional graph and so a much more expensive book.) These more complicated graphs are called **space-time diagrams**. (Even the high-school physics graph is a simpler kind of diagram of space-time.) Space-time diagrams can be used to represent all of history; everything that has ever happened or ever will happen can be fit into a space-time diagram somewhere. This particular diagram represents a dinosaur in the distant past and a person who is born in AD 2000. These objects stretch out horizontally in the graph because they last over time in reality, and time is the horizontal axis on the graph: the objects exist at different points along the horizontal time axis. They stretch out in the other two dimensions on the graph because dinosaurs and people take up space in reality: the objects exist at different points along the vertical, spatial, axes.

In addition to the dinosaur and the person themselves, some of their **temporal parts** are also represented in the diagram. A temporal part of an object at a time is a temporal cross-section of that object; it is that-object-at-that-time. Consider the temporal part of the person in 2000.

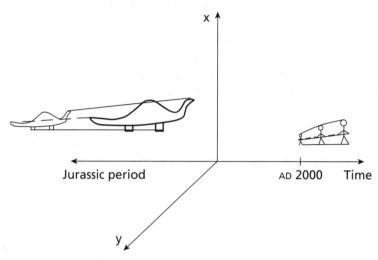

Figure 24.4 Space-time diagram

This object is the exact same *spatial size* as the person in 2000. But the temporal part is not the same *temporal size* as the person; the temporal part exists only in 2000 whereas the person exists at later times as well. The person herself is the sum total of all her temporal parts:

Notice how the person is tapered: the earlier temporal parts (those on the left of the diagram) are smaller than the later ones. This represents the person's growth over time.

In contrast to the ordinary conception of moving or flowing time, then, the space-time theory says that reality consists of a single unified space-time, which contains all of the past, present, and future. Time is just one of the dimensions of space-time, alongside the three spatial dimensions, just as it appears to be in the space-time diagrams. Time does not flow; time is like space.

Well, time isn't *completely* like space. For one thing, there are three spatial dimensions but only one temporal dimension. And time has a special *direction*: past to future. Space has no such direction. We do have words for certain spatial directions: up, down, north, south, east, west, left, right. But these are not directions built into space itself. Rather, these words pick out different directions depending on who says them. "Up" means away from the earth's center on a line that passes through the speaker; "North" means toward the Arctic pole from the speaker; "Left" picks out different directions depending on which way the speaker is facing. In contrast, the past to future direction is the same for everyone, regardless of his or her location or orientation; it seems to be an intrinsic feature of time itself.

Still, according to the space-time theory, time and space are analogous in many ways. Here are three.

First, in terms of *reality*. Objects far away in space (other planets, stars, and so on) are obviously just as real as things here on Earth. We may not *know* as much about the far-away objects as we know about the things around here, but that doesn't make the far-away objects any less real. Likewise, objects far away in time are just as real as objects that exist now. Both past objects (e.g. dinosaurs) and future objects (human outposts on Mars, perhaps) exist, in addition to objects in the present. Distant objects, whether temporally or spatially distant, all exist somewhere in space-time.

Second, in terms of *parts*. Material objects take up space by having different parts. My body occupies a certain region of space. Part of this region is occupied by my head, another by my torso; other parts of the region are occupied by my arms and legs. These parts may be called my spatial parts, since they are spatially smaller than I am. The corresponding fact about time is that an object lasts over a stretch of time by having different parts located at the different times within that stretch. These parts are the temporal parts mentioned above. These temporal parts are just as real objects as my spatial parts: my head, arms, and legs.

Third, in terms of *here* and *now*. If I say on the phone "here it is raining" to a friend in California, and she replies "here it is sunny" (Figure 24.5), which one of us is right? Where is the *real here*, California or New Jersey? The question is obviously misguided. There is no "real here". The word "here" just refers to whatever place the person saying it happens to be. When *I* say "here", it means New Jersey; when my friend says "here", it means California. Neither place is *here* in any objective sense. California is here for my friend, New Jersey is here for me. The space-time theory says an analogous thing about time: just as there is no objective here, so there is no objective *now*. If I say "It is now 2005", and in 1606 Guy Fawkes said "It is now 1606", each statement is correct (Figure 24.6).

Figure 24.5 Where is the "real here"?

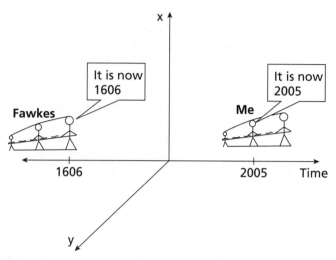

Figure 24.6 "Now" for me and for Guy Fawkes

There is no single, real, objective "now". The word "now" just refers to the time at which the speaker happens to be located.

Arguments Against the Space-Time Theory: Change, Motion, Causes

We have met two theories of time. Which is true? Does time flow? Or is time like space?

The space-time theory avoids the paradoxes of time's flow; that counts in its favor. But the believer in time's flow will retort that the space-time theory throws the baby out with the bath-water: it makes time *too much* like space. For starters, she may say that the alleged analogies between space and time suggested in the last section don't really hold:

> Past and future objects do *not* exist: the past is gone, and the future is yet to be. Things do *not* have temporal parts: at any time, the *whole* object is present, not just a temporal part of it; there are no past or future bits left out. And "now" is *not* like "here": the present moment is special, unlike the bit of space around here.

Each of these claims could take up a whole chapter of its own. But time is short, so let's consider three other ways the defender of time's flow might argue that time is not like space. First, regarding *change*:

Compare change with what we might call "spatial heterogeneity". Change is having different properties at different times. A person who changes height starts out short and then becomes taller. Spatial heterogeneity, in contrast, is having different properties at different *places*. A highway is bumpy at some places, smooth at others; narrow at some places, wide at others. How, if time is just like space, then having different properties at different times (change) is no different from having different properties at different places (spatial heterogeneity). Look back at the space-time diagram. Change is variation from left to right on the diagram, along the temporal axis. Spatial heterogeneity is variation along either of the two spatial dimensions. The two are analogous, according to the space-time theory. But that's not right! Spatial heterogeneity is wholly different from change. The spatially heterogeneous highway doesn't *change*. It just sits there.

Second, regarding *motion*:

> Things can move any which way in space; there's no particular direction in which they are constrained to travel, But the same is not true for time. Moving back and forth in time makes no sense. Things can only travel forward in time.

Third, regarding *causes*:

> Events at any place can cause events at any other place; we can affect what goes on in any region of space. But events can't cause events at just any other time: later events never cause earlier events. Although we can affect the future, we cannot affect the past. The past is fixed.

The first objection is right that the space-time theory makes change somewhat similar to spatial heterogeneity. But so what? They're not *exactly* the same: one is variation over time, the other is variation over space. And the claim that change and spatial heterogeneity are *somewhat* similar is perfectly reasonable. So the first objection may be flatly rejected.

The second objection is more complicated. "Things move back and forth in space, but not back and forth in time" – is this really a disanalogy between time and space? Suppose we want to know, for a certain true statement about space, whether the analogous statement is true of time. The twentieth-century American philosopher Richard Taylor argued that we must be careful to construct a statement about time that really is analogous to the statement about space. In particular, we must *uniformly reverse ALL references to time and space* to get the analogous statement. And when we do, Taylor argued, we will see that time and space are more analogous than they initially seemed.

To illustrate. Our true statement about space is this:

> Some object moves back and forth in space.

Before we can reverse the references to time and space in this statement, we need to locate all those references, including any that are not completely explicit. For instance, the word "moves" conceals a reference to time. When these references are made explicit, our statement becomes:

> *Moving back and forth in space*: Some object is at spatial point p_1 at time t_1, point p_2 at time t_2, and point p_1 at time t_3.

(See Figure 24.7.) Now we're in a position to construct the analogous statement about time – to reverse *all* references to time and space. To do so, we simply change each reference to a time into a reference to a point in space, and each reference to a point in space into a reference to a time. This is what we get:

> *Moving back and forth in time*: Some object is at time t_1 at spatial point p_1, time t_2 at point p_2, and at time t_1 at point p_3.

And we get the graph for this new statement (Figure 24.8) by swapping the "Time" and "Space" labels on Figure 24.7.

Our question now is: is this second statement correct? Can an object "move back and forth in time" in this sense? The answer is in fact *yes*, for a fairly humdrum reason. To make this easy to see, let's make the "moving back and forth in time" graph look like our earlier diagrams by flipping it so that its temporal axis is horizontal (see Figure 24.9). It should be clear that the diagram represents an object that is first, at t_1, located at *two* places, p_1 and p_3, and then, at t_2, is located at just one place, p_2. This sounds stranger than it really is. Think of a clapping pair of hands. At first the two hands are separated – one is located at place p_1, the other at p_3. Then the hands move toward each other and make contact. The pair of hands is now located at place p_2. Finally, suppose the pair of hands disappears at time t_2. This kind of scenario is what the diagram is representing.

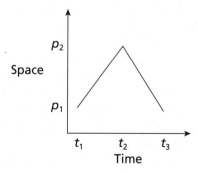

Figure 24.7 Moving back and forth in space

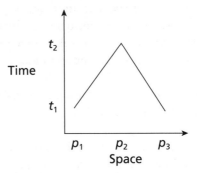

Figure 24.8 Moving back and forth in time, temporal axis vertical

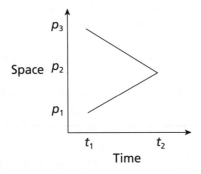

Figure 24.9 Moving back and forth in time, temporal axis horizontal

So things *can* "move back and forth in time", if that statement is understood as being truly analogous to "moving back and forth in space". We were deceived into thinking otherwise by neglecting to reverse *all* references to time and space. The statement "things move back and forth in space" contains an implicit *reference dimension*, namely time, for it is with respect to time that things move in space. When we construct the statement "things move back and forth in time", we must change the reference dimension from time to space. When we do, the resulting statement is something that can indeed be true.

The third objection is the most challenging and interesting. It is true that we do not actually observe "backwards causation", that is, the causation of earlier events by later events. This represents a *de facto* asymmetry between space and time – an asymmetry in the world as it actually is. But a deeper question is whether this asymmetry is built into the nature of time itself, or whether it is just a function of the way the world happens to be. The question is: *could* there be backwards causation? *Could* our actions now causally affect the past?

If time is truly like space, then the answer must be *yes*. Just as events can cause events anywhere else in space, so too events can in principle cause other events anywhere in time, even at earlier times. But this has a very striking consequence. If backwards causation is possible, then *time travel*, as depicted in books and movies, ought to be possible as well, for it ought to be possible to cause ourselves to be present in the past.

Time travel may never *in fact* occur. Perhaps time travel will never be technologically feasible, or perhaps the laws of physics prevent time travel. Philosophy cannot settle questions about physics or technology; for speculation on such matters, a better guide is your friendly neighborhood physicist or engineer. But if time is like space, there should be no prohibition *coming from the concept of time itself*, time travel should at least be conceptually possible. But is it?

A familiar kind of time travel story begins as follows: "In 1985, Marty McFly enters a time machine, sets the controls for 1955, pushes the button, waits, and then arrives in 1955 . . ." Any time travel story must contain this much: the use of some sort of time travel device and subsequent arrival in the past. But even this much seems to conceal a contradiction. The troublesome bit is the end: "and *then* arrives in 1955". The suggestion is that McFly *first* pushes the button, and *second* arrives in 1955. But he pushes the button in 1985, which is *after* 1955.

This is an example of a so-called paradox of time travel. One attempts to tell a coherent story involving time travel, but ends up contradicting oneself. Saying that McFly arrives in 1955 both after and before he pushes the button is contradicting oneself. And if there is no way to tell a time travel story without self-contradiction, then time travel is conceptually impossible.

This first paradox can be avoided. Is the arrival after or before the pushing of the button? *Before* – 1955 is before 1985. What about "and *then*"? Well, all that means is that McFly *experiences* the arrival as being after the button-pressing. Normal people (i.e. non-time travelers) experience events as occurring in the order in which they truly occur, whereas time travelers experience things out of order. In the sequence of McFly's experiences, 1985 comes before 1955. That's a very strange thing, to be sure, but it does not seem conceptually incoherent. (What determines the order of McFly's experiences? Later members of the sequence of his experiences contain memories of, and are caused by, earlier members of the sequence. When McFly experiences 1955, he has memories of 1985, and his 1985 experiences directly causally affect his 1955 experiences.)

Yet a more potent paradox lurks. Let's continue the story from *Back to the Future*: "Back in 1955, the dashing McFly inadvertently attracts his mother, overshadowing his nerdy father. As the union of his parents becomes less and less likely, McFly begins to fade away into nothingness." The problem is that a time traveler could undermine his own existence. He could cause his parents never to meet; he could even kill them before he is ever born. But then where did he come from? Back to paradox!

That McFly begins to fade away into nothingness shows that the writers of *Back to the Future* were aware of the problem. But the fade-out solves nothing. Suppose McFly fades out completely after preventing his parents from meeting. He still existed before fading out (it was he, after all, who prevented his parents from meeting). Where then did he come from in the first place? Whatever its literary merits, as a work of philosophy *Back to the Future* fails miserably.

Let's not be too hard on careless screen-writers and authors. (We can't all be philosophers.) Though it's not easy, paradox-free time travel stories can be told. The movie *Terminator* is an excellent example (spoilers included):[1]

> In the future, machines take over the world and nearly destroy the human race. But the machines are eventually thwarted by the human leader John Connor. On the verge of defeat, the machines fight back by sending a machine, a "Terminator", back to the past to kill John Connor's mother, Sarah Connor, before John is born. John Connor counters by sending one of his men, Kyle Reese, back to the past to protect Sarah Connor. The Terminator nearly succeeds, but in the end Reese stops him. (Reese dies, but not before impregnating Connor's mother, Sarah Connor. The baby, we later learn, grows up to be John Connor himself!)

This story never contradicts itself. It would if the Terminator killed Sarah Connor, since we are told in the beginning of the story that Sarah Connor lived and had a son, John Connor, whose future exploits are the cause of the presence of the Terminator in the past. But since Sarah Connor survives, the story remains consistent.

The failure of *some* time travel stories (such as *Back to the Future*) to remain consistent shows nothing, since other consistent stories can be told. The similarity of time and space has survived: there is no conceptual impossibility with backwards causation and time travel.

There are numerous close calls in *Terminator*. Again and again, Sarah Connor narrowly escapes death. It would appear that on any of these occasions, she could easily have died. Yet we know that she must survive, because her son is John Connor. So it seems that she is not really in danger; she cannot die. But there is the Terminator in front of her. The danger seems very real. Back into paradox?

Not at all. What is strange about a time travel story is that we are told the end of the story first. We, the audience, learn early on that John Connor exists in the future. Later we find his mother endangered before he is ever born. We, the audience, know she will survive (if we trust the screen-writers to be consistent!), but that does not mean that *in the story* her danger is unreal.

A very peculiar thing arises when the time traveler himself knows how the story will end. Think of Reese. He knows that the Terminator will fail, since he knows that John Connor exists: it was Connor that sent him back to the past. Yet he fears for Sarah Connor's life, works hard to protect her, and in the end gives his life to save her. Why doesn't he just walk away and save himself? He *knows* that Sarah Connor is going to survive.

Or does he? He *thinks* he remembers serving a man called John Connor. He *thinks* he remembers Connor defeating the machines. He *thinks* Connor's mother was named Sarah. He *thinks* this woman he's defending is the same Sarah Connor. He *thinks* this woman has not yet had children. So he's got lots of evidence that this woman he's defending will survive. But then he sees the Terminator advance. He sees it effortlessly killing everyone in its path, searching for someone named Sarah Connor. Now it advances on the woman he's defending. It raises its gun. Reese's confidence that this woman will survive now wavers. Perhaps she is not John Connor's mother after all. Or, if he's sure of that, perhaps she's already had a child. Or, if he's quite sure of that, perhaps he's made some other mistake. Perhaps all of his apparent memories from the future are delusions! Such self-doubt is ordinarily far-fetched, but it becomes increasingly reasonable with each step of the Terminator. As certain as he once was that Sarah Connor will survive, he has become equally certain about the danger presented by the Terminator: "It can't be bargained with! It can't be reasoned with! It doesn't feel pity, or remorse, or fear. And it absolutely will not stop, ever, until you are dead!" He thinks "I'd better be sure." He raises his gun.

Note

1. *Terminator 1*, that is. *Terminator 2* appears to be incoherent. It says in the beginning that Cyberdyne systems learned the technology behind Skynet by studying the hand of the corpse of a T-800 Terminator from the future. Then at the end, after the T-800 is melted (Schwarzenegger's thumbs-up to Furlong), the movie suggests that Skynet is never created and Judgment Day is avoided. Where then did the time-traveling Terminators come from? *Terminator 3* does better: it never suggests that Judgment Day is avoided. Yet there are remaining questions, for instance about the true date of Judgment Day. *Terminator 1* is by far the best of the three, from a philosophical (as well as cinematic) point of view.

25

THE PARADOXES OF TIME TRAVEL

David Lewis

Time travel, I maintain, is possible. The paradoxes of time travel are oddities, not impossibilities. They prove only this much, which few would have doubted: that a possible world where time travel took place would be a most strange world, different in fundamental ways from the world we think is ours.

I shall be concerned here with the sort of time travel that is recounted in science fiction. Not all science fiction writers are clear-headed, to be sure, and inconsistent time travel stories have often been written. But some writers have thought the problems through with great care, and their stories are perfectly consistent.[1]

If I can defend the consistency of some science fiction stories of time travel, then I suppose parallel defenses might be given of some controversial physical hypotheses, such as the hypothesis that time is circular or the hypothesis that there are particles that travel faster than light. But I shall not explore these parallels here.

What is time travel? Inevitably, it involves a discrepancy between time and time. Any traveler departs and then arrives at his destination; the time elapsed from departure to arrival (positive, or perhaps zero) is the duration of the journey. But if he is a time traveler, the separation in time between departure and arrival does not equal the duration of his journey. He departs; he travels for an hour, let us say; then he arrives. The time he reaches is not the time one hour after his departure. It is later, if he has traveled toward the future; earlier, if he has traveled toward the past. If he has traveled far toward the past, it is earlier even than his departure. How can it be that the same two events, his departure and his arrival, are separated by two unequal amounts of time?

It is tempting to reply that there must be two independent time dimensions; that for time travel to be possible, time must be not a line but a plane.[2] Then a pair of events may have two unequal separations if they are separated more in one of the time dimensions than in the other. The lives of common people occupy straight diagonal lines across the plane of time, sloping at a rate of exactly one hour of time$_1$ per hour of time$_2$. The life of the time traveler occupies a bent path, of varying slope.

On closer inspection, however, this account seems not to give us time travel as we know it from the stories. When the traveler revisits the days of his childhood, will his playmates be there to meet him? No; he has not reached the part of the plane of time where they are. He is no longer separated from them along one of the two dimensions of time, but he is still separated from them along the other. I do not say that two-dimensional time is impossible, or that there is no way to square it with the usual conception of what time travel would be like. Nevertheless I shall say no more about two-dimensional time. Let us set it aside, and see how time travel is possible even in one-dimensional time.

The world – the time traveler's world, or ours – is a four-dimensional manifold of events. Time is one dimension of the four, like the spatial dimensions except that the prevailing laws of nature discriminate between time and the others – or rather, perhaps, between various timelike dimensions and various spacelike dimensions. (Time remains one-dimensional, since no two timelike dimensions are orthogonal.) Enduring things are timelike streaks: wholes composed of temporal parts, or *stages*, located at various times and places. Change is qualitative difference between different stages – different temporal parts – of some enduring thing, just as a "change" in scenery from east to west is a qualitative difference between the eastern and western spatial parts of the landscape. If this chapter should change your mind about the possibility of time travel, there will be a difference of opinion between two different temporal parts of you: the stage that started reading and the subsequent stage that finishes.

If change is qualitative difference between temporal parts of something, then what doesn't have temporal parts can't change. For instance, numbers can't change; nor can the events of any moment of time, since they cannot be subdivided into dissimilar temporal parts. (We have set aside the case of two-dimensional time, and hence the possibility that an event might be momentary along one time dimension but divisible along the other.) It is essential to distinguish change from "Cambridge change", which can befall anything. Even a number can "change" from being to not being the rate of exchange between pounds and dollars. Even a momentary event can "change" from being a year ago to being a year and a day ago, or from being forgotten to being remembered. But these are not genuine changes. Not just any old reversal in truth value of a time-sensitive sentence about something makes a change in the thing itself.

A time traveler, like anyone else, is a streak through the manifold of space-time, a whole composed of stages located at various times and places. But he is not a streak like other streaks. If he travels toward the past he is a zig-zag streak, doubling back on himself. If he travels toward the future, he is a stretched-out streak. And if he travels either way instantaneously, so that there are no intermediate stages between the stage that departs and the stage that arrives and his journey has zero duration, then he is a broken streak.

I asked how it could be that the same two events were separated by two unequal amounts of time, and I set aside the reply that time might have two independent dimensions. Instead I reply by distinguishing time itself, *external time* as I shall also call it, from the *personal time* of a particular time traveler: roughly, that which is measured by his wristwatch. His journey takes an hour of his personal time, let us say; his wristwatch reads an hour later at arrival than at departure. But the arrival is more than an hour after the departure in external time, if he travels toward the future; or the arrival is before the departure in external time (or less than an hour after), if he travels toward the past.

That is only rough. I do not wish to define personal time operationally, making wristwatches infallible by definition. That which is measured by my own wristwatch often disagrees with external time, yet I am no time traveler; what my misregulated wristwatch measures is neither time itself nor my personal time. Instead of an operational definition, we need a functional definition of personal time: it is that which occupies a certain role in the pattern of events that comprise the time traveler's life. If you take the stages of a common person, they manifest certain regularities with respect to external time. Properties change continuously as you go along, for the most part, and in familiar ways. First come infantile stages. Last come senile ones. Memories accumulate. Food digests. Hair grows. Wristwatch hands move. If you take the stages of a time traveler instead, they do not manifest the common regularities with respect to external time. But there is one way to assign coordinates to the time traveler's stages, and one way only (apart from the arbitrary choice of a zero point), so that the regularities that hold with respect to this assignment match those that commonly hold with respect to external time. With respect to the correct assignment properties change continuously as you go along, for the most part, and in familiar ways. First come infantile stages. Last come senile ones. Memories accumulate. Food digests. Hair grows. Wristwatch hands move. The assignment of coordinates that yields this match is the time traveler's personal time. It isn't really time, but it plays the role in his life that time plays in the life of a common person. It's enough like time so that we can – with due caution – transplant our temporal vocabulary to it in discussing his affairs. We can say without contradiction, as the time traveler prepares to set out, "Soon he will be in the past." We mean that a stage of him is slightly later in his personal time, but much earlier in external time, than the stage of him that is present as we say the sentence.

We may assign locations in the time traveler's personal time not only to his stages themselves but also to the events that go on around him. Soon Caesar will die, long ago; that is, a stage slightly later in the time traveler's personal time than his present stage, but long ago in external time, is simultaneous with Caesar's death. We could even extend the assignment of personal time to events that are not part of the time traveler's life, and not simultaneous with any of his stages. If his funeral in ancient Egypt is separated from his death by three days of external time and his death is separated from his birth by three score years and ten of his personal time, then we may add the two intervals and say that his funeral follows his birth by three score years and ten and three days of *extended personal time*. Likewise a bystander might truly say, three years after the last departure of another famous time traveler, that "he may even now – if I may use the phrase – be wandering on some plesiosaurus-haunted oolitic coral reef, or beside the lonely saline seas of the Triassic Age".[3] If the time traveler does wander on an oolitic coral reef three years after his departure in his personal time, then it is no mistake to say with respect to his extended personal time that the wandering is taking place "even now".

We may liken intervals of external time to distances as the crow flies, and intervals of personal time to distances along a winding path. The time traveler's life is like a mountain railway. The place two miles due east of here may also be nine miles down the line, in the west-bound direction. Clearly we are not dealing here with two independent dimensions. Just as distance along the railway is not a fourth spatial dimension, so a time traveler's personal time is not a second dimension of time. How far down the line some place is depends on its location in three-dimensional space, and likewise the location of events in personal time depend on their locations in one-dimensional external time.

Five miles down the line from here is a place where the line goes under a trestle; two miles further is a place where the line goes over a trestle; these places are one and the same. The trestle by which the line crosses over itself has two different locations along the line, five miles down from here and also seven. In the same way, an event in a time traveler's life may have more than one location in his personal time. If he doubles back toward the past, but not too far, he may be able to talk to himself. The conversation involves two of his stages, separated in his personal time but simultaneous in external time. The location of the conversation in personal time should be the location of the stage involved in it. But there are two such stages; to share the locations of both, the conversation must be assigned two different locations in personal time.

The more we extend the assignment of personal time outwards from the time traveler's stages to the surrounding events, the more will such events acquire multiple locations. It may happen also, as we have already seen, that events that are not simultaneous in external time will be assigned the same location in personal time – or rather, that at least one of the locations of one will be the same as at least one of the locations of the other. So extension must not be carried too far, lest the location of events in extended personal time lose its utility as a means of keeping track of their roles in the time traveler's history.

A time traveler who talks to himself, on the telephone perhaps, looks for all the world like two different people talking to each other. It isn't quite right to say that the whole of him is in two places at once, since neither of the two stages involved in the conversation is the whole of him, or even the whole of the part

of him that is located at the (external) time of the conversation. What's true is
that he, unlike the rest of us, has two different complete stages located at the
same time at different places. What reason have I, then, to regard him as one
person and not two? What unites his stages, including the simultaneous ones,
into a single person? The problem of personal identity is especially acute if he
is the sort of time traveler whose journeys are instantaneous, a broken streak
consisting of several unconnected segments. Then the natural way to regard him
as more than one person is to take each segment as a different person. No one
of them is a time traveler, and the peculiarity of the situation comes to this: all
but one of these several people vanish into thin air, all but another one appear
out of thin air, and there are remarkable resemblances between one at his appearance and another at his vanishing. Why isn't that at least as good a description as
the one I gave, on which the several segments are all parts of one time traveler?

I answer that what unites the stages (or segments) of a time traveler is the
same sort of mental, or mostly mental, continuity and connectedness that unites
anyone else. The only difference is that whereas a common person is connected
and continuous with respect to external time, the time traveler is connected and
continuous only with respect to his own personal time. Taking the stages in
order, mental (and bodily) change is mostly gradual rather than sudden, and at
no point is there sudden change in too many different respects all at once. (We
can include position in external time among the respects we keep track of, if
we like. It may change discontinuously with respect to personal time if not too
much else changes discontinuously along with it.) Moreover, there is not too much
change altogether. Plenty of traits and traces last a lifetime. Finally, the connectedness and the continuity are not accidental. They are explicable; and
further, they are explained by the fact that the properties of each stage depend
causally on those of the stages just before in personal time, the dependence being
such as tends to keep things the same.[4]

To see the purpose of my final requirement of causal continuity, let us see
how it excludes a case of counterfeit time travel. Fred was created out of thin
air, as if in the midst of life; he lived a while, then died. He was created by a
demon, and the demon had chosen at random what Fred was to be like at the
moment of his creation. Much later someone else, Sam, came to resemble Fred
as he was when first created. At the very moment when the resemblance became
perfect, the demon destroyed Sam. Fred and Sam together are very much like
a single person: a time traveler whose personal time starts at Sam's birth, goes
on to Sam's destruction and Fred's creation, and goes on from there to Fred's
death. Taken in this order, the stages of Fred-*cum*-Sam have the proper connectedness and continuity. But they lack causal continuity, so Fred-*cum*-Sam is
not one person and not a time traveler. Perhaps it was pure coincidence that
Fred at his creation and Sam at his destruction were exactly alike; then the connectedness and continuity of Fred-*cum*-Sam across the crucial point are accidental.

Perhaps instead the demon remembered what Fred was like, guided Sam toward perfect resemblance, watched his progress, and destroyed him at the right moment. Then the connectedness and continuity of Fred-*cum*-Sam has a causal explanation, but of the wrong sort. Either way, Fred's first stages do not depend causally for their properties on Sam's last stages. So the case of Fred and Sam is rightly disqualified as a case of personal identity and as a case of time travel.

We might expect that when a time traveler visits the past there will be reversals of causation. You may punch his face before he leaves, causing his eye to blacken centuries ago. Indeed, travel into the past necessarily involves reversed causation. For time travel requires personal identity – he who arrives must be the same person who departed. That requires causal continuity, in which causation runs from earlier to later stages in the order of personal time. But the orders of personal and external time disagree at some point, and there we have causation that runs from later to earlier stages in the order of external time. Elsewhere I have given an analysis of causation in terms of chains of counterfactual dependence, and I took care that my analysis would not rule out causal reversal *a priori*.[5] I think I can argue (but not here) that under my analysis the direction of counterfactual dependence and causation is governed by the direction of other *de facto* asymmetries of time. If so, then reversed causation and time travel are not excluded altogether, but can occur only where there are local exceptions to these asymmetries. As I said at the outset, the time traveler's world would be a most strange one.

Stranger still, if there are local – but only local – causal reversals, then there may also be causal loops: closed causal chains in which some of the causal links are normal in direction and others are reversed. (Perhaps there must be loops if there is reversal; I am not sure.) Each event on the loop has a causal explanation, being caused by events elsewhere on the loop. That is not to say that the loop as a whole is caused or explicable. It may not be. Its inexplicability is especially remarkable if it is made up of the sort of causal processes that transmit information. Recall the time traveler who talked to himself. He talked to himself about time travel, and in the course of the conversation his older self told his younger self how to build a time machine. That information was available in no other way. His older self knew how because his younger self had been told and the information had been preserved by the causal processes that constitute recording, storage, and retrieval of memory traces. His younger self knew, after the conversation, because his older self had known and the information had been preserved by the causal processes that constitute telling. But where did the information come from in the first place? Why did the whole affair happen? There is simply no answer. The parts of the loop are explicable, the whole of it is not. Strange! But not impossible, and not too different from inexplicabilities we are already inured to. Almost everyone agrees that God, or the Big Bang, or the entire infinite past of the universe or the decay of a tritium atom, is uncaused and inexplicable. Then if these are possible, why not also the inexplicable causal loops that arise in time travel?

I have committed a circularity in order not to talk about too much at once, and this is a good place to set it right. In explaining personal time, I presupposed that we were entitled to regard certain stages as comprising a single person. Then in explaining what united the stages into a single person, I presupposed that we were given a personal time order for them. The proper way to proceed is to define personhood and personal time simultaneously, as follows. Suppose given a pair of an aggregate of person-stages, regarded as a candidate for personhood, and an assignment of coordinates to those stages, regarded as a candidate for his personal time. If the stages satisfy the conditions given in my circular explanation with respect to the assignment of coordinates, then both candidates succeed: the stages do comprise a person and the assignment is his personal time.

I have argued so far that what goes on in a time travel story may be a possible pattern of events in four-dimensional space-time with no extra time dimension; that it may be correct to regard the scattered stages of the alleged time traveler as comprising a single person; and that we may legitimately assign to those stages and their surroundings a personal time order that disagrees sometimes with their order in external time. Some might concede all this, but protest that the impossibility of time travel is revealed after all when we ask not what the time traveler *does*, but what he *could do*. Could a time traveler change the past? It seems not: the events of a past moment could no more change than numbers could. Yet it seems that he would be as able as anyone to do things that would change the past if he did them. If a time traveler visiting the past both could and couldn't do something that would change it, then there cannot possibly be such a time traveler.

Consider Tim. He detests his grandfather, whose success in the munitions trade built the family fortune that paid for Tim's time machine. Tim would like nothing so much as to kill Grandfather, but alas he is too late. Grandfather died in his bed in 1957, while Tim was a young boy. But when Tim has built his time machine and traveled to 1920, suddenly he realizes that he is not too late after all. He buys a rifle; he spends long hours in target practice; he shadows Grandfather to learn the route of his daily walk to the munitions works; he rents a room along the route; and there he lurks, one winter day in 1921, rifle loaded, hate in his heart, as Grandfather walks closer, closer. . . .

Tim can kill Grandfather. He has what it takes. Conditions are perfect in every way: the best rifle money could buy, Grandfather an easy target only twenty yards away, not a breeze, door securely locked against intruders, Tim a good shot to begin with and now at the peak of training, and so on. What's to stop him? The forces of logic will not stay his hand! No powerful chaperone stands by to defend the past from interference. (To imagine such a chaperone, as some authors do, is a boring evasion, not needed to make Tim's story consistent.) In short, Tim is as much able to kill Grandfather as anyone ever is to kill anyone. Suppose that down the street another sniper, Tom, lurks waiting for another victim, Grandfather's partner. Tom is not a time traveler, but otherwise he is just like Tim: same make of rifle, same murderous intent, same everything. We can even suppose that Tom, like Tim, believes himself to be a time traveler. Someone has gone to a lot of trouble to deceive Tom into thinking so. There's no doubt that Tom can kill his victim; and Tim has everything going for him that Tom does. By any ordinary standards of ability, Tim can kill Grandfather.

Tim cannot kill grandfather. Grandfather lived, so to kill him would be to change the past. But the events of a past moment are not subdivisible into temporal parts and therefore cannot change. Either the events of 1921 timelessly do include Tim's killing of Grandfather, or else they timelessly don't. We may be tempted to speak of the "original" 1921 that lies in Tim's personal past, many years before his birth, in which Grandfather lived; and of the "new" 1921 in which Tim now finds himself waiting in ambush to kill Grandfather. But if we do speak so, we merely confer two names on one thing. The events of 1921 are doubly located in Tim's (extended) personal time, like the trestle on the railway, but the "original" 1921 and the "new" 1921 are one and the same. If Tim did not kill Grandfather in the "original" 1921, then if he does kill Grandfather in the "new" 1921, he must both kill and not kill Grandfather in 1921 – in the one and only 1921, which is both the "new" and the "original" 1921. It is logically impossible that Tim should change the past by killing Grandfather in 1921. So Tim cannot kill Grandfather.

Not that past moments are special; no more can anyone change the present or the future. Present and future momentary events no more have temporal parts than past ones do. You cannot change a present or future event from what it was originally to what it is after you change it. What you *can* do is to change the present or the future from the unactualized way they would have been without some action of yours to the way they actually are. But that is not an actual change: not a difference between two successive actualities. And Tim can certainly do as much; he changes the past from the unactualized way it would have been without him to the one and only way it actually is. To "change" the past in this way, Tim need not do anything momentous; it is enough just to be there, however unobtrusively.

You know, of course, roughly how the story of Tim must go on if it is to be consistent: he somehow fails. Since Tim didn't kill Grandfather in the "original" 1921, consistency demands that neither does he kill Grandfather in the "new" 1921. Why not? For some commonplace reason. Perhaps some noise distracts him at the last moment, perhaps he misses despite all his target practice, perhaps his nerve fails, perhaps he even feels a pang of unaccustomed mercy. His failure by no means proves that he was not really able to kill Grandfather. We often try and fail to do what we are able to do. Success at some tasks requires not only ability but also luck, and lack of luck is not a temporary lack of ability. Suppose our other sniper, Tom, fails to kill Grandfather's partner for the same reason, whatever it is, that Tim fails to kill Grandfather. It does not follow that Tom was unable to. No more does it follow in Tim's case that he was unable to do what he did not succeed in doing.

We have this seeming contradiction: *"Tim doesn't, but can, because he has what it takes"* versus *"Tim doesn't, and can't, because it's logically impossible to change the past."* I reply that there is no contradiction. Both conclusions are true, and for the reasons given. They are compatible because "can" is equivocal.

To say that something can happen means that its happening is compossible with certain facts. *Which* facts? That is determined, but sometimes not determined well enough, by context. An ape can't speak a human language – say, Finnish – but I can. Facts about the anatomy and operation of the ape's larynx and nervous system are not compossible with his speaking Finnish. The corresponding facts about my larynx and nervous system are compossible with my speaking Finnish. But don't take me along to Helsinki as your interpreter: I can't speak Finnish. My speaking Finnish is compossible with the facts considered so far, but not with further facts about my lack of training. What I can do, relative to one set of facts, I cannot do, relative to another, more inclusive, set. Whenever the context leaves it open which facts are to count as relevant, it is possible to equivocate about whether I can speak Finnish. It is likewise possible to equivocate about whether it is possible for me to speak Finnish, or whether I am able to, or whether I have the ability or capacity or power or potentiality to. Our many words for much the same thing are little help since they do not seem to correspond to different fixed delineations of the relevant facts.

Tim's killing Grandfather that day in 1921 is compossible with a fairly rich set of facts: the facts about his rifle, his skill and training, the unobstructed line of fire, the locked door and the absence of any chaperone to defend the past, and so on. Indeed it is compossible with all the facts of the sorts we would ordinarily count as relevant in saying what someone can do. It is compossible with all the facts corresponding to those we deem relevant in Tom's case. Relative to these facts, Tim can kill Grandfather. But his killing Grandfather is not compossible with another, more inclusive set of facts. There is the simple fact that Grandfather was not killed. Also there are various other facts about Grandfather's doings after 1921 and their effects: Grandfather begat Father in 1922 and Father begat Tim in 1949. Relative to these facts, Tim cannot kill Grandfather. He can and he can't, but under different delineations of the relevant facts. You can reasonably choose the narrower delineation, and say that he can; or the wider delineation, and say that he can't. But choose. What you mustn't do is waver, say in the same breath that he both can and can't, and then claim that this contradiction proves that time travel is impossible.

Exactly the same goes for Tom's parallel failure. For Tom to kill Grandfather's partner also is compossible with all facts of the sorts we ordinarily count as relevant, but not compossible with a larger set including, for instance, the fact that the intended victim lived until 1934. In Tom's case we are not puzzled. We say without hesitation that he can do it, because we see at once that the facts that are not compossible with his success are facts about the future of the time in question and therefore not the sort of facts we count as relevant in saying what Tom can do.

In Tim's case it is harder to keep track of which facts are relevant. We are accustomed to exclude facts about the future of the time in question, but to include some facts about its past. Our standards do not apply unequivocally to the crucial facts in this special case: Tim's failure, Grandfather's survival, and his subsequent doings. If we have foremost in mind that they lie in the external future of that moment in 1921 when Tim is almost ready to shoot, then we exclude them just as we exclude the parallel facts in Tom's case. But if we have foremost in mind that they precede that moment in Tim's extended personal time, then we tend to include them. To make the latter be foremost in your mind, I chose to tell Tim's story in the order of his personal time, rather than in the order of external time. The fact of Grandfather's survival until 1957 had already been told before I got to the part of the story about Tim lurking in ambush to kill him in 1921. We must decide, if we can, whether to treat these personally past and externally future facts as if they were straightforwardly past or as if they were straightforwardly future.

Fatalists – the best of them – are philosophers who take facts we count as irrelevant in saying what someone can do, disguise them somehow as facts of a different sort that we count as relevant, and thereby argue that we can do less than we think – indeed, that there is nothing at all that we don't do but can. I am not going to vote Republican next fall. The fatalist argues that, strange to say, I not only won't but can't; for my voting Republican is not compossible with the fact that it was true already in the year 1548 that I was not going to vote Republican 428 years later. My rejoinder is that this is a fact, sure enough; however, it is an irrelevant fact about the future masquerading as a relevant fact about the past, and so should be left out of account in saying what, in any ordinary sense, I can do. We are unlikely to be fooled by the fatalist's methods of disguise in this case, or other ordinary cases. But in cases of time travel, precognition, or the like, we're on less familiar ground, so it may take less of a disguise to fool us. Also, new methods of disguise are available, thanks to the device of personal time.

Here's another bit of fatalist trickery. Tim, as he lurks, already knows that he will fail. At least he has the wherewithal to know it if he thinks, he knows it implicitly. For he remembers that Grandfather was alive when he was a boy, he knows that those who are killed are thereafter not alive, he knows (let us suppose) that he is a time traveler who has reached the same 1921 that lies in his personal past, and he ought to understand – as we do – why a time traveler cannot change the past. What is known cannot be false. So his success is not only not compossible with facts that belong to the external future and his personal past, but also is not compossible with the present fact of his knowledge that he will fail. I reply that the fact of his foreknowledge, at the moment while he waits to shoot, is not a fact entirely about that moment. It may be divided into two parts. There is the fact that he then believes (perhaps only implicitly) that he will fail; and there is the further fact that his belief is correct, and correct not at all by accident, and hence qualifies as an item of knowledge. It is only the latter fact that is not compossible with his success, but it is only the former that is entirely about the moment in question. In calling Tim's state at that moment knowledge, not just belief, facts about personally earlier but externally later moments were smuggled into consideration.

I have argued that Tim's case and Tom's are alike, except that in Tim's case we are more tempted than usual – and with reason – to opt for a semi-fatalist mode of speech. But perhaps they differ in another way. In Tom's case, we can expect a perfectly consistent answer to the counterfactual question: what if Tom had killed Grandfather's partner? Tim's case is more difficult. If Tim had killed Grandfather, it seems offhand that contradictions would have been true. The killing both would and wouldn't have occurred. No Grandfather, no Father; no Father, no Tim; no Tim, no killing. And for good measure: no Grandfather, no family fortune; no fortune, no time machine; no time machine, no killing. So the supposition that Tim killed Grandfather seems impossible in more than the semi-fatalistic sense already granted.

If you suppose Tim to kill Grandfather and hold all the rest of his story fixed, of course you get a contradiction. But likewise if you suppose Tom to kill Grandfather's partner and hold the rest of his story fixed – including the part that told of his failure – you get a contradiction. If you make *any* counterfactual supposition and hold all else fixed you get a contradiction. The thing to do is rather to make the counterfactual supposition and hold all else as close to fixed as you consistently can. That procedure will yield perfectly consistent answers to the question: what if Tim had not killed Grandfather? In that case, some of the story I told would not have been true. Perhaps Tim might have been the time-traveling grandson of someone else. Perhaps he might have been the grandson of a man killed in 1921 and miraculously resurrected. Perhaps he might have been not a time traveler at all, but rather someone created out of nothing in 1920 equipped with false memories of a personal past that never was. It is hard to say what is the least revision of Tim's story to make it true that Tim kills Grandfather, but certainly the contradictory story in which the killing both does and doesn't occur is not the least revision. Hence it is false (according to the unrevised story) that if Tim had killed Grandfather then contradictions would have been true.

What difference would it make if Tim travels in branching time? Suppose that at the possible world of Tim's story the space-time manifold branches; the branches are separated not in time, and not in space, but in some other way. Tim travels not only in time but also from one branch to another. In one branch Tim is absent from the events of 1921; Grandfather lives; Tim is born, grows up, and vanishes in his time machine. The other branch diverges from the first when Tim turns up in 1921; there Tim kills Grandfather and Grandfather leaves no descendants and no fortune; the events of the two branches differ more and more from that time on. Certainly this is a consistent story; it is a story in which Grandfather both is and isn't killed in 1921 (in the different branches); and it is a story in which Tim, by killing Grandfather, succeeds in preventing his own birth (in one of the branches). But it is not a story in which Tim's killing of Grandfather both does occur and doesn't: it simply does, though it is located in one branch and not in the other. And it is not a story in which Tim changes the past; 1921 and later years contain the events of both branches, coexisting somehow without interaction. It remains true at all the personal times of Tim's life, even after the killing, that Grandfather lives in one branch and dies in the other.[6]

Notes

1. I have particularly in mind two of the time travel stories of Robert A. Heinlein: "By His Bootstraps", in R.A. Heinlein, *The Menace from Earth* (Hicksville, NY, 1959), and "—All You Zombies—", in R.A. Heinlein, *The Unpleasant Profession of Jonathan Hoag* (Hicksville, NY, 1959).

2. Accounts of time travel in two-dimensional time are found in Jack W. Meiland, "A Two-Dimensional Passage Model of Time for Time Travel", *Philosophical Studies*, vol. 26 (1974), pp. 153–73; and in the initial chapters of Isaac Asimov, *The End of Eternity* (Garden City, NY, 1955). Asimov's denouement, however, seems to require some different conception of time travel.

3. H.G. Wells, *The Time Machine, An Invention* (London, 1895), epilogue. The passage is criticized as contradictory in Donald C. Williams, "The Myth of Passage", *The Journal of Philosophy*, vol. 48 (1951), p. 463.

4. I discuss the relation between personal identity and mental connectedness and continuity at greater length in "Survival and Identity" in *The Identities of Persons*, ed. by Amélie Rorty (Berkeley and Los Angeles, 1976).

5. "Causation", *The Journal of Philosophy*, vol. 70 (1973), pp. 556–67; the analysis relies on the analysis of counterfactuals given in my *Counterfactuals* (Oxford, 1973).

6. The present chapter summarizes a series of lectures of the same title, given as the Gavin David Young Lectures in Philosophy at the University of Adelaide in July 1971. I thank the Australian-American Educational Foundation and the American Council of Learned Societies for research support. I am grateful to many friends for comments on earlier versions of this chapter; especially Philip Kitcher, William Newton-Smith, J. J. C. Smart, and Donald Williams.

26

THE QUANTUM PHYSICS OF TIME TRAVEL

David Deutsch and Michael Lockwood

Imagine, if you will, that our friend Sonia keeps a time machine in her garage. Last night she used it to visit her grandfather in 1934, when he was still courting her grandmother. Sonia convinced him of her identity by referring to family secrets that he had not yet revealed to anyone. This left him stunned, but worse was to follow. When he told his sweetheart over dinner that he had just met their future granddaughter, the lady's response was both to doubt his sanity and to take offense at his presumption. They never married and never had the baby who would have become Sonia's mother (see Figure 26.1).

So how can Sonia be sitting here today, telling us of her adventure? If her mother was never born, how was she ever born? The real question is, when Sonia returns to 1934, can she or can she not bring her grandparents' romance to a premature end? Either answer creates problems. If Sonia can prevent her own birth, there is a contradiction. If she cannot, that inability conflicts with common sense, for what is to prevent Sonia from behaving as she pleases? Will some strange paralysis grip her whenever she tries to enact certain intentions?

Situations like this – a mild version of the classic "grandfather paradox," in which the grandfather is murdered by his time-traveling grandchild – are often regarded as ruling out time travel. Yet, surprisingly, the laws of physics do not forbid such adventures.

Another paradox, which often appears in science fiction, has been discussed by the Oxford philosopher Michael Dummett. An art critic from the future visits a 20th-century painter, who is regarded in the critic's own century as a great artist. Seeing the painter's current work, the critic finds it mediocre and concludes that the artist has yet to produce those inspired paintings that so impressed future generations. The critic shows the painter a book of reproductions of these later works. The painter contrives to hide this book, forcing the critic to leave without it, and then sets about meticulously copying the reproductions onto canvas. Thus, the reproductions exist because they are copied from the

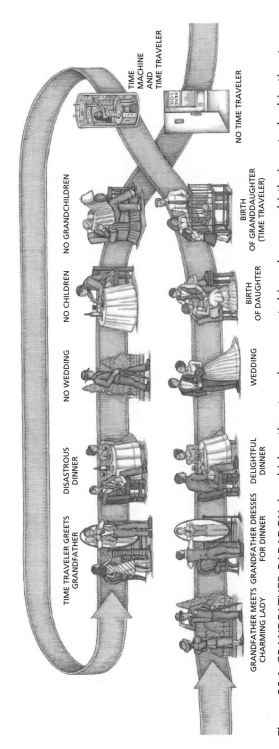

Figure 26.1 GRANDFATHER PARADOX, in which a time traveler prevents his or her own birth, is a stock objection to time travel.

paintings, and the paintings exist because they are copied from the repro-ductions. Although this story threatens no contradiction, there is something very wrong with it. It purports to give us the paintings without anyone's having to expend artistic effort in creating them – a kind of artistic "free lunch."

1.

Persuaded by such objections, physicists have traditionally invoked a chron-ology principle that, by fiat, rules out travel into the past. One-way travel into the future raises no such problems. Einstein's special theory of relativity predicts that, with sufficient acceleration, astronauts could go on a journey and return to the earth decades into the future, while physically aging only a year or two. It is important to distinguish between predictions such as this, which are merely surprising, and processes that would violate physical laws or independently justifiable philosophical principles.

We shall shortly explain why traveling into the past would not violate any such principle. To do so, we must first explore the concept of time itself, as physi-cists understand it. In Einstein's special and general theories of relativity, three-dimensional space is combined with time to form four-dimensional space-time. Whereas space consists of spatial points, space-time consists of spatiotemporal points, or events, each of which represents a particular place at a particular time. Your life forms a kind of four-dimensional "worm" in space-time: the tip of the worm's tail corresponds to the event of your birth, and the front of its head to the event of your death. An object, seen at any one instant, is a three-dimensional cross section of this long, thin, intricately curved worm. The line along which the worm lies (ignoring its thickness) is called that object's worldline.

At any point on your worldline, the angle it makes with the time axis is a measure of your speed. The worldline of a ray of light is typically drawn as mak-ing an angle of 45 degrees; a flash of light spreading out in all directions forms a cone in space-time, called a lightcone (see Figure 26.2). An important difference between space and space-time is that a worldline – unlike, say, a line drawn on paper – cannot be any arbitrary squiggle. Because nothing can travel faster than light, the worldline of a physical object can never stray outside the lightcone emanating from any event in its past. Worldlines that meet this criterion are called timelike. Time, as measured by a watch, increases in one direction along a worldline.

Einstein's special theory of relativity requires worldlines of physical objects to be timelike; the field equations of his general theory of relativity predict that massive bodies such as stars and black holes distort space-time and bend world-lines. This is the origin of gravity: the earth's worldline spirals around the sun's, which spirals around that of the center of our galaxy.

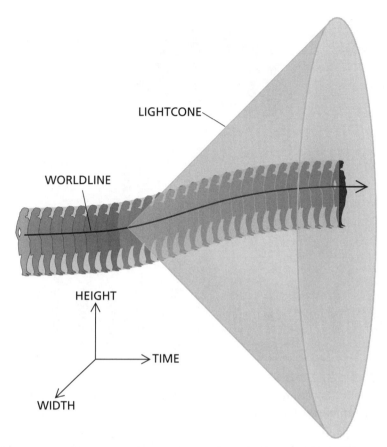

Figure 26.2 SPACE AND TIME are combined into one four-dimensional entity, space-time. Here we show two space dimensions and time. A worldline connects all events in our life in space-time; since we have some size, a person's worldline is more like a worm extending from birth to death than a line. The worldlines of light rays emanating in all space directions from an event trace out a cone in space-time, called a lightcone. The worldline of any object, such as the navel of this figure, cannot stray outside a lightcone emanating from any point in its past.

Suppose space-time becomes so distorted that some worldlines form closed loops (see Figure 26.3). Such worldlines would be timelike all the way around. Locally they would conform to all the familiar properties of space and time, yet they would be corridors to the past. If we tried to follow such a closed timelike curve (or CTC) exactly, all the way around, we would bump into our former selves and get pushed aside. But by following part of a CTC, we could return

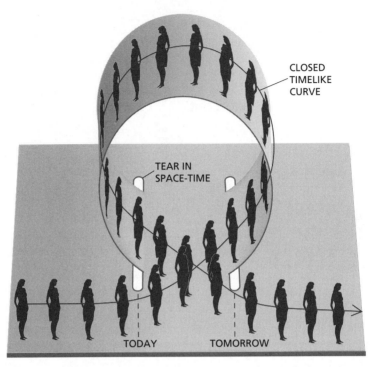

Figure 26.3 CLOSED TIMELIKE CURVE can be formed if space-time loops around. Entering such a curve tomorrow and moving forward in time, we can end up at today.

to the past and participate in events there. We could shake hands with our younger selves or, if the loop were large enough, visit our ancestors.

To do this, we should either have to harness naturally occurring CTCs or create CTCs by distorting and tearing the fabric of space-time. So a time machine, rather than being a special kind of vehicle, would provide a route to the past, along which an ordinary vehicle, such as a spacecraft, could travel. But unlike a spatial route, a CTC (or rather, the surrounding closed timelike tube) gets used up if repeatedly traversed; just so many worldline worms can fit into it, and no more. If one travels on it to a particular event, one will meet everyone who has ever traveled, or will ever travel, to that event.

2.

Does our universe now, or will it ever, contain CTCs? We do not know, but there are various theoretical conjectures about how they might be formed. The mathematician Kurt Gödel found a solution to Einstein's equations that describes CTCs. In that solution, the whole universe rotates (according to current evidence, the actual universe does not). CTCs also appear in solutions of Einstein's equations describing rotating black holes. But these solutions neglect infalling matter, and how far they apply to realistic black holes is a matter of controversy. Also, a time traveler would be trapped inside the black hole after reaching the past, unless its rotation rate exceeded a critical threshold. Astrophysicists think it unlikely that any naturally occurring black holes are spinning that fast. Perhaps a civilization far more advanced than ours could shoot matter into them, increasing their rotation rate until safe CTCs appeared, but many physicists doubt that this would be possible.

A kind of shortcut through space-time, called a wormhole, has been mooted by Princeton University physicist John A. Wheeler. Kip S. Thorne of the California Institute of Technology and others have shown how two ends of a wormhole could be moved so as to form a CTC. According to a recent calculation by J. Richard Gott of Princeton, a cosmic string (another theoretical construct that may or may not exist in nature) passing rapidly by another would generate CTCs.

We are at present a very long way from finding any of these CTCs. They may, however, become accessible to future civilizations, which might well attempt to enact time-travel paradoxes. Let us therefore take a closer look at the paradoxes to see what principles, if any, time travel would violate, according to classical and quantum physics.

Classical physics says, unequivocally, that on arriving in the past Sonia must do the things that history records her doing. Some philosophers find this an unacceptable restriction of her "free will." But as an argument against time travel within classical physics, that objection is unpersuasive. For classical physics in the absence of CTCs is deterministic: what happens at any instant is wholly determined by what happens at any earlier (or later) instant. Accordingly, everything we ever do is an inevitable consequence of what happened before we were even conceived. This determinism alone is often held to be incompatible with free will. So time travel poses no more of a threat to free will than does classical physics itself.

3.

The real core of the grandfather paradox is not the violation of free will but of a fundamental principle that underlies both science and everyday reasoning; we call this the autonomy principle. According to this principle, it is possible to create in our immediate environment any configuration of matter that the laws of physics permit locally, without reference to what the rest of the universe may be doing. When we strike a match, we do not have to worry that we might be thwarted because the configuration of the planets, say, might be inconsistent with the match being lit. Autonomy is a logical property that is highly desirable for the laws of physics to possess. For it underpins all experimental science: we typically take for granted that we can set up our apparatus in any configuration allowed by physical law and that the rest of the universe will take care of itself.

In the absence of CTCs, both classical and quantum physics conform to the autonomy principle. But in their presence, classical physics does not, because of what John L. Friedman of the University of Wisconsin and others call "the consistency principle." This states that the only configurations of matter that can occur locally are those that are self-consistent globally. Under this principle, the world outside the laboratory can physically constrain our actions inside, even if everything we do is consistent, locally, with the laws of physics. Ordinarily we are unaware of this constraint, because the autonomy and consistency principles never come into conflict. But classically, in the presence of CTCs, they do.

Classical physics says there is only one history, so try as she might to do other than what history dictates, consistency requires Sonia to act out her part in it. She may visit her grandfather. But perhaps when he tells Sonia's grandmother-to-be what happened, she becomes worried about his state of health. He is very touched and proposes to her; she accepts. Not only could this happen – under classical physics something like it must happen. Sonia, far from altering the past, becomes part of it.

What if Sonia is determined to rebel against history? Suppose she travels back to meet her earlier self. At this meeting, her younger self records what her older self says and, in due course, having become that older self, deliberately tries to say something different. Must we suppose, absurdly, that she is gripped by an irresistible compulsion to utter the original words, contrary to her prior intentions to do otherwise? Sonia could even program a robot to speak for her: Would it somehow be forced to disobey its program?

Within classical physics, the answer is yes. Something must prevent Sonia or the robot from deviating from what has already happened. It need not be anything dramatic, however. Any commonplace hitch will suffice. Sonia's vehicle breaks down, or the robot's program turns out to contain a bug. But one way or another, according to classical physics, consistency requires the autonomy principle to fail.

Now let us return to the story of the time-traveling art critic. We call this violation of common sense a "knowledge paradox" (the grandfather paradox is an inconsistency paradox). We use the term "knowledge" here in an extended sense, according to which a painting, a scientific article, a piece of machinery and a living organism all embody knowledge. Knowledge paradoxes violate the principle that knowledge can come into existence only as a result of problem-solving processes, such as biological evolution or human thought. Time travel appears to allow knowledge to flow from the future to the past and back, in a

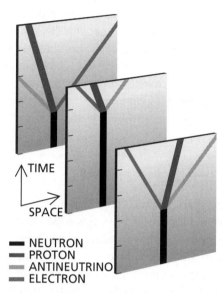

TIME

SPACE

- NEUTRON
- PROTON
- ANTINEUTRINO
- ELECTRON

Figure 26.4 NEUTRON DECAY can occur at any time, though some times are more likely than others. For each instant in which the neutron might decay, there is a universe in which it decays at that instant, according to Everett's multiverse interpretation of quantum mechanics.

self-consistent loop, without anyone or anything ever having to grapple with the corresponding problems. What is philosophically objectionable here is not that knowledge-bearing artifacts are carried into the past – it is the "free lunch" element. The knowledge required to invent the artifacts must not be supplied by the artifacts themselves.

In an inconsistency paradox, physical events seem to be more tightly constrained than we are used to. In a knowledge paradox, they are less tightly constrained. For instance, the state of the universe before the art critic arrives does not determine who, if anyone, will arrive from the future or what he or she will bring along: the generally deterministic laws of classical physics allow the critic to bring back great pictures, poor pictures or no pictures at all. This indeterminacy is not what we usually expect from classical physics, but it constitutes no fundamental impediment to time travel. Indeed, the indeterminacy would allow the classical laws to be supplemented with an additional principle, stating that knowledge can arise only as a result of problem-solving processes.

Yet that principle would land us in the same problem regarding autonomy as we encountered in the grandfather paradox. For what is to prevent Sonia from carrying new inventions into the past and showing them to their supposed originators? So although classical physics can, after all, accommodate the kind of time travel that is usually considered paradoxical, it does this at the cost of violating the autonomy principle. Hence, no classical analysis can wholly eliminate the paradox.

All this, however, is in our view academic. For classical physics is false. There are many situations in which it is an excellent approximation to the truth. But when closed timelike curves are involved, it does not even come close.

4.

One thing we already know about CTCs is that if they exist, we need quantum mechanics to understand them. Indeed, Stephen W. Hawking of the University of Cambridge has argued that quantum-mechanical effects would either prevent CTCs from forming or would destroy any would-be time traveler approaching one. According to Hawking's calculations, which use an approximation that ignores the gravitational effects of quantum fields, fluctuations in such fields would approach infinity near the CTC. Approximations are inevitable until we discover how to apply quantum theory fully to gravity; but space-times containing CTCs push current techniques beyond the limits where they can be confidently applied. We believe that Hawking's calculations reveal only the shortcomings of those techniques. The quantum-mechanical effects that we shall be describing, far from preventing time travel, would actually facilitate it.

Quantum mechanics may necessitate the presence of closed timelike curves. CTCs, while hard to find on large scales, may well be plentiful at submicroscopic scales, where the effects of quantum mechanics predominate. There is as yet no fully satisfactory theory of quantum gravity. But according to many versions that have been proposed, space-time, though it appears smooth at large scales, has a foamlike submicroscopic structure containing many wormholes as well as CTCs reaching about 10^{-42} second into the past. For all we know, time travel by subatomic particles may be going on all around us.

More important, quantum mechanics can resolve the paradoxes of time travel. It is our most basic physical theory and constitutes a radical departure from the classical worldview. Rather than predicting with certainty what we shall observe, it predicts all possible outcomes of an observation and the probability of each. If we wait for a neutron to decay (into a proton, an electron and an antineutrino), we are most likely to observe this in about 20 minutes. But we might observe it immediately or be kept waiting indefinitely. How are we to understand this randomness? Is there something about the internal state of neutrons, currently unknown, that differs from one neutron to another and explains why each neutron breaks up when it does? This superficially attractive idea turns out to conflict with predictions of quantum mechanics that have been experimentally corroborated.

Other attempts have been made to preserve our classical intuitions by modifying quantum mechanics. None are generally deemed to have succeeded. So we prefer to take quantum mechanics at face value and to adopt a conception of reality that straightforwardly mirrors the structure of the theory itself. When we refer to quantum mechanics, we mean its so-called many-universes interpretation, first proposed by Hugh Everett III in 1957. According to Everett, if something physically can happen, it does – in some universe. Physical reality consists of a collection of universes, sometimes called a multiverse. Each universe in the multiverse contains its own copy of the neutron whose decay we wish to observe. For each instant at which the neutron might decay, there is a universe in which it decays at that instant. Since we observe it decaying at a specific instant, we too must exist in many copies, one for each universe. In one universe we see the neutron break up at 10:30, in another at 10:31 and so on. As applied to the multiverse, quantum theory is deterministic – it predicts the subjective probability of each outcome by prescribing the proportion of universes in which that outcome occurs.

Everett's interpretation of quantum mechanics is still controversial among physicists. Quantum mechanics is commonly used as a calculational tool that, given an input – information about a physical process – yields the probability of each possible output. Most of the time we do not need to interpret the mathematics describing that process. But there are two branches of physics – quantum cosmology and the quantum theory of computation – in which this is not good enough. These branches have as their entire subject matter the inner workings of the physical systems under study. Among researchers in these two fields, Everett's interpretation prevails.

What, then, does quantum mechanics, by Everett's interpretation, say about time travel paradoxes? Well, the grandfather paradox, for one, simply does not arise. Suppose that Sonia embarks on a "paradoxical" project that, if completed, would prevent her own conception. What happens? If the classical space-time contains CTCs, then, according to quantum mechanics, the universes in the multiverse must be linked up in an unusual way. Instead of having many disjoint, parallel universes, each containing CTCs, we have in effect a single, convoluted space-time consisting of many connected universes. The links force Sonia to travel to a universe that is identical, up to the instant of her arrival, with the one she left, but that is thereafter different because of her presence.

5.

So does Sonia prevent her own birth or not? That depends on which universe one is referring to. In the universe she leaves, the one she was born in, her grandfather did marry her grandmother because, in that universe, he received no visit from Sonia. In the other universe, the one whose past Sonia travels to, her grandfather does not marry that particular woman, and Sonia is never born.

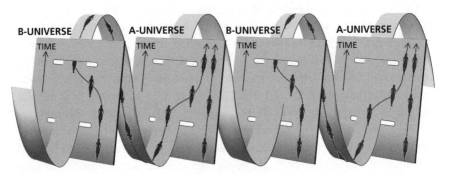

Figure 26.5 MULTIVERSE PICTURE OF REALITY unravels the time travel paradoxes. Sonia plans to enter the time machine tomorrow and travel back to today but resolves that if she emerges from the time machine today, she will not enter tomorrow. She is able to carry out this plan, without paradox. In a B-universe she does not emerge today and so enters the time machine tomorrow. She then emerges today, but in an A-universe, and meets her copy – who does not enter the time machine.

Thus, the fact that Sonia is traveling in time does not constrain her actions. And it turns out, according to quantum mechanics, that it never would. Quantum mechanics, even in the presence of CTCs, conforms to the autonomy principle.

Suppose Sonia tries her best to enact a paradox. She resolves that tomorrow she will enter the time machine and emerge today, unless a version of her first emerges today, having set out from tomorrow; and that if a version of her does emerge today, she will not enter the time machine tomorrow. Within classical physics, that resolution is self-contradictory. But not under quantum physics. In half the universes – call them A – an older Sonia steps out of the time machine. Consequently, just as she resolved, Sonia does not enter the time machine to-morrow, and each A-universe thereafter contains two Sonias of slightly different ages. In the other (B) universes, no one emerges from the time machine. So Sonia sets out and arrives in an A-universe where she meets a younger version of her-self. Once again, she can behave as she likes in the past, doing things that depart from her (accurate) recollections.

So in half the universes there is a meeting between two Sonias, and in half there is not. In the A-universes an older Sonia appears "from nowhere," and in the B-universes she disappears "into nowhere." Each A-universe then contains two Sonias, the older one having started life in a B-universe. Sonia has gone missing from each B-universe, having emigrated to an A-universe.

However convoluted Sonia's plans might be, quantum mechanics says the universes link up in such a way that she can carry them out consistently. Suppose Sonia tries to cause a paradox by traveling around the link twice. She wants to reappear in the universe she started from and join her previous self for a spaghetti dinner instead of the stir-fry she remembers having. She can behave as she likes, and in particular eat whatever she likes, in company with her younger self; however, the multiverse, by being linked up in a way different from that of the previous paradox, prevents her from doing so in her original universe. Sonia can succeed in sharing spaghetti with a version of herself only in another universe, while in the original universe she is still alone, eating stir-fry.

Time travel would make possible another curious phenomenon, which we call "asymmetric separation." Suppose that Sonia's boyfriend, Stephen, stays behind while she uses her time machine in one of the ways we have described. In half the universes, she enters it and never returns. Thus, from Stephen's point of view, there is a possibility that he will be separated from her. Half the versions of him will see Sonia departing, never to return. (The other half will be joined by a second Sonia.) But from Sonia's point of view, there is no possibility of her being separated from Stephen, because every version of her will end up in a universe containing a version of him – whom she will have to share with another version of herself.

If Stephen and Sonia follow a similar plan – entering the time machine if and only if the other does not first emerge – they can separate completely, ending up in different universes. If they carry out more complex intentions, each of them could end up in the company of any number of versions of the other. If time travel were achievable on a grand scale, competing galactic civilizations could use these asymmetric separation effects to have the whole galaxy to themselves. Also, an entire civilization could "clone" itself into any number of copies, just as Sonia did. The more often it did this, the likelier it would be that an observer would see it disappear from his universe, just as Stephen sees Sonia disappear from the A-universe when her "clone" appears in the B-universe. (Perhaps this explains why we have not yet encountered any extraterrestrials!)

In the art critic story, quantum mechanics allows events, from the participants' perspective, to occur much as Dummett describes. The universe that the critic comes from must have been one in which the artist did, eventually, learn to paint well. In that universe, the pictures were produced by creative effort, and reproductions were later taken to the past of another universe. There the paintings were indeed plagiarized – if one can be said to plagiarize the work of another version of oneself – and the painter did get "something for nothing." But there is no paradox, because now the existence of the pictures was caused by genuine creative effort, albeit in another universe.

The idea that time travel paradoxes could be resolved by "parallel universes" has been anticipated in science fiction and by some philosophers. What we have presented here is not so much a new resolution as a new way of arriving at it, by deducing it from existing physical theory. All the claims we have made about time travel are consequences of using standard quantum mechanics to calculate the behavior of logic circuits – just like those that are used in computers, except for the additional supposition that information can travel into the past along CTCs. The time travelers in this computer model are packets of information. Similar results have been obtained using other models.

6.

These calculations definitively dispose of the inconsistency paradoxes, which turn out to be merely artifacts of an obsolete, classical worldview. We have argued that the knowledge paradoxes would likewise present no obstacle to time travel. But one cannot make that argument airtight until concepts like knowledge and creativity have been successfully translated into the language of physics. Only then can one tell if the "no-free-lunch" principle we require – that it takes problem-solving processes to create knowledge – is consistent, in the presence of CTCs, with quantum mechanics and the rest of physics.

There is a final argument that is often raised against time travel. As Hawking puts it, "The best evidence that time travel never will be possible is that we have not been invaded by hordes of tourists from the future." But this is a mistake. For a CTC reaches only as far back as the moment it was created. If the earth's first navigable CTC is constructed in 2054, subsequent time travelers could use it to travel to 2054 or later, but no earlier. Navigable CTCs might already exist elsewhere in the galaxy. But even then we should not expect "hordes of tourists from the future." Given the limited capacity of CTCs and that our stock of them at any given time cannot be replenished in this universe, a CTC is a nonrenewable resource. Extraterrestrial civilizations or our descendants will have their own priorities for its use, and there is no reason to assume that visiting the earth in the 20th century would be high on their list. Even if it were, they would arrive only in some universes, of which this, presumably, is not one.

We conclude that if time travel is impossible, then the reason has yet to be discovered. We may or may not one day locate or create navigable CTCs. But if anything like the many-universes picture is true – and in quantum cosmology and the quantum theory of computation no viable alternative is known – then all the standard objections to time travel depend on false models of physical reality. So it is incumbent on anyone who still wants to reject the idea of time travel to come up with some new scientific or philosophical argument.

27

MIRACLES AND WONDERS: SCIENCE FICTION AS EPISTEMOLOGY

Richard Hanley

I've always been attracted to science fiction, in part because science fiction is so *imaginative*. The worldview of everyone around me always seemed like the horrible English/Australian cooking I grew up with: every day the same old stodge of meat-and-three-vegetables, which only seems like the best thing available if you doggedly refuse to try anything else. Now I live in the USA, and some things haven't changed. Most people around me eat absolutely disgusting food, and believe absolutely outrageous things for no good reason.

But could there be one kind of good reason – evidence – for belief in super-natural things? A minor philosophical industry has sprung up in recent years defending the possibility and epistemic utility of *miracles*: supernatural interventions in the world by a Christian God. By examining some staples of science fiction, I'm going to find a way to agree: miracles are possible, and could tell us something about reality. But don't get too excited: I doubt my conclusion will offer any comfort at all to traditional Christianity.

No discussion of miracles and wonders can proceed without mentioning David Hume, so let's get that out of the way.

Humeans on Miracles

Nobody is sure exactly what Hume himself thought, but there is an identifiable Humean tradition on miracles. It holds that you would never be justified in think-ing that a miracle has occurred, and it makes two main points.

First, by definition a miracle is in some relevant sense *beyond* what the laws of nature can describe and explain. It requires that something happen which is *contrary* to the laws of nature, standing in need of *super*natural expla-nation. Suppose something marvelous occurs, which is established as con-trary to our current understanding of the laws of nature. Then we have two choices: either accept that it is a miracle, requiring supernatural explanation; or else revise our understanding of the laws of nature. Humeans hold that it will never be more plausible to opt for a miraculous explanation. After all, we know too well from past experience that our understanding of nature is limited, so any occurrence, no matter how marvelous, at most ought to send scientists back to the drawing board to come up with better natural explanations.

The second point is intended to generally undermine claims of an established marvel which is contrary to our understanding of the laws of nature; to prevent a miracle claim even getting a toehold. Such belief would be based on testimony (either the testimony of someone else or the testimony of your senses), and it is never more likely that the miracle actually occurred than that the testimony is mistaken. So you would never be justified in believing a miracle had occurred.

These are powerful considerations, which I think in most cases of actual miracle claims easily win the day. But the second point seems overstated. Recall Arthur C. Clarke's Third Law, "any sufficiently advanced technology is indistinguishable from magic," at least at first. (I take it Clarke means by *magic* something that is not a mere conjurer's trick, impressive as that can be.) What *seems* like magic might just be beyond our current understanding, so surely there must be conditions under which it is plausible to believe that it had in fact occurred anyway.

In general, the more people who seem to see something, the more seriously we should take it. Not always, of course – even thousands of people, if they're all in the grip of some religious fervor or other, can convince themselves they see things that aren't there. So the sort of evidence we should take more seriously would be *robust*: corroborated reports from people of diverse backgrounds and beliefs, under different sorts of conditions.

(Consider for instance the oft-claimed phenomenon of near-death experience. I have no doubt that there is indeed a commonly experienced phenomenon here – such as the seeing of "the light" – but various claims like meeting one's dead relatives are very culturally specific, and nowhere near robust enough.)

Three Modern Miracle Mongers

What kind of robust evidence could do the job, and overturn the first Humean point as well? Here's C. S. Lewis (1986): "If the end of the world appeared in all the literal trappings of the Apocalypse; if the modern materialist saw with his own eyes the heavens rolled up and great white throne appearing, if he had the sensation of being hurled into the Lake of Fire, he would continue forever, in that lake itself, to regard his experience as an illusion and to find the explanation of it in psychoanalysis, or cerebral pathology."

Here's Peter Heath (1976): "If the stars and the galaxies were to shift overnight in the firmament, rearranging themselves so as to spell out, in various languages, such slogans as I AM THAT I AM, or GOD IS LOVE . . . would anyone lose much time in admitting that this settled the matter?"

Or consider William Dembski (1994): the "Incredible Talking Pulsar" is 3 billion light years away, transmits messages in Morse Code, and answers questions we put to it – in just ten minutes! The questions are hard, but the answers are checkable, and the Pulsar is always right. (Some proofs are uncomputable – such as Goldbach's Conjecture, perhaps – but are at least checkable if false.) Since there are questions we *know* are beyond the computational resources of the universe, the answers to them would be, according to Dembski, evidence of the divine.

Okay, that was three of the miracle monger's favorite things. Now let's examine three of mine, and put them all together.

Three of my Favorite Sci-Fi Things: Time Travel, Other Dimensions, and Simulations

The possibility of time travel is something I believe in. But most of the time travel stories in science fiction are impossible, since they fall for a three-card trick. They depict time travel as a means for *annulling* the past: for making it the case that (unrestrictedly) some event both occurred and never occurred. But that's a contradiction, and no machine or anything else can bring it about that a contradiction is true. So you don't need to be a Humean to conclude that any appearance of contradiction does not actually establish that a contradiction is true – it will *never* be on balance advisable to revise the laws of logic. (Of course, there's always someone who disagrees – see the relevance logic and dialetheism literatures, if you're interested in contradiction mongers.)

Consistent time travel may involve marvelous things: very specific knowledge of the future, advanced technology, people being in two places at once, people parenting themselves, and so on. But these will not disturb Humeans in the least. Roy Sorenson (1987) agrees, but he apparently thinks only the second Humean point needs to be made. That is, Sorenson thinks you could never have sufficient evidence that you or anyone else has time traveled. I'm more optimistic on that score. For instance, something like the Sports Almanac in *Back to the Future II* could in my view establish that information, if not the almanac itself, has time traveled. But I also think that the first Humean point stands.

Visitors from the future may, as we noted above, appear to be in possession of magical powers, given that our physics can give no account of them, and there are enough physicists around who believe anyway that time travel is physically impossible. But surely we should give credence to the possibility that the physicists are wrong, and that their understanding of nature needs revision.

So why doesn't Dembski give credence to time travel as a possible explanation of the incredible talking pulsar? Perhaps the incredibly fast exchange of information between us and the pulsar happens in physically possible ways, because time travel is involved. Why leap so quickly to the supernatural conclusion? Answer: because that's the hypothesis Dembski favors *before* ever considering the evidence.

Other-dimensional hypotheses expand our horizons a little more still. Consider Edwin Abbott's *Flatland*, the story of two-dimensional beings, perceiving two-dimensionally, inhabiting a two-dimensional world in a universe that is in fact three-dimensional. Suppose that a clever Flatlander conceives of the third dimension, and builds a house in the shape of an unfolded *hypersquare* (we would call it a cube). That is, he builds a house of six squares, four in a row, with two more attached one on either side to the second in the row. But he builds it on a fault-line, and (by analogy with the unfortunate protagonist of Robert Heinlein's *And He Built a Crooked House*), his house folds up into a cube, with one face in Flatland. Now he enters his house, and when he changes rooms (the rooms are now at right angles to each other, thanks to the folding), seems to the rest of Flatland to have *disappeared into thin air*. Were he to continue through the house, he might well *reappear* in Flatland, in a different location.

No doubt his fellow Flatlanders would suspect that magic is at work, but if they are imaginative enough, they will have to seriously consider the possibility of a third dimension at right angles to their familiar two. By the same token, the hypothesis of a fourth spatial dimension at right angles to our familiar three must be taken seriously when we are confronted with any marvelous occurrence. These will involve more than appearance and disappearance. For instance, the cube house appears to our Flatlanders as a square, but it will take on other two-dimensional appearances if it is rotated in a plane orthogonal to Flatland. Likewise, if we are three-dimensional beings in a four-dimensional world, also containing four-dimensional beings, we will have only the most benighted, skewed perspective on the more encompassing reality, *even if* we are aware of its existence. (Maybe we already have such evidence, like the two-slit experiment.)

And we should not just assume that we are ourselves merely three-dimensional. It may be that some Flatlanders are in fact three-dimensional, but their perceptions are limited to Flatland, hence they only ever see the skewed Flatland perspective on *themselves*.

One obvious way to understand time travel is as involving an other-dimensional hypothesis, with the fourth dimension being *temporal* rather than spatial. If so, then we may indeed be extended in four dimensions, but only perceive our extension in the three spatial ones. Looking at me now, you see only a tiny temporal part of a space-time worm that extends for longer (much longer, hopefully) than fifty years. Time travel would then be an alternative means of traversing this dimension (that is, in a manner other than the ordinary passage of time).

And we needn't stop there. Perhaps there is a further dimension of time – call it *hypertime* – and our four-dimensional universe is but one of many branches in a hyperverse. Hypertime travel would involve switching timelines, and so one might encounter all manner of otherwise unexpected marvels. A time traveler might appear to do the impossible and change the past, for instance. But this is no miracle, and no threat to Humeans. Add as many spatial and temporal dimensions as you like, and the world gets more wonderful, but no more miraculous.

Now to the third of my favorite things: *simulations*. I take seriously (a) the possibility of simulations, and (b) the non-negligible probability that we occupy one (see Chapter 2 by Nick Bostrom in this volume). Here's another possibility: simulations can have what I shall call *glitches*. Glitches can be accidental, systemic, or deliberate. An accidental glitch is one that is unintended, and is hard to anticipate, because it has no systematic explanation. It just happens from time to time. (My favorite fictional example is the "déjà vu" we see in *The Matrix*.) A systemic glitch is one that is unintended, but arises as a feature of the implementation of the simulation. (My favorite fictional example is the boundary of the full simulation in *The Thirteenth Floor*, where the details just run out – it's a bit like watching an incomplete animation.) A deliberate glitch is one that is intended by the simulators. (I don't have a favorite fictional example, because I don't have a fictional example. But I think the "bail-out" feature in the simulations described in Greg Egan's *Permutation City* comes close.) How will a glitch in the simulation manifest itself? *As a marvelous occurrence, apparently contrary to the laws of the virtual world.*

Simulation Epistemology and Metaphysics

Simulation hypotheses are usually interpreted as skeptical hypotheses, as Chalmers notes (Chapter 5 in this volume). The skeptical argument goes something like this:

1. If you know you're in the USA, then you know you're not in a simulation.
2. Since you don't know you're not in a simulation, you're don't know you're in the USA.
3. In fact, even if you're not in a simulation, anything you believe about the world outside your mind isn't *knowledge*, even if it's *true*, because you *might* be in a simulation.

Dan Dennett (1991) argued that skepticism can be defeated because we know we're *not* in a simulation. The computational resources required to maintain an interactive *world-like* simulation suffer from combinatorial explosion – they are fantastically beyond our present capabilities. However, this argument doesn't work, since (a) our evidence for combinatorial explosion might be *part of what is simulated*, so that we drastically overestimate what's required, and (b) our evidence for the limits of the capabilities of a simulation might be *part of what is simulated*, so that we drastically underestimate what's available!

Dembski either fails to consider the possibility of simulation (my favored diagnosis), or else makes *exactly the same mistake* as Dennett. If this is a simulation, then as things stand we simply have no idea whether or not the world of the simulators has the resources to compute things that we cannot. And if Dembski's Incredible Talking Pulsar were actual, then we should seriously consider that we are being simulated, in which case we might after all have evidence that the simulators are capable of computing things we cannot.

Let me repeat the charge against the miracle mongers. They are *unimaginative*, simply failing altogether to allow the opposition reasonable intellectual resources. So it is ironic that C. S. Lewis, for instance, accuses the "modern materialist" of dogmatically shutting his mind to the glorious possibilities that Christianity offers. Lewis imagines that the only possible rationalization for denial is explanation in terms of "psychoanalysis, or cerebral pathology." But I have outlined three different alternatives to Christian interpretation of marvelous occurrences, none of which involves the hypothesis of mental aberration. So even if it would be dogmatic to insist that *it* (the marvelous phenomenon) was an illusion, that is a very long way from establishing that *it* is evidence for the divine. *However . . .*

An Argument for Miracles

If the events Lewis imagines were actually to occur, and be robustly observed, how should a non-Christian like me respond? The simulation hypothesis seems well suited here, especially the hypothesis of a *deliberate* glitch. I regard typical Christian belief as including a lot of rather obviously false, even silly, stories about what we can expect in our futures. If the simulators know what Christians believe, and take a similar dim view of it, maybe they will *mess* with us, giving us the experiences Christians expect. (By the way, Lewis's sanguine assumption is that *materialists* will be cast into the Lake, but on the simulation hypothesis, there's no reason things have to go this way!)

The *simulation with a deliberate glitch* hypothesis seems a good general response to any miracle mongers. Our simulators would get a particularly good ROFL from producing Heath's phenomenon. What better way to have a joke at the expense of a bunch of sims who have the hubris to suppose that they are the most important things ever created?

Notice that the sims get something right, though – they *are* created. And by something a whole lot more powerful, knowledgeable, and generally impressive than they are. But does that mean *God*? Well, that rather depends.

David Chalmers (Chapter 5 in this volume) argues that if you have always been in a simulation, then the fact that you are in a simulation is no great threat to you knowing pretty much what you thought you did. It's not just that you *don't* have false beliefs about your situation, but also that you *do* have a lot of true beliefs about it, because a *sim's* beliefs are largely about virtual things – other sims and the like – and not about the underlying reality of the world of the simulators. To put it another way, when you think that you are in the USA, you can be correct, because the USA is *part of the simulation*, and not part of the world of the simulators. (Even if this is in some fairly intimate sense a simulation *of* the world of the simulators, *our* USA is not *their* USA, and our beliefs are about *ours*, not *theirs*. So even if I'm in fact not in their USA right now, nevertheless I truly believe that I am in ours.)

How does this metaphysical hypothesis help the miracle mongers? It's tempting to say that it doesn't change anything: the Humean can still respond that apparent miracles (glitches), including those of the deliberate kind, are *at most* evidence that the natural world is a lot bigger than we normally think. But consider two recent definitions from philosopher of religion Paul Draper (2005: 277–8):

(a) x is supernatural $=_{df} x$ is not a part of nature and x affects nature.
(b)   nature $=_{df}$ the spatio-temporal universe of physical entities together with any entities that are ontologically or causally reducible to those entities.

What exactly are the *physical entities*, if this is a simulation? They are whatever our physics successfully refers to, and by Chalmers's argument, those are part of the simulation. Hence, I submit, if Chalmers and Draper are both correct, then *the world of the simulators* is *supernatural*, since it is not part of the simulation, and causally affects the simulation. Hence, the right sort of glitch in the simulation will be evidence for the *supernatural*.

Perhaps it will be objected that the simulators are not benevolent (*I* grant this readily), but *Christians* better not say this, if they insist on the traditional claim that we don't have evidence against God's benevolence. Perhaps it will be objected that the simulators are not omnipotent. But what is the contrary evidence? No doubt the simulators are bound by logic and relevant mathematics, but only a *crazy* Christian denies that God is not likewise bound by logical necessity. Perhaps it will be claimed that simulators need not control every aspect of a sim's existence, at least not directly. Better to set up relatively self-directed programming, *delegating* much of the decision-making to the sims themselves. This might be regarded as a threat to both omnipotence and omniscience of the simulators. But again, we'd better not hear any *Christians* claiming that this gift of free will to the sims makes the simulators different from God. Perhaps it will be claimed that there is only one God – or one and three at the same time – but maybe there is only one simulator, or one and three at the same time.

(I have argued before that the Christian God is in the simulation business: in Hanley, 2005, I argue that only a very specific simulation hypothesis can meet the standard criteria for the Christian heaven. God would have to be up to his divine armpits in other science fiction staples, too. I argue in Hanley, 1997, that the Christian God would have to be in the teletransport business, in order to account for survival of bodily death. A further possibility I'd like to explore is that God himself is a simulation . . . hey – maybe it's simulations all the way down!)

Despite the fact that the simulator hypothesis apparently meets all the standard criteria of God (at least, given that Christians apply the criteria consistently, it does not definitely violate any of them), I doubt that the hypothesis would be met with anything other than horror by traditional Christians. So, oddly enough, Draper's definitions may disappoint theists and Humeans alike. The uncomfortable choice for both is to (a) come up with plausible alternative definitions, (b) eliminate the simulation hypothesis, (c) eliminate Chalmers's metaphysical hypothesis, or (d) grant that it is possible to have evidence of the supernatural, just conceived a little more *imaginatively*.

References

Dembski, W. A. (1994). On the Very Possibility of Intelligent Design. In Moreland, J. P. (ed.), *The Creation Hypothesis: Scientific Evidence for an Intelligent Designer*. Downers Grove, IL: Inter Varsity Press, 113–38.

Dennett, D. (1991). *Consciousness Explained*. Boston, MA: Little, Brown & Company.

Draper, P. (2005). God, Science, and Naturalism. In Wainwright, W. J. (ed.), *The Oxford Handbook of Philosophy of Religion*. Oxford: Oxford University Press, 272–303.

Hanley, R. (1997). *The Metaphysics of Star Trek*. New York: Basic Books.

Hanley, R. (2005). Never the Twain Shall Meet: Reflections on the Very First Matrix. In Grau, C. (ed.), *Philosophers Explore The Matrix*. Oxford: Oxford University Press, 115–31.

Heath, P. (1976). The Incredulous Hume. *American Philosophical Quarterly* 13: 159–63.

Lewis, C. S. (1986). *The Grand Miracle*. New York: Ballantyne.

Sorenson, R. (1987). Time Travel, Parahistory, and Hume. *Philosophy* 62: 227–36.

INDEX